A MAN OF INFLUENCE

A MAN OF INFLUENCE

The Extraordinary Career of S.G. Warburg

JACQUES ATTALI

translated by Barbara Ellis

ADLER&ADLER

Published in the United States in 1987 by
Adler & Adler, Publishers, Inc.
4550 Montgomery Avenue
Bethesda, Maryland 20814

First published in French in 1985 under the title *Un homme d'influence*
copyright 1985 Librairie Arthème Fayard
English translation copyright 1986 George Weidenfeld & Nicolson Limited

Library of Congress Cataloging-in-Publication Data

Attali, Jacques.
  A man of influence.

  Translation of: Un homme d'influence.
  Bibliography: p.
  Includes index.
  1. Warburg, Siegmund, Sir, 1902–1982. 2. Jewish bankers—Biography.
3. Bankers—Great Britain—Biography. I. Title.
HG1552.W37A8713 1987   332.1′092′4 [B]   86-28735
ISBN 0-917561-36-8

Printed in the United States of America
First U.S. Edition

Contents

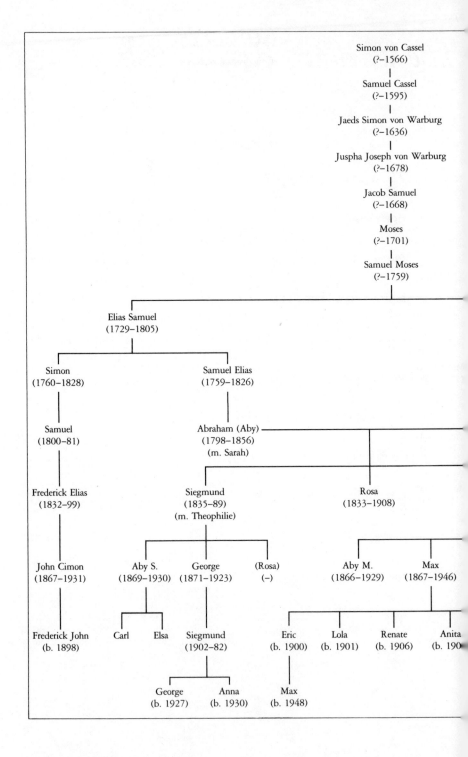

The Warburg Family Tree

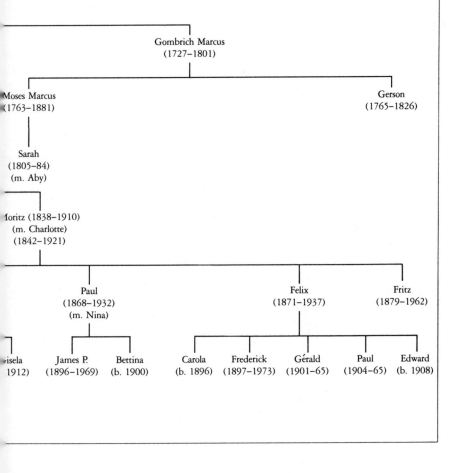

Gombrich Marcus
(1727–1801)

Moses Marcus
(1763–1881)

Gerson
(1765–1826)

Sarah
(1805–84)
(m. Aby)

Moritz (1838–1910)
(m. Charlotte)
(1842–1921)

Paul
(1868–1932)
(m. Nina)

Felix
(1871–1937)

Fritz
(1879–1962)

Gisela
1912)

James P.
(1896–1969)

Bettina
(b. 1900)

Carola
(b. 1896)

Frederick
(1897–1973)

Gérald
(1901–65)

Paul
(1904–65)

Edward
(b. 1908)

Acknowledgments

Bankers do not like to be talked about and S.G. Warburg & Co. is no different from the rest. Neither the bank nor Siegmund Warburg's family was associated with the writing of this book or the views expressed in it.

The archives of private banks and chanceries, secret by nature, were made available to me only with reservations, but I was able to benefit from exceptional evidence, written and oral. I should emphasize the difficulty of researching a story in which the main protagonist had unceasingly worked to obliterate any trace of it, leaving behind hardly any documents, correspondence or archives. True, Siegmund is mentioned in a few rare public documents, among them two notable family histories. The first, begun in 1923, almost ignores him; the second, in 1975, devotes only about ten pages to him. He granted only two interviews, a short one in 1975, and another very detailed one in 1980.

Also in existence is a kind of intimate diary, a collection of ideas rather than facts, to which I was the first to have access, along with other unpublished diaries or memoirs of certain family members, in particular those of his cousins Max and Elsa. Finally, he and his family have also been mentioned in many history books and in the international financial press since the beginning of the century.

These written sources are contradictory and often aim to embroider the role of a particular person. However, the essence of this story comes from evidence painstakingly collected and assembled from those who knew him well personally and professionally, and most of whom did not want to be quoted for attribution.

I also take responsibility for choosing a particular version of an event where several existed.

I thank Serge Waléry, assistant professor at the University of Paris IX, who was kind enough to help me prepare the bibliography; Margit Danel, who translated certain German documents for me; and Christiane Ademi, Christine Contini and Annick Proye, who undertook the difficult task of typing the successive drafts of this book.

Introduction

It was nearing noon on 22 March 1933 when Siegmund Warburg entered the imposing but familiar building of the Ministry of Foreign Affairs. He was worried. Two days earlier several of his friends— journalists and bankers—had been arrested at their homes without a warrant in the middle of the night, "to be taken to a place of safety in their own interest," as the police put it. The previous day he had attended the reopening of the new Parliament, housed since the Reichstag fire in the chapel of Potsdam fort, where Frederick the Great lay buried. There he had been horrified to see a Socialist spat on, jostled, then roughly ejected by the Nazis, who had deliberately omitted to invite left-wing members of Parliament to the opening.

It was hardly reassuring to see, daubed on the wall opposite the Foreign Ministry on Wilhelmstrasse, anti-Semitic slogans calling for Jews to be murdered. With things as they were, how could he go to New York the next day and leave his wife, Eva, and two children in Berlin? Two hours before, from his office at the bank, Siegmund had telephoned the foreign minister, Baron Constantin von Neurath, a man he had known since childhood and who was almost like an uncle to him. The call was not unusual. The two men had been working together for over a year on international financial affairs. Germany had been playing a cautious game in these matters for more than a century—and often winning, thanks to the Warburgs. Siegmund requested an urgent meeting and von Neurath agreed without even asking why.

As usual the baron received him warmly, coming out into the waiting room himself to welcome him. A cultured former diplomat and ambassador, the foreign minister combined the elegance of the Swabian nobility with the professional self-assurance so indispensable to politicians. His friend's visit was nothing out of the ordinary. Confirmed in his own post by the new chancellor, Adolf Hitler, von Neurath had asked Siegmund to go on helping him and had Siegmund agreed.

As soon as the two were alone, von Neurath began asking questions: "Where have you been, my friend—Amsterdam or Hamburg? I haven't seen you for days."

"Nowhere," Siegmund replied. "I have been here all the time, but busy preparing for my trip. You know I leave for New York tomorrow and that is why I wanted to see you. For once I want to talk to you about what is happening here, not abroad. What I am seeing here is dreadfully worrying. You are foreign minister—do you know that people are being arrested at their homes in the middle of the night and sent to prison without any warrant whatsoever? Are you aware of what happened in Parliament yesterday?"

"Yes, I know all that. Such things happen now and again these days. It is very unpleasant, but it is the price we must pay for the national revolution. Nobody regrets this more than I do, but you see I am foreign minister, not home secretary. What can I do?"

"What do you mean, what can you do? You know very well that these arrests are unconstitutional and that the chancellor who ordered them is violating the oath he has just taken on the Constitution. You can't let that get by. You must go and see President Hindenburg immediately and remind him that Article 19 of the Weimar Constitution authorizes him to dismiss this chancellor—indeed it obliges him to do so. He need have no fear—he is chief marshall of the army, which will support him, and it is well known that the armed forces minister, von Blomberg, is no Nazi. In fact I think he would make an excellent chancellor. Hindenburg has usually listened to you—he will again. You must go and see him at once."

Von Neurath looked at Siegmund for a long time without answering. Then, with lowered eyes and speaking very deliberately, he said, "Yes, it's true. You are right. That is what I should do, but I can't. You see, my young friend, as I am not a Nazi myself I am now considered politically suspect. I must therefore be very careful. No, I can't do anything." Then, looking Siegmund straight in the eye, he said, "Good-bye and good luck."

Siegmund got up without a word. On the way down Wilhelmstrasse he no longer even saw the banners, the swastikas or the slogans on the wall. Deserting his driver, he walked home without going back to the bank. "Politically suspect"—this was the end.

By the time Siegmund reached home his decision was already made, and it was as irreversible and matter-of-fact as all the others that would count so much in his life. He asked his wife to leave the same day with their children and go to her parents in Stockholm.

"You are never coming back here. Wait there for me. Take back your Swedish citizenship immediately. You never know: if you keep your German citizenship I might be stuck in Germany. I will tell you later where we will settle. As for me, I am going straight to Hamburg to see Max and from there to New York. I will telephone you."

In the two hours that followed, Eva, Anna and George Warburg left for Stockholm. They crossed the German border without hindrance. The same afternoon Siegmund took a train to Hamburg to see the head of the dynasty, Max Warburg, a cousin of his father whom he called uncle. The old banker received him late that evening in his mahogany-paneled office in the bank's magnificent building at 75 Ferdinand-strasse.

"Haven't you gone yet? Your ship is about to leave."

"I'm going, uncle, I'm going. But I shall never come back to Hamburg or Berlin. Don't be angry, but I am quitting. I don't know yet where I shall go after New York, but it won't be here. You must help me to set up somewhere else."

"You're mad—why are you doing this?"

"I have had enough. Hitler is going to do what he said he would do ten years ago: he will kill us all. I saw von Neurath this morning. Even he considers himself politically suspect and dares do nothing. Do you realize? Him 'politically suspect.' That is too much. Germany—our Germany—is lost."

"No, Siegmund, what you are saying is absurd. They will never touch us. Schacht is head of the Reichsbank again. That is a guarantee, isn't it? Only yesterday he told me we were protected and nothing would happen to us. Hitler doesn't want war and neither does Britain. Schacht told me."

"Schacht, Schacht! You are fooling yourself. You are wrong to go on working with him. He went over to their side more than a year ago, maybe without even knowing it himself. I don't believe a word of what he told you. I don't believe any of it anymore."

"Siegmund, you can't leave. You can't walk out on Berlin—there is a lot of work to be done there. And you will soon succeed me here. Besides, you can't leave Germany. Our family has been established here for more than three centuries. This is our country. We bear the name of a town in this country. What is more, we are responsible for the other Jews here. You can't desert them. Who will look after them if we don't?

You know very well what we have started with Palestine. It is a very delicate matter and I need you for that. You are the only one who knows the whole structure. We must stay. There are still many Jews to be got out of this country."

"No, uncle, you are making a mistake by staying. Seeing you working with Schacht and the others, people will think they are protected and will never be threatened. They cling onto the slenderest hope. You are not giving them a good example. I am going and you should think of leaving too—all the Warburgs should. Then people would see that they should all do the same before chaos descends."

Fifty years later on 12 January 1983 a ceremony took place at the Guildhall in London. In the presence of Lady Warburg, her two children and the entire staff of Europe's leading merchant bank, a portrait of Sir Siegmund Warburg, painted ten years earlier, was unveiled and officially presented by the family to the bank. The founder of the bank had died only a few weeks before. The ceremony was short. Three brief speeches were heard—one from the young successor-designate David Scholey, English to his fingertips; one from a friend from the bad old days, the German-Jewish financier Henry Grunfeld, who like Warburg had arrived almost penniless in the London of the 1930's; and finally, one from the new head of the bank, Eric Roll, a brilliant academic before becoming a lord.

After each of the speeches, an orchestra played one of Sir Siegmund's three favorite pieces—a Bach cantata, the adagio movement of a Mozart violin concerto and an air from Handel's "Water Music."[1]

The last words fell to Lord Roll, who quoted the well-known lines from Hamlet, "He was a man, take him for all in all, I shall not look upon his like again."

Siegmund was born in 1902 into a very old family of Jewish bankers that had been influential for over a century from Berlin to New York and from Hamburg to Tokyo. Like his celebrated ancestors, he began his career in Germany as a banker and government adviser. In the upheavals of the Weimer Republic that ruined his father, he took part in the torturous financing of German reparations. When the debt economy gave way to the war economy, the rise of Hitler sent him to London with little more than his name as capital. There Siegmund set up a small financial business and helped find ways of financing the wartime Allies and disrupting German sources of finance. Meanwhile,

Hitler was destroying the Jewish people and the bank that his family had taken more than two centuries to build up.

After the war, Siegmund brought his family name again to the fore, founding his own bank in London, S.G. Warburg & Co. Within twenty years he became the leading banker in the city. He devised the principal financial techniques in use today—from takeover bids to Eurodollar issues—and did business in New York, Frankfurt, Geneva, Hamburg and throughout the world. He revolutionized the methods of training top industrialists, and even the press and the automobile industry benefited from his involvement.

However, he also saw—long before others did—signs of the impotence of Europe, the revolt of the Third World, the rise of Japan and the difficulties of Israel.

From Switzerland, the base of his last adventure, he continued until his death to extend his influence, from New York to Cairo, from Tokyo to Jerusalem.

Siegmund was almost unique in his single-minded obsession with his name and his desire to prolong its influence even during the worst storms of this century. He was witness to a time of barbarism but never succumbed to defeat. A prince of finance and listened to by men of power without ever being one of them, he lived one of the great lives of our time.

A man of influence over those who in turn claimed power over events: this is how he liked to see himself—like his "uncle" Max who had such a profound effect on him, like Joseph in the Old Testament or like Thomas Mann, whom he ranked above all.

Concrete evidence of his influence is hard to find. Like seers in every age, on guard against threats to their world and discreetly advising princes, he liked to remain private as a protection against their thunder. His passion was for doing things rather than being seen doing them, and for succeeding in his work rather than signing it.

There have been men like Siegmund throughout history. Whether diviners, men at arms, money men or artists, they were more easily able than others to predict the future. Sometimes they were able, by a gesture, a command or an action to alter the course of events, change the law or at the least stay downstream of the flood of the time.

Often when they thought their vision, their strength or their motivation gave them power beyond the limits of the possible, they failed. Like all prophets they were then accused of the very evil they had tried to avert by forecasting.

During the last two centuries it is the financier far more than the artist or the industrialist whose influence has been unquestionable: the man who directly or indirectly finances princes. It may also be something of a surprise to discover that for better or worse, the Warburgs, Rothschilds, Schiffs, Lehmans, Melchiors, Hambros and Mayers have played as great a role as princes and politicians in our destiny—not to mention the part played by the Bards, Fuggers, Morgans or Barings, or individuals like Abs, Monnet, Cuccia or Rockefeller.

These enigmatic men of influence have always had to try to look far into the future, to imagine new sources of wealth, to get money into circulation in order to prevent its becoming worthless in time of war. Sometimes they have been mistaken, deluded by their own unbounded ambition, and have had a hand in the ruin of their world. Occasionally, too, they have seen the arrival of a worse catastrophe than the one they had delayed. As pioneers of capitalist rationalism and founding witnesses of the merchant order, they are essential links in our history and a magnificent reflection of the relative powers of money and of reason.

Among these men are some of the people of the Book, turned merchants by force of circumstance, forced to lend to princes in order to attract their protection, taking the risk of being creditors to the powerful to guarantee their own freedom, knowing that in doing so they might end up as scapegoats, and having learned in four thousand years of suffering to link ethics with action.

These men were forced into the financial world in order to keep their identity. They were more concerned with what they were doing than with the money they were making, trying their utmost to ensure that fair exchange prevailed over violence, circulation over immobility, life over death. Occasionally in the limelight and always punished for it, but most often hidden, they were practically the double of the powers they advised, yet almost always better informed about world events, and at the same time guardians of the communities that surrounded them. On the periphery of the obvious elites, they eventually organized themselves into a strange aristocracy, a kind of austere order, with implacable moral laws and savage rituals, in which a Name is the prime wealth and Land the ultimate vanity. Always in search of new places of refuge and the formation of new wealth, they might act either for some higher reason or because of political necessity.

This is their story, told through one of their number—for me one of the most brilliant men of this century, though far from being the only one whose life demonstrates better than any theory, in its ambition and final failure, that a world and a culture were drawing to a close—the end of a fancied compatibility between Words and Money.

This book is not a biography in the conventional sense since there is only the barest mention of the private life of Siegmund Warburg. It is foremost a detailed account of a life that would have supplied the material for more than a few novels. It is the story of a captain of finance seeking his fortune (in the wider sense of the word), and that of a man with a heritage. It shows that at a given time and place there did exist a just man of caliber and that despite appearances, the history of this century cannot be summed up as an age of barbarism.

Finally, and perhaps above all, this is a kind of *Book of the Hours* of the history of the Jewish people, on guard by nature and forced to be scapegoats, the central subject of my research for many years, which I shall one day publish in another work if I am granted the time to finish it.

Perhaps it will be said that to speak of such things is to make a gift to one's enemies. My belief is quite the contrary: it is when one lacks self-awareness that the threat from others becomes acute.

1

Fortune in a Name
(1559-1902)

A *Family Tree*

The Warburgs have always taken their name very seriously. They watch over it as over an estate, use it sparingly as with property and extend it like an empire. Today, it is well known that the name first entered the history of finance during the sixteenth century. It happened first in Italy, then in Germany, then in the other countries their enemies call "Warburg countries"—the United States, Russia, Palestine and Japan. The family itself has been following the development of the family tree attentively, and by means of careful alliances has ensured the survival of the name and its increasing influence.

It will be seen that in the midnineteenth century, in order to save an apparently hopeless situation, the family tree was used to define and prescribe the one marriage that would avoid the disappearance of the name from the portals of the bank.

The family tree unceasingly was kept up to date, studied, annotated and taught to children and newcomers. The women of the family loved to tell tales, which they sometimes wrote down for the inner circle only, of the wonderful adventures and scandals of the uncles in Germany, the financial geniuses in America, the magnificent aunts exiled to India, the crossed loves in Palestine. There were endless discussions on the limits of territory and reviews of the list of allied names. There was pride in the

1

name and in being Jewish, even though the name was not. In the middle of the nineteenth century a huge family tree was even distributed to all family members. This was done again at the beginning of the twentieth century when Siegmund was born, although by then the tree had grown extensively: to four thousand people, six hundred of them Warburgs—in Germany, Italy, Denmark, Sweden, the United States, Russia and as far away as Turkey and Shanghai. At that time men by the name of Warburg were in charge of the most influential banks in Germany, America and Russia. One Warburg had founded the American Federal Reserve, another the Jewish Agency. Others included several future advisers to United States presidents, a chemist—who was to win the Nobel Prize for medicine—and a professor of economics at Oxford.

Much later, ten years after the Second World War and with discreet pride, the family again took stock of its history. In four centuries the Warburgs had carried on more than thirty different professions in twenty-nine countries and almost always reached the peak of excellence.

By this time the tree was very difficult to read, and even more so to interpret, as the wish to keep the family to itself was carried to extremes by the repetitive use of certain "Warburg first names" for generation after generation.

As in the great dynasties, everything was codified: the eldest son would be named after his grandfather. He would go into the family bank, and assisted by a younger brother would be responsible for financing the careers of the other children. As for the girls, they would marry more of less as they pleased, though to other bankers—Jewish of course—and in parts of the world carefully chosen so as to extend the network of contracts, the business capital, the influence of the name and the family territory. Money, however, would not be a consideration. It was never an end in itself, even if it was sometimes a result, rather like a symbol of the value of reason.

If family members became rich, or even very rich, there would never be an ostentation: the main thing was to be Jewish, orthodox and strict, even if practice did become somewhat secularized over time in the Protestant world of North Germany. Ethics and culture would also always be of the highest importance. Holidays, every holiday, would be observed, and the family would keep to the Jewish calendar as much as possible without troubling about what non-Jewish clients might think. The synagogue would be visited at first every day, then only on Friday evening and Saturday morning, but always on foot. When wealth permitted, there would be a private synagogue in the home.

Whatever Siegmund himself thought or said, his destiny would be incomprehensible without a prior account of the history of his family. Just as a society cannot be explained independently of its foundations, tracking the path of a man—especially one as attached to his origins as Warburg—requires detailed knowledge of his heritage, his hopes and disappointments, as well as the revenge he took and positions he held.

Moneylending Jews

The Warburgs were basically Italians, though history records that the family's furthest ancestors lived in North Africa around the tenth century. When their protectors became fickle and their power weakened, they fled from the Arabs toward Italy, possibly spending some time in Spain at the beginning of the fifteenth century. The first person recognized by the family as an ancestor is Andrea del Banco,[1] a money changer in Pisa at the beginning of the sixteenth century, a time when Jews were allowed no other name than that of their profession or the place where they lived.

During that period pawnbroking was a standard occupation for many Jews, because it was one of the few left open to them. There was no particular Jewish inclination toward it. On the contrary, there was only the constraint of those who needed the service and who, knowing the hatred reserved for its practitioners, made sure the task went to their enemies. This was nothing new. From the earliest times fate had forced the Jews to become bankers. The profession was necessary to others and authorized by Jewish law. Among Jews the lending of money was actually allowed by the Bible, whether for purchase of land or goods for the house of Israel. However, a highly codified system of loans and moratoriums forbade the accumulation of fortunes by lenders, who were no more than servants of the community, and arranged at regular intervals for the cancellation of debts, thus maintaining the original distribution of land and power among the twelve tribes.

Here in brief is the history of these predecessors of the Warburgs, a minority among Jews and a minority among bankers. Their fate illustrates the tradition that the Warburgs were to take as their law.

At the time of the kings, some of these predecessors, in association with the Phoenicians, had control of lending to international trade expeditions—especially those underwritten by the monarch—reaching as far as the west coast of India.

After the Exile, the Jews lost their land, and their dispersal to Babylon and elsewhere made them ideal agents for international trade and the lending of money such a trade. Here again, they were forced into the profession.

Among the records kept by one of the world's first lending institutions in Babylon, the House of Murashu, were seventy Jewish names and a number of contracts signed on equal terms between Jews and Babylonian businessmen.[2]

The fall of Jerusalem dispersed the Jews still further and pushed them even more toward professions concerned with the circulation of goods, ideas or money—professions of intellect, and the only ones open to them outside their communities. At the same time they did need their community. A Jewish life is not lived singly. It entails butchers, bakers, teachers and religious courts, and communities move around in the wake of their richest members. So in Alexandria at this time, along with a few very powerful Jewish bankers, there was a large Jewish community.[3]

In Rome Jews obtained protected status, in return for which their bankers were to ensure financing for princes and to lend with interest to merchants—something Christians were forbidden to do.

Under constraint from the earliest days of money lending, Jewish communities set themselves up along its power lines. When the Roman Empire divided, they organized around the empires of the East, financed their trade and gave birth there to the capitalism of risk and profit, using calculation and reasoning in the service of commerce.

Jews had to pay very dearly for their security. Thus in the third century a Jewish banker in Baghdad justified special taxes, which he saw as "ensuring his existence"—"By abolishing them, you would unleash the propensity of the population for spilling the blood of Jews."[4] By the third century, Jewish communities were already spread throughout the world, and they secured trade links from the north of Germany to the south of Morocco, as well as from Italy to India and China, perhaps even to Japan and Korea.[5]

In the Byzantine Empire, which became the center of the world a little later, Jews became pawnbrokers or dealers in precious stones. They controlled the minting of money, exchange, deposits and credit, and were also in charge of the unpopular task of tax collecting.[6] Since their communities provided one of the best information networks of the period, whether in Baghdad, Cairo, Alexandria or Fez, they were indispensable as royal advisers. Already in these first centuries of their influence they suffered at regular intervals from the violence of their debtors and the whims of their masters.[7]

In the fifth century Jews established themselves, again as bankers, in the main villages of Christian Europe and financed the business matters of convents, monasteries and cities. Gregory of Tours mentions Azmentarius, a Jewish banker to whom the Count of Tours and his vicar owed money.[8]

Two centuries later, when Islam invaded the Arab world, the Jews became *dhimmis*, protected by a new set of princes, whose trade with the rest of the world they also managed through their network. In the ninth and tenth centuries their contacts extended from the north of Europe to China.

However, the Jewish people remained mainly eastern, and it was not until the awakening of the West in the eleventh century that they were drawn westward and their financiers were encouraged to circulate money from the heart of the East toward this seething periphery. It was at this time an unkind expression came into many languages, "to judaize,"[9] which meant to receive interest on money.[10]

By the eleventh century, capitalism crept into internal social relationships, for example, at the Champagne and Cologne fairs and at the markets of Antwerp and Venice.[11] And despite the Church's interdicts, many besides the Jews entered the world of finance: merchants from Lombardy or Cahors became the financiers of towns in Italy and the Netherlands and competed with the Jewish bankers who, always on the lookout for new prospects, were fleeing the threatening East to establish themselves in fragile cities from the North Sea to the Mediterranean. The young merchants of Europe who saw them as a source of trade and therefore of profit did their best to attract them in exchange for the protection of a "bill of rights," a gift of land or privileges. In 1004, for example, a bishop of Speyer named Rudiger granted a charter to the Jews in his city: "I think," he wrote, "that I shall increase the honor of our locality a thousandfold by bringing the Jews to live here."[12] In Champagne, on the Rhine, in Northern Italy and in Poland several hundred communities were thus established, which until then only communicated with the outside world through their financiers.[13]

So ended more than one thousand years of almost complete—and totally involuntary—Jewish control of international finance. From this time onward the power of the Jews remained immense, but they were no longer the main financiers of capitalism. Calculated risk became a means to wealth, and Jewish financiers partly gave way to other merchants and other bankers.

The Norman Conquest drew the Jews to England, where their financiers helped the new kings to establish themselves, by acting as intermediaries for their trade, agents for their taxes—always incurring the hostility of those who had to bear the costs. As soon as they arrived an English cardinal noted, "The money a prince obtains through the expedient of the income of a usurer makes him an accomplice in the crime."[14]

At the end of the eleventh century many Jews were massacred in the wake of the first Crusade, whether or not they were bankers or creditors of lords who had gone off to adventure: the first in Europe of a long series of anti-Semitic massacres that were the pretext for a moratorium on debts.[15]

In the twelfth century the Jews of Europe regrouped in four regions: the newer towns on the North Sea coast, those in Italy and Spain that were vying to be the centers of nascent capitalism, and between these three zones, the towns of South Germany, a place of transit on the way to fairs and silver mines.[16]

Jews now began to be on their guard and demanded greater protection from these towns if they were to accept their hospitality. So, for example, in order to attract lenders and international merchants, Reggio had to guarantee a financial indemnity to the Jewish bankers in case of an attack by the people.[17] They worked more and more with the savings of other Jewish merchants established in towns of lesser importance nearby and lent townspeople and peasants the means to meet their commitments in exchange for jewels, boats, houses and goods.[18] Their power increased, and some of them then made loans against land and or even estates. The moneylenders also busied themselves with the repair of second-hand clothes and other items they had taken as pledges, which they would resell if the borrower defaulted: the second-hand trade therefore was very closely linked to money lending.

New banking families, Jewish and otherwise, now began their reigns, succeeding the old financial dynasties of North Africa or the Orient that fled the Islamic decline. Italy saw the rise of the Volterras, the Tivolis, the da Pisas and the del Bancos, alongside the Bardis of Florence, who controlled a bank first in Italy and then in London and Tunis until the sack of their palace much later by the Medicis and their ruin by Edward III of England.

The names of other banking families began to appear: Abecassis in Portugal, Mendes in Spain, Lincoln in England and Suissa in the

Netherlands.[19] At the same time, Beer and Lehman[20] appeared in Germany in Trier, Mainz, Nuremberg, Ulm and Speyer, towns of the wheat and silver trade.

But in Italy, and then elsewhere, religious interdicts became blurred by the rise in profits, exacerbating competition from bankers from Cahors, Catalonia and Lombardy. In England, around 1275, when rates reached 40 percent, Italian bankers came in to replace the Jewish financiers, one of whom, Aaron of Lincoln,[21] had gained enormous influence with Edward I. Yet in 1290, Edward went so far as to expel the ten thousand Jews in England to Bohemia, Hungary or Poland, where the protection of other princes awaited them—before other massacres.

The Del Bancos

At the beginning of the fourteenth century, the Jewish merchants made a choice that was to affect their descendants for hundreds of years: moving to the West rather than the East. The center of gravity of their people swung with them. They established themselves wherever there was a mercantile order: Antwerp, Bruges, Trier, Nuremberg, Venice[22]—as well as in all the courts—supplying money for the enterprises of the Iberian monarchs, such as Alfonso III against the Moors. Among them were Judah ibn Ezra, banker to Alfonso VII, Joseph ibn Shoshan, banker to Alfonso VIII, ibn Zadok, tax collector to Alfonso X, Abraham el Barchilon, financier to Sancho IV, Beneviste de Porta, banker to Jaime I of Aragon, Judah Halevi and Abraham Aben-Joseph, "tax farmers" to Charles II and Charles III of Navarre.[23]

Then with the major economic crisis in the midfourteenth century, the persecutions began again: in Germany, despite the efforts of Pope Clement VI, the Black Death served as the pretext for the massacre of Jews, who fled to Poland and Lithuania. France also put to flight the Jews who were working there, and only Italy and the Netherlands, less affected by the crisis, remained places of refuge with the agreement of the popes and the merchants. It was there that some emigrants, whose ancestors had left two centuries before to try their luck in Germany or Spain, found the del Bancos, who had apparently stayed where they were.

In the fifteenth century the Jews tended to arrive in the vanguard of wealth and established themselves in fabulous cities of luxury, gaiety and excitement—in Bruges, Antwerp, Venice and Genoa. Many still continued to play important roles at the court of Spain: Luis de la

Cavallerai was chief treasurer to Juan II of Aragon; Diego Aria de Avila, and then his son, were secretaries to Henry IV of Castile; Abraham Senior, then Isaac Abrabanel, were first bankers to Alfonso V in the war against Granada, and later became financial advisers to Isabella la Catholica.[24]

It was at that time that the Fugger dynasty began, descended from a family of Catholic weavers from Augsburg. In 1507 Andreas Fugger, then controlling European banking from Lisbon to the Baltic, lent twenty thousand florins to Maxmilian and in 1519 ensured the election of Charles V as emperor against François I—proof if it were needed of the growing power of the "gentiles" in the financial world of the time.[25]

At the end of the sixteenth century, as at the end of the previous century, and for the same reasons, Spain closed its doors on the Jews as had Germany, France and England. There was a tremendous dispersal of power and knowledge: Isaac Abrabanel left for Naples; others, the Pintos and the Lopez Suissas, as well as the Mendeses, left for Antwerp. From there Joseph Mendes Nasi went to the East where he became very influential with the Turkish sultan. Diego Texeira de Sampaio of Spain became financial adviser to Christina of Sweden;[26] his son Manuel would later settle in Hamburg, which had been growing since the reign of Charles V.

At the beginning of the sixteenth century, financiers no longer lent to lords except in places like Poland and the principalities of Germany.[27] Elsewhere they lent only to merchants. There was a widening gap between the two kinds of Jewish communities: those of Southern Europe and Italy and those of Northern Europe and Russia. The former were comprised mainly of Sephardic Jews who had come from Spain or North Africa with their wealth to take part in economic life, but who lived in seclusion, cut off from the Christians. The first ghetto was created in Venice in 1516,[28] a year before Luther nailed his ninety-five theses to the door and began a revolt against money, among other things. The Ashkenazic Jews from Northern Europe and Russia were freer and better integrated, but far less wealthy and influential.

The history of the Warburgs is that of a Sephardic Jewish banking family switching from the South to the North at the exact moment when the north gained access to wealth. In fact it was around 1520 that the del Bancos moved toward Germany, as Ashkenazic country, where the fate of the family would be played out first under the name of von Cassel, then von Warburg and finally plain Warburg.

From von Cassel to von Warburg

At the beginning of the sixteenth century North Germany was a land of great hope. Cassel, where the family settled, was then a small town in Westphalia on the Fulda. There was trade in silver and corn from Bruges and Antwerp to Venice and Genoa. The merchants and clergy of the town had long been trying to attract Jewish merchants to establish themselves as moneylenders to the rich peasants and corn merchants of the surrounding area. After all, nearby Speyer and Trier both had their Jews, why not Cassel? So the town made every effort to welcome them properly. The richest men took them under their protection and, in exchange for regular royalties, offered them commercial and religious privileges. And, as with all other Jewish moneylenders received in this way, they were asked to take the name of the town that welcomed them. So the del Banco family changed its name to von Cassel. Not that this meant that such Jews were any less hated or martyred than the others. The threat was always there; for example in 1538 the clergy of Hesse issued a libelous document that compared Jewish pawnbrokers to "a sponge which sucks up the wealth of people to spit it out into the Prince's Treasury."[29]

In 1557, Simon von Cassel, the son of the original emigrant, did not feel at ease as a "money-changer and lender against agricultural goods" in the town and did not care for the ghetto life imposed on him,[30] so he decided to move fifty kilometers away to Warburg, where a few hundred Jews had already been established for half a century.

Warburg, at the time still called Warburgum, was a large market town on the eastern frontier of Westphalia. Founded by Charlemagne in 778, as legend has it, the town kept records from 1001 onward, which show that at the time Simon settled there trade in wool and beer was flourishing.[31] Life was unpleasant for Jews: they did not have to live in ghettos, which was increasingly the case in Central Europe and even in Frankfurt, where the Rothschild saga was to begin a century later.

Upon arrival in the town, Simon was registered as a "money-changer and lender of funds against grain." In 1559 the protector of Warburg, the bishop-prince of Paderborn, granted him the right to stay for ten years and to take the name of Simon von Warburg.[32] His family was to stay for a whole century and to keep the name to the present day.

Simon died around 1566, several years after moving to Warburg. His son Samuel, and later his grandson Jacob Simon, took over as heads of the small business. Lending on security to the merchants of the

bishopric enriched the family, whose name became known in the surrounding area. They offered money—either their own or borrowed from
other Jews—at reasonable rates of about 20 percent; they did not ask for
excessive security and were well advised: if they financed something it
would be reliable. Jacob Simon von Warburg's fortune grew because of
earnings from interest, commissions, and pledged goods. He made
friends. He became the leading light and the head of the small Jewish
community in Paderborn.[33] A pious and charitable Jew, every morning
he brought together all the men in the town for prayers in his house.
After many years, in 1615, he became rich enough to have a beautiful
synagogue built in his own home, the first in Paderborn.[34] Men came
long distances on foot, sometimes every morning, or at least every Friday
evening, to spend the whole of Saturday there in prayer.

For these Jews, rich or poor, life was austere even if they were better
received here than elsewhere in Europe, where the counter-reformation
was then raging. But the Thirty Years War was the source of all evil, and
as always the Jews were held in suspicion. Moreover, in the small
principalities they were less well protected than were some of the
families at the great German and Austrian courts: the Lehmans in
Alberstadt, the Beers in Frankfurt, the Kaullas in Stuttgart, the
Seligmans in Munich or the Suess Oppenheimers in Vienna. The von
Warburgs, even though they belonged to one of the older families, were
somewhat looked down on by the Jews of these cities. They lent to
peasants and merchants, or at best to the bishop, and not to princes or
kings.

After Jacob Simon's death in 1636, his eldest son, Juspha Joseph,
brought up in the same tradition and with the same ambition as his
father, went into the profession and won an extension of the charter. He
strengthened the family influence among the merchants of the region
and became the richest Jew in the town. This much is known because,
according to the records, he paid the highest protection duty to the
bishop.[35]

The extent of the bishopric was no longer enough, however. Juspha
Joseph wanted to play a bigger field, to widen the range of his clients
and to lend more. He could not do this from Warburg, which was too
isolated. Where could he go? Further west, Europe was not yet welcom-
ing enough. The East was opening up but was too poor. Since he spoke
only Hebrew and German, he wanted to stay in German territory. He
also realized that for a banker wealth could only come from international
trade. To do better he would have to be at the source: in a port.

So, in 1647, he asked his eldest son, Jacob Samuel, to settle in Altona, a port to the north of Warburg.

The Warburgs of Altona

Altona, the twin city of Hamburg, was then a principality under Danish protection.[36] The city was more receptive to foreigners than Warburg, as is usual for a port. Religious and community life was freer. A few Portuguese Jews had been established there for some time with their judges, cemeteries and schools. Altona was also the capital of the Jewish communities in the region, and the seat of the rabbinic court for the surrounding Hanseatic towns,[37] where freedom reigned, along with pride in being without rulers.

The departure of the Warburgs for this northern town reflects a wider phenomenon of the time: shortly before the Mediterranean gave up its claim to shaping the course of capitalism in favor of Amsterdam and London,[38] the Jewish communities of Europe shifted en masse toward Northern Europe—the Jewish bankers, sensitive and alert to prosperity, going ahead of them as pathfinders.

Amsterdam, where Menasseh ben Israel published his extraordinary *Hope of Israel* in 1659,[39] therefore became a major center of Jewish banking, even before the fall of Genoa, the last Mediterranean metropolis.[40]

At the same time another banker—this time a Juguenot named Samuel Bernard—was playing a notable role at the Versailles court of Louis XIV, whose excesses he financed.

The day after the wedding of Charles II and Catherine of Braganza in 1662, there arrived in London the Sephardic Jewish bankers Jacob Henriques and Samson Gideon, who were already deserting Amsterdam for the "center" of the future.[41]

In Altona Jacob Samuel felt happy immediately. His pawnbroking business opened up for the family the new universe of the sea. He was successful and branched out to Hamburg in 1647. He urged his father to join him, but Juspha was reluctant: he was after all the most influential Jew in Westphalia. He even became the collector of taxes from Jews in Warburg. Certainly not. Why should he leave?

When Jacob Samuel died in 1668, Juspha decided to go to Altona.[42] He closed down his business in Warburg, left the town regretfully and went to Altona to look after the education of his grandchildren and take over his son's affairs. He was to die ten years later, leaving one of his grandsons, Moses, in sole charge of the business.[43]

There was a complete break with the past. Almost all the Warburgs moved to Altona and retained from the past only their name—no longer von Warburg—but Warburg. It was now possible to be a Jewish moneylender in a German town without necessarily carrying its name like a collar around one's neck.

The family, which would settle for two and a half centuries in this area of a few square kilometers, already had a long history behind it, longer than that of other bankers: the Barings would not begin their operations until 1717 in Exeter, the Rothschilds not until 1785 at the court of Prince William, landgrave of Hesse and Casel.[44] This was also the period when other non-Jews, such as the Fuggers and the Bardis, disappeared from the firmament of European bankers.

But their long history would never quite wipe out their origins. They had begun in the country and were always made to feel it. It would take the extraordinary longevity of the family, the intense pressure to acquire an education and the dedicated way of caring for the "sacred flame," to take the family to unimaginable heights.

Little is known of what Moses Warburg did, except that at his death in 1701 his son Samuel Moses took over the business from him. Samuel was married late in life, in 1772, to the daughter of a Hamburg banker, Elias L. Delbanco, originally from Vienna. The wedding took place in Hamburg, which was now more prosperous, and in 1725 settled there as a money changer. He did not close down the Altona business, which he left in the hands of Warburg cousins.[45] The small establishment he then opened was to stay in the same city and under the same name until 1941 and, as we shall see, was to play an extensive role in the history of finance.

Settling in Hamburg

Samuel's short move is easily understood. The business of lending changed with each center of power: London had become the rival center to Amsterdam.[46] Hamburg appeared to be the third most important European port or, it was hoped, perhaps the second, and tomorrow the first. Granted a charter of freedom in 1189, the city agreed in 1256 to join the Hanseatic League in order to preserve its overseas markets.[47] It lived on its exports to England and the Netherlands.[48] It was on the lookout for everything that moved, and from 1525 it accepted the Reformation. In 1558 a stock exchange was set up. In 1567 it granted privileged rights of establishment to merchant adventurers and in 1612 to Portuguese Jews. Foreigners had freedom to settle and to associate.

Italians, Jews and Portuguese arrived en masse to import their own goods.

Hamburg then became the leading cereal market in northern Europe, the leading importer of English cloth, the main market for beer on the Continent, and as a city was tolerant of even the most advanced ideas and practices.[49] In 1617 it rejected the protection of the Duke of Holstein and had itself recognized as a free city within the empire.

In 1619 the city's first, the Hamburger Bank, opened, ten years behind Amsterdam's. It was set up by thirty merchants to secure a network of finance for the northern courts. This was a place where people were proud to be "citizens," subject to no one.

The Hanseatic League did not survive the Thirty Years War. Its membership was reduced to Hamburg, Bremen and Lübeck, and soon dissolved, but this was no loss for the bankers—quite the opposite—as the city kept control of trade.

The banking profession eventually became diversified all over Europe. England, which bowed to the power of the English goldsmiths who took deposits of gold and made them bear fruit, saw the birth of deposit banks,[50] and the Bank of England was set up in 1694 by William III, then at war with Louis XIV. The Hamburg banks made their guarantee techniques known to the rest of the world by sending some of their people to London, Berlin and even America. Observing these techniques, the great British merchants stopped participating directly in long-distance trade, because they were able to make a better profit by financing[51] loans granted to other less well-known traders who took the actual commercial risk. In this way merchant banks were created in London in the image of banks. Baring Brothers was the first in 1762. Others imitated them a little later: Anthony Gibbs, Arbuthnot Latham, then Schroder and the Hambros, also from Altona.[52]

The business of lending or guaranteeing loans for international trade developed as far as America, even before her independence: thus Asher Levy, David Franks and Haym Salomon were to finance exports and later the American Revolution. In France, Spain, Germany and Italy the new breed of banker also appeared, financing international trade by doing no more than guaranteeing the loans granted by others.

This was not yet the ambition of the Warburgs, who had only just arrived in Hamburg. When Samuel Moses settled there in 1725, the city had become the main crossroad between Northern Europe and the Mediterranean, an exit to the Channel, the Atlantic and the American continent, and finally a center of trade in bills of exchange and money for

North Germany.[53] Portuguese Jews played an important economic role, particularly in trade with the Netherlands and the Iberian peninsula.[54]

The Jews were well favored. In 1671 the Jewish communities of Hamburg, Altona and Lübeck united, under the protection of the Senate, to form the largest and most secure Jewish community in Germany, led as always by the richest merchants.

In addition to his daughters, Samuel Moses Warburg had two sons: Gombrich Marcus, born in 1727, and Elias, born in 1729, direct ancestors of all the contemporary Warburgs.[55] He passed on the "sacred flame" to both. The elder son, having returned to live in Altona for a while, went into his father's bank as a trainee in 1750 (to be followed two years later by his brother, Elias),[56] and married the daughter of another of Hamburg's Jewish bankers, Ruben Heckscher.

The Warburg bank was still small. With fewer than ten employees, it made all kinds of loans on security, to shippers who were exporting, or to merchants who were importing. Life was not exactly restful for the two trainees. They were sent to the docks to count merchants' bales or into the city to enquire about the reputation of the shippers. The family had a network of contacts in a number of places. Thus one of the Altona cousins, David Warburg, moved to Frankfurt and would later leave for London, having sold his business to Meyer Amschel Rothschild.[57]

On the death of Samuel Moses in 1759, his son Gombrich Marcus, who had been with the firm for ten years, took control, with his brother, Elias, as deputy.[58] They were to continue building up the business for forty years. In 1773 they established themselves permanently in Hamburg, leaving Altona altogether. At that time Hamburg was beginning a privileged relationship with London, where numerous banking families from the Continent had settled as a result of the French Revolution. G.M. Warburg, as it was now called, was still only a family business, lending against security from 1 Market Street. It was not yet even a company, let alone a true bank.

In London, Paris and Hamburg the business of money lending was continuing to diversify. Some lenders advanced their own money to ventures and in exchange had control of their capital; others found money elsewhere, took deposits and became commercial banks. Everywhere banking was becoming more structured, and Jewish banks no longer occupied such an important position, except in long-term lending, providing financial advice and underwriting international trade.[59]

In 1797, four years before his death, Gombrich Marcus handed over responsibility for the business to two of his sons: Moses Marcus and

Gerson.[60] His younger brother, Elias, was still alive and had two sons, Samuel and Simon, also working in the business, though as subordinates to their cousins, as required by the family's laws of succession. More will be heard later of this kind of succession, and of the scars it could leave behind.

Moses Marcus and Gerson

Gombrich handed the firm over to his two sons during the time of great trouble for Hamburg: Europe was at war, France had just annexed the left bank of the Rhine, the trade links of Europe were severed; trade was worsening everywhere. However, because of the blockade of France and Holland by the English, Hamburg became the center of transit for British goods on the way to Europe.[61]

At the end of the century, when a payments crisis threatened London, the Bank of England stopped guaranteeing the loans of any merchant bank too heavily involved in international trade, disrupted as it was by the war. In Hamburg the banks that were very bound up with their London counterparts found themselves dangerously off balance— short of the money to guarantee their own loans. This crisis was to last ten years.

Nevertheless, elsewhere in Germany, then in the midst of industrialization, the main Jewish banking dynasties were consolidating or growing. In Frankfurt the Speyers, one of the leading dynasties in the country, were then said to be worth 420,000 florins. A member of this family, Philip, who settled in the United States, much later financed the federal government during the Civil War. In Frankfurt again, Joseph Mendelssohn established his firm in 1795, Salomon Oppenheim opened his in Cologne in 1789 and Samuel Bleichroeder set up his in Berlin in 1803 (his son succeeded him and became the influential adviser and political agent of Bismarck).[62]

In Hamburg the Warburgs were beginning to reach a place in the sun, even though they were not yet admitted into the inner circle of great merchant families known as the "pepper sacks" after the origins of their wealth. Warburg was by now one of the top names in Continental finance, and the richest banks in Europe, Jewish and otherwise, did business with them. There was no anxiety over anti-Semitism, either in Hamburg or elsewhere.

The two brothers who took over the bank at the beginning of the nineteenth century were exact opposites: Moses Marcus, the elder, was extremely prudent, while Gerson, the younger, was bold and daring; the former was reserved, the other a man about town.[63] Their association, however, began harmoniously. In 1798 they asked permission from the Senate for the family firm to be turned into a company. This was granted and the trade register shows that the company M.M. Warburg, money changer of Hamburg (M.M. stood for Moses Marcus) replaced the "moneylender G.M. Warburg." The two brothers were the sole shareholders, with equal holdings.[64]

However, the war that exacerbated the financial difficulties of Europe stirred conflict between the two brothers. On this subject diaries kept by some members of the family contain an astonishing story: when Napoleon entered the city in 1804 the merchant banks withdrew the gold they then held in the Hamburg Giro Bank. In order to force the companies to pay a special tax, Napoleon imposed martial law and imprisoned the richest citizens as hostages. Among them was Gerson. Furious at this blackmail, Moses Marcus refused to pay the tax, in defiance of an agreement made by the leading citizens of the city. This shocked everyone. He gave in only after a delegation of rabbis from the community officially ordered him to do so.

This episode left a bitter taste within the family. There followed five years of sulking and negotiation, in which the rabbis played a great part. The two brothers were at last reconciled on 22 June 1810, when they signed a veritable peace treaty, drafted in Hebrew and Aramaic, before the highest religious authorities in the city. The treaty provided that at the death of either brother, the other would become sole owner of the bank, without interference from the city's civil or religious authorities. The treaty added that in the future, only two family members, a descendant of each of the two signatories, would be eligible to become partners in the bank.

This process showed, at the beginning of the nineteenth century, how a family took steps to protect its name against its own members. It also gave the defense of the institution it had created precedence over its own heirs.

That same year, 1810, an imperial decree dated 10 December named Hamburg the French "départment des Bouches-de-l'Elbe." On 18 March 1813 it was captured by the Russians, and six months later, reconquered by Louis Nicolas Davout, only to be evacuated once more by the French on 14 March 1814.

In spite of the wars, and its numerous changes of political status, Hamburg continued to develop and to strengthen its banking ties with England. The Jews lived in peace in the quarter reserved for them. The house of Warburg came through the troubled years as a middle-rank firm. Even though the Warburgs were already among the richest Jews in Hamburg, they were not yet admitted into high society, and there were no Warburgs on the list of the forty biggest taxpayers in the city. Besides, they made no attempt to distance themselves from Jewish tradition—quite the contrary.[65] Once the two brothers were reconciled, Gerson bowed to the demands of religious orthodoxy imposed on him by his elder brother. Each evening they went to a religious service together, and on Fridays they went on foot.[66] The brothers still spoke Hebrew fluently and associated frequently with other Jewish citizens in the running of community affairs: the court of law, the school, social work and the synagogue.

Since—at least as far as money was concerned—success in trade required acceptance by the richest people, the Warburgs did their utmost to be recognized as a financial force to be reckoned with. Thus, on 14 June 1814, after the French finally had left and the city's official Hamburg Giro Bank was trying to guarantee the banco mark as the new currency, M.M. Warburg hastened to be among the first institutions to redeposit the sacks of precious metal that had been hidden since the arrival of the enemy. This act of good citizenship opened society's doors to the Warburgs and won them many a client in Protestant circles.

The following year, as a result of the Congress of Vienna, several states came together to form a German confederation (the Austrian Empire, the kingdoms of Prussia, Hanover, Saxony, Bavaria and Württemberg, and several grand duchies, principalities and self-declared free cities, Hamburg among them)—a rather vague entity, endowed with a powerless assembly based in Frankfurt and dominated by Austria.[67]

Hamburg, however, had no intention of being integrated into any sort of Continental body. It had always been wary of the East and the South and its links had always been primarily with England, rarely with Prussia or Austria, and still less with Poland or Russia. So once the speeches were over, the city Senate decided to keep its distance from all the Germanic structures, and especially from the Zollverein, or customs union, for which the plans emerged in 1818 in Prussia.[68]

By then established at 277 Peterstrasse, the M.M. Warburg bank was strong enough to do business with some of the biggest institutions in Europe. In 1817 M.M. Warburg made so bold as to take up its first contact with the Rothschilds of London,[69] who were then triumphant after their successful speculations on Waterloo. In order to supply them with gold for the London market, Moses suggested that he should become their correspondent in Hamburg, promising to act "as efficiently as anyone else on the spot—no matter who."[70] The Rothschilds, already aware of the growing reputation of these former country moneylenders, accepted the offer and admitted the house of Warburg to the first circle of international finance.

At the same time the family's Judaism now was taking a more secular turn. Together with others, the Warburgs were making Hamburg the center of a major religious reform, aiming toward a Judaism that was far more integrated into the contemporary world and the Lutheran environment. Thus in 1818 Gerson played a major role in the building of a new temple where the prayers, said in German, no longer evoked the return to Zion or the coming of the Messiah.[71] This did not change anything fundamental to Judaism: the strength of practicality, the power of the Law and omnipresence of education.

Marriage for Sarah

With the end of the Napoleonic wars, trade picked up, markets reopened, exchanges started up again, money circulated. Though bullion was still the standard currency in many countries, an English law of 1816 stipulated that payments above 40 shillings must be made in gold at a rate of 77 shillings and 10.5 pence per ounce. In 1821 another law established the convertibility of English notes into a precious metal, without specifying which. These two laws together gave birth to the gold standard, the basis of convertibility of currencies and a means of regulating international exchange rates for more than a century.[72]

The two brothers grew old and their relationship soured. Gerson had remained a bachelor. Moses had only one daughter, named Sarah or Särchen. They saw that the agreement they had made in 1810 after much negotiation and such solemn declarations would give the bank to Sarah and therefore to her husband, and that the family would thus lose it.

When Gerson died first in 1825, without an heir, Moses Marcus was no longer young, but Sarah was only twenty-one. A decision had to be made. She was not particularly pretty, but she was intelligent and assertive.[73] So at the beginning of the following year Moses Marcus brought the family together to discuss the best way to save the name without breaking the pact. One suggestion was to consult the family tree and marry Sarah to a Warburg. There were several possible choices. Moses chose the Warburg nearest to him: Abraham Samuel Warburg, known as "Aby," then a young employee of the bank, was the son of

Samuel Elias and the nephew of the Simon who had gone into the bank at the same times as Moses. Aby was twenty years old. His physical condition was not bad, though he had a rather weak constitution, and he was fairly intelligent. The decision was taken without either of the participants being consulted. The next day Aby was made a partner in the bank and introduced to Sarah.[74] Two years later on 11 February 1829 they were married. The succession was safe, but it had come back to the descendants of Elias against all expectations.

This happened just in time, for Moses died a year and a half after the wedding of his daughter, on 18 November 1830.[75] Aby, with Sarah, then became sole owner of the bank, and took as a partner one of his distant cousins, another Samuel. The latter left after five years to set up his own firm, went bankrupt and has left to this day in the family a horrifying memory of failure and an example not to be followed, only to be spoken of in order to frighten children.

Aby in Business

On 1 January 1834 the Zollverein came into being among the majority of states in the German confederation and Prussia, and gradually became dominant.[76] The Warburg bank was now making loans to major concerns, along with another Jewish bank in Hamburg, that of Salomon Heine, uncle of the poet. In Vienna, Frankfurt and London, Warburg worked with the Rothschilds, in Berlin with the Bleichroeders and Bischoffsheims, and in Antwerp with the Goldschmidts. Once more established in Marktstrasse, the bank still had no more than twenty employees in addition to six members of the family.[77] The business was in money changing and long-term lending, the management of money for merchants and shipowners and investment for ventures affecting all parts of Europe.

The family had become rich, indeed very rich, but theirs was not ostentatious wealth. They kept to themselves with a great sense of formality, discretion and a single obsession: the education of their children.

Then came the revolutionary year of 1848. On 13 March liberal demonstrators drove Metternich out of Vienna. On 19 March riots forced Frederick William IV, who had been king of Prussia since 1840, to promise to call an Assembly (the Diet), which declared itself constituent on 18 May in Frankfurt with six hundred German delegates. On 29 June a provisional government opened the debate on a constitution for Germany.[78] This lasted six months, with the supporters of Austria opposing those of Prussia—moderates against radicals. In January 1849 the supporters of "little Germany" prevailed. Austria was to be considered a foreign state and Parliament decided to create a German empire. The constitution was promulgated on 27 March, but the state had no political reality. Frederick William IV, preferring to be a despotic monarch in Prussia rather than a democratic prince in Germany, refused the offer of the imperial crown on 15 May and recalled the Prussian delegates. The other German states did the same. On 30 May the Parliament, down to 110 members, was transferred to Stuttgart, and on 18 June the government of Württemberg had it dispersed by military force. The first glimmer of German unity had lasted only a year.[79] However, it brought advantages for the Jews of Hamburg, who during that year became citizens of the city and were no longer forced to live in the ghetto. This was an enormous change, which was to open all doors to them.

In August 1849, as a substitute for the empire, Frederick William IV set up a "limited union" of twenty-eight German states. Six months later, on 31 January 1850, he organized elections for a parliament of the limited union, which was also short-lived: in September first Saxony and then Hanover withdrew. On 29 November 1850, having occupied Hesse, Prussia allowed Austria, which was supported by Czar, a return to the 1815 confederation and the rebirth of the Diet of Frankfurt. As a delegate for Prussia, Bismarck attempted to render the assembly ineffective, to drive out Austria and deprive the confederation of any *raison d'etre*. At the same time Frederick William IV was strengthening the Zollverein, which was gradually making Prussia the dominant economic power in Germany.[80]

For the time being peaceful Hamburg remained aloof from the political turmoil.[81] Jews were by then fully accepted everywhere and the house of Warburg became a bank like any other, but not in name. In 1853 its headquarters moved to the city center, 36 Neuer Wall.[82] Aby, who was then in charge, did not leave much of an impression on the family. He is remembered as a lazy man who had a small room built behind a secret door in his office, complete with bathroom and leather sofa, so that he could sleep in comfort. From then on this room was always reserved for the least zealous partner.

Banking Comes to Capitalism
London was then at the heart of Western capitalism and dominated world industry. Its bankers, insurers, shipowners and captains of indus-

try supplied the country with raw materials and organized the export of textiles, machinery and capital. Britain produced more than half the world's industrial goods, and the increasing earnings of its shipping fleet, its banks, insurers and merchants more than compensated for its external trade deficit, which worsened throughout the century. These surpluses were not put into industry, however, but were invested directly abroad and earned even more, to the point where income on capital alone came to balance the trade deficit. The surpluses fed the extensive need for capital of the woolen and cotton mills, the shipyards, steelworks, railways, paper mills and rubber manufacturers of the world.[83]

London's business center, known as the City, became the major world foreign exchange warehouse. The pound attained the status of an international currency, even draining off savings from the Continent to finance the industrialization of faraway countries. The City consisted of a number of increasingly distinct financial institutions: alongside the commercial banks, special departments or separate merchant banks were developing, lending over the long term and advising commercial concerns.[84] In order to buy or sell British shares on the stock exchange, these banks had to go through intermediary brokers and jobbers, although they could operate freely in foreign shares.

The British merchant banks thus became bankers to the great of Europe and America: the Baring bank, founded in 1762, was official financier not only to the imperial family and the Russian government, but also to the whole of South America. The English Rothschilds fixed the world price of gold and financed most of the governments of Europe. Morgan Grenfell, founded in 1833, forged links with the United States through the Morgan family which had emigrated there and managed British investments in America. Hambros Bank, named after a family that had come from Altona at the beginning of the century, took up an interest in Scandinavia, where it had originated.

Banking was becoming organized. In 1844 a law introduced by Robert Peel gave the Bank of England a monopoly on the issue of banknotes, banned the creation of any other issuing institutions and defined the steps to be taken to maintain the country's gold reserves.

Amsterdam, Hamburg and Paris received their share of the money from England, and thanks to this were able to finance ventures in Northern Europe, Germany and Russia. At this time also the United States saw the birth of firms specializing in long-term lending to companies and advising shareholders. The first of these American merchant banks was set up in 1826 in New York by Nathaniel Prime; the second,

set up on 1830 in Baltimore, was Alex Brown and Sons. The same year
Vermilye and Co. made its appearance, and a little later Jay Cooke set
up his bank in Philadelphia.[85]

During those years a number of German Jews arrived in the United
States to do business. Some later became investment bankers, such as
the three Lehman brothers—Henry, Emmanuel and Mayer—who came
from Frankfurt to be cotton brokers first in Alabama, then in New
Orleans and New York, before launching themselves into banking.[86]

Sarah, Savior of Hamburg

On the death of Aby on 8 July 1856 his widow became, at fifty, sole
owner of the firm. She had two sons and a daughter. The eldest child,
Siegmund, grandfather of our subject, was then twenty-one years old.
That year he joined the bank with the pompous title of "director" under
the "counsel" of August Sanders, a merchant and friend of the family
who was helping Sarah with the business. The younger brother, Moritz,
was to join later as a trainee. The daughter, Rosa, married in the same
year a Hamburg banker name Paul Schiff who went to work for the
Creditanstalt in Vienna, where he would become director-general.[87]

Sarah took on the running of the firm. She was an authoritarian and
intelligent woman. The female members of the family did not remember her fondly,[88] perhaps because she was quite forceful and very
demanding of her children. She was well acquainted with the business;
her husband had for a long time treated her like a partner. However, his
legacy was not exactly flourishing. Many of the bills of exchange in the
portfolio were unrealizable, and the Rothschilds, along with other European bankers, showed less confidence in the Warburg bank.[89]

In 1857 Europe was hit by a very serious financial crisis—the first in
the history of industrial capitalism—which affected every market. In
order to support twenty years of uninterrupted economic growth, all the
economies of Europe and America had become indebted, and for a time
the Crimean War kept up the expansion and speculation, feeding the
debt with military successes. When the battles were over, however, the
inadequate earning power of these economies became apparent. There
was panic in all the capital markets; interest rates fluctuated enormously
from one day to the next and banks had difficulty in guaranteeing their
loans.

Critical pressure came from an outpost of the financial world, the
United States, where farmers especially were heavily in debt. On 25
August 1857 a regional insurance company, the Ohio Life & Trust Co.,

suspended payments after an avalanche of claims, followed on 17 October by 150 American banks.[90] Rumors of failure spread to the railways, and at the beginning of October their shares fell by one-third. Illinois Central Railroad, followed by other companies, was unable to meet its commitments. In turn the investment banks, which were heavily involved in this sector and unprotected by any local or federal guarantee, also stopped payments. Count Sartigues, financial counselor at the French Embassy in Washington, noted in his diary that the prime cause of the crisis was that "in the commercial community of the United States, borrowing is supported only by other borrowing, and takes only a lack of confidence in a small part of this community—either banks, companies, or even isolated individuals—for the whole credit market to come to a halt."[91] The American economy as a whole was affected, in particular in the North. Europe, too, which held a major share of the securities in American enterprises, was damaged—mainly the British, who held half the shares in American railways. At the end of September worried European capital withdrew from British banks and the businesses were unable to finance their current operations. Reality was grim: there was large-scale unemployment in Manchester, Leeds, Nottingham and Glasgow. There was no hope for business in Great Britain, where the 1844 Peel law was no longer in force and where at the end of October 1857 the banks were obliged to repatriate all funds invested abroad quickly—especially in Hamburg[92]—in order to meet their commitments.

Hamburg was then placed in a very difficult situation as its banks had borrowed from British banks in order to lend to ventures in Northern and Western Europe and South America. The crisis spread to Austria, Bohemia, Scandinavia, Italy and France.[93]

In Hamburg the situation rapidly became untenable. With desperate creditors and sluggish debtors, the banks were unable to guarantee their own commitments. Panic set in. Indeed, for the first time since its establishment, M.M. Warburg was threatened with failure. The city Senate intervened, determined not to allow the ruin of its hard-won financial reputation. In October it brought together the city's leading bankers, who came to the conclusion that they would need to find 8 million marks within a month in order to secure payments on a continuing basis. The Senate then decided to set up the Garantie-Discontoverein, a loan guarantee bank, capitalizes at 8 million marks.[94] Within a few weeks the city's banks poured in 5 million marks, but they still needed 3 million more. Bankers and industrialists explored every contact: the hunt was on. November was a month of frenzy. With Europe in crisis, nobody was willing to lend such a large amount to a center in breach of its payments. The Berlin government refused—why help a free city that had ignored the Zollverein? Banks in Paris, London, Stuttgart, Frankfurt and Milan all refused; there were too many problems. The due date for payments came very close: Hamburg was threatened with bankruptcy.

The solution came at the beginning of December—from Vienna, but through the Warburgs. Siegmund, the latest to join the bank, and very worried about its future, decided to write to Vienna, where Paul Schiff, the husband of his sister, had become director-general of the Rothschild's Creditanstalt bank.

He explained that he had to get together 3 million marks mainly to keep the city from bankruptcy, but also to save M.M. Warburg, which was in the front line of this crisis. Paul Schiff was tempted to accept, and not only to please his wife. Helping the city of Hamburg was a risk worth taking. Still, like every good banker, before granting such a sizable loan to a foreign bank, he consulted the minister of foreign affairs. On 6 December he also informed Franz-Joseph in person the same day. Franz-Joseph, only too happy to have an opportunity of countering the influence of Berlin in Hamburg, immediately authorized the loan for six months at 6 percent. Three days later a train carrying crates of silver bars worth 3 million marks left Vienna for Hamburg. The bullion arrived in Hamburg on 15 December. Its entry into the station was enough to restore confidence.

Moreover, in the United States the crisis began to subside and British capital gradually returned to the Continent. In January 1858 the situation eased around the world; on 11 February the discount rate in London fell back to 3 percent. Hamburg was saved. Four months later, on 15 June, the bullion was sent back to Vienna unopened, with interest.[95]

The Warburgs had saved the city. This family of Westphalian money changers had finally been admitted into the ranks of leading European financiers. Clients flocked in. More than half a century of halcyon days and power lay ahead.

A Cake for Bismarck

In 1858, barely two years after the death of Aby, M.M. Warburg was out of the red where Aby had left it. That same year Sarah appointed

Siegmund her partner and put him in sole charge of the running of the firm, but kept all the important business and three-fifths of the profits for herself. The rest was for Siegmund. Moritz, the younger brother, remained an employee of Siegmund until 1862 when he came of age and—despite the 1810 agreement—became a partner with a one-fifth share in the profits, taken from his mother's share. Sarah continued to control the bank. Her two sons, along with the then director Hans Dorner and their guardian August Sanders, did no more than carry out her instructions.

The two brothers were very different from one another. Siegmund was very unconventional, and although his grandson and namesake never met him, he spoke of him with some pride. He was a great banker.

"Of the two brothers, he was the entrepreneur," said his nephew Max.[96] Quick-tempered and hard to please, far less academic than the rest of the family, he loved riding, hunting and singing opera, and was fond of society life whether in Hamburg, London or Berlin. He attended services and observed Jewish law but did not care for the dietary rules that forbade him access to the restaurants he enjoyed. He had his own synagogue at his home at 18 Alsterufer.[97] One day he shocked his brother, who had suggested dismissing an employee who had fathered a child, by snapping back, "Certainly not, we are keeping him! And I trust the mother is pretty!"

Hamburg was still a free city, but not for much longer. On 2 January 1861 Wilhelm I became King of Prussia and on 23 September 1862 appointed Prince Otto von Bismarck chancellor. The latter sought a confrontation with Austria, having first secured the neutrality of Russia through the Alvensleben Convention of 6 February 1863.

On 2 April 1862, in Wiesbaden, Siegmund married Theophilie Rosenberg, the daughter of a Russian banker from Zhitomir. Her mother was from the Günzburg family of Russian bankers, located in Kiev and St. Petersburg and with ties to many European banks. One of Theophilie's sisters was married to Leon Ashkenazi, founder of the Ashkenazi bank in Odessa; another to Baron Joseph von Hirsch-Gereuth, a partner in the Bischoffsheim and Goldschmidt bank of Berlin, Paris, London and Antwerp. As was customary in the family, it was decided that two-thirds of the dowry would be added to the capital of the M.M. Warburg bank. The young couple had seven children, two of them boys and one of whom became the father of Siegmund G. Warburg.[98]

Thanks to the first Siegmund, the firm them moved into the top rank of city institutions. It earned a lot of money from lending, either alone or with syndicates, a major Hamburg innovation of the time.

Sarah was still the real boss; she knew how to judge the market and the worth of companies issuing securities. Every morning, before the arrival of her two sons, the mail was opened by the youngest employees. Every evening, Siegmund and Moritz went to report to her on the day's business. If Sarah was not satisfied with what she heard, she would say, "Now account for your actions. I am listening, Siegmund."

Family tradition says that Sarah "thought like a man," and often imposed her decisions on Siegmund, who became increasingly rebellious.[99] At home, and even toward her children, she kept to strict etiquette and protocol. Her highly luxurious life-style equaled that of the mayor of Hamburg. She entertained at her home everyone of note in Germany—from shipowners to bankers, from Heinrich Heine, who dedicated a poem to her, to Otto von Bismarck, the new chancellor with whom she corresponded regularly. Each year she sent him a cake at Passover, except when she did not approve of what was being done to the Jews—for example, when the emperor's chaplain preached sermons she considered anti-Semitic.[100]

The family was received in the most exclusive circles. In February 1862 Siegmund was elected a "citizen of Hamburg," the city's equivalent of a title of nobility, and the only one the family would allow, reluctantly. He also became a respected member of the city council.

Two years later Moritz became a partner in the bank and on 12 June 1864 married Charlotte Oppenheim, the daughter of a great Frankfurt goldsmith, whose maxim bears repeating: "Selling a pearl you own to someone who wants to buy it is not doing business. Selling a pearl you haven't got to someone who doesn't want it—that's doing business."

Moritz also had seven children: five boys and two girls. He settled in Mittelweg, another part of the city, and his branch of the family became known by that name.

By this time the family had extended its branches throughout Europe via an exceptional network of relationships and a series of well-planned marriages. The Schiffs in Vienna, the Rosenbergs in Kiev, the Günzburgs in St. Petersburg, the Ashkenazis in Odessa, and the Oppenheims, Bischoffsheims and Goldschmidts in Germany itself were all either relatives or associates.

Moneylender Turned Banker

In 1863 (some less reliable sources say 1867) the firm obtained from the Senate the right to change its legal status: from M.M. Warburg, money changer, to M.M. Warburg, bankers at 47 Hermannstrasse. This was also an important change from the viewpoint of social status. That same year Sarah moved to a house in the best residential part of town, the Rothenbaumchaussee. Life became still better. The family had a great number of servants. While remaining very Jewish, some members of the family ventured into politics—a sign of the ease and freedom of the times. A cousin, Samuel Warburg, a grandson of Elias, was elected member for Schleswig-Holstein in the Danish Parliament, which still rules there.[101] In 1864 Siegmund had his first son, the premature and delicate Abraham, who would be known as Aby S.

On January 1865 Sarah, aged sixty, retired from the bank. Shortly afterward the capital was divided equally between the two brothers. Until her death twenty years later she would continue to follow the business of the house of Warburg and to draw a princely pension from her two sons.

Germany was then once more attempting to unify. At the beginning of March 1866 Bismarck persuaded the Prussian council of ministers to accept the principle of a war against Austria and entered into a military alliance with Italy, which hoped to recover Venice. On 9 April he proposed the election of a German assembly by universal suffrage. On 7 June Prussian troops invaded Danish Holstein. All the German states, except the small northern ones, took the side of Austria. On 15 June Bismarck announced that he considered the German confederation dissolved.

Prussian military victory was swift, and the peace treaty signed in Prague on 23 August 1866 marked the end of Vienna's German ambitions.[102] Prussia then set up a North German confederation north of the Main, over which the king of Prussia became hereditary ruler. Samuel Warburg, who had been elected to the Danish Parliament, became a member of the German Parliament.[103]

At the same time, wherever it was still in use as a monetary standard, silver gave way to gold. Following the discoveries of gold in California and Australia, and also as a result of the American Civil War, the gap between the values of gold and silver had considerably diminished. However, the discovery of silver mines in Nevada led to a quintupling of world production within the space of a few years, and consequently the price of silver collapsed. It was also thought at the time that gold was becoming more rare, although its production was increasing even faster than that of silver: "Silver came into disrepute basically for psychological reasons: people ceased to believe in its monetary role. . . . The disavowal of silver led to the victory of gold."[104]

Birth of Kuhn Loeb & Co.

The midnineteenth century saw the first appearance of those who would be the leaders of American investment banking: the Morgans, who organized British investment in America, and others, like Kidder Peabody. In addition, after the riots of 1848 a number of German Jews left for the United States and became bankers alongside Speyer, Belmont, Lehman and Salinger, who were already established there.[105] At first they financed the federal government during and after the Civil War; then they became way stations for capital coming from Europe to finance the development of the American continent.

So it was that two brothers-in-law, Abraham Kuhn and Salomon Loeb, left Worms around 1850, to become wholesale textile merchants in Cincinnati. On 1 February 1867 they made their way to New York with the $500,000 they had earned and set up a bank at 31 Nassua Street.[106] It was a well-timed move. The Civil War was over, steelworks were being built and the telegraph operated across the whole continent. The railways under construction opened up enormous sources of profit for the banks. The Union Pacific was progressing westward and the Central Pacific eastward, and the federal government put $60 million at their disposal for the purchase of land.[107] The banks were needed to organize groups of investors to finance the rest of the operation, and there was much money to be made from forming "syndicates" of potential lenders and charging commission on these loans.

This led to specialization among certain banks. Jay Cooke, J.P. Morgan and Kuhn Loeb made loans to railways and steelworks, while the Lehman Brothers and Goldman Sachs financed the distribution of goods. The first guaranteed loan was made in 1869 by Jay Cooke for $2 million to the Pennsylvania Railroad. To pull in money from Europe the American banks strengthened their agreements with London banks; for example, J.P. Morgan with Morgan Grenfell, Kidder Peabody with George Peabody, and Kuhn Loeb with Rothschild.

In the opposite direction, European banks began to establish offices in New York and Boston, and other German Jewish bankers, attracted by American expansion, emigrated to these two cities. The Guggenheims and Lewisons all opened businesses with great expectations.[108]

The Time of Siegmund

By the end of the 1860's, the function of the investment bank, making long-term loans and advising investors, had become increasingly distinct from that of the commercial bank, which took in money from individuals, made short-terms loans and advised on cash management. However, the distinction varied from country to country.

Siegmund became an eminent person. As an elected member of the "governing body" of the city, he was in charge of organizing the transfer to the state of taxes previously paid by the Jews to their community.[109] On 1 June 1869 he was elected a member of the association of vendors of securities and on 14 December 1870 appointed a deputy to the city Senate.[110]

The Warburg's family history, like untiringly repeated biblical stories, was a safeguard against immoderate ambition, luxurious tastes or an appetite for power. The Warburgs were not fond of parvenus, Siegmund no less than others. A century later his grandson would remember one of his adages: "It was the Warburgs' good fortune that whenever they were on the point of becoming very rich, something happened that made them poor again, and forced them to start over from the beginning."[111] This is what would happen to his grandson fifty years later in the turmoil of Weimar.

For the moment, however, all was well. Siegmund was running the bank successfully under the severe eye of his mother and with the help of his brother. The families of the two brothers rivaled each other in brilliance and wealth. In the city they were known by their respective addresses: Siegmund's family was known as the "Alsterufer Warburgs" and Moritz's as the "Mittelweg Warburgs." This rivalry explains much that lay behind the destiny of the Warburgs in the next century. At the time they were Germany's *haute banque*. They helped new banks in Hamburg or Berlin to develop and assembled "syndicates" to guarantee and issue loans in Germany and throughout the world.

The money they loaned came from friendly bankers or private fortunes. This earned them a great deal of money, even though enrichment was not always their motive. Siegmund was then on the best of terms with Lionel Rothschild in London, with Pereire in Paris, with Günzburg in St. Petersburg and with Salomon Loeb in New York.[112]

In 1870 the Franco-Prussian War gave Bismarck the opportunity to achieve the unification of Germany. The states of Saxony, Baden, Württemberg and then Bavaria joined the confederation. On 18 January 1871, in Versailles, the Confederation of North Germany became the German Empire.[113] Each state retained its constitution, laws and administration. The government of the empire, dominated by Prussia, took charge of foreign affairs, the army, mail and telegraph, trade, customs and communications. Two-thirds of the members of the Reichstag were Prussian. The kaiser (emperor) was the king of Prussia; the chancellor was Bismarck, the German architect of this confederation, formed against the royal will.[114]

Only then did Hamburg, the last financial center still free of Prussian control, join the empire. Nevertheless, it remained a city apart, international by inclination, a natural outlet for North Germany to England and the Netherlands and turned more toward London and New York than Berlin or Frankfurt.

After the end of the 1870 war and the creation of the German Empire, France was obliged to pay heavy reparations. In 1871 Siegmund participated in the Rothschilds' organization of the loan floated by France in order to repay Prussia for war damage. Fifty years later the firm would do the same thing, but in the opposite direction, to pay reparations due from Germany.

This was the year that Siegmund's second son was born: George, who would be the father of Siegmund George. Some time later a daughter, Rosa, was born, followed by four others: Elsa, Anna, Olga and Lilly.[115]

The Schiffs Appear on Wall Street

For the Warburgs, a future link between their bank and America was in the making: in 1871 Abraham Kuhn, who had set up a bank in New York with Salomon Loeb, returned to Germany with the intention of retiring to Hamburg. There he met Jacob Schiff, a young man of exceptional ambition, whose father was a stockbroker in Frankfurt.[116] If family legend is to be believed, he was descended from a fourteenth century Frankfurt money changer named Uri Phoebus Schiff, who himself had claimed to be a descendant of King Solomn. In 1864, at age eighteen, Jacob outraged the community by going to America without his parents' knowledge to try to open a brokerage office. He failed and returned to Germany five years later, humiliated. His family then sent him to Hamburg to work in the offices of the newly established Deutsche Bank. Even so, he did not give up his American dream. In 1872, when he met Abraham Kuhn, just back from the United States, he asked him for help to go back there.

Abraham gave him an introduction to Salomon Loeb, who was still in New York. Overjoyed, Jacob seized his chance and left immediately. Salomon liked him and took him on. His success came with lightning speed: three years later in 1875 he became the partner of Salomon Loeb and, the following year, married his daughter.[117] He was very soon recognized as the true head of Kuhn Loeb, became one of the richest men in America and remained in charge of the bank for nearly half a century—a role that led to his association with two of the children of Moritz Warburg.

In 1873, fifteen years after the first major financial crisis of capitalism, a second began. The center of the industrial world moved across the Atlantic. As a sign of this threat to British power, the British copper market collapsed. Chile and the United States were now the leading copper producers. To stay in business, British copper trading companies like Brandeis-Goldschmidt sought to enter the markets for more precious metals.

British banks were unable to switch from the financing of raw materials and textile technology to oil production or electrification, and so were damaged by the crisis.

On 8 May 1873 a wave of panic hit the stock exchange in London, and then in Vienna, with repercussions in France and Germany. For some years the German banks, among them Warburg's, remained in a precarious position. The strength of the industrial world was becoming concentrated in America. Boston and New York vied with each other for control. America saw the lightning-speed development of the steel industry, shipyards, electricity and the internal combustion engine. The first long-distance telephone line between New York and Boston was inaugurated in 1884. Money was needed to finance these rising industries. Capital poured in from around the world in search of greater profits, while the issue of currency remained free, barely controlled by a federal law of 1875.[118]

The new power of America could be gauged from its balance of payments: its foreign trade was in surplus, as were its payments, and both stayed that way, with some variation, until 1898, and thereafter without the shadow of a deficit for more than sixty years.

Britain, however, remained the financial heart of the West for another twenty years. John Maynard Keynes was to write that in the second half of the nineteenth century London's influence on the terms of credit throughout the world was such that the Bank of England was able to act as the conductor of the international orchestra. By adjusting the terms of its loans it was able to determine in large part the terms of credit offered abroad.[119]

So the international monetary standard was not as quickly replaced as the industrial capital, and responsibility for this in fact became a lasting burden to Britain. The pound remained the major international currency, and transactions among foreign countries continued to be settled in sterling, which was detrimental to the cost of Britain, which felt obliged to support the value of its currency against the interests of its own exporters.

Thus the City continued to concern itself with the finance of other countries, not that of Britain, attracting the wealth of Europe toward America, Indonesia, Nigeria, Kenya and South Africa.[120] At the request of the City, in 1881 William Gladstone granted preferential rights to certain colonial companies to assist these exports of capital: the British North Borneo Co. was set up in 1881, the Royal Niger Co. in 1886, the Imperial British East Africa Co. in 1888 and the British South Africa Chartered Co. in 1889.[121]

In Moritz's Day

In 1889, Siegmund, who had brought the bank to greatness, died in Baden at the age of fifty-four—four years after his mother—leaving two sons, Aby S. and George, and five daughters. Despite the full power of attorney held by Aby S. and the large family left by Siegmund, the "Alsterufer" Warburgs were relegated to the sidelines for many decades by the "Mettelweg" Warburgs. It was Moritz, at fifty-one, who found himself at the head of what remained of the M.M. Warburg bank. From then on, and up to the time of Siegmund George, the history of the name is intermingled with the history of Moritz, and the quite extraordinary story of his five sons.

Aby S., a diabetic, initially went through the tough regimen of a young trainee. Like his forebears a century earlier, he went down to the docks at dawn to count the bales received as security, wrote up accounts and supervised debtors. He became a director of the family bank, then a partner, but in effect fell imperceptibly under the authority of his uncle Moritz. As he did not have the "sacred flame," he surrendered his right of seniority to others better able to run the bank.

Two years later his younger brother, George, who was suffering from unbearable encephalitis, gave up the idea of a banking career, to the great joy of the Mittelweg Warburgs. George would have liked to study history, but his headaches led him to make a decision that was unprecedented for a Jew in high society at the time: to live in the country. Aby S. used a small part of his inheritance in 1891 to buy his brother a fairly large property, "Uhenfels," near Urach, not far from Stuttgart, and much farther south than the town of Warburg in Swabia. George was something of a recluse but nevertheless was welcomed by neighbors such as the Heusses, the von Neuraths, and the Kaullas, a very eminent family of bankers and lawyers. With the help of several farmers, he became an agricultural expert, growing maize and rye. Because he retained a share in the profits of the bank, he was fairly rich.

Quite different from his older brother, Siegmund, Moritz was conservative and orthodox. Upon coming of age in 1857 he chose the motto, "*Labor et Constancia*," which said it all. In a private, unpublished diary circulated much later within the family, his son Max wrote of him, "He attached more importance to the reputation of the firm than to financial gain. Moritz was a very orthodox Jew."[122] He was bald, and the memory of his pride in a stunning collection of wigs lives on. Anxious to be fully integrated into the city, he schemed to gain acceptance as a trumpeter in the Hamburg and Warburg militias, and once enrolled he stayed for years. These small vanities aside, he was a very great banker, concentrating on the large-scale ventures he called "higher banking." Unlike other bankers in the city, he accepted few private clients and preferred to finance his undertakings either with his own money or with that of the banks he syndicated. Moreover, his area of influence was able to extend throughout Germany, which Bismarck was then seeking to unify militarily, judicially, fiscally, economically and monetarily. In 1875, to replace the Royal Bank of Prussia, the Reichsbank was set up as the supervisory institution for all banks within the empire, and a standard mark was put into circulation.[123] Moritz, as yet no more than a provincial worthy, was to follow—or even run ahead of —the exceptional financial and political growth of the new Germany.

Childhood of the Five

Between 1866 and 1879 Charlotte and Moritz had five sons: Abraham, known as Aby M. (to distinguish him from his cousin Aby S.), Max, Felix, Paul and Fritz, and two daughters: Olga and Louisa. It was then that the fine clockwork of the banking dynasty began to run awry. For the first time in the history of the family, several children of one father rebelled against the fate assigned to them by their positions on the family tree.

By clan law, and insofar as Siegmund's sons stood aside, Aby M. was to succeed his father as the head of the bank. Max and Paul were to become his assistants, Felix was to join the business of maternal grandfather, Oppenheim the goldsmith, and Fritz was to become a lawyer. But from their very first discussions, the children decided otherwise. At the age of eleven, Aby M., who had a passion for the arts, gave up his right of seniority to Max in exchange for the promise of as many books as he would wish to read in the future.[124] The extraordinary thing is that in later life neither Aby M. nor Max changed their minds.

Forty years later Aby M. would become one of the great art historians of the century, and with the help of his brother, who had become the leading financier in Germany, he would set up the first multidisciplinary library in the world: the Warburg Institute, now in London, which was endowed during his lifetime with tens of thousands of books.[125] Whereas Aby M. was withdrawn and physically resembled his father, Max took after his mother. Like her, he was blond and blue-eyed, and because of this and his name many people came to forget that he was a Jew: occasionally, he too, forgot. When, after two years of trying, Aby M. managed to get his father to accept his refusal to enter the bank, Max began the classic route of a Warburg bound for an executive role in the enterprise. He finished his formal studies and began training as a clerk in the family firm; then he went to Dreyfus in Frankfurt and finally to Wertheim & Gompertz in Amsterdam. There, in 1888 (he was twenty-one), he succeeded in having the family bank appointed a correspondent bank to the Nederlandsche Bank, the greatest Dutch bank at that time.[126]

On the death of his uncle Siegmund in 1888, Max committed the only undisciplined act in his life: he joined the 3rd Bavarian Regiment of Light Cavalry, with the idea of becoming an officer and giving up banking. When he wrote to his father to explain his intentions, Moritz replied succinctly that he did not know whether to think it worse to have a son who wanted to be an officer because he had forgotten that he was a Jew, or to have a son condemned never to be an officer precisely because he was a Jew.[127] After a year of stubborn persistence, Max gave up his idea, resigned from the army and went back to banking.

Two months later, on 29 March 1890, Wilhelm II "dropped the pilot," Bismarck, and appointed General Alfred von Schlieffen chief of staff in place of Field Marshal Alfred von Waldersee. Germany was working toward expansion and planning for war to maintain its industry. Max went back to live in Hamburg. He became friendly with another influential Jew, not much older than himself, Albert Ballin, who had started out with nothing but by then ran the Hamburg-America Line, which he would build into one of the leading German concerns.[128] Max admired him greatly: he was the confidant of the kaiser—in fact the only man the kaiser would visit at home. As the kaiser reigned unilaterally, influencing him meant influencing the fate of Germany. Chancellors succeeded one another, each one weaker than the next: Caprivi, Hohenlohe—then Bülow. In fact Albert Ballin was more powerful than all of them, and Max began to dream of something all previous Warburgs had avoided: politics.

After his military interlude, Max did not stay in Hamburg for long. To give him a change of scene his father sent him to the Imperial Ottoman Bank in Paris, where he spent a year, at the same time taking classes at the Sorbonne. Quite the dandy, Max left Paris regretfully in 1891 to finish his apprenticeship with N.M. Rothschild & Sons in London. He thought he was doing the right thing by arriving in the City at nine in the morning.[129] In the style of the "House of Sarah," he even went to open the mail with the young employees, as he had seen young trainees do at home. Anxious to prevent him from discovering too many trade secrets in this way, the bank quickly explained to him that no gentleman arrived in the City before ten o'clock, and that he should leave before four. Max adapted well to this schedule. He soon became a young man of fashion, the darling of the British aristocracy and more English than the English.

At the end of 1891, however, just when he was preparing to make a tour of the correspondent banks around the world, his father recalled him urgently to Hamburg, to help him manage the firm. Moritz had been heading it for two years and it was going through a bad phase. A bank owned by Siegmund's wife's family, the Günzburg bank of St. Petersburg, had sunk 7 million marks borrowed from M.M. Warburg into the Lena mines of northern Siberia, which turned out to be worthless. The Günzburg bank was unable to honor its commitments.[130] Worse still, the following June, Rosa, one of Siegmund's daughters and a cousin of Max, was to marry the banker involved, Baron Alexander de Günzburg, to whom she had been engaged for two years. Their wedding had been delayed by the death of her father, but it was too late to break the engagement off. So despite the large accounts already committed, Moritz decided to guarantee all the bills that came from Günzburg, without limit. The risk was not taken in vain: managed with an iron hand, the Günzburg bank recovered.[131] Some years later the baron and Rosa repaid all their creditors at a sumptuous dinner held at their St. Petersburg mansion. Here each guest found the amount owed set out on his plate in gold coins, and a silken sack to put the coins in after counting them.[132] Such was the sumptuous generosity of the Russian barons, whose splendor dazzled the abstemious Huguenots of Germany.

Once the emergency had passed, Max stayed in Hamburg. His first years with his father were difficult. Then cholera broke out in a big Hamburg import-export firm that was a major client. Several employees of M.M. Warburg caught the disease and died, and for two dreadful months only Max and two volunteer employees continued working at the bank. By this courageous action, Max compelled his father to recognize him as second-in-command, and at thirty he became in fact the true head of the firm.[133]

That same year Max's brother Paul, one year his junior, joined the bank. Intellectual, serious, melancholy and somewhat inhibited by the two elder brothers who outshone him in society, Paul, too, had begun his training as a banker early. He started with his uncle in Hamburg, then went to Samuel Montagu in London, to the Russian Bank in Paris and finally to his cousins-to-be, the Günzburgs in St. Petersburg. He then made the round-the-world trip that completed the education of every Warburg and in 1893 returned to Hamburg to his father, who appointed him a director.[134]

Felix, Moritz's fourth son, was born in 1871. Unlike Paul, Felix was no intellectual. A lover of beautiful things and beautiful women, quite detached from religious orthodoxy, he kept up appearances only to avoid hurting his mother. It bored him to have to eat kosher food while traveling. In 1893 he was sent as a trainee to Oppenheim in Frankfurt, where he had a fine time. At the age of eighteen he became the lover of Clara Schumann, who was more than three times his age. It was in Frankfurt, during a party at the Dreyfus home the following year, that he met Frieda, the daughter of Jacob Schiff.

At forty-seven Jacob, the emigrant who had become the son-in-law of Salomon Loeb, was then the most famous Jew in New York and one of the richest men in the world. The year before he had managed the impossible; he reorganized the Union Pacific, which was on the edge of bankruptcy, and made an enormous amount of money out of it. In 1894 he had moved Kuhn Loeb to 27 Pine Street[135] and now had just arrived in Europe on holiday with his wife and daughter. He hated Germany but had to go there, if only to be seen by those who had known him when he was poor. So he came to Frankfurt where his daughter met Felix Warburg. It was love at first sight. That evening Felix wrote to his parents, "I have met the girl I want to marry."[136]

Moritz was very upset. Here was his son in love with an American girl and ready to follow her to that land of savages where it was impossible to live as a good Jew. Furthermore, Moritz loathed the sea, and the idea of having to cross the Atlantic terrified him.[137] Jacob Schiff was just as enraged to see his daughter take an interest in "that boy." He had no wish to see her settle in Germany and considered the Warburgs far too modest a match for her. But the two young people insisted, and for the first time among the Warburgs a love story exploded in public.

The two angry families finally agreed to meet, but on neutral ground. Sir Ernest Cassel, correspondent of Kuhn Loeb and N.M. Rothschild in London, a friend and adviser to the Prince of Wales, and linked to both families, was chosen as intermediary. After many trials and allegedly chance meetings at the races at Longchamps and the baths at Bad Gastein, Sir Ernest managed to organize a dinner for the families in Osten. This turned into calamity when lobster was served. Jacob was furious that Felix did not seem shocked by this violation of Jewish law. The parties separated without having discussed anything. After many more attempts, Sir Ernest at last found a compromise: it was agreed that once a week Felix would write to Frieda and Frieda to Felix, under the censorship of their respective parents, to whom the letter would be read aloud before mailing.[138]

This did not discourage the two sweethearts, and letters were exchanged for a year. Then the families gave in, and the wedding was agreed to. Felix would live in New York and work with his father-in-law. The ceremony, in March 1895, was the occasion for Hamburg society and many European bankers to cross the Atlantic.[139]

That, however, was not the end of it: Paul was best man to his brother, and the bridesmaid was the young sister of Frieda's mother, Nina Loeb, who was the same age as her niece. So another romance now entwined Nina Loeb and Paul, who until then had been courting his cousin Rosa Warburg, and led to a second wedding. Paul thus became his brother's uncle and a year later also moved to New York, where he in turn became a partner with Kuhn Loeb.

Within two years Max lost two of his brothers, even though they remained German citizens and partners in M.M. Warburg for another ten years. Although they regularly crossed the Atlantic in both directions with a full complement of cooks, valets and waiters,[140] both would play an extensive part in the financial history of the United States, which along with Russia then became a "Warburg country."

The destiny of the last of the five brothers was also altered. Fritz, who was meant to become a lawyer, studied law in Berlin and Rostov, but following the departure of three of his brothers, gaps at the bank had to be filled, and he went to train with the Disconto-Gesellschaft in Frankfurt, which had become one of the major German institutions.[141] He spent some time with Brandeis-Goldschmidt & Co., which had become the biggest metal trading company in London, the head of which, Paul Kohn-Speyer, had just married his sister Olga. Then he settled in Hamburg and in 1893 took charge of the credit department of M.M. Warburg.

The five brothers were on their way, and their extraordinary adventure was beginning. Without exaggeration, their destiny could be said to embrace a major part of international financial life in the first half of the twentieth century.

The Rise of Max

In 1893 Max became his father's partner and gradually took on a decisive role within the bank. He was strong enough to have old family laws broken. Using the excuse of Aby S.'s illness, he had his own brother Paul appointed a partner, despite opposition from Theophilie, Siegmund's widow. The balance between the two branches of the dynasty was thus upset.

The financial crisis that had accompanied America's seizure of industrial power was over. America, the "heart" of industry, was not yet competing with London for control of the international financial movements. America also profited more than any other country from the discoveries of gold in South Africa: currencies secured by this gold allowed the expansion of world trade to be financed.

In Europe the rise of German economic power began, backed by the national banks and by dynamic private banks, whether these were all-round banks like the Deutsche Bank or investment houses like M.M. Warburg. Thanks to its reputation and international networks, the latter was now able to take advantage of economic conditions and, using money from Germany and London, to finance industrial exports and the import of raw materials. M.M. Warburg now managed money for the great men of Europe: businessmen, ministers and even writers, such as Marcel Proust.[142] Max steered the bank's activities in the three most profitable directions: the acceptance of bills of exchange, the finance of international trade and the management of money on stock exchanges and the foreign exchanges, which were beginning to fluctuate considerably.[143]

By now he had numerous partners around the world: Kuhn Loeb in New York; Rothschild, Kayser and Japhet in London; Albert Kahn in Paris; Henriques in Copenhagen; and Stockholms Handelsbank in Sweden. He himself had succeeded in entering the Swedish market— which was nearby but had been neglected by the family, in his opinion, because the Warburgs were afraid of not finding any kosher food in Sweden.[144]

In contrast, connections with Russia started to become strained. Certainly there was still support for the family banks, Günzburg and Ashkenazi, but Moritz and Max were enraged to see the growth of anti-Semitism and the beginning of pogroms in the Ukraine, Galicia and Muscovy. Understandably, the Warburgs did not care for this. They detested even more what they read form the pens of journalists and writers such as Dostoevsky. "Today the Jew and his bank dominate everywhere, Europe and its lights, all of civilization, especially socialism, for with its help the Jew will eliminate Christianity and destroy Christian civilization. Then there will be nothing left but anarchy. The Jew will rule the universe."[145]

The family's somewhat dormant Jewish consciousness awoke and turned with hatred on the "Russian devil." But this was no more than opposition to virulent anti-Semitism they themselves had yet to experience. So in 1897 when Theodor Herzl laid the foundations of the Jewish nationalist movement at the first Zionist conference held in Basel, his speech left the integrated Warburgs unmoved.

The family established itself in luxury and power. In 1896 Moritz bought a huge parcel of land overlooking the Elbe at Kösterberg on the outskirts of Hamburg, where he built alongside a magnificent eighteenth-century mansion several large houses for guests and members of the family. Summer was spent there, and winter at Mittelweg.[146] It was a time of great expansion for the business: each year for the next twenty years the bank's turnover rose by one-third. Moritz had then reached the pinnacle of local influence; the Senate consulted him on all municipal matters and he was the undisputed leader of the sixteen thousand Jews in the city.[147]

In 1899, the year of the retrial of Alfred Dreyfus, the bank lavishly celebrated its centenary. It now had a relatively modest thirty-six employees, of whom four were "directors." However, its influence was not to be judged by the number of employees. It owned a portfolio of securities worth more than 9 million marks, and made an annual net profit of more than 1.5 million marks, a margin of 27.6 percent.[148] So everything was going very well for the family except for the scandal caused that year by the eldest son, Aby M., the first Warburg who wanted to marry a non-Jew, Mary Herte. There was a dreadful family storm. Aby persevered.[149] Despite opposition from his father and brothers, the wedding took place, away from Hamburg. For a time Aby M. had to go into exile with his wife in Florence.[150]

As for Max, he continued to climb the social ladder in Hamburg and also in Berlin, the place to be. Everyone in the family recognized his preeminence, though some worried that he was overexposing the name by trying to place himself in the reflected glory of the powerful. His father, tired out before his time, handed the business over to him. His cousin Aby S., the elder son of his father's elder brother, who had been married, widowed and remarried, all but abandoned the bank and lived in a magnificent villa at Cap-Martin. In 1897 Max was elected to the board of the city's Commercial Tribunal. On 29 December 1898 he married Alice Magnus, from a family connected with the Altona Warburgs, whose inactive bank he bought in order to integrate it with the Hamburg bank.[151] With his brother Fritz he now moved to Kösterberg. Paul and Felix also owned a magnificent house there, which they visited from time to time. Their properties were a sort of a private luxury village, with a swimming pool and tennis courts, where guests were lavishly received. In 1900 Alice and Max had their first child there— their only son, Eric.

In Stuttgart that same year Max's cousin and Siegmund's father, George, then age thirty, met his future wife, the mother of Siegmund, Lucie Kaulla.[152] The daughter of a Stuttgart lawyer, Luz, as she was known, had been educated at the best schools and was an excellent pianist. They were married on 1 December 1901. Like George, she came from a strict and highly moral background. Siegmund was to write in a note to friends at the time of her death:

> For my mother, her parents' home in Stuttgart had been a severe and rather spartan school. Whenever an action was needed, it had to be accomplished with maximum attention to detail and gravity; whenever thought was needed, it had to be carried to its ultimate consequence .... My mother told me that her father liked to tell her

repeatedly, "My child if you have to choose between two paths, ask yourself which is the most arduous, for that will be the right one . . . ."[153]

She and George settled in the country, far away from Hamburg. Although Paul spent most of his time in New York where he became a partner in Kuhn Loeb, he was appointed a citizen of Hamburg in 1902, a rare honor that the slighted Max did not receive until a year later.

The family was therefore universally recognized as one of the most powerful in Germany when Siegmund George was born in Urach, son of the Warburg who loved his simple agricultural life.

2

Power at Court

(1902-1933)

The Education of Siegmund

When Siegmund was born in the house at Urach on 30 September 1902, the first and only child of George and Lucie, the family name was at its zenith. Bülow, who replaced Hohenlohe as chancellor of a flourishing Germany, consulted the family increasingly concerning world affairs.

Siegmund's father was rich and happy. He was teaching agronomy at the University of Tübingen. His fortune was estimated at 6 million marks. He had a few servants and numerous tenant farmers, whose number would later diminish, as his business worsened. With a passion for the land he worked and the history he studied, he lived—probably the only one in Europe at that time—the unusual life of Jewish gentleman farmer.

The family remained religious, but in an undemonstrative way characteristic of this part of Germany. "Almost all year, the synagogue was deserted," wrote Fred Uhlman, who lived in a neighboring town during the same period.

Only twice a year, for New Year and the Day of Atonement, it was overflowing . . . . Most Jews belonged to the liberal synagogue [George among them]. But some were orthodox, ate only kosher food, observed the sabbath and refused to do any work whatever on that day. They did not travel, pick up the telephone receiver or wear anything to keep up their trousers, even braces.[1]

George looked on such Jews with remoteness. The food at Uhenfels was still kosher as far as was possible in that distant place, but greater importance was attached to Jewish morality than to religious practice. "My father was a good gardener," Siegmund would say much later. "He thought one should prune branches twice a year and leave the rest to God."[2]

George acquired a still greater taste for solitude when his uncurable headaches grew worse. He went out less and less, except for long walks with his son in the wild and bleak countryside of Swabia. At the very beginning of Siegmund's education he was much in evidence and passed on to him his passion for books. He conveyed to him his disdain for money.

George went often to Stuttgart, Berlin or Frankfurt and spent long summer months with the Rothschilds, the Oppenheims or the Mendelssohns, where wonderful musical evenings brought together the richest families; and he also visited Aby S. in Hamburg, where he took Siegmund, who played the role of Orestes in the family performances of *Iphigenia*.

Gradually Lucie became the real master of Urach: it was she who kept the accounts, managed the property, concerned herself with the families who worked there, received innumerable guests and supervised the education of their son. This life was a change from her bourgeois childhood in Stuttgart, as Siegmund wrote:

> The years of her youth had in no way prepared her for the tasks incumbent on the mistress of a house. She mobilized all her energy to take her share in the work of the house and the farm in order to support her husband, and as was then the custom in country areas and patriarchal societies, to play a role of attentive benefactress towards the famlies living on our land and in the surrounding village communities.[3]

Siegmund's childhood was therefore primarily a long dialogue with his mother; all witnesses to his later life would report that he often spoke of this, referring ceaselessly to the moral principles that guided it—the heritage of a very strict Germanized Judaism.

Until he was seven his mother took complete charge of his education; she taught him to read and write German, gave him lessons in the rudiments of theology and Hebrew and made him say his daily prayers in Latin.

> Prayer was an essential point among my mother's principles of education, even though it was approached in a totally nonconformist way. For my mother, neither the Jewish religion nor any other church or sect had any real importance from a religious point of view. She was very devoted to Jewish tradition and to the moral teachings of Judaism, but her piety was fed on elements of belief which she found in a myriad of religions and philosophies, and especially in her dear Goethe. She firmly rejected any form of dogmatism. The main thing, for her, in religion was to believe in a supreme and supra-terrestrial power and to maintain permanent contact with that force by means of prayer and daily actions.[4]

She also taught him to play the piano and to love music; she herself composed. "Each of her compositions," wrote Siegmund proudly, "whether it was a march, an andante, a minuet or a lullaby, was the clear and powerful expression of her lively and positive view of the world."

At the age of eight he was sent as a boarder to a school a few miles away in Reutlingen. Every Sunday he came back to Urach, and his mother continued her close supervision of his education.

> During the first five years of my school life . . . my mother made me work regularly. She thought that for her son work at home was even more important than work at school, and she was strongly against the idea of leaving this task to even the best of governesses. . . . She thought learning by heart essential for the training of the memory. . . . My mother was firmly convinced that in the end all our actions are subject to the amount of effort and will that goes into them.

Siegmund was therefore a happy child, even though he received little pocket money and his mother kept a tight rein on its use. One day when he was eight she reproached him for spending the money on chocolate rather than a book.[5] He never forgot this criticism of "shallowness" that would constitute in his eyes much later a major weakness of men and nations.

He would also always remember that on the eve of his bar mitzvah his mother said to him:

> My dear boy . . . From tomorrow on, you have to pray for yourself. When you pray the most important thing is to think very hard about

all the wrong things you have done during the day. And if you cannot think of at least five or six or seven things you have done wrong, then something is wrong with you.[6]

The bar mitzvah was the occasion for a great but not very orthodox celebration, and the speech he made—studded with moral undertakings—was in Latin. Seventy years later, shortly before his death, he would still know it by heart. In 1914, he began his secondary education at the Evangelical seminary in the town, the first Jewish student to do so. This institution was one of the oldest in Germany, founded in 1479, and the poet Eduard Mörike had been a pupil there.[7] Siegmund received a thoroughly classical education, which left a lasting impression on him and made him much more a man of culture than of money. He also acquired a taste for style and elegance. For him, elegance was synonymous with simplicity. "A classical education is a wonderful thing. One learns from it that abstruse authors are not necessarily the most profound and that simplicity does not exclude profundity."[8] Later his *ex libris* plate was inscribed with a similar saying of Butler's: "Progress in thought is progress toward simplicity."

It was also at the seminary that he discovered the world of Greece and Rome from their language and culture. From Greek literature he was to acquire fatalism. Watching for signs of the times, he would always expect the worst, was always surprised to live another second more.

There was no lack of warning signs throughout his long life. He was to say that he had learned from a painful experience[9] in Berlin at the beginning of the 1930s that bankers could see a crisis coming but could do nothing to prevent it. Still later, in New York, he was to describe himself as a "pessimist surrounded by risks, listening to the hints of fate."[10] At about the same time, he asked his associates in London to learn to listen to the voice of destiny and act accordingly. Later in Blonay, speaking of a man in a hurry, he said. "He does not know the difference between *Kairos* and *Chronos*."* After Siegmund's death, some of those who had known him intimately confirmed having heard him call himself "pessimistic, sometimes even superstitious."[11]

*Kairos the proper time; Chronos time in the abstract.

The Warburgs in Berlin

During Siegmund's austere childhood his uncle Max, who was anxious to break the family's embargo on politics, filled his own father, Moritz, with dread by entering the leading circles of imperial society. Whether in Hamburg, Kiel or Berlin, Max was completely at ease. He was conscious of being German and only German. His name, after all, was that of a small German town and most of his friends in finance, industry, the army or at court ignored the fact that he was a Jew. He even became envied, indeed hated, by the Jewish elite of the time. Chaim Weizmann, the future first president of the State of Israel, would cruelly write of Max twenty years later what many already thought. "He was the archetypal Court Jew, more German than the Germans, obsequious, superpatriotic, anxious to anticipate the designs and plans of the masters of Germany."[12] A harsh judgment that was also unjust. Max was no courtier: if he loved power it was because he saw the empire as the only form of government capable of saving Germany, whose financial and religious freedom had been the strength of his family. So he intended to help the empire, but also to steer it in what he saw as the "right direction," to turn it away from the anti-Semitic czar and commit it to colonial adventure, full of promise and an outlet for the ambitions of the military, and finally to reinforce the powers of the Reichsbank in order to put the German banking system beyond the reach of politics.

To do all this Max needed an introduction to the kaiser, and he did his utmost to get one. In 1900 he was at last noticed by the court when he succeeded in placing in New York one of the very first European loans, which brought 80 million marks into the German Treasury, thus reversing the time-honored flow of world savings. In 1903 the kaiser asked Albert Ballin to bring Max to him.[13] The audience did not go well. The kaiser did not ask Max, as he had expected, for his opinion on possible future reforms of the empire's financial system but questioned him on the economic future of Russia, which he believed on the verge of bankruptcy.[14] Max confirmed his disquiet about the shortcomings of St. Petersburg's financial management but said that in his view there was nothing to indicate the impending failure of the Russian state. He also asked the kaiser to protest the pogroms to the czar. Otherwise, he said, the weakness of the Romanov dynasty would be plainly revealed and the revolutionary threat would grow. The kaiser shrugged his shoulders in complete skepticism, and the interview was cut short.

Some time later, after the Russian uprising in 1905, the kaiser recalled him and admitted him to his circle of advisers with the remark, "Well, Mr. Warburg, must you always be right?" Thus began a relationship that would be severed only by the fall of the empire.[15]

To begin with, the kaiser invited Max to the annual regatta on the Elbe; the talk was of finance and beautiful women. Then Max went to court and saw the monarch regularly, with or without Ballin. The banker and the shipowner, both from Hamburg, benefited from each others contacts and became inseparable.[16] The first private telephone line to be installed in Germany was the one between their two offices.[17] From Hamburg, both influenced a powerful empire and profited greatly from organizing loans and opening up shipping routes in the interests of the Reich.

Max knew how to maintain the family's century-old network of well-informed contacts. He saw many people, wrote letters to every part of the world and protected his sources. He was now in business with scores of banks, among them A. Kayser in London, Albert Kahn in Paris, H. Henriques, Jr., in Copenhagen, Svenska Handelsbanken in Stockholm and Kuhn Loeb in New York.[18]

He also strengthened the staff of the bank. In 1902 he took on as legal adviser a young Hamburg lawyer, Carl Melchior—the brother of the husband of Elsa, one of his cousins—a strange character who alongside Max was to play a large part during the Weimar republic in an effort to stop Europe's gradual slide toward catastrophe. In 1905 came recognition: the bank was at last admitted to the Consortium of Reich Loans, the preserve of the very highest German finance. In 1906, at Ballin's invitation Max joined the board of the Hamburg-America Line and very successfully organized an increase in the capital of the company from 100 to 125 million marks.[19]

The Warburgs in the United States

Felix and Paul, the two brothers in America, led quite different lives from their relatives in Europe. Millionaires, they were under the stern authority of Jacob Schiff—father-in-law of one and brother-in-law of the other—at home as well as in the bank. They worked under his orders and every Friday evening the three families dined together at 932 Fifth Avenue, where Jacob Schiff had built a palatial mansion. Jacob said the prayers and the family listened in silence. English was spoken even though all those present were of German origin. Like Jacob and most of the German Jews who had become Americans, Felix was turning his back on Germany.[20] His children were educated at the best Protestant schools. Having become almost as rich as his father-in-law through inheritance and dowry, he was more a squash player than a banker, more a man of the world than a court Jew. An opera lover, he financed the establishment of the Juilliard School of Music and the New York Philharmonic Society. He was one of the first Americans to own a yacht, his own polo grounds and racehorses. When he sailed to Europe, he took with him a butler, a maid and a cook. He was a friend of Albert Einstein and from 1906 onward entertained the elite of New York either at his Tudor-style castle in White Plains—with separate houses for each guest—or in the five-story mansion he had built at 1109 Fifth Avenue, which was crowded with Dürers, Rembrandts and Botticellis.[21]

Paul, in contrast, took his profession very seriously; a partner with Kuhn Loeb, he became a high-level associate of Jacob and a theoretician of international finance. He lived well, but far less ostentatiously than his brother. He did not give up his ties with Germany. On the contrary: he often went back. In fact he handled the German loan of 1900 that opened the kaiser's door to Max. Still, in 1907 he decided, like Felix, to give up his partnership with Warburg and settle permanently in New York.

From then on Max ran the firm alone, with only three partners: his cousin Aby S.—Siegmund's son who should really have been the head of the firm, but who was being edged out because of his worsening health—his brother Fritz and, above all, Carl Melchior, who became his main associate.

Paul, Founder of the Federal Reserve System

At the beginning of the century the United States became a great power and the dollar a great currency. The dollar was based on gold, even though the Gold Standard Act of 1900 did not completely exclude silver from the American monetary system.

Twenty years after its rise to industrial power, and in the same way that every nation that becomes a storehouse of goods soon becomes a storehouse of money, the United States began to invest and lend its currency to companies and other countries. The investment banks of Boston and New York not only continued borrowing from Europe to lend to America, but also began to operate in the reverse direction.[22]

Kuhn Loeb, for example, was still importing European capital to finance American industry; in 1906 it borrowed $48 million in France to finance the Pennsylvania Railroad and in 1909 was the intermediary through which a French group loaned $5 million to the Southern Pacific. To do this, Schiff used his links with Rothschild and Warburg. However, Kuhn Loeb also invested American money in loans for Shell and for the governments of Sweden, Germany and Japan.

At the time of this reversal of financial currents, which was to last three-quarters of a century, the American banking system was still very rudimentary. There was no central organization; the banks, whatever their activity, set up anywhere they wanted to and their growing interconnection made their failures contagious. Since the 1880 crisis about twenty of the biggest banks in the country had made a habit of consulting together regularly to harmonize their policies, but there was no mutual guarantee, and no control over the issuing of bank notes. So when banking panics broke out they led to numerous bankruptcies that were difficult to limit.

To remedy this, Paul Warburg suggested to Jacob Schiff in 1903 the creation of a control system along German lines. He published a short book, *Plan for a Central Bank*, in which he suggested—in the image of what had existed in the German Empire since 1875—the creation of a Central Bank, serving as a mutual guarantee to the private banks, and owned in equal shares by the government, the big private banks and about ten regional federal banks that alone would be authorized to issue banknotes, backed by gold. His plan aroused much interest on Wall Street and in Washington, and Paul gave many lectures on the subject in the United States. But he was perceived only as a rich German banker living six months of the year in New York. His plan was not put into effect.

Everything changed in the autumn of 1907. The collapse of the Knickerbocker Trust Co. and the threat hovering over Trust Company of America brought about a particularly severe crisis: the banks were accused of making too much money by giving ill-considered loans and of not having foreseen the crisis.[23] Paul's plan became topical again.

In 1910, at the age of forty-two and after many hesitations, he finally became an American citizen. That same year the Association of New York Bankers gave official support to his plan, which he was continuing to advocate everywhere. Though the previous president, Theodore Roosevelt, had not consulted him, Nelson Aldrich, an influential U.S. senator from Rhode Island, saw Paul often and took an interest in his ideas. Aldrich, the father-in-law of John D. Rockefeller, Jr., was an adviser to President Taft and chairman of the National Monetary Commission of which Paul was also a member. In addition, the financial situation in America was beginning to be problematical and there was pressure to put the banks under supervision.

In 1912 the Money Trust Investigation Committee of the Senate investigated the activities of Kuhn Loeb, J.P. Morgan, Kidder, Lee Higginson and the National City Bank. Some states passed laws to control banks.[24]

In November 1912 President Wilson, only just elected over Taft and Roosevelt, asked Paul to draft a law based on his book and was pleased with the result. He decided to submit it to the Senate as quickly as possible. Everything was settled at a secret meeting at the beginning of 1913 at Sea Island, Georgia, between Paul Warburg, the president of the National City Bank of New York and Senator Aldrich. The bill proposed by Paul was introduced in the Senate by Robert Owen of Oklahoma and in the House by a representative from Virginia, Carter Glass, and thus became the Owen-Glass Act. Passed in the summer of 1913, it set up a Federal Reserve Bank in twelve districts and a Federal Reserve Board in Washington.

Paul thus managed to organize the American banking system in German style. The main architect of this structure, he was nominated by Wilson for the chairmanship of the Federal Reserve Bank. But as a German Jew only just naturalized, he thought the honor inappropriate and would accept only a vice-chairmanship, even though the chairman had not yet been appointed. Benjamin Strong, the son-in-law of J. Pierpont Morgan, was appointed to the chairmanship of the regional bank of New York, the immediate rival of the central bank.

Samurai Armor

At the beginning of the century Japan was forcing the pace of its modernization. Robbed of its conquests in China in 1894, it attacked Russia on 8 February 1904 without declaring war. To the amazement of the Europeans, Japan then revealed itself as a modern military power; but in order to win, it needed money. A vice-governor of the Bank of Japan and financial commissioner to the Japanese government, Baron Korekiho Takahashi, was therefore sent to London and New York in June 1904 to ask the bankers of Europe and America to subscribe to a loan to the imperial Japanese government of £30 million sterling at 4.5 percent. Jacob Schiff had been trying to arrange a financial blockade of the czar, whom he had called "the enemy of humanity" since the pogroms of 1894, and agreed with pleasure to finance this war. That year he even refused to participate in a Wall Street loan to France for fear that the money might go to the Russians, who were great borrowers in Paris at that time.[25] Jacob Schiff then wrote to Max Warburg to ask him to join in the loan to Japan. Max, as always, assured himself that such a loan would not go against the foreign policy of Berlin. He noted in his diary, "I did what every good banker would do in this case: I went to the Ministry of Foreign Affairs in Berlin."[26] He was immediately given the green light, as Krupp, who was then playing an extensive role in affairs of state, hoped that this participation in the loan would lead to orders from Japan for German arms.[27]

Max then received Korekiho Takahashi. On 28 March 1905 he undertook to place £1 million of the loan. He immediately placed £900,000 in Germany, which led to a considerable profit, since M.M. Warburg earned a commission to 1.5 percent of the amount of the loan.

On 11 July of the same year, just as the war began to turn in its favor, Japan floated a second loan, this time of £30 million. M.M. Warburg, in association with the Deutsche Asiatische Bank, undertook to place one-third in Germany itself. The attempt was a huge success: the loan was ten times oversubscribed. A few months later Japan's victory was complete and the Portsmouth treaty awarded her control of Manchuria and Korea.

Max Warburg and Jacob Schiff then became officially appointed suppliers of capital to Japan. The following year Jacob Schiff made a triumphal tour of the country, and the daughter of Baron Takahashi went to live for a time with the Schiffs in New York.[28] Takahashi himself later became finance minister, then prime minister before being assassinated in 1936.

Max and Jacob also became industrial advisers to the great family groups in Japan. In 1906 Baron Mitsui, the owner of a large part of Japanese industry, went to Hamburg by the Trans-Siberian railway in order to meet Max. As family tradition has it, the conversation went like this:

Mitsui: We are a great family with many business interests, and so are you. Tell me, how do you manage not to fight among yourselves?
Max: To tell the truth we do fight among ourselves, all the time.
Mitsui: I did not come all the way across Siberia to hear that!
Max: Let's be serious. To avoid problems, I advise you to group all your family's activities into one holding company and to give control to a single authority. We Warburgs did this long ago, and it is working very well.

Thus was born the Mitsui group, one of the foremost in Japan. Upon his return the baron sent Max a magnificent fourteenth-century Samurai suit of armor, which today still occupies a place of honor in a glass case in the Ferdinandstrasse building.

Two years later Max undertook the financing of the Chinese railways, which was initially entrusted to the Deutsche Asiatische Bank, then to a German-American-Franco-British group headed by Jacob Schiff. Negotiations with the Chinese state were difficult.[29] Jacob wrote to Max in 1910, "I am sorry China is giving us so much trouble. Still God knows there are enough people and space in China to justify much financing in the future." The fall of the Manchu dynasty in February 1912 rendered all these efforts void. Max Warburg also lost his business openings in Japan when the Deutsche Asiatische Bank of Berlin acquired a monopoly on financial relations between that country and Germany.

Despite the losses it suffered like everyone else during the 1907 crisis, M.M. Warburg retained its prestige. That year the bank managed to place in Germany half of a 30 million mark loan issued by the Bank of Sweden to rescue a struggling Swedish company, and this added to the reputation of M.M. Warburg in Stockholm.[30] It became the leading issuing house in Hamburg and brought thirteen new issues to the city's stock exchange. The bank grew very quickly, even outstripping the substantial growth of Germany itself. Between 1902 and 1910, turnover tripled, and so did the family's income.[31]

Moritz, who had long been on the sidelines, died in 1910. Max then became the official head of M.M. Warburg, seconded by his brother Fritz and, distantly, by his cousin Aby S. He chose as his motto: "*En avant!*" The bank became the leading German bank in commercial and overseas loans.

In 1911 Carl Melchior, who was increasingly influential with Max, became a director.[32] The same year M.M. Warburg opened an office in London and entrusted it to Pieter Vuyk, a Dutchman. In Paris Lionel Hauser, who had represented the interests of M.M. Warburg for some years, set up his own firm—"Lionel Hauser et Cie"—with capital from Max. In 1912 Max joined the board of Blohn & Voss, the main German shipbuilder. He continued working in Austria with the Creditanstalt, in the United States with Kuhn Loeb, and in Scandinavia and Germany with Siemens-Schuckert-Werke, Deutsche Bank, Disconto-Gesellschaft and Deutsche Orientbank. That same year Carl Melchior joined the board of directors of Norddeutsche Hütte in Bremen.[33] Over the next few years other directors of the Warburg bank would join the boards of all the major German companies that were its clients, including those in the Ruhr, increasingly a competitor of North Germany.

The Colonial Adventure

Britain remained an enormous power by colonial standards. Her fleet was still the biggest in the world, equal to those of France and Germany combined. Her investments abroad still brought in £200 million a year. Her industry was still the most productive in Europe, and she accounted for 60 percent of world industrial exports.

America, however, was about to leave Britain far behind. Also, an expanding Germany was keen to be seated at the colonial feast, either through her dependencies, or in Europe itself. Her population had reached 67 million. Her fleet and trade were the second biggest in the world. Her foreign trade still showed a deficit, partly balanced by income on capital invested abroad. Germany was also in search of the nonferrous metals she did not produce. The country had almost reached the point where its growth could only be sustained through colonial ventures, and therefore needed a maritime policy: "Our future is on the water," said Wilhelm II in 1898. Because of this, Admiral Alfred von Tirpitz built an enormous battle fleet.

The Warburgs did not like war, and they chose to push for colonial development to deflect and avert violence. In an effort to extend the empire, Max collaborated closely with the new chancellor Theobald von Bethmann-Hollweg, who had come to office in 1909. He developed ways of financing purchases of raw materials. For this Fritz Warburg established links with Brandeis-Goldschmidt in London and with Guggenheim in New York. This work made a large profit for the bank.

However, Germany immediately clashed with the identical, and older, ambitions of France and Britain. This happened first in Morocco. The Algeciras Conference of April 1906 recognized France and Spain's special rights while confirming Morocco's independence. Despite this diplomatic defeat—in fact a victory for the Banque de Paris et des Pays-Bas—Germany did not give up her stand on the matter. In 1909 Max set up the Colonial Institute of Hamburg, then in 1910 established the Hamburg-Morocco company, with Carl Melchior as chairman and Wilhelm C. Regendanz as director. Regendanz, a former senior civil servant in the colonial department of the Ministry of Foreign Affairs, had previously been appointed a director of M.M. Warburg.[34]

On 21 May 1911, when the French occupied Fez in violation of the Algeciras agreement, Regendanz suggested to the German Ministry of Foreign Affairs that by way of reprisal it should establish a German presence in Agadir. So that the government should not be in the front line in this matter, he proposed sending out someone from the private sector, a joint representative of M.M. Warburg and Mannesmann, the Ruhr-based producer of guns and steel tubing.

In May the Wilhelmstrasse bank agreed, and a mining engineer from Mannesmann left for Agadir on 15 June. He arrived on 3 July, two days after Regendanz arrived to "protect German interests." Nationalist reactions in France and Britain were very strong. To calm things down, Sir Ernest Cassel hired a ship and brought together on a Nordic cruise those who wanted to avoid a war between Britain and Germany: Colonel Wilfred Ashley, Ballin, Max and their wives.[35] At the beginning of September the French banks organized a financial boycott of Germany that caused the German stock exchanges to fall steeply. On 4 November despite opposition, French Prime Minister Joseph Caillaux agreed to a compromise with Bethmann-Hollweg. In exchange for recognition of the French presence in Morocco, France would cede part of the Congo to Germany. In Berlin the colonial leagues protested against this agreement, which they considered inadequate since it excluded Germany from Morocco. However, Chancellor Bethmann-Hollweg did not think he was ready to stand against France and Britain and that the partial victory would have to do. Regendanz, whose bluff had given Germany the Congo, even if he had been aiming at Morocco, was decorated by the kaiser.[36]

In England, colonial ambition was just as voracious, and the British banks played their part. In 1910, for example, N.M. Rothschild and Kuhn Loeb organized a loan to the Dominican Republic guaranteed by the customs duties of that country. Jacob Schiff cabled Sir Ernest Cassel, "If they do not pay, who will collect these customs duties?" Cassel replied, "Your marines and ours."[37]

Everywhere in Europe finance, industry and armies fed one another's development. To reinforce the German army under Field Marshal Helmut von Moltke and Erich Ludendorff, railway lines were built eastward, and new rifles were introduced and tested in the Boer War and the Russo-Japanese conflict. The German general staff thought that a war should be won as quickly as possible in the West, where a peaceful front would then allow a leisurely conquest of the East. Most of the German financial world was hostile to the idea of war, even though some banks were closely bound up with the military industry of the Ruhr. In 1908 the Deutsche Bank took control of Mannesmann, while the Stein bank of Cologne, run by Kurt von Schröder, who had come from Hamburg, linked up with the prowar factions in the City and on Wall Street through its branches in London and New York. The dream of these people was an alliance of Anglo-Saxons against Austria, France and Russia.

In 1911 Gustav Stresemann, an employee of a German industrial consortium, along with Albert Ballin and Max Warburg, came up with the idea of a German company for world trade. From this idea came the foundation in the following year of the Deutsche Amerikanischer Wirtschaftsbund, with Stresemann as chairman. In 1913, the year in which the bank finally moved into a magnificent building, still on Ferdinandstrasse, Regendanz, in the name of M.M. Warburg, attempted to go further. He proposed that an "overseas projects syndicate" to conduct financial transactions in Africa should be set up by the leading banking and shipping companies in Hamburg (M.M. Warburg, Hamburg-America Line, Woermann Shipping Line, F. Rosenstern & Co., Norddeutsche Bank), Berlin (Berliner Handels-Gesellschaft, Deutsche Bank, Disconto-Gesellschaft and Brisk & Pohl), and including Fried Krupp.[38] The syndicate was quickly formed and the kaiser asked Max to head it.

The syndicate's first move, at the end of 1913, was to send a mission consisting of engineers, bankers and imperial officials to study the feasibility of building a railway between Angola and German Southwest Africa. The expedition was still in Angola when the First World War broke out and the project had to be abandoned.

Meanwhile Max and Regendanz did not give up the idea of a German presence in Morocco and, to bring this about, pushed for an alliance with Britain against France. In February 1914 they went to London to set up with Lord Milner—a former high commissioner in South Africa—an Anglo-German bank for Morocco called the Bank of North-West Africa; it would be established with half-English and half-German capital. Max Warburg was to run the bank. Here again the agreement was on the point of being signed when the war broke out and put an end to the plan.

Simultaneously, the "Hamburg group" tried to take control of a territory in West Africa almost as big as Great Britain: Nyasaland, owned by the Nyasa Company, which itself belonged to Nyasa Consolidated Ltd., a British firm. The group contacted Nyasa Consolidated, which agreed to sell the territory after asking for authorization from the Foreign Office, which took scant interest in the region. In March 1914 a price was set: £150,000. The money, assembled by Max, came mostly from German banks: Deutsche Bank and Berliner Handels-Gesellschaft each supplied 25 percent, M.M. Warburg and the Disconto-Gesellschaft 16.66 percent, Mendelssohn and Bleichroeder 8.34 percent.[39] The sale document was signed in London on 28 May 1914 and Pieter Vuyk, Warburg's representative there, received the deeds on deposit.

This was undoubtedly the high point of Warburg power in Germany: in two months, at the head of a consortium of largely Jewish banks, they had bought for the kaiser 400,000 square kilometers of Africa. However, when war broke out the deeds of Nyasa Consolidated were still in London. They were confiscated as enemy assets and Max's office was closed.[40]

At the same time, in London, the Accepting Houses Committee was established, bringing together all the City's best merchant banks, controlled by the British and active internationally. The bills accepted by these banks were in the last resort rediscountable by the Bank of England and counted in its reserves. Much later Siegmund G. Warburg was to be the most brilliant star in this merchant banking constellation.

Averting War

Europe's slide toward another war was neither necessary nor inevitable. Russia, France and Britain became allies. Germany and Austria feared that Russia would carve up the Turkish Empire, where the nationalities were restive, to its own advantage. North and South Germany did not always have the same attitudes: the industrial capitalism of the Ruhr chose the prospect of war, which could alone—it was thought—keep the factories working at full capacity. The more financially minded North, turned more toward the Atlantic, was hostile to war. Max thought that a war would kill "his" Germany and did his utmost to oppose the Ruhr in Berlin.[41] Like the whole of German banking, Max himself was not without responsibility for the circumstances that led to war. To keep up his profits he actually lent money to industry and to the state to finance armaments.

In 1912 the hostilities between Italy and the Ottoman Empire, and the first Balkan War, exercised both men and armies. Then the size of the forces on either side of the Rhine increased. From then on, Conrad von Hötzendorff, chief of staff of the Austrian army, and Moltke, who had just replaced Schlieffen at the head of the German army, wanted a quick war. They knew that Britain did not yet have an army worthy of the name, and that France had disturbingly been rebuilding its own for some time. Chancellor Bethmann-Hollweg was also on the side of those who wanted to wage war in Europe in order to gain territory, give work to industry and maintain the social order.[42] He used Max, without realizing it fully, to try to obtain British neutrality and American support in the conflict to come.

Thus in 1913 he sent Max to New York to request a loan for the German war industry. In America the bankers, like the rest of the public, were split among neutralists, supporters of Britain and supporters of Germany.[43] Max got only a little money from friendly banks, among them Kuhn Loeb of course. Soon afterward, feeling that war was coming and wanting to avoid involving Britain, Max Warburg with Albert Ballin and Walther Rathenau, a brilliant young industrialist who had taken over from his father as head of the huge Berlin trust AEG, made every effort to neutralize Great Britain toward Germany. At the beginning of 1914 Ballin went to see the first lord of the admiralty, Winston Churchill, in an attempt to reach an agreement and obtain a guarantee of peace.[44] It was in vain.

The Conflict Begins

In June 1914 all the armies of Europe were on the alert and the economies of the Continent were working only for them or through them. Peace was at the mercy of an incident, and that one should occur was in the interest of many. Max went to London three times, twice at the beginning of the month, then again on 27 June, after a discussion with the chancellor and the kaiser.[45] On 28 June the assassination in Sarajevo, Bosnia, of a liberal Austrian prince, Archduke Franz-Ferdinand, a nephew of the kaiser, allegedly by a Serb, passed almost unnoticed. The next day, as he did every year, the kaiser left for the Kiel regatta, the chancellor was on holiday and Moltke was taking the waters at Carlsbad.[46] However, still convinced of British neutrality, Bethmann-Hollweg and the German general staff thought to profit from the incident by launching a lightning attack on Serbia, then on Russia, supporting an Austrian response to the assassination to "finish the Serbs." But the Austrians did not seem determined to fight and it was difficult for Germany to declare war if the ally "offended" by the outrage had not done so itself.

At the end of July, a strange month of waiting with everything at stake, the kaiser met Max once more in Kiel. "Should we declare war or wait, Mr. Warburg?" "Wait, Sir. Every year of peace strengthens Germany and gives us more means of winning. Waiting can only be beneficial."[47]

Max knew then that war was inevitable, for there were too many pressures in favor of it and the kaiser had weakened. Warburg knew that "his" Germany was almost certainly finished. Resignedly he cut back his operations and cashed in his securities, before the stock exchange fell as he knew it would. On 28 July the cable link between Germany and the United States was cut. Max Warburg moved his London representative, Pieter Vuyk, to Amsterdam. On the same day Austria, urged on by Bethmann-Hollweg, finally declared war on Serbia.

The war began in confusion. Serbia believed it was supported by Russia, which in turn believed it had French support. On 30 July Russia mobilized the whole of its army, the czar having been convinced by his general staff that partial mobilization was impossible. Seeing this, Austria did the same on 31 July. That evening Jean Jaurès was assassinated at the Café du Croissant in Paris. The dice were rolling.

The same day there was a rush for gold on all the European exchanges and currency rates fell. The Hamburg exchange was closed. The world's leading currencies suspended convertibility to gold and began to float: the barely established gold standard was thus inoperative. It would be restored only for a few short years after the war.

In Germany companies asked the state for a moratorium on their debts. On 1 August Max, with other bankers, tried his best to calm the situation. But matters had gone too far. That day, Germany declared war on Russia and on 3 August on France; on 5 August Austria declared war on Russia. At the beginning of August the Germans still believed that Great Britain would not enter the conflict against them.[48] When on 12 and 13 August Paris and then London declared war on Austria, this was the beginnng of what would become the First World War, to the dismay of financiers, the misery of nations and, soon, the twilight of the eagles.

The Beginnings of War

The German press, largely controlled by Ruhr industrialists, mobilized public opinion and created a special association that tried to obtain, from the banks and the government, cheap loans and a moratorium on debts. On 6 August Max Warburg and other bankers called to Berlin by the chancellor opposed any general moratorium, which they said would ruin the banks or require huge public spending to support them. Instead, Max proposed the establishment of banks specializing in "war lending," with more flexible lending rules and lower rates than others. Bethmann-Hollweg took up the idea and imposed it on the Ruhr. Carl Melchior and Max Warburg set up the first bank of this kind, the Hamburgische Bank; others followed throughout Germany. In August, Fritz Warburg left Hamburg to become commercial counselor at the German Embassy in Sweden. Aby M., a committed pacifist, then fell very ill and left for Switzerland.

At the beginning of August the German armies had made a breakthrough. On 24 August they were threatening Paris, and by 29 August they had beaten the Russians at Tannenberg. Germany saw itself as already victorious and aspired to the role of "pilot of Europe."[49] It was then that Bethmann-Hollweg, with the financier Arther von Gwinner and Walther Rathenau, who had become his adviser, drafted a peace treaty under which Germany would establish its dominance over Europe from Brest to Moscow and would annex all the Belgian and French colonies.[50] This was the high point of German imperial hopes. Ahead lay three years of gradual decline and one year of collapse.

The Battle of the Marne began on 6 September, to be lost by the German army on 10 September, and the front then stabilized. By the end of the year everything had become less simple for everyone. The Germans sought a separate peace with the Russians, making contact through Franz von Mendelssohn, a German-Jewish banker who had relatives in banking in Russia. It was in vain. The czar refused.[51] Later, Max was to play the same role as Mendelssohn in the West and Fritz in the East.

The M.M. Warburg bank became a central component in the new German economy, which was being transformed into a war economy under the growing authority of Walther Rathenau.[52] It organized war loans in Germany and abroad and set up agencies specializing in marine insurance and in the purchase of strategic metals abroad.[53] The Warburg family, like the rest of their class, invested a large part of its wealth in the empire's war loans. At the end of 1914 the government sent Max to Holland and Belgium to investigate the capacity of these countries to help Germany financially. Carl Melchior went to Bulgaria and Rumania to negotiate supply contracts, and with the Hamburg-America Line, M.M. Warburg helped set up a department in the Ministry of the Interior to import food. In order to finance these imports Melchior set up two specialized financial institutions, one in Berlin and the other in

Hamburg, run by Max, to discount the purchase certificates on these goods with American banks, especially Kuhn Loeb.

The War Seen from America

America held on to its neutrality and President Wilson forbade any American public organization to lend to any of the combatants, but, faithful to liberalism, he authorized loans by private banks. Each bank then took sides and most joined that of the allies against Germany.

So at the beginning of August 1914, Morgan placed $2 billion worth of securities for the allies, while Kuhn Loeb was able to place only $35 million worth for Germany.[54]

The British, French and Germans sent mission after mission in search of money. At the end of 1914 Lord Reading, formerly Rufus Isaacs and a future viceroy of India, came to New York to borrow from the American banks in the name of Britain. Jacob Schiff, who was approached, set as a condition for participating in the loan that the money should neither directly nor indirectly go to Russia, an ally of London and the main exponent of anti-Semitism in Europe. As Lord Reading was unable to give this guarantee,[55] Kuhn Loeb did not participate in the loan. Mortimer, Jacob's son, subscribed in his personal capacity. The German Jews of America were thus very divided.[56] Jacob stuck to American neutrality, as did Paul, who still went to Hamburg from time to time, and remained close to German circles in Washington. He was annoyed with his brother Felix, who had chosen the British and French side and was campaigning among the richest Jews in New York for help for the Jews of Eastern Europe, who were still under German control.

Felix had changed. He was no longer just a dandy, a man of the world, but had become more and more militant concerning the right of Jews throughout the world to be totally free. He took the lead with the main Jewish charitable organizations in New York in order to federate them. His example was followed in all the large American cities. To arrange aid to the Jews of Eastern Europe he set up and later became chairman of the Joint Distribution Committee.

War Economy

With the beginning of the war, industrialists and military personnel replaced shipowners and bankers as the men of influence in Berlin. Albert Ballin and Max Warburg lost much of their authority with the kaiser and the chancellor. Though they were still used to maintain a link with the United States, and more generally to loosen the Allies' economic and financial grip on Germany, they were shunted to the sidelines. At the end of 1914, scenting the danger of an American involvement, Bethmann-Hollweg even suggested that Max should become German ambassador to the United States. Max hesitated, but in the end declined. An ambassador, he thought, has as little influence "as the manager of a bank branch."[57] Besides, how could a German Warburg be in anything but an unsound position in Washington vis-à-vis his two brothers in New York? Count Johann-Heinrich von Bernstorff went instead, but Max agreed to go to Washington to negotiate American aid to Belgium, Bulgaria, Rumania and Sweden so that these countries would remain favorable to Germany.

The war favored America by increasing her exports to Europe. As a result her balance of payments moved into ever increasing surplus and huge amounts of capital piled up.

Meanwhile, across the Atlantic, on either side of the front there was only a weakened Europe that was killing its youth. This old continent, short of food, raw materials and money, was forced to end the convertibility of its currencies and become indebted to the bourgeoisie of the neutral countries. That year, for example, the German Treasury had a deficit of 60 billion marks, two-thirds of it financed by state loans and the rest by printing money.

Everywhere arrangements were being made for a long war. The state took control of imports. To this end Walther Rathenau set up a Bureau of Raw Materials. People dug in for the winter. In February 1915 the war spread. Germany controlled Central Europe. Italy came into the conflict.[58] On 23 May 1915, after the Dardanelles defeat, Asquith, the British prime minister, dismissed Churchill but kept Kitchener as minister of war.

Unlike the German Court, Max was pessimistic. He thought that time was against Germany, that its economy could not sustain such indebtedness and that the longer the conflict lasted, the greater the risk that America would enter the war. He thought he would be able to win people over to the idea of a peace without victors or vanquished, through which Hamburg would become a very important world economic center.[59] Nobody would listen. The general staff believed it was going to win and wanted war to the bitter end. In March 1915 Max was astounded when Admiral Tirpitz, unhappy to see his fleet still unused on the kaiser's orders, asked his opinion on what America would do if Germany used its submarines against the merchant ships supplying the

Allies. Max was sure—and told the chief of the general staff so—that this would bring the immediate entry of America into the war, and within six months the defeat of Germany.[60]

Tirpitz shrugged. "America will not dare. She is pacifist by nature and even if she wanted to go to war Germany will win first, thanks to its submarines, by cutting Britain off from her supplies."

On 11 May 1915 Germany declared an embargo on all shipping bound for England. Six days later a German U20 sank the first civilian vessel—in fact secretly carrying arms for Britain—the *Lusitania*: 1,200 died, among them 124 Americans. The result was tremendous ill feeling toward Germany in America. Wilson threatened to enter the war but did not do so, despite pressure from the prowar lobby in New York and in Congress.[61] Germany slowed down its submarine war in order not to upset America further. The two Warburg brothers again tried to calm things down—Paul with Wilson and Max with the kaiser. Felix also kept in touch with Max, but this was to urge him to concern himself with the fate of the Jews in Galicia, who were increasingly ill-treated, and to intervene for them to be allowed to emigrate to Palestine.[62] Max did agree to try and asked the German minister of foreign affairs, Gottlieb von Jagow and his secretary of state, Arthur Zimmermann, to intercede with the Turks, allied to Germany, to open Palestine to Jewish immigration. Of course he was badly received. The Turkish Empire was too important in the war against Russia for anyone to antagonize it. Von Jagow asked Max to concern himself instead with financing the war and protecting German interests in the neutral countries, which was becoming increasingly difficult because of the Allied blockade.

In July 1915 Max joined the board of a new body set up by the Reichsbank and the ministries of Finance and the Interior, with the aim of securing the country's supply of food. He and Carl Melchior traveled across Europe to negotiate supply contracts for various ministries. Three times during 1915 Bethmann-Hollweg sent him to Sweden to see Knut Wallenberg, the Swedish minister of foreign affairs, on the pretext of financial negotiations, but actually to try to persuade Wallenberg to help Germany secretly, or at least allow the transit of goods banned by the Allies. Though he doubted the effectiveness of his approaches, Max nevertheless went to Stockholm. His efforts were in vain. Sweden intended to remain neutral. Its capital was then a pivotal city, a refuge for émigrés: German, Russian, English and French. In Stockholm Max met with his brother Fritz, who had been living there with his family for a year. His title was "honorary commercial attaché to the German embassy;" he was, in fact, negotiating regular supplies of Norwegian and Swedish agricultural products for Germany. Officially independent, he was actually in close contact with the German embassy in Stockholm. In addition to his commercial activities, he became involved in an abortive peace negotiation between Germany and Russia.

That year the czar became anxious at seeing his crown wobble because of the war and tried to strengthen his control by leaning on the supporters of Germany against the Duma. Under the influence of Rasputin, he replaced prime minister Ivan Gormikin with a committed Germanophile, Stürmer. Aleksandr Protopopov, the new minister of the interior, was also very much a Germanophile and wished to seek a separate peace with Berlin. In August 1915 he went to Stockholm, requested a meeting with Fritz Warburg, whom he knew through the Günzburgs and proposed ending the conflict between Germany and Russia. (Fritz turned to Max, who informed Foreign Minister Zimmermann, who then authorized negotiation of this unexpected offer.) However, when at the end of the year Germany recognized the independence of Poland, Protopopov was disowned by his own government and the talks were cut short.[63]

In Germany war fever grew; there were few pacifists. Even the socialists, with Philipp Scheidemann, voted for military credits. The chancellor himself was overwhelmed by the military, especially Marshals Hindenburg and Ludendorff and Admiral von Holtzendorff, chief of the navy general staff, who wanted all-out war.[64] At the end of 1915 Holtzendorff asked Max to reflect on what the United States might do if submarine warfare against merchant shipping broke out anew. Max played for time, promising a report that he finally delivered two months later. Once again he clearly came out against such a strategy, explaining that a submarine war would force the United States either to start a financial blockade of Germany, which would lead to its economic suffocation, or to enter the war, which would cause its military defeat.[65] In both cases, he concluded, the war would be lost for Germany within a fairly short time. Few people then thought as Max did, and in military circles he was said to be too attached to American interests not to be suspect. He knew he was now less credible and was silent. There was nothing anti-Semitic, he thought, in this suspicion, and he resigned himself to seeing less and less often the American ambassador in Berlin, James W. Gerard. Max was the first Warburg to be "politically suspect," but not the last.

Urach in the Rearguard

In February 1916 Germany became bogged down in its Verdun offensive. The Allied blockade was effective; inflation picked up and shortages threatened. Bread was rationed: two hundred grams per person per day.[66] The German public began to mutter. In March Tirpitz resigned. In August Ludendorff became Hindenburg's deputy, replacing Erich von Falkenhayn, who had himself succeeded Moltke at the head of the army. Walther Rathenau took over at the head of the bureau of raw materials and brought in a sort of war socialism, austere and egalitarian.

Life was increasingly difficult for young Siegmund, as it was for all children of his age. At school there were now only very old teachers.[67] Food was scarce and there were no men to work in the fields. The children brought in the harvest, collected waste and dug shelters.[68] One of the buildings at Uhenfels became a center for the wounded and for refugees. Coming home on the weekend from the seminary where he boarded, young Siegmund found his mother harassed and his father ill. "All the responsibility of managing the various houses, which was added to her duties as regards her immediate family, sometimes exceeded her strength."[69] His father's fortune, largely invested in war loans, was depleted, and his already fragile health was worsened by financial worries. He was, wrote Siegmund,

> affected by a serious nervous illness, the symptoms of which had already shown themselves earlier. One of my mother's main aims in life was then to care for her husband and relieve him as much as possible of his work and his worries. During his illness it was more and more difficult to prevent my father from sinking into phases of deep depression, or becoming agonizingly agitated. The years of my father's illness were the hardest in the life of my mother.[70]

Siegmund never said any more about this to anyone. But he must have had painful memories.

"Finis Germaniae"

America was still benefiting from the war and did not yet wish to take a stand. She was selling wheat, raw materials, machinery and arms to both sides. Her banks competed in ingenuity in lending money to whoever wanted it, in exchange for huge commissions. Even Kuhn Loeb, heavily committed to the German side, was attracted by the profits to be made and issued loans for the British Royal Dutch Petroleum and for the big

French cities (Paris, Bordeaux, Lyon and Marseilles) alongside the loans it continued to make to Germany and to the big American companies (Westinghouse, American Smelting and Refining Co., Baldwin Locomotive Works, US Leather Co., US Rubber Co., Western Union Telegraph).[71]

Only one change could threaten this prosperity: the interruption of trade to Europe if the seas became unsafe. The sinking of the *Lusitania* was all but forgotten, however, as the German submarine war largely stopped in the autumn for lack of submarines.[72] Germany then tried once more to divide the Allies. After the failure of talks with Russia on a separate peace, Bethmann-Hollweg now attempted to negotiate with Belgium, France and Great Britain. Although he tried to obtain territory in exchange for a cease-fire in each case, negotiations bogged down.

By the beginning of 1916 all the combatants were exhausted, and conscription had reached young people aged sixteen. Max's son, Eric, knew that he would have to go to the front the following year and Siegmund, who was fourteen, was also threatened with call-up if the war continued. For the general staff, especially Ludendorff, only one solution remained: to strangle Britain as quickly as possible by a total blockade on food. After some German economists had undertaken learned calculations of the calories consumed by the British at breakfast, the general staff concluded that if two hundred additional submarines were put to sea, it would be possible to cut off British supplies before America had time to enter the war. The Junkers, the right-wing parties and public opinion all fell in with this view.[73] Construction of the vessels began. When consulted, Count von Bernstorff, the German ambassador in Washington, showed great hostility to this idea and predicted that America's entry into the war would be far more rapid than Berlin thought. He counterproposed that Wilson should be asked to mediate in the pursuit of an honorable peace with Britain. On 16 October 1916 the Parliament in Berlin backed Ludendorff and called for an immediate start to submarine warfare.[74] However, Bethmann-Hollweg was increasingly hesitant. The German navy was too unreliable, he thought, something the British naval victory at Jutland confirmed.

In December 1916 Wilson proposed that the combatants meet to negotiate a "peace without victory." Germany rejected these proposals. When instructing the devastated Bernstorff to convey his refusal to the American president, Secretary of State Zimmermann asked him to add that Germany "did not want to risk being cheated of its hopes of winning that war."[75]

At that point imperial Germany condemned itself to win or perish. The army and the court understood that if victorious the Allies would demand onerous indemnities, inevitably leading to complete social upheaval and the end of the Hohenzollerns. The die was cast. No one, neither the financiers nor even Bethmann-Hollweg, could any longer prevent or even delay the submarine war. On 9 January 1917 Admiral von Holtzendorff presented the kaiser with a report assuring him of victory before the summer if the 154 submarines already built, which could sink 600,000 tons per month,[76] were launched into battle immediately. Hindenburg supported this view, but Bethmann-Hollweg, finally won over by Max Warburg and Bernstorff, openly changed sides: 154 submarines were too few. We would not be able to finish off Britain, he said, before the United States could enter the war, and that would be a catastrophe. The general staff insisted. If the blockade started by 1 February 1917 at the latest, it was possible to win before the summer.

That evening the kaiser assembled the general staff and at the end of a dramatic meeting gave his assent to the start of a blockade. On leaving the room the defeated Bethmann-Hollweg murmured somberly, "*Finis Germaniae.*"[77]

Max, whom he informed, thought the same, and the following week on 15 January, the very day on which General Edmund Allenby took Jerusalem from the Turks despite German aid, he fiercely opposed a resolution passed by the Hamburg Chamber of Commerce calling for submarine warfare. Although this decision was already made, it had not yet been revealed to the public.[78] On 1 February America was informed of the blockade. The same day Wilson received a secret telegram from Bethmann-Hollweg begging him not to enter the conflict despite the blockade and giving an assurance that he would be able to lift this as soon as "the basis of a peace acceptable to Germany"[79] was defined. But Wilson had just received a copy of an intercepted telegram from Zimmermann to the Mexicans, promising them Texas if they declared war on the United States.

That month, Max, who was running the bank more and more on his own, asked Carl Melchior to become his partner. Melchior accepted, becoming the first non-Warburg partner, although he did belong to an allied family.[80]

At the outset the blockade was very effective. On 15 March the submarine war caused the first deaths among American sailors. In this time of turmoil, as Russia moved into revolution, the French general

Robert Georges Nivelle launched an abortive offensive on the Chemin des Dames, and mutinies increased among the armies of Europe. America, reacting violently to the death of its sailors, entered the war very quickly, much more quickly than the German general staff had expected. On 6 April Congress voted 373 to 56 in favor of a declaration of war on Germany. Count von Bernstorff left the Washington Embassy for that of Stockholm.

The Warburg brothers were cut off from each other. For nearly two years they were unable even to write to one another. Letters sent some months before via England would remain there. Felix gave up his share in the Hamburg bank. In a letter to President Wilson, which will be mentioned again, Paul wrote the fine phrase,"Brother must confront brother." However, this did not prevent him from using his contacts to keep his son, Jimmy, a volunteer, from going to fight on the European front.[81]

With the declaration of war, loans to Germany were stopped on Wall Street and the New York banks mobilized to sell war bonds issued by Washington. To do this they created enormous nationwide sales networks that forced the pace of selling far beyond what was reasonable.[82] In this way they invented sales techniques that would later be used in peacetime to sell American company securities to the public.

By June 1917 the blockade set up by the Allies was strangling the German economy. Foreign exchange was running out, the last free capital was leaving the country, tax revenue was poor and there was almost no saving. The German state was forced by lack of resources to indebt itself more and more to its central bank. Inflation, which had been relatively contained until then, flared up, gradually reducing the value of the mark on the few foreign exchange markets still open.

Max sensed the coming disaster. He drafted a plan proposing to strengthen exchange control and float long-term loans abroad in order to consolidate German debt. He knocked on every door and submitted the plan to the governor of the Reichsbank and the minister of finance.[83] It was brushed aside despite the support of Bethmann-Hollweg. Max made known his deep bitterness. On 6 July 1917 before the Reichstag, which had asked for his views, he made a brilliant speech, predicting the failure of the submarine war, defeat and the economic disaster awaiting the country if his plan were not implemented. A good many members were won over by his speech. On 12 July an exhausted Bethmann-Hollweg resigned. On 19 July the Center party and the Socialists passed a resolution in favor of peace. Overwhelmed by events, the kaiser appointed Dr. George Michaelis to the Chancellery, though Hindenburg and the army were in fact running the country.

German banking at that point essentially consisted of placing war loans and financing what little international trade survived. Nevertheless, the archives of M.M. Warburg covering this period also show signs of a rather strange transaction.[84] Karl Hagenbeck, a friend of Max who had a magnificent collection of wild animals, no longer had the means of feeding them. Max lent him 8,000 marks, taking a rhinoceros as security! After the war, the animal was sold to the Budapest zoo in order to repay the loan.

That summer Max Warburg noted in his diary:

> Never has our financial destiny been so closely linked to the political destiny of Germany. This has clearly demonstrated the invalidity of the idea that a private company can remain independent of the political and economic situation of the empire in time of war. Probably no single German private bank has guaranteed more German Empire loans than we have. From this point of view, we have certainly contributed to financing the war, particularly by giving our guarantee for purchases from neutral countries.[85]

Max knew that this unavoidable situation was as much a death trap for his firm as it was for the empire. As he wrote in September to Carl Melchior, who was working more and more frequently for Berlin, he knew that if Germany lost the war the Reichsbank would be unable to honor its commitments and "it will only remain to put a notice in the papers stating, M.M. Warburg suspended payments on the field on honor."[86]

In October, after long negotiations in Amsterdam, Melchior, in the name of the German government, signed a huge trade finance agreement with Holland and its colonies, opening up a new source of supply of raw materials for Germany.

In November the radical turn in the Russian Revolution was costly for the bank. When Nikolai Lenin's government nationalized industry and the banks, it rendered worthless the enormous portfolio of Russian securities that M.M. Warburg had held from the time family links with the Günzbergs were established. Baron Alexander de Günzburg and his wife, George's sister, the magnificent Russian nobility who had been kept at great expense for so long, then emigrated to Germany and moved in, together with other refugees, with George and Lucie Warburg in Urach.

At the same time, in London Foreign Secretary Lord Arthur Balfour made a declaration in favor of a Jewish national home in Palestine. In Paris on 16 November in the midst of military uncertainty and despite his differences with Raymond Poincaré, the President of the Republic, Georges Clémenceau took power. On the 26th of that month Russia requested an armistice from Germany. The German Empire saw a breathing space, even eventual victory. In fact it was entering its death struggle.

End of the Empire

In January 1918, even though Wilson had made known his Fourteen Points peace plan, Germany relaunched the war in the West. Italy was defeated. Russia signed peace in Brest-Litovsk on 3 March 1918. Count George von Hertling replaced the kindly but ineffectual Michaelis as chancellor and made every attempt to negotiate an end to hostilities with America. In May he called Max to Berlin and asked him to go to Holland, to see the American ambassador and to propose peace. Max went in June, but the ambassador refused to receive him. Ludendorff, who had not been warned of this step, accused Max of trying to deal with the enemy and reproached him vehemently for his ties to his brothers in America.

Max was not the only Warburg to suffer because of his name in that month of June 1918. In Washington Paul's post as vice-chairman of the Federal Reserve Bank came up for renewal. Though his dream was to continue to help govern the monetary institutions he had set up, Paul wrote to President Wilson offering the advice that he should not be reappointed because political problems might arise if a former German citizen were renamed as an officer of the Federal Reserve. In fact, however, he hoped that Wilson would still confirm him in his duties.[87] He was indeed sure of it. When the president accepted his resignation, he took it very badly. Embittered, he returned to Kuhn Loeb. On that day the *New York Times* wrote that none more than he could claim the title of founder of the Federal Reserve System. He was the second Warburg after Max to become "politically suspect."

On 15 June in Berlin, Max, back from Holland, was again heard by the Reichstag on "economic and monetary policy after the war." He announced that, loaded with short-term debt, Germany was threatened by inflation that would ruin its creditors, i.e., the bourgeoisie and the middle class. He again proposed that this debt shold be consolidated immediately by long-term borrowing abroad.[88] He then met Friedrich

Ebert, chairman of the Social Democratic party and a future president of the Weimar Republic. Ebert, who was impressed by Max, had not expected him to be so critical of the imperial regime, or to find himself in agreement with a man he knew as the adviser most heeded by the kaiser for the previous fifteen years.

Destiny now was played out by force of arms. Halted at Armentières in April, Germany was pushed back to Rheims in July. All was lost; the summer brought a gradual disintegration of the front. On September 28 Chancellor Hertling resigned. The next day, on the advice of Ebert and Max Warburg, the kaiser called his brother-in-law Max von Baden to the Chancellery. The latter invited Warburg to Dessau and asked him to be his minister of finance. Max refused. As a Jew he did not want to be in the front line in such times.[89] He did agreed to be the chancellor's adviser. He stayed in Berlin until the end of October, working incessantly with von Baden on an economic recovery plan. His friend Walther Rathenau, with whom he had constructed the German war economy, joined the government as minister of industry and immediately declared, "We are not beaten." Siegmund met Rathenau at that time at Max's home in Hamburg and would retain a strong memory of this energetic, brilliant and charming man.

Chancellor von Baden had no real power over the country and economic stabilization was no longer possible. From the beginning of September, "to protect his army," Ludendorff had wanted the quickest possible peace with honor, albeit without victory.[90] At his request von Baden wrote to Wilson on 3 October to propose an armistice. He would only accept "a peace compatible with honor," he said. On 8 October without advising either France or Britain, Wilson replied, setting out very harsh peace terms: the return of all territory occupied since 1870 and the payment of indemnities to the Allies—the amount to be fixed later.

Von Baden knew by 12 October that the war was lost. With a heavy heart he accepted Wilson's terms. The army thus blamed the shameful defeat on the politicians. Austria capitulated on 22 October. The next day Wilson added a further condition: the kaiser had to go. This was too much for Ludendorff, who resigned. The army was in revolt. On 3 November, the day Austria signed the armistice, German sailors mutinied in Kiel. Councils of workers and soldiers were being set up everywhere. Max and others urged the kaiser to abdicate in order to avoid the threat of revolution. Albert Ballin was distraught. His firm was on the edge of bankruptcy. Panic was at its height. On 5 November

1918 a revolutionary committee took power in Hamburg. Such was the prestige of Max Warburg that once the committee members had taken him hostage and forced him to tell where the city's money was, they protected his family, invited him to dine at the city hall and treated him as an adviser.[91]

Max von Baden resigned and on 9 November Ebert, in the name of the Socialists, signed a secret agreement with the general Staff defending the country's unity against "bolshevik" revolts. That evening Wilhelm left for Holland after abdicating as kaiser but not as king of Prussia. The next night, unable to bear ruin and defeat, Albert Ballin committed suicide.[92] Max would never really recover from this tragedy.

In the turmoil of riots by the extreme right and the extreme left, the kaiser was kept prisoner in the Netherlands, while the Spartakists began their revolution and Philipp Scheidemann proclaimed a republic. Ebert headed a provisional government.

On 11 November the armistice with the Allies was signed. The empire was dead. However, the front ostensibly had held and the army was apparently not compromised in the defeat, which was to weigh heavy on the shoulders of the civilian population for some years.

Communications between Germany and America became possible again after four years of near silence. Jacob Schiff wrote to Max:

In the last few days I have received a good number of letters that you wrote at the end of 1915 and at the beginning of 1916. They were held back by the British censor and have only just been freed. Some of the letters sent me good wishes for the engagement and wedding of Carola who today has a little daughter of three. In the two and a half years we were unable to talk, your children have grown up, as shown by the little photograph Frieda received and has shown us.[93]

Warburg, Melchior and Keynes Against Versailles

Then began the dreadful years of the imposition of absurd reparations on an already drained Germany, reparations that destroyed the newborn Republic and helped germinate Nazi barbarism and the next war. Some men immediately saw this madness and tried to warn those in power. But their influence ended. In fact it was almost nonexistent: rational financiers were ignored by the vengeful spirit of politics.

America was now more powerful than ever. The leading world producer of wheat, coal and steel, she also held half the world's gold. The dollar was the only currency really convertible into gold. An ounce of gold was still worth $20.70. The US balance of payments was in ample surplus. By contrast, in Europe all the currency rates were floating in an attempt to return theoretically to prewar parities. Inflation was everywhere. During the war the supply of notes in circulation multiplied by six in France, fourteen in Great Britain and twenty-five in Germany. Both victors and vanquished had lost many of their finest men and most of their industrial base, and both were weighed down with debt.

The situation was especially disastrous in Germany. Unemployment and poverty had taken hold, financial activity was wiped out and the value of the mark remained undefined.[94] A few days after the armistice, on 16 November, the Ebert provisional government in Berlin asked Max Warburg to lead the financial delegation to the peace treaty negotiations that were soon to start at Versailles. He agreed to be a member of the delegation but asked that the leader be Carl Melchior rather than himself, to avoid bringing the name of his bank—one of the few German financial institutions still more or less upright—too much to the fore.[95] The government agreed. Kauffmann, chairman of the central bank, was to go with them, and Max would stay in the background. The delegation to the political talks led by Matthias Erzberger, a Catholic member of Parliament, was in the same situation. They were all to be treated like prisoners, allowed only a few walks in a corner of the park around the château.[96]

Facing the Germans in the British financial delegation appointed by Lloyd George, the prime minister, was the young Cambridge professor John Maynard Keynes, who would describe the conference in various writings, among them a striking essay devoted to Carl Melchior published in 1920,[97] and another more theoreticaly work giving a lucid and prophetic account of the economic consequences of the war and peace.

When he met Melchior, even before the negotiations began, Keynes was very impressed and described him thus:

> A very small man, exquisitely clean, very well and neatly dressed, with a high, stiff collar which seemed cleaner and whiter than an ordinary collar, his round head covered with grizzled hair shaved so close as to be like in substance to the pile of a close-made carpet, the line where his hair ended bordering his face and forehead in a very sharply defined and rather noble curve, his eyes gleaming straight at us, with extraordinary sorrow in them, yet like an honest animal at bay . . . . This Jew, for such, though not by appearance, I afterwards learnt him to be, and he alone possessed dignity in defeat.[98]

Carl Melchior, like Max, was an exceptional visionary. "His national feeling towards Germany," Siegmund was later to say of him, "had nothing to do with a conventional patriotism or the slogan 'my country right or wrong.'" Carl Melchior considered himself a loyal member of the German community. He was deeply attached to the German language of which he had a clear and precise command, but this did not prevent him also turning a lucid gaze on the weaknesses of his country.[99]

Fascinated by Melchior, Keynes did not at first notice Warburg, who however picked him out immediately and noted in his diary:

> On the inter-Allied Commission, Keynes was by far the most gifted. At the close of a session he always gave us the opportunity to give him our joint impressions. He was an obvious seeker after truth. Understanding and insight marked his every word."[100]

The negotiations began in the utmost confusion. The conditions were very ill-defined and the Allies' interests very contradictory. To start with the question of the blockade, which had been in force since 1915, the November armistic anticipated that this would also continue since reparations were not fixed. The complementary armistice negotiated in December 1918 by the French alone forbade the Germans to use their gold or bonds for purchases abroad, as these were considered security against the reparations to come. Keynes was furious:

> The blockade took four years to design and it is a perfect instrument. Now its creators have come to love it for itself . . . [thinking] it is the only instrument by which we can impose peace terms on Germany and that if it were raised it could not be brought back into force.[101]

But what should be demanded from vanquished Germany? Should anything be exacted? These were the great questions of the day. Instead of accepting that times were hard for the whole of Europe and trying to rebuild the devastated continent together, all the victors in their own way took the selfish and pointless way out. They forced Germany, already burdened with war debt, to pay reparations, even though it meant she would become even more indebted to them and would drag them down in her fall. Europe plunged deeper into a debt economy, which was known to be at the root of the war that had just ended.

The talks began at Versailles on 12 January 1919 in the middle of Germany's "bloody week," when the extreme Socialists Karl Liebknecht and Rosa Luxemburg were murdered. Their revolution failed and their Spartakist party was crushed. A constituent assembly elected on 19 January met the next month in the municipal theater of Weimar, a small town in Thuringia, and worked out a constitution. The Social Democrats allied themselves with the Catholic center and with the Democrats against the extremists, and on 11 February Ebert, who had tried to save the monarchy, was elected president of the Republic. Scheidemann, another middle-of-the-road Socialist, became chancellor, and Erzberger, the Catholic who had headed the political delegation to Versailles, became first minister of finance, then foreign minister.

At Versailles the German delegation, which had been anxiously following developments at home, hoped its new government would give them some sort of mandate. In fact this did not happen and the confusion that reigned in Berlin was reflected at Versailles in a disoriented, undisciplined delegation, itself out of control. One day in February Melchior was looking for a place at the Hotel des Reservoirs, where they were housed, to hold a private conversation with Keynes. He went into a room where three young Germans were idling, one playing the piano. When he asked them to give up the room, they shouted vulgarly at him that this was the hour when music was permitted. "Here you have a picture of Germany in revolution," Melchior told Keynes. "These are my clerks."[102]

In the course of this month Max Warburg, Melchior and Keynes held long conversations that the latter related with subtlety:

> Melchior's emotions were towards Germany and the falsehood and humiliation which his own people had brought on themselves rather than towards us. I also understood most clearly for the first time how dwellers in East Germany look to the East and not Westwards. The war for him had been a war against Russia; and it was the thought of the dark forces which might now issue from the East which most obsessed him. I also understood better than before what a scrupulous man he was, a strict and right moralist, a worshipper of the Tablets of the Law, a rabbi.

Melchior feared Germany's insincere acceptance of impossible conditions it did not intend to carry out; Germany "would be almost as guilty to accept what she could not fulfill as the Allies to impose what they were not entitled to exact—it was violating one's word that so much wounded him."[103]

At the end of February 1919 just as Kurt Eisner, the Bavarian prime minister, was assassinated, Melchior and Warburg returned to Berlin to prepare the peace conference documents. They knew that Germany was to be asked for large sums, and fantastic figures were circulating in the chancelleries. How much could they agree to pay? And how could they pay? They asked the Scheidemann government not to agree to just anything. The thing to do, they told Berlin, was to pay as little as possible and obtain long-term loans in order to keep the means of buying the raw materials needed for reconstruction.[104] Their report was ready by April.

On 7 May the conference resumed, and the Allies presented their terms. Even Max, the most pessimistic of the German negotiators, had not foreseen that they would be so harsh: the loss of the colonies, neutralization of the left bank of the Rhine, abandonment of all German investments abroad and of most of the merchant fleet, payment within two years of 20 billion gold marks, 5 billion of which to be paid before 1 May 1921 in exchange for supplies of food and raw materials with further reparations still to be determined.

Max was certain that if the Treaty of Versailles were signed on these terms Germany would be ruined and would drag down the rest of Europe. It would also be a disaster for the French and he warned them of this. (*"La France fera faillite un jour après nous"*)—"France will default the day after we do"—he told the negotiators.[105] Keynes recognized the absurdity of the situation. In order to pay reparations of this magnitude, he told the Allied delegates, Germany would need a trade balance, allowing it to export half as much again as it imported, therefore driving from the world market some of the major industries of Great Britain.[106] On 20 May, when the delegates refused to heed him, Keynes left Versailles and withdrew to his university, where as an economist of great influence he would carry on his work and denounce the blunders of his time.

The Allied blockade, however, accompanied by revolts of every kind, was forcing the worried German government to give in. Even so, Max made several trips to Berlin to ask them to hold out. The consequences of the agreement would be worse for the young democracy than those of a rejection, he said. At the beginning of June he wrote to his wife, "One thing is certain: we shall never be able to sign this peace in earnest."[107]

On 17 June, when Wilson had denied Italy the annexation of Fiume and Dalmatia, the Allies handed the Germans a final draft. Under this plan Germany would lose one-eighth of its territory and one-tenth of its population. East Prussia would be cut off from the rest of

Germany, which was also to lose all its colonies. Germany would lose 25 percent of her steel and coal, 75 percent of her iron and 15 percent of her agricultural land. Her general staff would be dissolved. Military service would be abolished. Heavy artillery, submarines and tanks were banned and the army was to be limited to a hundred thousand men. The Allies were to occupy the left bank of the Rhine for the next five years. The plan also required the delivery of equipment, the payment of 20 billion gold marks before 1 May 1921 and the forfeit of assets abroad. In its political section, the treaty called for the demilitarization of both banks of the Rhine for fifteen years, "in order to ensure the payment of reparations;" the amount was to be determined by a reparations commission that was to be set up. The treaty also envisioned the creation of a League of Nations, from which Germany would be excluded.

Faced with this crushing burden, the German financial delegation unanimously asked the chancellor on 18 June not to sign "this peace that would inevitably lead to the ruin of Germany," and threatened to resign if he were to sign. Scheidemann, as outraged as they, refused to sign and resigned on 20 June. Gustav Bauer, who replaced him, did not feel in a position to refuse. On 22 June 1919 the Weimar Parliament ratified the terms of the Treaty, signed on 28 June by the German government and initialed the same day at Versailles, by Clemenceau, Wilson, Lloyd George and the other victors. Neither Max nor Carl were any longer with the German delegation.

On 11 August, at last, the Weimar constitution was promulgated, article 48 of which allowed government by decree. By terrifying the Socialists and the army, the Spartakist revolution had thus made possible the instrument that Hitler would use fifteen years later to seize power.

Surprisingly, the American Senate refused on 19 November to ratify the treaty, believing it to be too harsh toward Germany and in contradiction of the Fourteen Points proposed by Wilson. Thus, the agreement never had legal validity, though it was to blight the postwar period.

Siegmund Joins M.M. Warburg

In common with all Germans of their class, the Warburg family came out of the war seriously damaged. Aby M., who had been very hostile toward the war from the start, thought the defeat well deserved. From 1916 onward he was tubercular and had been admitted to a sanitorium on the Swiss border where he now suffered from persecution mania.

Fritz, back from Sweden, was again working at the bank with the older brother of George, Aby S.

As for George, he was very ill. His headaches were growing worse and no one could find the cause.[108] His fortune had evaporated in the empire loans that Weimar would never repay. His farm property was largely abandoned, the Günzburgs still huddled there with destitute workers and peasants. His wife was wearing herself out with domestic work.

George's son, Siegmund, had now finished his secondary school studies. A charming but proud young man, he asked nothing of anyone. Money did not interest him and finance was scarcely an attraction. At no time did he think of making banking his career. His father had often enough told him of the boredom of life in Hamburg and the austerity of M.M. Warburg; and his distant cousins had never really given the impression of enjoying themselves.

His passion was politics, and he was quite determined to take courses at the nearby University of Tübingen in order to become a professor before launching himself into politics. His mother agreed with him.

However, Max, who well knew the financial difficulties of his provincial cousin—difficulties he had not done much to ease until then —asked Siegmund to come to Hamburg one evening in August 1919. He hardly knew this young man of seventeen. However, as head of the family, following the example of all those who had preceded him in that role during the two centuries, Max wanted to do something for the last of the "Alsterufer" Warburgs. Some also say that Max had other reasons to be interested in Siegmund, as he doubted the worth of his own more direct successors. He questioned him:

"Well, Siegmund, what do you want to do now?"

"Study history and philosophy in order to go into politics."

"A very good idea, but why not start by coming to work with me in the bank for a while? You would have a salary and be able to help your mother. You are not too young. All the Warburgs come in at eighteen. My son Eric has just done it."

Siegmund hesitated.[109] He would really have preferred to become an academic or a writer like his father's cousin Aby M. or his second cousin James, the son of Paul in New York.

Max was charmingly insistent. "Anyway, begin by training here just for a year or two. If you are the best, you will have all the scope there is; and if you don't like this business there will still be time to go back to the university. Besides, if you come and work with me in Hamburg, you can go to as many university lectures here as you like."

This meeting greatly impressed Siegmund and was a turning-point in his life. The only time he agreed to talk about himself to a journalist, more than sixty years later, he spoke of it in a very precise way. "Max told me that the bank would prepare me for a lot of other things. He had great authority, great charm and I was a rather shy, reserved young man. . . . I agreed that it could be of interest to work in that bank for a year or two."[110]

In fact his hesitation was partly because the politician Matthias Erzberger had just invited him to campaign on his behalf in Swabia. It was also because he knew his father would have liked him to take over the running of the Urach property. When he returned home, however, his father advised him, whatever he might have said previously, to go to work in Hamburg. Siegmund hesitated still, then after two months moved to Hamburg, but without giving up his initial ambitions.

As soon as he arrived he did in fact take up politics, supporting liberal candidates, writing speeches for his uncle's friend Walther Rathenau, then minister of industry, and for Gustav Stresemann, another family friend who had gone into politics. He was very interested in literature, took part in the intellectual life of the city and devoured book after book. On one occasion, he wrote to Stefan Zweig in Vienna to express his admiration for Zweig's biography of the French author Romain Rolland. To Siegmund's great surprise Zweig replied with a long letter, the start of an unusual friendship that would last as far as London, their common place of exile, and until the death of the writer.

During those years most of Siegmund's life was taken up with the role of a trainee in the house of Warburg. He drafted letters, learned accounts, went to religious services and opened the mail. He worked with his father's cousins Max, Fritz and Aby M., his second cousin Eric and with Carl Melchior.

During the first interview I had with Carl Melchior, I felt at first rather intimidated by his obvious authority [he wrote later]. Soon, however, he revealed qualities of human understanding and inner calm which undeniably encouraged the much younger boy that I was to confide in him and often ask his advice. . . . Carl Melchior was one of those rare men who show complete objectivity. He had that higher form of impartiality which is acquired through great struggle, with passion and at the cost of great inner conflict. This consists of self-control almost to the extent of quasi masochism, with the aim of dominating one's own impulsive subjectivity, without, however, repressing the intensity of personal feeling.[111]

Melchior taught Siegmund to write business letters, and made the style then known all over Europe as *haute banque* an absolute requirement in his life.

An important client had to be told that his proposal was being rejected and young though I was, I was responsible for writing the reply. In my draft I drew up a detailed table of the reasons for our negative stand. When I gave it to Carl Melchior for him to read, he crossed out the entire list of reasons I had mentioned and said, "We should, on the contrary, simply express our regret at not being able to participate in this venture and at the same time express the hope that we shall undertake another together on another occasion. The recipient will thus be far less hurt then if we troubled to explain the reasons for our rejection, which in any case he would not understand."[112]

A Central Bank for the "Warburg Countries"

On 15 June 1919, even before the signing of the Treaty of Versailles, Max and Melchior had returned to Hamburg disappointed and humiliated, but determined to rebuild the drained bank. In June 1919, as Max von Baden had done in October 1918, Ebert asked Max and then Melchior to become finance minister in the Bauer government. Each refused in order to return to work at M.M. Warburg. They had to find employees, reestablish contact with clients and, even more urgent, obtain payment of overdue debts. Max was in anguish. As he had predicted in 1917, without new capital his bank was headed for failure. Where could he find money except in America? He therefore wrote to his two brothers asking them to help him. Paul and Felix did not hesitate and came to Europe. Max arranged to meet them in Switzerland, where he was sent by Scheidemann in July to request a loan for Germany from the Swiss government and banks. The brothers met in St. Moritz in August 1919 for the first time in six years.[113] Max asked them for 6 million marks, a huge amount, to save the bank. Paul and Felix advised him not to be obstinate but to close down the bank and join them in America.

"Germany is lost as you well know—you refused to sign at Versailles. Europe will go backwards and tip over into Communism. What are you staying for?"

"No, look, we shall become a great bank again and Hamburg will
be the new capital of industrial Germany."

They parted without coming to a decision. Felix went back to New
York. Paul stayed on in Europe for some time, in search of a part to play
in organizing the financing of European debt. For him this problem was
likely to lead to a world catastrophe. Instead of lending to Europe over
the short term, a sort of international central bank should be established,
to organize these movements of capital in the form of long-term loans.

He believed this would not be done without bringing in private as
well as public funds and banks. Paul went first to Basel, then Amsterdam, where at the beginning of October and partly on his initiative a
group of British, French, American and German bankers and academics
met for the first time since the war (among them Keynes and Max
Warburg).[114] They discussed the coming reparations and their consequences for the European economy. Paul floated the idea of a bank
specializing in financing the reparations, which would be used to revive
international trade. Several institutions eventually were to be born from
this idea, including today's Bank for International Settlements and the
World Bank.

Paul's plan was much discussed during the Amsterdam meeting,
but without any immediate result. On 12 October Keynes, who was
still there, telegraphed Melchior in Hamburg asking him to come and
see him. On 15 October Melchior arrived in Amsterdam and he,
Keynes and Paul Warburg went walking in the city, which Melchior
knew well. Back at their hotel, Keynes read them a passage from the
manuscript of his book, *The Economic Consequences of the Peace*, in which
he spoke harshly of Wilson and his defeat in Congress over the Treaty of
Versailles.

> I noted its effect on the two Jews [wrote Keynes]. Warburg for
> personal reasons hated the President and took malicious pleasure in
> his discomfort; he laughed and thought this an awfully good re-
> proach. But Melchior, as I read, grew ever more solemn, until at the
> end he appeared almost to be in tears. This then was the other side of
> the curtain; neither profound causes, nor inevitable fate nor magnifi-
> cent wickedness. The Tablets of the Law, it was Melchior's thought at
> that moment, had perished meanly.[115]

The Amsterdam meeting greatly affected all those who took part in it.
All the bankers present saw the urgent need to link Germany with the

Allies and put Europe back on its feet by consolidating short-term debts. All participants had the feeling that it was to the advantage of America, no longer supported by the war economy, that the European market should be revived. If not, she might see her own financial markets gasping for breath.

Returning to Hamburg in November 1919 Max found a country in ferment. The popular press clamored for the murder of "the November criminals," in other words, the Republicans, the Socialists and the Jews. The right accused him of having agreed to negotiate at Versailles and of having betrayed the country there. He had to go into temporary hiding. The economic and political situation was not improving—far from it. The far left attempted a revolution in Bavaria and several hundred Communists were shot. The far right attempted a *coup d'etat* in March 1920. Revolts by workers in the Ruhr and Saxony were harshly repressed in June. The Weimar government played a delicate game relying on the army against the starving people.

Nevertheless, for a time it was possible to believe that things would get better. The German economy was slowly coming back to life and international credit was returning, though on a small scale. The big companies increased their capital and mergers began again.

That year Max Warburg refused to take on as a trainee a brilliant young German named Hermann Abs—who will be mentioned later—because Abs would not agree to stay with the bank after his training period.[116] The mark stabilized at one-tenth of its prewar value. However, the government overestimated its own strength and showed excessive optimism. In the spring of 1920, with the help of the Reichsbank, it indemnified the banks for their war loans to the Treasury, and the Ruhn industrialists for the loss of Lorraine, but without requiring a productive counterpart, and therefore simply printing money.[117]

As Bethmann-Hollweg, Prince von Baden and Scheidemann had done before him, Ebert again asked Max to be either minister of finance or ambassador to the United States, where Harding had just replaced Wilson. Max refused both posts, the first because he still thought that it was not good for a Jew to be in the government; the second because he was more used to "giving orders than to obeying."[118] Then, in Berlin, he meet with Hjalmar Schacht, who had just joined the Reichsbank as one of its directors, after being a banker in Kiel, Berlin, Munich, Leipzig, Paris and London. During the war Schacht had been part of the banking team working on the occupation of Belgium, and the two men had conferred. Schacht, a Christian and a freemason, thought as Max did that Germany urgently required a long-term loan, to enable it to pay off the first 5 billion marks of its debt.

In America, financial institutions were developing and consolidating. The stock exchange firm set up by Charles E. Merrill in 1910 merged with Edmund C. Lynch's firm to create Merrill Lynch, while the J.P. Morgan bank joined with that of Harold Stanley.[119]

Paul was now determined to set up on his own and create a sort of international central bank, which he called the International Acceptance Bank, in order to guarantee loans granted by American banks to international trade ventures. He wanted to bring into it the big public and private banks of Europe. It took Paul several months to convince a number of banks that it was in their interest to join in this venture. The banks involved were Svenska Handelsbanken, Skandinaviska Kredit Tiebolaget, National Provincial Bank, N.M. Rothschild, Credit Suisse in Zurich, Dreyfus Sons in Basel, Hope & Co., Handel Maatschappij and M.M. Warburg in Germany.

The International Acceptance Bank opened in April 1920 and Paul's son, Jimmy, went to work there with his father. An intellectual who had joined the marines in 1917 straight from Harvard, he had written under a pseudonym the book for a successful musical, *Fine and Dandy*, as well as several books on cotton, leather and finance.

But the International Acceptance Bank was merely a stopgap. The growth of world trade reawakened in this way would never be strong enough to repay the loans or the war debt. Paul would later realize that he had done no more than delay the catastrophe.

Germany Raises Her Head

After the summer of 1920 there were changes in Europe. Alexandre Millerand replaced Paul Deschanel, who had beaten Clemenceau for the presidency of France. Germany paid in cash the amounts agreed for 1919 and the beginning of 1920. However, after that she would do her utmost not to keep to the due dates set at Versailles, and would not pay the reparations, for which illusory amounts and theoretical methods of payment would be set by conferences in city after city over the next ten years.

The first of these conferences at Spa on 5 July 1920 determined the percentages each victorious country should receive: 52 percent for France, 22 percent for Great Britain and 10 percent for Italy; the remainder to go to Japan, Rumania, Belgium, Greece, Serbia and Portugal. The price of the coal Germany was to deliver to the victors by way of reparation also had to be decided. In theory the price should have been very low, but two German mine owners, Hugo Stinnes and Otto Wolf, refused to deliver even a kilo of German coal to France unless the price were fair. They only agreed to sell at one gold dollar plus ten dollars of loan per ton of coal delivered, which was actually a first-rate price, comparable to those on the international market.[120]

Max took over as head of a campaign to rehabilitate Germany. He asked for her admission to the recently formed League of Nations and called for a big international loan for reconstruction. That same year, to get around the Treaty of Versailles and avoid confiscation of the Zeiss and Krupp subsidiaries abroad, he disguised them as British and Dutch companies by having them bought out by two M.M. Warburg companies that had reopened in London and Amsterdam (Merchant & Finance Corporation and M.M. Warburg & Co.). In March he issued the first postwar German industrial loan of 100 million marks on behalf of the Elektrizitäts-Gesellschaft of Berlin. The Guggenheim Bank in New York took a quarter of this from him.

Also that year, with Mendelssohn in Berlin, he set up a small international bank to attract foreign investment to Germany, Deutsche Warentreuhand AG, and financed the purchase of new ships for the "Line," which he had saved from collapse after the death of Ballin. One of the ships would bear his name and another that of Carl Melchior.[121] Siegmund, who had been working with Max for about a year, was fascinated by all this.

At the end of 1920 negotiations began to determine the amount of reparations. Carl Melchior, with a group of experts, made proposals in the name of Germany that were rejected by the French in January 1921 at a conference in Paris. The Allies demanded 226 billion marks in forty-two annuities. At the beginning of March, Germany refused and proposed paying 30 billion, in addition to the 20 billion she maintained had already been paid since the war. Furious, France occupied Düsseldorf and Duisburg on 8 March, as a sanction. On 27 April at the resumed London conference, the Allies reduced their claim to 132 billion marks. If she agreed to this amount, Germany would have to pay out 2 billion marks a year and give up one-quarter of her export receipts, or more than the total budgetary revenue of the German state, which was obviously impossible. The Germans rejected this demand, despite an ultimatum from the Allies, who threatened to reoccupy all of South Germany. Deadlock was total.

In Germany the blockade continued and poverty worsened. In June the politician Dr. Josef Wirth was appointed chancellor. Social unrest increased, capital took flight and commercial and banking contracts were more and more often qualified in dollars. The Reichstag then agreed to the Allied ultimatum. Wirth signed the London agreement and to begin to pay off the 132 billion gold marks. Great quantities of gold and foreign exchange were sold, reducing still further the solvency and the borrowing capacity of Germany. Max Warburg was still telling anyone who would listen that the only reasonable solution would be for the Allies to agree to make Germany a long-term loan of the money to pay the reparations, since these were now unavoidable.[122] He himself did not manage to raise such loans, however, apart from a small amount from the International Acceptance Bank: $9 million lent to M.M. Warburg to finance imports to Germany of essential cereals.

Germany therefore continued to live on short-term borrowing. With the shortfall in production and the size of this borrowing, inflation, contained for a time, began to accelerate in the spring of 1921. This meant intense activity for the German banks, because as prices rose there had to be regular increases in the capital of the major groups, and loans had to be issued for Krupp, Daimler or the Hamburgische-Elektrizitätswerke.[123] M.M. Warburg, like other banks, earned a good living from this; but inflation was eroding the value of its own assets and those of savers, and the mark was falling rapidly: the dollar went from 63 marks in June 1921 to a little under 100 by December. People lost no time in withdrawing their money from the banks. In the course of that year the capital and reserves of the German banks fell by 70 percent, amounts on deposit and in current accounts fell by 80 percent. Several private banks failed and a few public bodies took a share in the capital of some of them.

Progressive Slide toward Hitlerism

Thanks to the help of Max's brothers in America, M.M. Warburg was one of the few surviving German institutions to avoid seminationalization. By the end of 1921 it had been able to settle most of its prewar debts.

This was not the case in the rest of the country. Only six months after accepting the London agreement, Chancellor Wirth declared Germany incapable of meeting the payment due in January 1922 and called for a moratorium on her debt. He would not hear of a loan that would turn Germany into a vassal state.

At the beginning of the year another conference opened in Cannes, where Walther Rathenau, still minister of reconstruction, explained the desperate state of his country. The disquiet of the British bankers faced with the risk of German bankruptcy impelled prime minister Lloyd George to propose a compromise. At first Aristide Briand, the French prime minister, agreed, but the president, Millerand, disowned this on 12 January 1922. Briand resigned and was replaced by Poincaré, while the amount of reparations remained at the figure set in London: 132 billion marks.

In February Wirth called Max and Melchior to Berlin and asked them to prepare for a new European Economic Conference, arranged for April in Genoa by Lloyd George. Max refused to go to Genoa and warned Melchior to be careful there. He wrote to him:

> I would find it incorrect for our firm to be strongly represented at this conference. I would like to ask you in advance to leave the conference immediately if in reference to a possible international loan there is any talk of putting Germany under financial supervision. Whatever the circumstances, I would not wish to see us linked to the abdication of our financial independence and in any case I would expect no result from such supervision.[124]

Inflation was now acknowledged. In February 1922 the mark lost another 25 percent of its value against the franc and 10 percent between 15 and 31 March 1922. In April the Wirth government attempted a stringent stabilization policy. Just as Walther Rathenau, by then minister of foreign affairs, was signing the Rapallo agreement with Moscow, which put an end to Germany's isolation, Wirth asked Max to join the government.

For the fifth time in two years Max refused, explaining once more that given the general atmosphere it was not desirable for him and Rathenau—two Jews—to be in the same government.[125]

A month later, on 24 June, Walther Rathenau was assassinated by two anti-Semitic nationalists belonging to a secret organization named "Consul." That day in the Reichstag, Gustav Stresemann, who had become chairman of the People's party, declared, "The enemy is on the right," outraging the conservatives. Siegmund, like many liberal and intellectual Germans, attended Rathenau's funeral. He would never forget the speech made by Felix Deutsch, Rathenau's successor as chairman of AEG: "Each man has the shortcomings of his merits but few have, as he had, the merits of their shortcomings."[126]

This assassination and the threat of a total occupation of the Ruhr by the Allies caused severe unrest in Germany and led to the failure of Wirth's attempt at stabilization. Violence reached a peak. In August 1922 the Hamburg police chief again warned Max against threats of an attack and asked him to change his habits, surround himself with bodyguards or even leave the country—at least for a few weeks. Max left Hamburg for two months traveling to America for the first time since the war.

In October 1922 Benito Mussolini took power in Italy and Lloyd George was out of office. In November, under pressure from the Ruhr led by industrialist Hugo Stinnes, Wirth was replaced by Wilhelm Cuno, who had earlier replaced Ballin at the head of the "Line." Despite the chaotic situation, France continued to demand the payments stipulated earlier in London.

Hyperinflation

Then began a dreadful year. Because Germany had not paid, on 11 January 1923 French and Belgian troops occupied the whole of the Ruhr. The economic and financial position of the country became completely catastrophic—the mark collapsed with exchange rates changing by the minute. Max Warburg noted in his diary, "The mark no longer merits the name of currency; it has become an illusion, pure and simple."[127] The Jews, the middle class and the bankers were attacked *en masse* by the press. In March *Hammer*, an anti-Semitic newspaper, accused Max of having financed the Russian Revolution and having betrayed Germany at Versailles. As Germany was still a state based on law, Max sued the paper for defamation and won compensation. In April Cuno decided to start paying the amounts due again and in order to do this floated a gold loan for 500 million marks. But who would lend to Germany in this situation? Only 168 million was subscribed for, and this was immediately taken by the creditors. Inflation was out of control. There was no way out: on 13 June one dollar was worth one million marks. By August it was worth 100 million.

On 12 August 1923, Gustav Stresemann, the leader of the right wing of the national liberals, became chancellor and formed a coalition government with the Social Democrats. The mark was worthless: thirteen hundred paper mills and two thousand printing plants were working round the clock to supply banknotes. Morale was at a low point and cynicism was rampant. The middle class and the bourgeoisie evaporated. This became the crucible of Nazism.

In September banking activity became increasingly complex, requiring more and more employees. In order to protect its assets and honor its commitments abroad, M.M. Warburg then switched its capital and its profits into foreign currencies. The economy was becoming more and more "dollarized" or was managed in pounds. These were the beginnings of "Eurodollars." Even local authorities paid their civil servants in foreign currencies and borrowed from the banks in order to do so. Thus in September 1923 M.M. Warburg advanced £50,000 sterling to the city of Hamburg in order to pay the dockworkers.[128] On 15 October 1923 the dollar was worth 2,520 billion marks, and 4,200 billion by 5 November."[129]

In the same year, Vice President Calvin Coolidge succeeded Harding in the White House.

On 18 October 1923 Siegmund's father, George, died in Constance at the age of fifty-two, almost mad and on the verge of ruin. He was buried on his estate.[130] His wife had been beside him to the end:

> The worse his illness became, the more they shared the least experience, down to the smallest details. In the three years preceding the death of her husband, my mother was not separated from him for a single day . . . . After the death of my father, my mother at first had great difficulty in giving a new direction to her life. Now that my father had left this world . . . she was determined to carry on, as far as possible, his work on the estate and maintain his contacts with neighboring communities. There was also the need to look after guests who came to the estate; our house sometimes seemed like a hotel. More than one visitor who had expected to stay just a few days would spend weeks, even months with her."[131]

Max Warburg, Hjalmar Schacht and Others Save Weimar

In the insane turmoil of the time the outline of a solution began to appear. Another currency had to be created in place of the bankrupt mark. No one really knows who was the first to have had this idea. It is usually attributed to Schacht, though Walter Funk, Dr. Hans Luther and Rudolf Hilferding, successive ministers of finance, would also describe themselves as the inventors of the new currency.[132] In any case it is certain that Paul and Max Warburg both played a major, role though discreet, in implementing the idea.

At the end of September 1923 on the initiative of Paul and Max, three Hamburg banks (M.M. Warburg, the Norddeutsche Bank and the Dresdner Bank) joined with most of the big industrial companies in the city to set up the Hamburger Bank. This institution issued its own banknotes backed by gold and rediscountable in dollars through M.M. Warburg at the International Acceptance Bank in New York. The new mechanism worked. As had happened sixty-six years before, Hamburg was saved by foreign money brought in by the Warburgs thanks to a marital connection not in Austria this time, but in America.

But this ingenious plan, which was to save Weimar, still had to be made known to the rest of the country. Schacht was the man who did it.[133] With two years at the Reichsbank behind him, he suggested to Stresemann that a new currency be created for the whole of Germany. This "rentenmark" would be backed by the German economy as a whole, and would be strictly controlled by a new issuing institution independent of the state, the Rentenbank, with a capital of 3.2 billion rentenmarks.

On 9 November 1923 in Munich, Hitler and Ludendorff attempted a *putsch* and failed miserably. A few days later, Schacht became commissioner for the currency of the Reich and a month later chairman of the Rentenbank. The following year he would become chairman of the Reichsbank, with ministerial rank, and would attend cabinet meetings. For Schacht the rentenmark was only a stage on the way to reestablishment of the mark's convertibility into gold.[134] Stabilization was fairly speedy. On 17 November one rentenmark was worth one trillion paper marks.

On 23 November, deserted by the Socialists, Stresemann resigned from the Chancellery but remained minister of foreign affairs for a further six years. He was replaced on 30 November by Wilhelm Marx, the leader of the Catholic party.

In December the mark's exchange rate stabilized.

On 30 December 1923 Max Warburg wrote to a young banker friend in London, Carl H. Henriques:

> I have become philosophical: it is the only way to keep one's pleasure in living, appetite and sense of humor—some of the few things not to be taxed. We shall certainly not fall back into the catastrophe of inflation. But there will be a very long convalescence before we can put anything like economic order in our house.[135]

For a time, Weimar was saved.

Siegmund lived through these frantic years in Hamburg with Max, who kept him informed of everything. He also worked with Walther Rathenau, and after Rathenau's assassination, with Gustav Stresemann and Hjalmar Schacht, on either speeches or memoranda. By now Siegmund had decided to stay with the bank, thrilled by what he was learning. He always remembered Max saying at that time that in such a whirlpool "the bank has only been able to survive by constant attention to the slightest problems," adding a quote from his brother Aby M., the magnificent phrase of an aesthete, "God lives in details."[136]

The Dawes Plan—The First Dollars for Europe

America, beginning to understand the dangers of Germany's weakness, now wanted to help Weimar. Since breaking the London agreement in December 1921, Germany had paid almost nothing, apart from the proceeds of the undersubscribed loan of April 1923. The Reparations Commission established by the Treaty of Versailles finally met on 30 November 1923 and chose Charles G. Dawes, an American banker from the Midwest, to rethink the reparations at a realistic level. It is true that at the beginning of 1924 monetary stabilization caused a return of confidence and the beginnings of German economic renewal. However, Schacht's monetary stringency limited bank lending, since he insisted that any new lending should be preceded by repayment of existing loans.[137] Bankruptcies increased. Unemployment replaced inflation and Germany still did not have the means of meeting the payments set in the London conference.

Early in 1924, when Schacht saw Charles G. Dawes for the first time, he explained that Germany was willing to pay reasonable amounts, but on condition that she did not have to borrow abroad on a short-term basis in order to do this. Schacht stressed that he wanted to encourage foreign investment in Germany and urged German companies to borrow abroad to bring in foreign exchange, which would improve the economic situation. In the spring of 1924 the Dawes Commission, after three months' work, recognized that it was in the interests of the Allies that the German economy should recover, even if this meant agreeing to reschedule the payment of reparations. This had been the view of Max Warburg and John Maynard Keynes ever since Versailles. It had taken nearly five years for the Allies to accept it.

In April Dawes proposed that America grant an initial loan of 800 million gold marks at 8 percent in exchange for Allied control of the railways and the Reichsbank. The indemnity was still set at 132 million gold marks (but with annuities increasing from 1 to 2.5 billion);[138] Germany was to pay this off over five years.

Also in April M.M. Warburg and the International Acceptance Bank in New York put together some loans to German companies in rediscounted dollars. Among these was a rediscounted loan for first $5 million and then $25 million to the Golddiskontbank, whose board Max joined.[139] In the same month Hugo Stinnes died, leaving behind huge holdings in banks, steel, cement and paper.

The other European currencies, still floating in search of a theoretical return to prewar parities, were hit by the previous year's German inflation.

In France, despite the exchange control introduced in 1918 and strengthened in 1924, the victory of a left-wing alliance set off speculation against the franc, especially from Hamburg. M.M. Warburg's role in this has not been established.

The Lazard and Morgan banks then financed counterspeculation, and by throwing its full weight into the battle, the French government managed to stabilize the exchange rate of the franc. In May the Hamburg speculators suffered such heavy exchange losses that in order to save companies that had speculated, Max Warburg was forced to arrange a support fund of £110,000, subscribed by the city's leading banks.[140] A little later, in 1926, a government of national unity brought the value of the dollar in France down from 40 to 25 francs.[141]

On 30 August 1924, as provided for in the Dawes Plan, a new law simplified and unified the German banking system under Allied protection. The Rentenbank was abolished and the Reichsbank again became the sole issuing institution, completely independent of the government, with a ruling council consisting of seven Germans and seven foreigners. Max Warburg was appointed a member at the request of Schacht, whose friend and adviser he was gradually becoming. The bank's capital was 300 million gold marks. The reichsmark once more became the national currency, backed by gold. In fact the notes in circulation were only 40 percent covered by the bank's reserves, and one-quarter by foreign exchange. Parity was set at one reichsmark, or one trillion paper marks, to 0.3583 gram of gold.[142]

The Dawes Plan was ratified on 1 September 1924 by a vote of the new Reichstag, elected in May. The Ruhr was then evacuated by the Belgians and the French, and Germany was to live for five years on loans from America, reaching $250 million a year. These loans were arranged by Dillon Read and the International Acceptance Bank in New York,

Sullivan & Crownwell, headed by John Foster Dulles in the United States, and Schroder in London.[143] Half of the money would go through the big three German banks: Deutsche Bank, Commerzbank and the Darmstädter Bank, and the rest throught three investment banks, among them M.M. Warburg, which profited handsomely. The greater part of these loans went to Krupp and Stinnes, into steel and coal. In order to issue the loans in dollars, arrange the bank syndicates and place the securities, the German and American banks set up a network of experts in Berlin and Hamburg. Among them were Max's second cousin Siegmund and Schacht's private secretary, Gert Weismann, who will be mentioned later.

The pound and dollar market born during hyperinflation now developed around these loans, but it was still too narow to influence the exchange rates of the still floating pound or the dollar, as its descendant —the Eurodollar market—would do forty years later.

By October 1924 the International Acceptance Bank had run its course. Paul no longer believed in the concept. He saw debt and speculation rising everywhere. Money was going into the markets more than into investment, a bad sign. Max, however, still needed more capital to keep his firm going, and he founded the American and Continental Corporation in New York with a number of American banks, including Kuhn Loeb. The aim of the corporation, with capital of $10 million, was to arrange loans and industrial investment for Germany.[144]

With the implementation of the Dawes Plan, the German economy consolidated its debt to some extent, making it possible to increase the issues of shares or bonds. M.M. Warburg made substantial money by investing the fortunes acquired by some German companies thanks to inflation or gambling on exchange rates. The investment went either into long-term bonds or foreign exchange. M.M. Warburg also arranged the merger of Ossag-Werke and Shell and about this time put together an agreement between German and American groups for the construction of a communications cable between Germany and the United States.[145]

The Grand Illusion

The Swiss franc and the pound stabilized. One after another currencies came back to a more stable gold parity, and each one tried to reach its prewar level—an illusion of happier times. In Germany the expected recovery picked up speed. At the end of 1924 the Reichsbank withdrew the measures taken in 1923 against the flight of capital and lowered the discount rate. The stabilization of exchange rates reduced the need for complex bookkeeping, and as a result the number of staff employed by M.M. Warburg was reduced.

After four years on the verge of bankruptcy, Max had brought his bank back into the first rank of German finance. He had extricated it from the abyss, in part because of his influence on the financial options of successive German governments, but especially because of his brothers in America for whom Hamburg had become what St. Petersburg had been to Max before 1914: a city where Warburg cousins were at risk of ruin. Though he was a discreet man, less visible than Schacht or Melchior, nobody in Munich or Berlin was unaware of his role in public life. So when in March 1924, at the trial that followed his *putsch* attempt, a little-known fanatic, Adolf Hitler, denounced the constitution coming from a government "which has sold out and whose finance Minister will be a Jew." Everyone knew he was thinking of Max Warburg.

At the elections in December 1924 the far right and far left weakened while the moderates benefited. Marx, hated by the Nationalists, stepped down on 15 January 1925 to be replaced by Luther, the mayor of Essen. The army dropped the Socialists and allied itself with the right.

In the United States Prohibition was at its height. In London the prime minister, Stanley Baldwin, together with Churchill, the chancellor of the exchequer, made a nonsensical decision that would affect the whole of Europe. In May 1925 they reestablished the gold standard and the 1913 parity of the pound. There was to be no free striking of coins and convertibility was to be accepted only in four hundred-ounce bars.

This decision was immediately criticized by Keynes, who thought that the parity selected was far too high. Once again he was right. British industry was not ready to cope with its currency being brought back to absolute convertibility, and for six years, by means of deflation, successive governments would try to hang on to this anachronistic parity of the pound, causing unemployment and recession.

The Dawes Plan was now working fully, and dollars flowed into Germany from the rest of Europe and America in exchange for the reparations paid by the Reichsbank. M.M. Warburg's main activity was to raise capital in New York and London to finance German companies and cities. Max set up another investment company in New York with Dulles and Hayden Stone & Co.—European Shares Inc.—to invest in German industry, but it was a failure and the company went into liquidation soon afterward. But quickly he set up another one in London, The Industrial Finance and Investment Corporation Ltd., with the main British merchant banks (N.M. Rothschild & Sons, Kleinwort Japhet), the Prudential Insurance Co. and the International Acceptance Bank in New York.

In the summer of that year, during a dinner with Schacht, Max met Paul von Hindenburg, who had just been elected president of the Republic on the death of Ebert.

At the request of Felix Warburg, he also met Chaim Weizmann in Berlin, and at Weizmann's request passed on American funds to the Jewish communities in Poland. He also made use of his influence at every level in order to develop German trade with the USSR. The German government sent him to Moscow at the head of a consortium to open a credit line of £300,000 for a Soviet trading company that wanted to buy from Germany.

Everything seemed to be going well. Max was delighted that Gustav Stresemann signed the treaties at the Locarno Conference in October 1925; he hoped to see peace established in Europe at last. The bank's offices grew and now took up a good stretch of the Ferdinandstrasse. By the end of that year the staff of M.M. Warburg was down to 327 employees.[146]

Next Year in Jerusalem

The family recovered slowly from its war losses. Aby M., well again, took over the running of his institute in Hamburg in 1925. Fritz had come back to work with Max and Max's cousin Aby S., further weakened by diabetes.

Eric, Max's son, returned exhausted from the front where he had been sent in the final days of the war. After training in the Hamburg bank, he went to Kuhn Loeb in New York in 1921, then to Brandeis-Goldschmidt and Rothschild in London. Back in New York in 1923, he spent a year with his uncle Paul at the International Acceptance Bank and became a permanent resident of the United States. Despite a brief period of rebellion, for fifteen years he was to be "his father's voice," coming and going between New York and Hamburg.[147]

Paul was concerned only with his own bank and no longer set foot in Kuhn Loeb, then at its zenith. Felix stayed there with Otto H. Kahn, Mortimer L. Schiff, the son of Jacob, and Jerome J. Hanauer.[148] Felix was joined by Sir William Wiseman, an Englishman who had come to

America in 1917, after being gassed at the front, to run British psychological warfare in the United States. Kuhn Loeb drew off $9 billion a year in the form of issues, two-thirds for the railways and the rest for industry and foreign borrowers.[149] To be a partner brought one more than $1 million a year.

Felix had become one of the richest Americans of his time, a man to whom the conductor would bow when he attended the Metropolitan Opera. He was no longer the prewar dandy, however. Passionately interested in Jewish affairs, he had been transformed. He presided over the Joint Distribution Committee, which gave extensive help to the poor communities of the Diaspora, and established it throughout the world. He took part in the foundation of the United Jewish Appeal, which coordinated fundraising for the Joint and the United Appeal for Palestine.[150] In the last fifteen years of his life, he would give more than $13 million to Jewish charities, becoming one of the foremost philanthropists.[151]

The situation in the Middle East was very fluid. British and American Zionists were struggling to establish a Jewish agency that would organize the settlement of Jews in Palestine. In 1920 the British authorized its creation. In July 1922 Britain was entrusted by the League of Nations with a mandate over Palestine, thanks to the action of Lord Balfour.

Felix was not a Zionist, but the fate of the Jews interested him passionately and he was bent on backing every action in their favor, including those of which he did not approve. He did not approve of anything that was happening in Palestine where, according to him, Russian Jews were bringing in communism. In the spring of 1923 in New York he met for the first time a British chemist who had been born in Russia, Chaim Weizmann. He had become director of the laboratories of the British Admiralty during the war and was a friend of Foreign Secretary Balfour. From London, where he lived, he was trying to obtain financial and political help for Zionism from the American Jewish communities. The future president of the State of Israel gave the following account of his first meeting with Felix:

> Felix was an exceptional man, charitable in the highest degree, and a central figure in the American Jewish community, though not in close contact with its base. There was something of the "good prince" about him. . . . Soon after my arrival in the spring of 1923, I was a little surprised to receive an invitation to lunch with him at the

headquarters of Kuhn Loeb on William Street. Installed in one of the most splendid rooms of this mansion, I found myself in the presence of an extremely charming and gracious man, very much the lord, but full of kindness. I decided that this lunch would be at once a duty and a pleasure. I had judged too quickly. We spent about an hour and a half together and for almost the whole of that time Mr. Warburg gave me a report on what, according to his information, was happening in Palestine. To be frank, I have never heard a more fantastic gibberish from a person inspiring confidence: bolshevism, immorality, waste of money, inertia, inefficiency, and all on the basis of hearsay.[152]

Weizmann suggested that Felix should go to Palestine and make up his own mind:

To my astonishment, he took me at my word! "That is a good idea," he said. "I will talk to my wife about it and if possible I will go to Palestine immediately." I was even more stupefied to see him keep his word and sail for Palestine with Mrs. Warburg a fortnight after this first conversation. I telegraphed Kisch to show them round the country.[153]

This journey transformed Felix.

He returned to the United States with his wife while I was still there, burning with the desire to help us by all possible means. I was once more invited to lunch, this time at their home. I listened to them and this time heard nothing but praise for Palestine and for our ventures. I have rarely witnessed a more complete conversion. . . . I believe that this conversion was the real point of departure for the participation of [Felix] Warburg in our work. Incidentally, it was also the beginning of a long friendship which withstood the strain of very different opinions. These arose from the fact that we did not see Palestine from the same viewpoint. For us Zionists it was a movement of national renewal; for him, at least when he began to concern himself with it, it was just one of his fifty-seven philanthropic activities—more important and more interesting than the others, perhaps, but hardly different in kind. His whole education was opposed to his sharing our views; moreover his colleagues in innumerable ventures in which he was involved constantly warned him of the risk he was running in identifying too closely with the Zionists. Warburg was one of the most valued attributes of their community and they greatly feared losing him to a new idea which might capture all his attention in principle and in substance.[154]

At Weizmann's request Felix in 1923 set up a committee with the aim of financing the birth of the University of Jerusalem, which had existed in embryo on Mount Scopus since 1918. He devoted much money and energy to this. "In autumn 1923, during my second journey to America that year," Weizmann wrote, "after attending the thirteenth Zionist congress in Carlsbad, Mr. Warburg raised a million-dollar-fund for the Hebrew University through the American Committee of Jewish Physicians."[155] In October 1924, Felix went to the inauguration with Weizmann and Einstein, members like him of the first administrative board of the university. The three men immediately disagreed on the aim of the institution. Felix wanted a University of Judaism, Weizmann and Einstein, a Political Institute of Zionism. Felix won. The others countered by setting up what would later become the Weizmann Institute near Tel Aviv.

Felix's five children were no more interested in finance than he was. His first son, Frederick, came to Max as a trainee in 1920, just as Siegmund and Eric had. In 1925 he returned to Kuhn Loeb.[156] But his real passion was horse breeding, and he settled in Middleburg, Virginia, where he had a stud farm, and rarely went to New York. Gerald, Felix's second son, became a cellist and conductor. The others were equally lukewarm about banking.

Siegmund around the World

After three years in Hamburg, where he learned all sides of banking, saw the difficult birth of Weimar and the dreadful death of his father, Siegmund went abroad.

In common with all young Warburg bankers in the past century, he went first to London, in 1924, to N.M. Rothschild, with whom it had become the family custom to exchange young trainees. He discovered the City. It was true that the war had transferred the economic center of the world to the other side of the Atlantic, and it was also true that the British balance of payments had moved into deficit and that services and income on capital no longer balanced foreign trade, but the City was still the leading financial center. Its services still brought Great Britain almost as much as the cost of the raw materials she needed to import; and she continued to lend the world the wherewithal to pay for the machinery it bought from her.

Britain was then in the hands of the Conservatives, who had won an overwhelming majority in the election on 29 October 1924. Baldwin was prime minister, Churchill chancellor of the exchequer, Austen Chamberlain foreign secretary and Neville Chamberlain minister of health. In the City, Baring and Rothschild, the two greatest British merchant banks of the period, dominated the twelve others admitted with them to the Accepting Houses Committee, the holy of holies set up in 1914.

Siegmund was fascinated by this elite and surprised at its way of life, apparently so relaxed and so different from that of Hamburg. He made contact with the British intelligentsia and lived the life of a dandy, invited to the homes of the Rothschilds and the other great banking dynasties, the Hambros and the Barings. He also met, at concerts, a young German banker who would later count for much in his life: Hermann Abs, himself also working as a trainee in London after a stay in Amsterdam. At the end of 1924, Siegmund went back to the Hamburg bank.

In spring 1925 Siegmund met Eva Maria Philipson, daughter of the managing director of a big Stockholm bank closely connected with his uncle Fritz, with whom she had come to stay at Kösterberg in order to learn German. They soon decided on marriage. The wedding was in January 1926 in Stockholm. Siegmund then stayed a year in Hamburg, leaving again at the beginning of 1927 to continue his apprenticeship, first in Boston with the lending accounting firm of Lybrand, Ross Bros. & Montgomery. It was here, the same year, that his son was born and named George after Siegmund's father. Siegmund spent the following year in New York, first with Paul at the International Acceptance Bank, then with Felix at Kuhn Loeb, working on American loans to Germany.

Siegmund would never forget this training with bankers who, like his family in Hamburg, did not consider money the main aim in their lives. "The satisfaction of giving service was more important than the profit received. Banking for them was a positive accomplishment, an intellectual sport."[157]

He rediscovered the old family tradition, somewhat overlooked in the turmoil of Weimar, by which profit is a by-product of business well done and not an end in itself. He made the acquaintance of everyone of note in New York and became friendly with Charles Lindbergh, who had just crossed the Atlantic, and more especially with Lindbergh's father-in-law, Dwight Morrow, a partner in the Morgan bank and a friend of Franklin Roosevelt. He would long remember one of Morrow's sayings, "The world is divided into people who do things and people who get the credit. Try if you can to belong to the first class. There is far less competition."[158] Siegmund himself would follow this advice.

The Debt Economy

Starting in 1926 there were three years of growth during which all the world's bankers heightened the economic crisis by their lending, believing they were thus deferring it. These were years of illusory affluence.

Exchange rates were again fixed and seemed guaranteed by the direct or indirect convertibility into gold of the main currencies. Thanks to a series of loans, international trade grew. America was expanding fast. The investment banking business became very profitable, and the commercial banks actively competed for it.[159] Thanks to networks set up during the war to sell public bonds and which of course were easily convertible to private purposes, the American banks issued loans hand over fist to companies of every kind: manufacturers of radios, automobiles and airplanes. Americans invested unreservedly. The scale of issues increased, reaching $25 million, against $1 million before the war. Competition among the banks was fierce and their earnings were sizable. Kuhn Loeb was involved in everything from investment banking to investment management, and its clients included among others the future Pius XII, Cardinal Pacelli, for whom it would invest $200,000 in US Steel.[160]

Germany was then restoring the bases of her power, from the Ruhr to Berlin; Luther had become chancellor, Stresemann was still at the Ministry of Foreign Affairs and that year received the Nobel Prize for peace along with Briand, a year after Dawes and Austen Chamberlain. At the end of that year, 1926, Carl Melchior was nominated German representative to the finance committee of the League of Nations, to which Germany had just been admitted. The meeting at Thoiry between Stresemann and Briand, a last attempt at a Franco-German agreement on reparations and territory, was fruitless.

In the heart of Germany, a hundred miles away from the Anglophilia of Hamburg, the industrial concentration of the gun merchants began again. The Rhine-Elbe-Union belonging to Hugo Stinnes, youngest son of the man of the same name who had died two years before, merged with Thyssen, Phoenix and Rheinische-Stahlwerke under the name United Steelworks. All the elite of the Ruhr were involved: Fritz Thyssen, Werner von Siemens and Heinrich von Stein.[161] Their power was extensive. They had representatives in all the big companies and in all the major banks like the Berliner Handels Gesellschaft. They used American money borrowed either under the Dawes plan or directly from the New York market. Thus in 1926 Hugo Stinnes, in order to obtain dollars, sold shares in United Steelworks to two fictional companies he had set up for this purpose in New York, Hugo Stinnes Industries and Hugo Stinnes Corporation.[162] Other German industrialists did the same, and German industrial power actually began to dominate Europe once more.

On Wall Street and on the Stock Exchange, owing to his contacts, Max was still able to place his German loans better than anyone else. Thus he floated two long-term loans in New York, one for $5 million for the city of Hamburg and the other for $10 million for industry, then a third in London for £2 million, again for industry. He also continued to play an important part in transactions between German companies, the State Bank of the USSR and the various Soviet administrative bodies.[163]

At the beginning of 1927, resigning himself to the fact that Germany's center of gravity had swung to Berlin, he opened a small office there. The year went by without any remarkable happenings. At that point the family was very united and—a rare occurence—almost all its members were in Hamburg: Fritz, Max, Aby M., Aby S., Eric and Siegmund—before he returned to the United States in 1927—and each had a house, either at Kösterberg or Travemünde. Aby M. was very ill, and Aby S. was increasingly troubled by diabetes. Paul and Felix still came often to Hamburg. Kuhn Loeb was to slip away from them as new partners like George Bovenizer, W. Wiseman and L. Strauss came into the firm.

More than ever, the economy of the old continent was held up only by debt. Max, who saw the catastrophe coming, urged the Germans to invest in America in order to earn real income and not depend on loans that would have to be repaid one day. For what had to happen was happening: the market began to be uneasy and lenders withdrew. Short-term interest rates rose around the world, and more than half of Germany's debt was made up of loans lasting less than six months.

Max began to be on his guard against certain clients and refused to place loans for some companies. He still considered his bank invulnerable, though. He knew that Paul's International Acceptance Bank and Felix's Kuhn Loeb would give him unlimited help. Both, for different reasons, urged him to liquidate everything and join them in New York.

Paul because he foresaw a world financial crisis; Felix because he sensed the threats hanging over the Jews of Europe.

The year 1928 was better for Germany. At the Reichstag elections on 20 May the Nazis polled only 801,000 votes and won fourteen seats. But the Communists gained strength and the moderate parties weakened. Hermann Müller became chancellor, still with Stresemann at the Foreign Ministry, and in August adhered to the Kellogg-Briand pact solemnly renouncing war.[164]

The bank's staff stabilized at 289 employees. The small Berlin office needed ever-increasing effort but brought in more and more money. The bank's international openings again became reliable. In order to attract more capital to Germany, Max set up a new international investment company in Amsterdam, VN Nederlandsche Crediet, with Dutch, Swiss, American, Austrian, German and British shareholders. In August the Hamburg-New York telephone line for which he had arranged financing was inaugurated. After Stresemann, Max was the second person to use the line. He spoke to his brother and to his cousin, Siegmund, then in the United States, and arranged a loan of $3 million to M.M. Warburg.

The pace of business was picking up. In December in New York, with the help of Jimmy and Siegmund, Paul merged the International Acceptance Bank with the Bank of Manhattan and made the new company, the International Manhattan Bank, an even greater source of finance for his shareholders, especially the Warburgs.

In 1928 Paul decided to send one of his men to Hamburg to keep an eye on what was happening at M.M. Warburg. He chose a young German who was then their agent in Istanbul, Rudolf Brinckmann, who will be mentioned later.

The Jewish Agency

Meanwhile, Felix was increasingly concerned with Jewish affairs, and especially with the Jewish Agency set up by the British some years earlier. This was still no more than a club.

> The Jewish Agency [wrote Weizmann] brought together a group of the most distinguished personalities. All classes of society and all works of the human spirit were represented, from Léon Blum the great socialist leader to Marshall and Warburg, people of the right; from Lord Melchett one of the major industrialists of Great Britain, to Albert Einstein and the poet Chaim Nachman Bialik.[165]

Felix urged the rest of the family to take an interest. On his advice Max visited Palestine for the first time in 1928 and set up the German branch of the Jewish Agency in Berlin.[166] In 1929 its executive council left London and settled in Jerusalem with a Zionist bank born in London at the same time as the Agency: Bank Leumi.

Felix was uneasy at seeing Weizmann become chairman of the Agency's board. He saw him as a "sort of Mussolini," to be mistrusted, and actually threatened to pull out if he was not given control.[167] Relations between the two were strained, but they maintained a common façade against the British. When, following the Arab riots of 1929, the MacDonald government imposed restrictions on Jewish immigraton to Israel, neither Felix nor Weizmann hesitated to resign in protest from the council of the Agency. They did not return to their posts, together, until the British prime minister removed the restrictions. The British, however, often played off Felix, who accepted the idea of a "home," against Weizmann, who dreamed of a nation. In 1929 Felix wrote to Lord Melchett, previously Sir Alfred Mond, "I am for action which shows we want to reach agreement with the Arabs and for action which expresses our reduced ambitions plainly."[168] Later he would regret his attempts at conciliation.

The Young Plan—Birth of the BIS

Europe was now dependent on America to make ends meet. The US, however, was not yet conscious of its responsibilities and Europe was to pay dearly. As Michel Aglietta writes:

> ... the replacement of British loans by American loans in order to support the fragile banking systems of Central Europe and Latin America put the latter at the mercy of a speculative wave set off by the purely nationalist monetary policy of the United States, a phenomenon which came about from 1928 onward.[169]

As for Britain, she was still clinging to her absurdly fixed parity.

At the end of 1928 the Allies thought that the time had come to reopen the question of reparations. From February to June 1929 another conference in Paris brought together France, Great Britain, Belgium, Germany, Italy, Japan and the United States—Herbert Hoover had just arrived in the White House—to attempt to give a final ruling on the matter. Owen D. Young, the chief executive at General Electric, was appointed chairman. Schacht, determined that Germany should cease paying these excessive installments, came to Paris on 11 February

1929 to lead the German delegation himself, without giving up his duties in Berlin.[170]

In April, in the name of the Allies, Young asked Germany to pay amounts even higher than those provided for by the Dawes Plan. He proposed the creation of a sort of world bank to manage the loans needed to finance the reparations. Schacht accepted the principle, but not the amount. In the end there was agreement on a reduction of the reparations to 38 billion gold marks, payable in thirty-six annual installments—instead of the 132 billion of the Dawes Plan and the London agreement—and on a mechanism for issuing international loans to pay for the reparations, to be organized by a new semipublic, semiprivate international institution, to be called the Bank for International Settlements.[171]

What Paul had tried to do with his International Acceptance Bank was therefore now being carried out on a larger scale. The plan was initialed by Young and Schacht in the name of Chancellor Müller on 7 June 1929, despite the furious opposition of Hitler.

On 3 October 1929, Stresemann died and Max wrote, "This is a hard loss for Germany and for all those in search of a new and better world."[172] On the same day a committee chaired by the American banker Jackson E. Reynolds worked out the final form of the BIS. Its capital was to be guaranteed by the central banks of Germany, Belgium, France, Great Britain, Italy, a group acting for the Bank of Japan and a group of three American banks (J.P. Morgan & Co., The First National Bank of New York and the First National Bank of Chicago). Other central banks would be able to subscribe within two years.[173] The following month in Rome, governors of the banks of signatory countries signed the agreement for the BIS,[174] which established itself in Basel. The agreement was officially adopted at The Hague conference in January 1930, and France undertook to evacuate the left bank of the Rhine before the end of June of that year. The international inspections of Germany and the reparations commission of the Treaty of Versailles were abolished. On 11 March 1930 the Young Plan was adopted by the Reichstag at the end of a stormy debate. On 17 May the BIS began its work, in the midst of the Great Crash.

Many people then began to see what Paul had been trying to establish for more than ten years: a world central bank.

A week after it came into being the spirit and outlook of the BIS were outlined at a lecture in Paris by Jacques Rueff, a young and unknown French inspector of finance, then financial attaché in London. He summed up:

> The Bank spares the governments concerned from having to guarantee their foreign payments themselves, and to this end keeping the various reserves in foreign currencies required by these payments— reserves which would duplicate those of the issuing banks, set up with exactly the same object in mind.... This brings us to the concept of a real "BIS currency," freely convertible into any currency at that currency's rate of exchange.[175]

This was an illusion of reason, which would be swept away like everything else in the maelstrom of crisis.

The Crisis of 1929—the End of Reparations

At the beginning of 1929 Aby M., Max's elder brother, died of tuberculosis. Eric became a partner in the bank at the same time as Ernst Spiegelberg, the second partner from outside the family. Hans Meyer and Siegmund Warburg, back from New York in January, were given power to sign for the bank. As Max saw it, Ernst Spiegelberg and Siegmund, rather than Eric, were the two best hopes of the firm, even though one was not a member of the family, and the other was from a rival branch. M.M. Warburg was doing well. The bank was represented on the boards of eighty-six companies in Europe and the United States.

Max noted in his diary:

> We were unquestionably the leading banking firm in Hamburg. The growth of our business is illustrated by the fact that our balance sheet total was 382 million marks—the Vereinsbank's was 127 million and Schröder's was 191 million . . . or 318 million marks altogether —in other words 20 percent above the worth of the other two banks combined.[176]

In fact not everything was as rosy as that, since Max had taken big risks in real estate and retailing in Hamburg and Berlin.

There was also euphoria in New York. Paul was almost alone in expecting a crisis. He thought that world debt was too great, with companies borrowing ever more in order to meet annual payments on earlier debt. In New York share prices and speculation raced ahead, and Paul knew that when money goes for the short term rather than the long, the economy is in danger. Everyone was trying to speculate on stocks and shares; more than one million Americans were playing the market. In February almost $10 billion was in speculative positions. The demand for speculative capital was such that interest rates went up to 9 percent, but despite this, $500 million worth of stock was still placed each month. To get in on the issue market, the commercial banks increased the number of their investment agencies across the country.

Paul realized that his own efforts had done no more than postpone the day of reckoning, and that a time would soon come when the general indebtedness of the country, worsened by speculation, would have to have to be paid for, whether by the debtors or the creditors.

At the beginning of 1929, in the last annual report of the International Acceptance Bank, shortly before it became the International Manhattan Bank, Paul wrote:

> The rise in Stock Exchange prices, in the majority of cases, bears no relationship to the growth of the companies, their assets or prospects of profit and if this orgy of uncontrolled speculation is not slowed down the final collapse will affect not only the speculators, but will cause a depression affecting the whole of the country.

He had said it all. Paul then warned his friends to get out of the market and sell their shares. Some did, among them Max and Felix, in part. Most sneered.

The volume of trading on Wall Street reached a high point on 3 September. That month Max relaunched Warburg & Co. in Amsterdam with a capital of 5 million florins, to represent the interests of M.M. Warburg and those of the International Manhattan Bank of New York.[177] Paul was appointed managing director. On 24 October Wall Street began to falter. Bank intervention held up prices for five days, but on 29 October they could no longer hold and collapsed: 16,419,000 shares changed hands. In ten days the market lost $30 billion.

After that, 1930 was a nightmare year for American banks. Stuart, Merrill Lynch and Blyth scarcely suffered, but Kuhn Loeb, Goldman Sachs, Kidder Peabody and Lee Higginson almost had to stop payments. In September, 305 American banks were in liquidation; in October, 522.

Weimar at Bay

The American financial crisis hit Europe very quickly. In Germany it threatened the Müller government. Two million unemployed at the beginning of the year had grown to three million by the end. The government did nothing to allay the crisis, being only too happy to use it as an excuse to refuse to pay the first installments due under the Young Plan.

Once again there had to be a review of the terms for payment of the war reparations. Another commission, still chaired by Young, but in which the Germans participated, was set up in January 1930 at The Hague. Agreement was reached, this time to spread the payment over fifty-nine annual installments instead of thirty-six, increasing in value until 1988. However, the chancellor refused to ratify this plan although it was accepted by Schacht, and the latter resigned from the Reichsbank on 7 March 1930. Müller in turn resigned from the Chancellery on 27 March, to be replaced by the former minister of education, Heinrich Brüning, a Catholic, branded by Siegmund as a weak character.[178] Schacht left for America. He, too, was resigned to halting reparations payments and nonimplementation of the Young Plan, which he had negotiated.

In the spring of 1930 Max went to New York to ask for help from Paul and Felix once more. He wrote from there that what "neither I nor anyone else foresaw was the extent and the dynamism of the crisis."[179] He added that during this trip his brothers told him they were "opposed to the firm remaining independent and even to its keeping its own name."[180] According to the historian Eduard Rosenbaum, however, the American Warburgs nevertheless then took "a further financial interest"[181] in the old Hamburg firm.

That spring Siegmund's daughter, Anna, was born in Hamburg. His mother was still at Urach and he often went to see her:

> That time was the source of new joys, thanks to the existence of her daughter-in-law and her grandchildren. She naturally wanted the four people who were closest to her to be with her at the estate as often and for as long as possible.[182]

In May Carl Melchior was appointed, along with Reichsbank chairman Hans Luther, to the board of the recently-formed BIS. Max could have had an appointment but refused. On the same board were Gates W. McGarrath for the United States, Sir Charles Addis for Great Britain and Clément Moret for France. The BIS began to function:

> The bank began to receive and distribute the monthly reparation payments made by Germany under the Young Plan and to intervene on German markets, reinvesting in reichsmarks part of the installments received and buying reichsmarks in periods of tension.[183]

Nevertheless, in order to pay all the reparations installments due in June 1930, Chancellor Brüning agreed to borrow $351 million at 5.5 percent on nine different markets. M.M. Warburg had a 4 percent participation in the German *tranche* of 36 million reichsmarks, and Warburg & Co. in Amsterdam participated in the Dutch *tranche*. Because Germany's international credit rating was at its lowest, only $302 million came in, of which one-third went to the German government, while the other two-thirds went to the six creditor governments in accordance with The Hague agreement.[184] There was great doubt that Germany would ever repay, and the price of the loan very quickly fell below its issue price, which caused big losses for those who had subscribed.

Everything was going badly. Foreign depositors withdrew the few foreign exchange deposits they held with German banks in order to cover their losses in New York. To meet a growing budget deficit, the German government then increased direct and indirect taxes, cut civil service salaries and unemployment benefits by 20 percent, increased unemployment taxes and cut prices by 10 percent.

In June 1930 at Ferdinandstrasse, competition between Hamburg and Berlin was making the atmosphere so unbearable that Siegmund, by now a partner in M.M. Warburg, left with his wife, son and daughter for Berlin to run the bank's office and take responsibility for "all the interests of the parent company in Germany outside the Hamburg region."[185] His "importance in the firm was growing rapidly,"[186] said Charles Sharp, an observer at the time, and even Max was now a little uneasy about being overshadowed by his much younger cousin.

All tolerance then went out of German political life, as though the democratic graft had not taken. In the elections of September 1930 the Nazis won 6.4 million votes and 107 seats and to their own surprise became the leading party in Germany. The moderate parties collapsed. The Socialists lost ground but the Catholics held steady. Brüning remained chancellor with the support of the Social Democrats. The Communists considered the "Social Fascists" their main enemy. The Republicans, the right, the Communists and the Nazis S.A. all fought one another. The banks, though increasingly under state control, were nevertheless still dominated by their founding families, but the Fürstenbergs, Goldschmidts or Wassermanns who had played major roles in the Berliner Handels Gesellschaft, the Darmstädter Bank or Deutsche Bank, were like Max more and more the target of Nazi insults and threats.

Siegmund made his small office a center of Berlin life. He also, for the first time, opposed Max. In Berlin he again met up with his friend from London, Hermann Abs. After banking posts in Paris and New York following his training in London, Abs had returned to the German capital in 1928 to work with an influential private bank, Delbrück, Schickler & Co., former bankers to the kaiser and Krupp.[187] Siegmund wanted to employ Abs. Max was against it; he remembered Abs's refusal in 1920. Also why widen the circle again to a stranger to the family? Siegmund did not insist. However, the friendship between these men, who were later to become the two leading bankers in Europe, would last all their lives.

Siegmund met a number of other people in Berlin who would count greatly for him in the future: a Briton, Andrew MacFadyean, who had come from Malaya to lead the British financial delegation, before becoming private secretary to the prime minister, Baldwin, in London; some industrialists, especially the two brothers Hugo and Edmund Stinnes, heirs to a strange destiny; and above all the Fürstenberg family, who presided over the fate of the Berliner Handels Gesellschaft, one of the few banks, along with M.M. Warburg, to have remained completely outside state control. It was also then that Charles Sharp first met him. "I have only a visual memory of that interview. I see again the A.E. Wassermann office in Berlin where it took place and the serene, smiling face of Siegmund G. Warburg, full of interest and always slightly ironic."[188] Siegmund also often met Schacht's former secretary, Gert Weismann, whose father had become the Prussian minister of the interior.

At the end of 1930 Germany's financial situation became critical. She now owed 15.9 billion reichsmarks abroad, mostly on terms of less than three months, and nearly half of it to the United States.[189] The number of unemployed, which had grown from two million at the end of 1929 to three million in 1930, reached 4.35 million in 1931. Brüning, who thought to pressure Germany's creditors in this way, did next to nothing to increase employment or reduce the deficits. Panic grew from 21 to 31 December 1930 and M.M. Warburg had to pay out 80 percent of its currency deposits and 50 percent of its mark deposits. The country was near bankruptcy. At the end of the year its assets abroad were worth no more than 5.3 billion reichsmarks, only half the amount of its external short-term debt.

The die was cast and nothing now could stop the coming events. In three years, German debt would topple whatever democratic institutions were standing. The weight of a crisis that had come from America would cause the collapse of the Weimar regime, a democracy built on loans from America to meet a debt imposed by, among others, America.

For M.M. Warburg the only success of the year came from Amsterdam: the placing of a loan by the Norges Kommunalbank of 40 milliion Norwegian crowns at 5 percent. In Berlin, Hermann Abs and Siegmund both fought to avoid the bankruptcy of their two firms, which were at risk in the collapse of the biggest German department store group and over some risky real-estate loans.

Meanwhile Schacht, away from any position of power, was despairing of a democracy that had played with fire by using unemployment to avoid paying its debts. Gradually he was attracted by the Nazis, whom he saw as a force for order, and in October 1930 he went to see New York bankers, among them Felix Warburg. According to the reports of some witnesses—though not all[190]—he told them that they should show more regard for Hitler.[191] Did he do this thinking he could use Hitler for his personal ambitions and thus save the mark, which was once more threatened by crisis? No one knew then and no one will ever know.

In December 1930, through Strauss, a banker who was already openly a Nazi, he had a first meeting with Hermann Goering, who introduced him to Hitler in January 1931. In February 1932 he officially joined the Nazi party.[192] From then on Schacht was to serve whenever necessary as financial guarantor for the monster.

Then began the dreadful time when men of influence joined the madness of those they were supposed to restore reason.

Currency Crisis: British Shallowness

When the crisis from America hit Britain, the Labour party had just gained power. James Ramsay MacDonald had been prime minister since the elections of 30 May 1929, with Arthur Henderson as foreign secretary and Philip Snowden, chancellor of the exchequer. In order to defend the absurd parity, still under threat, Labour, like the Conservatives before them, followed a policy of deflation, under fierce pressure from the Bank of England. The numbers unemployed rose from 1,164,000 million in June 1929 to 2,319,000 in December 1930. At the same time income from assets abroad fell, as did that from international shipping. For the first time in two centuries the British balance of payments moved into deficit.

The whole of Europe was rocked by crisis. On 11 May 1931 the biggest bank in Austria, the Creditanstalt Verein in Vienna, which belonged to the Rothschilds, closed its pay desks following the withdrawal of French deposits in March and difficulties with Boden Kreditanstalt, an agricultural bank. Later, Siegmund would maintain that the biggest Austrian bank had failed because the chancellor of Austria had forced it to take on the losses of the agricultural bank. "It was fantastic. People everywhere had said it could never happen. Well it did happen. There were brilliant people all over Europe who foresaw the great crisis, but did not act."[193]

The advance of the National Socialists in Germany and the crisis in America then drove foreigners, particularly Americans, to speed up repatriation of any capital deposited in Germany. In the first half of 1931, 3.5 billion reichsmarks left the country, and between the beginning of April and the middle of July the twenty-eight main German banks had to pay back 1.25 billion reichsmarks to foreign creditors. In June withdrawals from the big Berlin banks reached 2.25 billion reichsmarks. Between 2 and 17 June the gold and foreign exchange reserves of the Reichsbank were almost halved.

On 20 June President Hoover, who had just set up the Reconstruction Finance Corporation to guarantee the banks, proposed a one-year moratorium on all intergovernmental debt—in other words those of all the European countries.

France acquiesced. All countries including Britain waived payment of their war debt for one year, which would halt the reparations machinery provided for in the Young Plan and forbid any further borrowing in America by a European state.

Britain's position was not improved by this concession, however. At the beginning of July 1931 the Macmillan committee on finance and industry had published figures showing the catastrophic state of the British economy and the pound's credit standing. Speculation redoubled. Withdrawals of gold reached £2.5 million a day.

That same month yet another international conference began in London on the reparations, bringing together Germany, Belgium, the United States, France, Great Britain, Italy and Japan. It recommended maintaining the volume of credit previously granted to Germany, despite the ban on reparations payments. Also, in order to help Germany, the conference decided that the creditor countries would suspend repayment of the loans Germany would eventually contract for.

Despite this, on 13 July panic reached Berlin. The Darmstädter Bank had to cease operations. The same evening credit institutions and exchanges were closed by decree. On 15 and 18 July, to control the flight of capital, Brüning ordered that all exchange operations be centralized at the Reichsbank. In this way the gold parity of the reichsmark was maintained and the outflow of capital was checked. Max and Siegmund took part in drafting all banking legislation. One of the partners in M.M. Warburg, Ernst Spiegelberg, in fact, represented all the big German banks during the drafting of official orders in July 1931 in the midst of monetary turmoil.[194]

The situation was also worsening in England. Despite an austerity policy and support from the Bank of France and the American Federal Reserve Bank, the Bank of England found itself on the verge of ceasing payments. The parity of the pound was untenable and gold was being withdrawn. Then on 24 August Labour Prime Minister MacDonald formed a coalition government consisting of four Labour members, four Conservatives and two Liberals. However, speculation had the upper hand. On 21 September the pound sterling, artificially supported for too long, was separated from gold, floated and fell appreciably, dropping from $4.86 in August to $3.40 in December.

Along with this devaluation, the coalition government reduced wages, abandoned free trade and nationalized air transport and transport in London. These measures provoked massive withdrawals from the banks with the volume of deposits falling by half. The state then took responsibility for the insurance of export credit, threatened by the weakness of the banks, and entrusted this to a public body, the Export Credit Guarantee Department.

Weakened by competition from American banks, the British merchant banks were dealing more and more with foreign banks and less than ever with British industry. That year the Macmillan Report would cause talk by recalling what Disraeli had said half a century earlier: that the City's loans to foreign governments were far too large in relation to those made to domestic industry.

Siegmund was as shocked by this abandonment of sterling convertibility, which ruined lenders, as he had been by the parity chosen five years before. For him this return to a floating pound was a serious setback, wholly attributable to the "shallowness" of the Bank of England and, he thought, likely to lead to a thousand catastrophes.[195] He saw in this a confirmation of what was taught by old Jewish wisdom and by what he recollected about pogroms, in other words the inevitable plundering of the lenders, sacrificed without fail to the borrowers and the owners of materials goods.[196]

He was right. After this abandonment a number of countries would follow the pound and allow the currencies to float. The gold standard was dead, international credit lost all value and the world would again turn imperceptibly toward war.

In the election of 27 October 1931 the national government won an overwhelming majority, with Conservative domination. Despite the Labour rout MacDonald remained prime minister, but this time at the head of a Conservative Cabinet with Neville Chamberlain as chancellor of the exchequer.

Meanwhile the last pretence at reparations collapsed. On 19 November 1931 after a series of intergovernmental talks, it was acknowledged that crisis-torn Germany would no longer be forced to pay anything whatsoever. In accordance with the Young Plan, the BIS convened a special committee responsible for examining "the steps to be taken should Germany's economic life be threatened,"[197] as was indeed the case. The committee met in Basel, recognized Germany's right to suspend transfer of installment payments for one year and expressed concern at the unprecedented seriousness of the crisis, "the extent of which unquestionably exceeds the relatively short depression envisaged in the Young Plan and for which the safeguards it contains were designed." The conclusion was that

> an adjustment of intergovernmental debts as a whole [reparations and other war debt] should take place without delay if further disasters are to be avoided . . . is the only lasting measure capable of restoring the confidence which is the very condition of economic stability and a true peace.[198]

This death certificate for reparations, recognized here as the cause of "disasters," appears in hindsight to be a masterpiece of unintentional black humor.

Siegmund and Jimmy at the Bedside of Weimar

The Warburgs in America were more worried than ever about the fate of the Warburgs in Germany and the other Jews in Europe. In 1931 Felix sent the Deutsche Bank, then headed by Oscar Wassermann, $3 million he had collected for the Jews who were victims of the pogroms in Galicia.[199] As for Paul, he was worried about the financial future of the family. He no longer trusted Max, who had been very rash in 1930 in real estate, or Eric, who was exactly like his father. He only valued the opinions of Siegmund and Rudolf Brinckmann—who had been made a signatory for the bank, over Max's reservations—and especially those of his son, Jimmy, despite the latter's losses on Wall Street. In spring 1931 he sent Jimmy to get a view of the situation first hand. In Berlin, Siegmund emphasized to Jimmy that the German banking system was on the edge of failure. The two men then proposed a relief plan for the country's main banks, for which they calculated they would need 50 million marks.[200] In August Max arranged a meeting for them with Chancellor Brüning. The chancellor gave his endorsement without understanding much about the plan and sent them to see Luther, chairman of the Reichsbank, who identified Jacob Goldschmidt's Darmstädter Bank as the institution most in danger and the first to be helped.[201] But the plan was curtailed for lack of guarantees on the bank's accounts following some questionable transactions by President Hindenburg's own son.

Jimmy, very worried, wrote his father to say that he was expecting the failure of the Warburg bank in Hamburg at any moment. Siegmund and he then tried to shore up the bank in Berlin by getng the backing of another, stronger German bank. In autumm 1931, with Jimmy's acquiescence, Siegmund negotiated a closer relationship between the Berlin subsidiary of M.M. Warburg and the Berliner Handels Gesellschaft of his friend Hans Fürstenberg—one of the few big German banks not to have suffered greatly from the crisis. Like M.M. Warburg, it had not yet appealed for state aid. With 5 million reichsmarks from each bank the negotiators set up a joint subsidiary, hoping to make it the leading bank in Berlin.

In Hamburg the family bank nonetheless came through this dreadful year more or less intact. Despite considerable losses in real estate, the financial reputation of M.M. Warburg had remained unblemished. The bank was thought to have unlimited access to American capital and to play a major role, through Max and Carl Melchior, in most of Germany's international negotiations—as much in the BIS as in all discussions on reparations payments. But the reality was that this time Paul and Felix had not been far from letting the bank go under.

The situation then reached a plateau. The Bank of England stabilized the pound at a rate close to that of 1926, letting it float and intervening on the rate via an exchange stabilization fund.

In the United States the crisis period claimed two victims in the family. Mortimer Schiff died in 1931 leaving his son John $7.6 million in cash plus securities in eighty-one companies. The securities, valued at $28.7 million when he died, had dropped 54 percent by the time they were distributed among his heirs.[202] Then Paul Warburg, who had been forced to delve deeply into capital to save Jimmy from some unwise investments, died in early 1932. He left only $2.5 million, a small amount for a Warburg.[203] On his death, Walter Lippmann wrote, "He was one of the chief architects of what is strongest in our central banking system and the truest critic of its weaknesses. He foresaw the latter, he spoke out in time."[204]

Overall the family fortune was then sizable: Max was richer than Jimmy, and Felix much richer still. Felix's son Frederick, a partner in Kuhn Loeb since the previous year, bought a magnificent estate at Westport, Connecticut. Aby S. and Fritz were also fairly rich. But Aby S.'s only son, Karl, was languishing at the bank; he did not have the "sacred flame." Siegmund, meanwhile, began to restore Uhenfels, where his mother was still living surrounded by servants, now in the charge of an openly Nazi steward.[205]

Max was able to write in the bank's annual report published at the end of the year, "For 1932, it is not appropriate to make remarks on each of the firm's departments. We are in a defensive position everywhere."[206]

That year Benjamin Buttenwieser, who had joined Kuhn Loeb as an employee, became a partner, along with Hugh Knowlton. The latter, a friend of Paul's, with whom he had created the International Acceptance Bank, wanted nothing more to do with the International Manhattan Bank.

Advent of Hitler

On 13 March 1932, at the end of his mandate, Hindenburg offered himself for reelection. Hitler, only just naturalized as a German, stood against him. In the first round involving several candidates Hindenburg won 18.6 million votes, less than an absolute majority; Hitler got 11.5 million. In the runoff on 10 April Hindenburg was elected by 19.2 million votes against Hitler's 13.5 million.

Brüning, who had supported the marshal, remained chancellor and continued to make unemployment—now over five million—the reason for demanding final cancellation of the reparations.[207] In May 1932, to save the United Steelworks from bankruptcy, he had the state buy part of the concern and thus saved the shareholders' money. Later that month he resigned, having failed to deal with armed political gangs that roamed the streets. Franz von Papen then took over, at the head of a cabinet of civil servants and "barons" who made every effort to include as many Nazis in the majority as possible in preparation for new elections.[208]

Siegmund then met up once more with his childhood neighbor, Baron von Neurath, a friend of his father's just back from the London Embassy and appointed minister of foreign affairs. He became a close friend, and Siegmund often went to Wilhelmstrasse to inform the minister of various financial negotiations and the political situation in the West. He also passed on through banking friends several messages to the United States for von Neurath: "We are in control of the situation. Hitler is no more than a puppet. The Nazi tide is beginning to turn."

The German government confirmed that it was unable to resume reparations payments after the end of the Hoover moratorium. The countries in dispute met in Lausanne in June and von Papen obtained a final cancellation of the reparations in exchange for a promise to pay 3 billion marks to a European reconstruction fund. The agreement was signed but not ratified, just as it would never come into force and the 3 billion would never be paid. That was the end of the functions of the BIS under the Young Plan.[209] But it continued imperturbably to service the Dawes and Young loans until two years later when Germany unilaterally suspended all payments. Later the bank would find other, less glittering tasks.[210] Schacht, still out of power, forcefully approved of this cancellation, now final, of the Young Plan.[211]

In the legislative elections of July 1932 that followed the 4 June dissolution, the Nazis won a further 123 seats, bringing their number to 230 out of 607. Schacht then fell in behind Hitler. Von Papen remained chancellor. The growing Nazi success impelled industrialists to concern themselves more with the National Socialist party. Until then they had contributed little by way of money to the Nazis. Thyssen had paid them one million marks in 1931, but that was because he financed all parties without distinction. In 1932, of the millions of marks he gave to political groups, he paid only 3 percent to the Nazis against 8 percent to right-wing parties, 6 percent to left-wing parties and 83 percent to center parties.

In the autumn of 1932 the country became ungovernable. Unrest redoubled. There were now six million unemployed. Hindenburg decided on a further dissolution in November. The Nazis lost thirty-four seats. General Kurt von Schleicher was appointed chancellor. Schacht called for bankers to give financial support to Hitler. Von Papen then tried to persuade the old marshal to give Hitler the post of vice-chancellor. On 28 January 1933 Schleicher asked Hindenburg to dissolve the Reichstag once more. The president refused and Schleicher resigned. On 30 January, at the request of von Papen who hoped to be able to manipulate the future führer, Hindenburg named Hitler chancellor, with only three Nazi ministers out of eleven.

Neither Max nor Siegmund realized that there had been such a total change, though they were already thinking of getting Jewish capital out of Germany and reflecting on ways of organizing very complex networks to do this.

The German industrialists then joined Hitler, after a fund-raising meeting in Berlin on 8 February 1933 and a meeting at the home of Reichstag President Goering on 20 February. Among these were Frederick Flick, Hermann Röchling, Siemens, Westruck, Hugo Stinnes and Wilhelm Zangen, president of the German employers' association, and especially the Krupps.

Then, on 27 February agents provocateurs set fire to the Reichstag, on 28 February at Hitler's request the president suspended civil liberties and had Communists arrested. Hindenburg called elections for 5 March 1933, at which the Nazis won 44 percent of the votes. Hitler was confirmed as chancellor.

Now everything really did change completely for the family as well as for the rest of the country. The Warburgs still did not fully believe what was happening: that Germany, "their" Germany, could become "that" Germany. "I have never seen my mother so distraught," Siegmund noted. "She could not imagine that the German people would let themselves be dragged so far in the wake of Hitler as happened from 1933 onwards."[212]

Max was sixty-five years old. For many people that is retirement age. Perhaps that was what Siegmund had been hoping for. In any case, Max was now alone, or almost, in the midst of turmoil. His son, Eric, was in New York. Still with him were Aby S. and Melchior, both ill. But Fritz in America and Siegmund in Germany were on the alert. Yet everything was to take a turn for the worse—and very quickly.

On 14 March 1933 Max learned that the mayor of Hamburg would no longer consult him on the financial problems of the city because he had received numerous petitions against the Warburgs' "dictatorship." Max was scarcely worried. His friend Schacht was in charge of the financing arrangements for the March election campaign, and on 17 March he would actually resume the chairmanship of the Reichsbank, which he had left three years before. This was reassuring.[213] Schacht was very quickly becoming all-powerful. That day he proposed that Hitler should raise indirect taxes and military spending for a few years so as to get the economy and employment moving, giving them time to put foreign trade in order, then to build up exports.[214] Hitler followed the suggestion without hesitation.

There was no question of Schacht's harming the Jews—they were too important, he told anyone who would listen, to the health of Germany's international finances. He repeated this to Max on the day of his appointment, and Max was once more reassured. Nevertheless, the next day, 18 March, another distinguished Hamburg Jew, Leo Lippmann, had to resign from the city council. Max, realistic for once, commented darkly in his diary, "Death is coming fast."[215] On 21 March the new Parliament met in Potsdam. On the following day the conversation between Siegmund and von Neurath that is quoted in the beginning of this book took place.

Furious at Siegmund's departure from Germany, Max Warburg, like almost everyone else in the Jewish community, was still incredulous. He did not believe that the Nazis really believed what they were writing and saying against the Jews. Nevertheless, the party program announced on 24 February 1921 had clearly said that all foreigners, and therefore all Jews—i.e., anyone with a Jewish grandparent who had entered Germany after 2 August 1914—would be expelled. Point 17 of the same program clearly mentioned a ban on the immigration of Jews into Germany, and foreign status and expropriation for any who were already there.

Later Max, who was usually quite self-satisfied and ready to hide anything that troubled him, would write in his memoirs, "I thought it was absolutely inconceivable that this man could have become the sole leader of one of the most powerful, creative and hardworking nations in the world."[216]

3

War Money
(1933-1945)

Choosing London

"Very deep is the well of the past. Should we not call it bottomless?" So begins "The Tales of Jacob," first book of the monumental *Joseph and His Brothers*, by Thomas Mann, which Siegmund began to read on the boat taking him from Hamburg to New York in the spring of 1933. Attentive since childhood to premonitions, the young man was surprised to discover such an obvious one in this splendid account of the alliance of a family and a people around a Name and a Word, and how it was played out from generation to generation. The alliance was apparently broken by the youngest son, exiled to Egypt by his jealous brothers, who became a seer and a man of influence, then finally the savior of the family that had abandoned him, drawing them into a happy refuge, which then turned into a place of slavery.

At the dawn of his own exile Siegmund saw an exact picture of the opportunities and of the risks he was taking for himself and for those who belonged to him. Remembering that particular Joseph, he would strive to become a seer in another time of great trial, an exile and savior, a man of influence abroad, at once faithful to his name and his land. And, more than half a century later, he would still know by heart the first twenty pages of the Thomas Mann novel.

Perhaps he would have thought it a sign of equal importance had he known that at exactly the same time Klaus Mann was telephoning from Munich to his father, in Switzerland, to tell him, "The weather is bad," meaning that he should not return to Germany.

However, Siegmund's voyage did not lend itself to serene reading or to an interpretation of signs. The day before his departure he had arranged for his wife to leave Berlin for Stockholm with the children, with no hope of returning. He abandoned Germany, with the few pounds and few thousand dollars he managed to carry without attracting attention. This was the second time he had lost everything. The first time was after the fall of the kaiser. Now it was after the fall of Weimar. Siegmund was burning to start again, to succeed elsewhere in a life of high adventure, free at last of the fascinating but stifling history of the family, though he knew that he would never be able to go into politics as he had dreamed of doing in Germany.

He had not yet decided where to settle and did not know when he would see any of his family again: his wife, his children or his mother, who would not leave Urach, despite the long telephone conversation he had had with her shortly before embarking.

He was a man who made decisions fast; the decision to leave Hamburg took two hours. It would take him a few weeks to choose a final place of exile: a Jew never returns to a place of misfortune.

Siegmund was glad to be returning to America, where he had recently spent three happy years, but he did not intend to stay. On his arrival his first act was to send von Neurath a laconic message, thanking him for "having shown him a sign."

He then concerned himself with getting settled. The America he had arrived in was not flourishing. There were fifteen million unemployed. The big drop in prices, particularly farm prices, worsened the already heavy debt load of the farmers. Franklin D. Roosevelt had been sworn in as president on 4 March. The dollar situation was growing worse, since the speculation that had swept away British parity had carried through to the American currency—its parity, fixed at $20.70 to the ounce since 1913, was becoming less and less credible. A devaluation was generally expected and many people exchanged bills for gold while it was still possible. On 6 March, after his inauguration, Roosevelt prohibited any transactions involving gold and later obtained authorization from Congress to devalue the dollar by half. On 5 June the federal government freed the dollar rate from that of gold and from July onward sold American, then international, gold at $31.36, then $34.35 per ounce. In this way a new permanent price gradually became fixed.

At the same time the New Deal was being introduced. This meant reviving domestic production, which led to developing investments, and which in turn led to strengthening the banks. The investment banks, though, were at death's door—as they had been in the prewar crisis—badly hit by stock speculation. The administration and the press did not mince words in criticizing them, considering them responsible for the excessive speculation. Just before Roosevelt took office President Hoover had set up a committee to investigate "banking errors." This committee revealed that the Morgan Bank had sold stocks at cut-rate prices to famous Americans from Calvin Coolidge to General Pershing and from Charles Lindbergh to J.W. Davis.[1] The resulting scandal sped the passage in May 1933 of two acts: the Glass-Steagall Act, prepared by Paul Warburg before his death, instituting the separation of commercial and investment banks, and the Securities Act. The banks were given a year to choose between investment or commercial bank status and were prohibited from engaging in interstate banking. Morgan then split in two; Morgan Stanley became an investment bank and Morgan Guaranty a commercial bank. Mortimer Schiff, who then was in charge of Kuhn Loeb, had to make a crucial choice. He initially thought of making the firm a commercial bank, keeping an investment subsidiary; after considering the legal difficulties, he chose to remain an investment bank and closed his clients' accounts.[2]

It was in this climate that Siegmund arrived on Wall Street. He went first to see Felix Warburg, then Schiff. Schiff's mother, the daughter of Salomon Loeb and sister of Nina Warburg, had just died, leaving Schiff a $4 million fortune in addition to the $6 million charity fund left by her husband, Jacob, which she had managed.[3] Mortimer offered Siegmund a place with Kuhn Loeb, but he refused. He wanted his own bank and was already thinking of setting it up somewhere in Europe, to be near Germany, without living in the shadow of anyone else.

Siegmund then went to see his second cousin Jimmy, who had been very busy since his return from Germany. A friend of James Roosevelt, the president's son, Jimmy had just turned down the post of undersecretary of state.[4] He refused because he would have had to sell his mother's banking shares, which would have greatly disturbed her.[5] However, he was helping Henry Morgenthau, secretary of the treasury, work out a plan to assist the banks. Jimmy agreed to go to London with presidential advisers Raymond Moley, former Ohio governor James M.

Cox, and secretary of state Cordell Hull, to represent Roosevelt at an economic conference organized by the League of Nations. Jimmy believed in the importance of this conference and had great hopes for its success. In June Siegmund decided to go with him.

Siegmund and Jimmy hoped for a return to a system of stable currencies, all based on gold and guaranteed by a World Central Bank, able to create international money, covering transactions and capable of having changes in parities accepted: in short, a sort of synthesis of Paul's International Acceptance Bank and Max's Bank for International Settlements.

The conference began in August 1933 at the Geological Museum in Kensington, chaired by British prime minister Ramsay MacDonald. Sixty-five countries were represented. Whole days and nights were spent talking of recovery, inflation, unemployment, protectionism and exchange stabilization. Speech followed speech. Each country brought its own doctrine, from the laissez-faire of Britain and France to German and Italian regulation—now also taken up by America with the emerging New Deal. But there was no progress. Each monetary zone rejected the domination of any other. Each accused the others of protectionism. Moley blocked any return to gold or free trade, which might reduce the independence of Roosevelt's new economic policy.

At the end of weeks of discussion five very vague resolutions were adopted, emphasizing the need for monetary cooperation and the opening up of international markets. The central banks should realize, the resolutions said, that "in addition to their national functions, they also have an international task to accomplish."[6] The wish was also expressed that there should be "close and continuous cooperation among central banks," the role of the Bank for International Settlements in this being "more and more important, not only in favoring relations among the banks, but as an instrument of concerted action."[7] At the last minute agreement was reached on a short text recommending the temporary stabilization of the relative values of the dollar, the pound and the franc. Jimmy Warburg, who had written and negotiated this, was pleased with it, but President Roosevelt, alerted by Moley, rejected this text that indicated acceptance of American responsibility in the management of the international economy. Jimmy angrily walked out of the conference, left Siegmund in London and went to Hamburg to see Max. He then returned to Wall Street to write a book called *The Money Muddle* in which he fiercely attacked Roosevelt's economic policy, especially in monetary matters.

After some months of a damaging policy of gold buying, Roosevelt next tried to demonstrate America's independence by breaking with the gold standard. On 15 January 1934 he asked Congress "to invest the nation's government with proprietary rights over all the gold within its frontiers and to convert this gold into bars rather than coin."[8] From then on the role of gold was limited to guaranteeing notes, carrying out international settlements and defining the dollar, and America was able to pay its debts with its own currency. Thus began the monetary hegemony of the United States. Several days later, on 30 January 1934, the Gold Reserve Act authorized the dollar to be fixed at between 40 and 50 percent of its value at the beginning of 1933, and to be altered subsequently within these limits if judged necessary. The next day the rate was set at $35 per ounce of gold. It was to remain unchanged for nearly forty years.

The same year the Johnson Act prohibited the sale or purchase in America of any security from any of the European countries, including allies, which had defaulted on their war debts toward the United States —and this was the case with all of them. As will soon be seen, this act would weigh heavily in the financing of the war to come.

Siegmund stayed in London. He knew he would settle in Europe, but was still hesitating. There was London, where he had nothing except a few friends; Amsterdam, where Max had just set up a Warburg & Co.;[9] and Stockholm, where his wife was waiting for him at her parents' home, having resumed her original citizenship.

At the end of 1933 he chose London. He rented a small flat but would not really move in until after a year of travel and preparation.

Why this choice? Siegmund always refused to say. He certainly had a lasting appreciation of what he called "English good manners," which he had first encountered ten years before. He probably acted for the same reasons as many other German Jews, for whom Europe was home. And for someone from Hamburg, there was no city like London.

For a year he lived alone, organizing things and traveling. He first set up a small bank in Amsterdam, then another in London, both with the enthusiastic help of émigré friends and the reluctant help of M.M. Warburg. Max, angry that Siegmund had left Germany, would later do all he could to be obstructive to Siegmund through his own London subsidiary. During the first year of Nazi power, however, Max had plenty of worries of his own.

Max in Danger

On 23 March 1933 Hitler had himself voted full powers for four years and opened Dachau, the first concentration camp. He decided to govern by decree, using Article 48 of the constitution, ironically drafted to protect democracy from coups d'état. On 1 April the government called for a boycott of Jewish businesses; Nazi party officials began a surveillance of comings and goings at Ferdinandstrasse and noted who were habitual visitors.[10] Several important clients began keeping their distance from the Warburgs, and the brilliant dinners at Kösterberg lost their regulars. However, Max clung to any belief that still allowed optimism: Hitler was only there by chance—in six months Hindenburg, Schacht and von Papen would have the better of him.[11] But one after another came racist laws, explicit and unequivocal, in an impressive and lugubrious blizzard. On 7 April a decree ordered the dismissal of all Jews employed in administrative or university posts, with the exception of war veterans, or children of war victims. Only those with more than ten years of service were to be compensated.

This time Max was worried. A week later he dined in Berlin with Schacht,[12] who reassured him:

> Oh no, that decree will not be implemented, nothing will happen to you or to the German Jews. Primarily because they are Germans. Then because even the craziest Nazis know quite well that Germany needs them and their contacts abroad. It has to be understood that order must be established, rearmament must be speeded up, and that requires a revolution, with all its mistakes and rough edges. For the moment Hitler has the majority of the people with him and he is the only man capable of bringing order in Germany. But in two years, when we are back at the industrial level of France, I shall be able to redirect production toward consumer goods and all this absurd excitement will stop. Don't worry; Goering has no real power. He talks a lot, but I am the one in control of everything through the Reichsbank.[13]

Max worked increasingly with Schacht, particularly on the board of the Reichsbank where he had been a member for ten years; some witnesses say he even toyed with the idea of becoming to Schacht what Albert Ballin had been to the kaiser: a court Jew.

Also, despite the opinions he received from New York and London, Max decided to stay in Hamburg. "I was resolved to defend my firm like a fortress," he noted in his diary, written ten years later and never published.

> My family was of a contrary opinion. My American brother Felix did his best to persuade me to sell everything and emigrate. My wife and son also thought that the time had come to emigrate. They were convinced I was in danger. But I remained intractable. I was sure that such a sacrifice would not be in vain. Melchior believed the situation was much more serious than I thought, but that was perhaps because he had always been a pessimist. I was conscious of the fact that we were at the beginning of one of the numerous periods of suffering that the Jews have had to bear, but I was inwardly convinced that this period would be very limited in time. Therefore, I had enough energy to continue.[14]

Most German Jews thought as Max did, believing that the Nazi wave was actually beginning to ebb. This was so even among the international financial elite of Frankfurt, Berlin and Stuttgart. To quote the historian Edward Rosenbaum:

> In the beginning the official spokesmen for the Jewish community saw these laws as an indirect means by which they would be able to secure a bearable, if somewhat restricted existence for most of their people. However, increasing pressure within the Nazi party for a far-reaching offensive against the participation of Jews in all spheres of national life, notably the economy, was to dash these feeble hopes.[15]

Nevertheless, other leaders of the German Jewish community understood much better the tragedy that was taking place. Several left the country very quickly, like Siegmund, Hans Fürstenberg and Jacob Goldschmidt. Others delayed, delaying with a view to staying as long as possible. At the beginning of April, a few days after the creation of the Gestapo, three Berliners of note, W. Alexander, W. Senator and L. Tietz, set up a Central Committee of German Jews to organize large-scale emigration and represent German Jews in negotiations with other Jewish communities in Europe and America. In May Alexander wrote to the chairman of the Joint Distribution Committee, Felix Warburg, in New York, to inform him of their aims:

> We wish, through this committee, to preserve and defend the economic position of the Jews in Germany, to help groups who intend to leave Germany go to other countries in Europe or overseas, or return

to their countries of origin, and to help those who wish to settle in Palestine.[16]

Tietz died a little later the same year and Senator settled in Palestine; they were replaced at the head of the committee by F. Borchardt and M. Kreutzberger, then by S. Alder-Ruel. Max was not yet a member, completely taken up as he was with helping Schacht to establish the financial and banking system of the Reich. Little by little the governor of the Reichsbank was taking full power over the German banking system; a law dated 2 June 1933 even invested him with powers traditionally devolved on a central bank: control of the financial markets and a monopoly on the financing of foreign trade. Despite his financial omnipotence, Schacht was not at all free politically, nor as much a defender of the Jews as he claimed to be, and in order to protect his power he showed no hesitation in giving Hitler the pledges he expected. True, he ostensibly kept close to the few leading Jewish technical experts at the Reichsbank.[17] But he strongly advised his former assistant Gert Weismann to leave Germany for Switzerland, which he did. He also became a reluctant enforcer of the racist laws.

That spring of 1933 was very painful for an ailing Carl Melchior. He was threatened by the Gestapo, who mistook him for the author of the Treaty of Versailles—an extreme irony. In a few days he lost all his official posts and in June had to leave the German headquarters of the Bank for International Settlements, which he had helped to found and to which he had devoted so much effort.

As he had at the end of the previous year, the führer reproached Schacht for his relationship with Max. Twice-warned, Schacht in September asked Max to leave the board of the Reichsbank "in their common interest." This was a staggering blow for Warburg.[18] The Reichsbank he had fashioned during the period of inflation, ten years earlier, and that he had so much helped to develop—how could it exclude him simply because he was a Jew? It was not only ridiculous, it was odious.

In addition, this ousting unleashed all the other prohibitions against Max. In the autumn he was forced from the board of the Deutsch-Atlantische elegraphen Gesellschaft, which he had founded; then from the Hamburg Chamber of Commerce, which had decorated him some years before, and of which his grandfather had been benefactor; then from the board of the Philharmonic Society financed by his grandfather almost a century before; and then from the Board of Higher Education for which he had done so much. Finally at the end of October came the greatest insult. Max was ousted from the board of the Hamburg-America Line, the firm he had built up over thirty years with Albert Ballin, then with Cuno, and had saved from bankruptcy in 1918. Here, so that Max's departure should not seem too much the result of the racist laws—which the German upper classes still refused to take seriously and which nobody dared say applied to him—the board of the Line had the good taste to decide that on the same day two other elderly directors would also leave.[19] Good taste stopped there. When the board met at a farewell dinner to mark the three departures, Max expressed with irony his regret at having to leave, not of his own volition, the firm he had loved so much for three decades. When nobody replied, he got up, walked slowly round the great table, stood opposite his own still empty seat and made his own reply, thanking himself for his services, especially when at the end of 1918 he was the only one who had been able to find the money to rebuild the fleet destroyed during the war. It was a painful episode that several witnesses remembered, though in differing ways.

Then began a descent into oblivion for the bank. It was no longer consulted by local or national authorities and that year lost two-thirds of its clients, who fell in number from 5,241 to 1,875.[20]

And as though everything had been planned to end quickly, an already dreadful year ended tragically: Aby S. Warburg and Carl Melchior died on the same day, 30 December 1933. Rosenbaum wrote as an epitaph:

> Many reponsibilities in dealing with personal problems had been entrusted at Ferdinandstrasse to Aby S. Warburg, because of his long experience as senior partner in the firm and his intelligent perception of men and matters. In particular, in his last years, he had devoted himself with much generosity to the traditional Warburg interests in all sorts of public service and philanthropic work . . . . Dr. Melchior, who had been literally worn out by his ceaseless traveling and the exhausting negotiations he had had to carry on for Germany, died of a heart attack. A few days previously, in case he might be arrested by the Gestapo, he had given power of attorney to a long-standing friend and highly trusted colleague Dr. Kurt Sievelsing.[21]

On one of the last nights of the year the library of Aby Warburg's Institute was sent to London: sixty thousand books and twenty thousand photographs in 531 crates were loaded onto two ships. According to family tradition, throughout the night of loading Aby M.'s widow served hot drinks to the movers, Communists who had taken the risk of spiriting away the finest art history library in the world, just before the great book burnings began.

Despite these mournful days and terrible threats, Max continued to hope he had a future in Germany. More and more isolated, he noted in his diary at the beginning of January 1934:

> The past year has been one of retrenchment. As reconquest is not possible for the moment, we can only defend our fortress, while trying to retain our German and foreign clients. In this respect, minor measures may turn out to be important. Not one of the board seats withdrawn from us should be considered finally lost, and we should seize every opportunity to regain these posts, long though we may have to wait for success.[22]

The Palestine Network

Max may have wanted to stay in Germany in the hope of better days ahead, but this did not stop him from helping other Jews to leave—his own clients first. He may not have advised anyone to leave, but he gave assistance to those who wished to do so.

When Hitler came to power there were still nearly 550,000 Jews in Germany, and nearly 100,000 left in the Nazis' first year.[23] From early 1933, even before Siegmund left, and despite strict border and exchange controls, Max was helping the rich Jews to get their money out and the poor to emigrate. One group was taken care of through the bank, and the other through Jewish organizations. Max acted as a community leader, but at the same time as a financier fully aware of his own business interests. The growing number of would-be emigrants were ready to pay any price to anyone who could get them out of the country. Siegmund and Max were not short of ideas on how to do this. Neither made any profit, quite the reverse in fact. However, all this activity kept the bank busy and gave Max the illusion that things were carrying on as before.

At that time emigrants were still in an ambiguous position. Exchange control was very tight and in theory the export of capital was prohibited, but the reality was that Schacht would use the foreign subsidiaries of German banks whenever it suited him, even if they were owned by Jews. For example, with Nazi blessing, the Amsterdam subsidiary of the Mendelssohn bank gathered in the foreign holdings of some major German companies—among them Bosch in America—so as to avoid any risk of confiscation if war should break out.[24] And these banks also played an important part in arranging to get Jewish money out of Germany, sometimes with the complicity of top Nazi officials.

While the rest of the world was mobilizing, the first program of Jewish emigration to Britain was set up with a fund jointly established for this purpose by the Jewish community there and Carl Melchior just before his death. The Jewish communities in America were also very active. Felix, with other rich American Jews, financed the settlement there of some of the poorest Jews as well as a number of Jewish artists and writers who were having difficulty in finding a country of asylum.

Though not a Zionist, Felix also helped in the movement of German Jews to Palestine. He was still very critical of the Jewish Agency, which in his eyes was not more than an anarchic and ungovernable body. He said, "If the Jewish Agency had the money for one new colony [kibbutz], it would decide to create two and trust to the future to complete them."[25] He was increasingly convinced that a Jewish state would be condemned to death because its neighbors would never accept it. He even said in 1934, "If a State of Israel ever came into being it would be coming cap in hand every year to Kuhn Loeb for another loan."[26] At the time, he wrote to Chaim Weizmann, with whom he was in growing disagreement on the way Jewish affairs should be run, "As long as the Jews crow 'Jewish State' and 'National Land' your efforts to get on a better footing will not be taken very seriously by the Arabs."[27] He dreamed instead of replacing the British mandate with a binational state in which both Jews and Arabs would come to an understanding and live together harmoniously.

Just before Siegmund's departure from Germany, he and Max had had the idea of setting up a bank to help German Jewish companies get their money out of the country. The idea ripened during the summer of 1933, and in October Siegmund went from London to Amsterdam to meet Max and two other German friends who had just left Germany: Edmund Stinnes, the brother of Hugo, who had gone over to the Nazis, and Hans Fürstenberg, who had run the Berliner Handels-Gesellschaft and with whom Siegmund had established a joint subsidiary in Berlin some years previously.

From this meeting came the idea of taking a small group of banks —some of them German—and establishing an organization to be called the Dutch International Corporation (DIC). It would receive any capital the emigrants were able to get out of Germany and then help them to use it first in the Netherlands, then in Britain or the United States, or even Palestine. It was in operation by the beginning of 1934, and thanks to the DIC Siegmund helped to get capital out of Germany for several German Jewish companies and for most of his former clients in Berlin and Hamburg.

With Max, Fritz and A.E. Wassermann in Berlin, the DIC also organized a direct link with Palestine, the Palestine Fiduciary Company, which helped emigrants transfer their funds. The transfers were activated by the purchase of German goods by Palestinian companies or by the sale to Germany of Palestinian goods at low prices.[28]

The system was quite complex and required numerous agreements with the German customs and tax authorities. Before leaving Germany the emigrants sold goods chosen by a Jewish Agency office, the Havana Company, to German firms for reichsmarks. Delivery was in Tel Aviv. On arriving in Palestine the emigrants were reimbursed in pounds sterling by the Havana Company, itself financed by the American Jewish community. The system also worked in the other direction. Palestinian produce was delivered to Germany and paid for by the Jewish Agency, the only German contribution being the authorization to take out emigrant capital. M.M. Warburg and A.E. Wasserman in Germany and the DIC in the Netherlands undertook all the banking work. This "Palestine connection" after four months of negotiation allowed the bulk export to Nazi Germany of Jaffa oranges (1934–1935 harvest). Rosenbaum wrote:

> Other possibilities for transfers arose along the same lines, by means of financing imports from Turkey. The many activities of the network, and a series of consultancy agreements with companies whose owners wished to liquidate their assets in order to emigrate, were a source of new clients and new business for Warburg and Co., but also and especially a source of stern warnings in so far as their own future was concerned.[29]

These systems worked badly, however. For some time it had been getting more and more difficult for people to get their money out of the country. A decree dated 18 May 1934 stipulated a fine of one-quarter of the assets of anyone who wanted to leave with more than 50,000 marks, or who had earned more than 20,000 marks a year.

Max now became chairman or board member of the leading German Jewish organizations: the Reich Representation of German Jews, the League of Rescue to German Jews, the Hamburg Community Association. "He busied himself from morning to night," wrote

Rosenbaum, "supporting Jewish compatriots and providing them with acceptable living conditions in circumstances which were deteriorating considerably."[30]

In May and June Max went several times to see Vice Chancellor von Papen in Berlin, hoping for his help. At Max's request von Papen went to Hitler on 28 June to protest the anti-Jewish measures, but two days later only just escaped the Night of the Long Knives when a number of his friends were killed by supporters of the führer. He then went to Vienna as ambassador.

Max felt increasingly isolated. Of his patrons, only Schacht was still in office. On 30 July 1934 Schacht became minister of the economy in place of Kurt Schmidt. He was then essentially responsible for the economy, as a four-year plan was beginning to be worked out. According to his own memoirs, *My First 76 Years*, and contemporary accounts,[31] he was shocked by the purges. Though he still thought Hitler was the only one who could bring about German recovery, Schacht found that many things were not as he would have wished. He did not care for the plundering of public money by the party, or for the violence perpetrated against the Jews and the churches. But he was unable to do anything, either against the ever-worsening anti-Semitic policy or against the economic policies of the fanatics, such as Wilhelm Kappler, Hitler's economic adviser. When Kappler set up a development agency for the production of raw materials without consulting him, Schacht was furious.[32]

On 2 August 1934 Hindenburg died. On 19 August, after a plebiscite, Hitler combined the offices of chancellor and president. That summer Max continued to develop his emigration network. With Hexter, the director of the Jewish Agency—a former Harvard professor taken on by Felix—who had come from Palestine for this purpose, Max met the Nazi in charge of exchange control at the Ministry of Finance and obtained from him authorization for visas for the Palestine network, against a promise to pay $10,000 into a secret account in London. This senior official was to leave Germany the following year, also to take refuge in England.[33]

That year three out of four clients had left the bank, which had also lost half its board seats. Its turnover fell significantly, and there seemed to be nothing to prevent imminent bankruptcy.

Apart from helping Jews who wanted to leave, or participating in state loans floated abroad, the bank was doing no businesss to speak of. Faced with collapse, Max again called on Felix for help but was told that he should sell out and leave. Siegmund, also consulted in Amsterdam, was of the same opinion. Max refused. He would not leave the firm he had built up. He was a German and nothing else. His family had stayed in Germany under all regimes and had no reason to break with its history, even to flee from a regime as crazy as this one. Rudolf Brinckmann, Kuhn Loeb's man in Germany, agreed with him.

Once more Felix, ill and resigned, agreed to take from his own money the amounts needed by Max and Fritz, his last two German brothers, to uphold the name. In exchange he insisted that Max should reduce his commitments and keep cash at a maximum to guard against any contingency.

Max's life became very difficult. He was now permanently followed by the Gestapo; his circle of friends shrank even more. Kösterberg became a solitary fortress. Every day papers like Julius Streicher's *Stürmer* accused him of having betrayed the country at Versailles, and of being the cause of Germany's misfortunes.

By the end of 1934, however, M.M. Warburg's financial situation had stabilized—thanks to Felix. Max wrote in his diary at this time that "the road to reconquest could have been open, but it was blocked by National Socialist policy."[34]

Siegmund in London

London had changed since Siegmund's first stay there ten years earlier. The crisis was beginning to fade. For the first time annual production exceeded the 1929 level, while the number of unemployed fell. British opinion was divided over Hitler. A very small minority among the upper middle class were not displeased by the arrival of this man who had "saved Germany from the Red Menace." The rest, like the working class, saw the danger of Nazism, which had destroyed the German Left.

The Jewish community in London was then fairly small but thriving, and it welcomed the refugees who were beginning to flow in. In March 1933 Otto M. Schiff, a distant relative of Jacob's, set up the Committee of Jewish Refugees, and in April 1933 Lionel Rothschild set up the Central British Fund for German Jewry.

As soon as he arrived, Siegmund found family, friends and some financial backing. There were then living in London several descendants of the Altona Warburgs who had emigrated first to Scandinavia in 1790, then to London in 1841. Some were associated with Sir Ernest Cassel at N.M. Rothschild, but Siegmund did not know them. There was also his uncle Paul Kohn-Speyer, who had become chairman of

Brandeis-Goldschmidt and who had been married to one of his cousins, Max's sister Olga who had come to London in 1903 and died the following year following the birth of Edmond. Brought up in England, Edmond in 1928 had been a trainee under Max at the same time as Siegmund. There was also his uncle Frederick's second cousin, the son of Sir Oscar Emmanuel Warburg, Frederick-John Warburg, born in 1898, who had become a publisher. A few months after Siegmund moved to London, he would be joined by his cousin Anita, Max's third daughter, who married Max Woolf, a journalist on the *Manchester Guardian*. Finally there was the staff of the M.M. Warburg subsidiary, Merchant and Finance Corporation, several of whom had been to Berlin, but would now become his business rivals.

At the beginning of 1934, now settled in a small flat near the Thames, Siegmund sent for his wife and two children in Stockholm. Life was hardly easy for him. He had come to London as the father of a family, almost penniless, ten years after living there as a rich Rothschild trainee. He was of course welcomed in *haute banque*, where his name meant something. But for other people he was nothing but a fairly poor German Jew, speaking English with quite a strong Swabian accent.

Siegmund on his part admired the tradition of freedom that had made Britain great. He had much respect for its sense of fair play. He used to say that the word "kind" and its meaning existed only in English and that it could not be translated into German or French. But he hated the shallowness, lack of courage and snobbery of the City. He often said that although in Germany the middle class had brought Hitler to power, in Britain by contrast this was the healthiest, most human, responsible and honest element in the country. He was still a little breathless, having come out of the hellish atmosphere of Nazism, and quite astonished to encounter freedom again.

Two other emigrants who left Germany at the same time as Siegmund wrote of London as it was then. One was Stefan Zweig, his friend of fourteen years, who had arrived a month before him and whom he would see almost every week for the next eight years. The other was the painter Fred Uhlman, born near Stuttgart like Siegmund, who knew him slightly, and who came to London a few months after him. "After a few days I felt indescribably satisfied in London," wrote Zweig. "Only one thing was important to me: to get back to my work again, to maintain my freedom of thought and action . . . . What was really salutary was the sense of again being in a civil, courteous, unexcited, hateless atmosphere."[35]

Everything seemed strange to me," said Uhlman. "Beyond relief, there was regret and fear."[36] Siegmund, like them, worried about what he had left behind.

"My friends were far away," wrote Zweig, "the old circle was destroyed, the home with its collections and paintings and books lost. Everything which I had attempted, achieved, learned, enjoyed in the meantime seemed wafted away."[37]

Siegmund was distressed to see how carefree Britain was. Having been such a critic, in Berlin, of Churchill's monetary policy and its outcome in the sterling disaster, he found British blindness to mounting political danger hard to bear. As an emigrant he was astonished to see that the British were just as naive as his uncle Max, clinging like him to simple minded hopes.

"It was painful to stand by," wrote Zweig, "when the greatest virtue of the English—their loyalty, their honest desire to believe anyone until proved a liar—was being abused by a masterfully conducted propaganda."[38]

New Trading Company

The City remained a financier of governments and a charterer and insurer of ships. More than half of international business was still transacted in British currency, once more stabilized in relation to gold, through the workings of an exchange stabilization fund.

However, the collapse of international trade had reduced the scale of the City's operations. Britain no longer had much to lend. Its small, sheltered and badly organized banks had to borrow dollars in New York and convert them into pounds before relending them in the Empire or elsewhere. Moreover competition from bankers and insurers in New York was becoming fierce.

Now that he was in London, Siegmund was thinking of making his name again, a great name in the profession he knew, *haute banque*. He considered various ways of giving himself a base: setting up his own London subsidiary of M.M. Warburg, but Max opposed this; or setting up a Kuhn Loeb subsidiary, but he had not sought Felix's agreement and undoubtedly would not have obtained it. So he decided to set up his own company and call it not Warburg but New Trading Company, a partial translation and adaptation of the name Berliner Handels-Gesellschaft (Berlin Trading Company). This was the company that ten years later would become S.G. Warburg & Co. It is worth telling in some detail the story of the birth of what is today one of the foremost investment banks in the world. There are several versions.

According to Edward Rosenbaum, who interpreted Max's account, it was the Dutch International Corporation that set up the New Trading Company in London with initial capital of £120,000, "the most active board member being S.G. Warburg."[39] Gradually, M.M. Warburg reduced its stake in Dutch International Corporation but increased its stake in New Trading Company, which was part of a series of structures abroad intended to serve the clients of M.M. Warburg & Co., and to help German Jews who had already emigrated to resume work. And another of its growing tasks was to finance medium-sized British companies.

This account does not seem accurate. In fact Siegmund alone wanted the New Trading Company and created it for himself, against the wishes of the rest of his family, in this way. Once the Dutch International Corporation was set up at the beginning of 1934, Siegmund thought of completing an exit chain for capital from Germany by setting up another company of the same kind in London with the same partners. Siegmund therefore sent for his two friends, Hans Fürstenberg, still chairman of the Berliner-Handels Gesellschaft, and Edmund Stinnes. He sounded them out on setting up another bank with him, one that would be a more sensitive operation in London than in Amsterdam. If he were a director himself, he would have to show his nationality at birth on the letterhead of the firm, and being German in London in 1934 was not an advantage in business. Moreover, he did not want to give offense to Max, the head of the European family and master of the name. Therefore he decided not to give his name to the new bank, at least for the moment.

It took Siegmund more than six months to organize everything. He brought some thoroughly British people into his venture, beginning with an old acquaintance, Andrew MacFadyean, chairman of Rio Tinto Zinc. Then came Richard Jessel and Harry Lucas, members of related families, one of stockbrokers and the other of bankers very well connected in London, and friends of Anthony Eden and Winston Churchill.

Siegmund then set up with them the equivalent of the establishment he had opened in Amsterdam but gave it the same name as the bank set up earlier in Berlin with Fürstenberg. So was born in the heart of the City on 30 October 1934 the New Trading Company, with five shareholders—Siegmund Warburg, Harry Lucas, Richard Jessel, the Dutch International Corporation and the Berliner Handels-Gesellschaft

—with a capital of £120,000 of which Siegmund held 10 percent. Andrew MacFadyean was appointed chairman; Harry Lucas, Siegmund and a secretary were the only employees. As a telegraphic address, they chose "Nutraco," still used by the bank today.

They moved into offices lent by Paul Kohn-Speyer, chairman of Brandeis-Goldschmidt, on King William Street, the street designed in the nineteenth century to link the Bank of England with London Bridge.

Brandeis-Goldschmidt was a strange firm. One of the directors kept a revolver on his desk and sometimes threatened new employees with it. Smoking was prohibited, and the hours were strictly those of the London Metal Exchange. These offices were at No. 9. On the second floor was a narrow corridor, in which were the fire hose and the telephone switchboard, and which linked No. 9 to No. 8, where there were three offices, also accessible from the street via an odd triangular elevator. These were the offices made available to the New Trading Company. They were so small that Siegmund had his own office elsewhere, a short distance away on the same floor, within Brandeis-Goldschmidt.

His German friends soon had to move on. At the end of 1934 Hans Fürstenberg went to Locarno. Edmund Stinnes stayed a few months more to help Siegmund, then left to teach political economy in Philadelphia. Siegmund had no capital, no clients and no goodwill, and he did not want to use his main asset—his name. So he took on the sort of small business that city bankers like N.M. Rothschild did not want. This was primarily from emigrants who were arriving with some money, or from referrals by Brandeis-Goldschmidt, passed on to him by Paul Kohn-Speyer. By the following year he was employing five people: K.L. Guinness of the brewing family; Sir Louis Sterling; Henry Grunfeld; E.G. Thalmann, a Berlin banker who had become Argentinian; and Eric Korner, a former officer under the Austrian monarchy.

It was in June 1935 in Amsterdam that Siegmund had first met Henry Grunfeld, who was to become his alter ego for nearly fifty years. Born in 1904 in Silesia into a well-to-do steel family, Grunfeld spent his youth in Berlin. He had revived his father's business, which was much weakened by Weimar inflation, and made it one of the foremost steel companies in Germany. In Berlin, like everyone else, he heard talk of the Warburgs, their wealth and power. But like many German Jews at that time, he did not even know that the Warburgs were also Jews. When he decided to emigrate to London at the beginning of 1935 and set up his own financial company, he sought to contact Siegmund. He asked two leading German steelmen, with whom he had worked, and who had known Siegmund in Berlin, to give him an introduction. The meeting took place on 17 June 1935 in Amsterdam at a DIC gathering. It lasted only ten minutes. Siegmund was in a hurry. He and Henry decided to see each other again in London a month later, where they talked at much greater length. They decided that the New Trading Company would become a shareholder in the company Grunfeld would set up. It was obvious what the two men had in common. Henry was not yet a banker, but he had all the qualities of a *haute banque* professional as these were understood in Hamburg: intelligence, freedom of spirit, strict morality, the will to succeed, a broad view of things, caring more about doing something well than merely making a profit. Neither man considered money a motivating force in his life. They had quite different characters, however. While Siegmund was brilliant and charming, Henry was shadowy and retiring, more concerned with paperwork.

On 6 June 1984, at a reception given for his eightieth birthday, Henry Grunfeld confided to a few friends:

> What we had in common was that we had the same comfortable family background, that in 1923, as a result of the inflation, both our family fortunes had been largely lost, that he and I at a relatively young age had positions of considerable responsibility and that we both had been successful and had established a name and reputation for ourselves. Then, after 1933, we suddenly found ourselves faced with having to leave everything behind and start afresh in another country from absolutely nothing. We both had the burning ambition and determination to get back to the position which we had had in Germany and to show to the world and to ourselves that we could do it.[40]

In August 1937, having seen much more of him, Siegmund suggested to Henry that he should leave his own business and come to work with him. Henry agreed and sold his firm—which still exists today—and took 5 percent of the capital of the New Trading Company. They were to work together for half a century, until the death of Siegmund. Each one knew he could do nothing without the other, and each would accept being overshadowed by the other. "Nobody else has the same status as alter ego in Siegmund's entourage," Pierre Haas, a Frenchman who worked with him, was to say.

Later it was said in London that "Siegmund is the first to agree that Grunfeld is the most brilliant mind in the City, much more brilliant than himself."[41]

Berlin under a War Economy

In 1935 the fine structure Wilson had wanted at Versailles was disintegrating everywhere. The Anglo-German naval treaty in June and the Stresa conference had nourished the hope of peace, but the crisis in Abyssinia in October, rumblings from Spain, Mussolini's ranting and the strong-arm tactics of Hitler, who reintroduced military service, worried the few sane democracies in Europe.

By now more than 150,000 Jews had left Germany. The League of Nations instructed a high commissioner, James MacDonald, to investigate their problems and coordinate aid to them. For this purpose the American Jews set up a consultative committee of private organizations in New York, grouping together the representatives of the various international Jewish organizations. Felix Warburg headed it and at first opposed the admittance to the committee of the Zionist leader Nahum Goldmann, whom he considered too extreme; after the intervention of James MacDonald he withdrew his veto. Felix helped a number of intellectual European Jews to settle in America and financed the foundation of an Art History Department at New York University, which was to receive a part of the Jewish cultural elite of Europe.

Not all Jews received such warm welcomes, and governments in the democracies showed no great enthusiasm. In Holland, Switzerland, France and Canada quotas were quickly filled, and many Jews from Germany and elsewhere were turned back. Some, from all walks of life, who were received in America, were to find only poverty there, such as Béla Bartók, who died in New York, alone and destitute.

The Jews remaining in Germany were becoming organized. After the first departures the situation seemed to stabilize for those who were left. Their official central body became the Reichsvertretung der Juden in Deutschland. It would help indirectly and unconsciously, as did all its counterparts in Europe, to create the concentration camp economy to come.

Promulgation of anti-Jewish laws slowed down, to the point where Schacht believed he had persuaded Hitler to return to a more moderate policy and boasted of this everywhere.[42] Supported by part of the Reichsbank administration and by the Ministry of Economics, which feared that the persecution of the Jews would lead to flight of capital,

Schacht kept his chief assistants at the Reichsbank, who were Jews, and continued to consult with Max Warburg. But meanwhile the Nazi party was preparing a final solution to the "Jewish problem" through extermination, without ever calling it that.

As 1935 began, Schacht, still master of the economy, wanted to maintain growth to reduce unemployment. He encouraged German industry to become more concentrated—the number of industrial groups dropped by half—launched big road-building projects, encouraged rearmament, stopped the latest interest payments on the Dawes and Young loans and set in place a kind of war economy. To finance this he created special credit bonds, with discount guaranteed by the central bank, called Mefo bonds; these were reserved for arms companies, allowing them to borrow on the money market. They had a term of four years and could be underwritten by companies with a capital of one million marks. The total of these bonds remained a state secret. In the eyes of Schacht, this was credit from the Reichsbank to industry and would have to be paid back at the end of the term; he intended to put an end to such monetary financing of investment as soon as full employment was achieved.[43] He dreaded the inflationary nature of this printing of money, knowing that it would lead to excessive imports. He therefore took control of German foreign trade, subsidizing exports and giving the mark as many as forty-five different exchange rates, and containing imports as much as he could. This policy was very successful and opened up markets for German industry as far away as Latin America, as well as in Southern Europe.

Schacht also put the German banking system completely under his own tutelage. In 1934 the Bank Deutschen Arbeit set up controlled credit for the construction industry and for small companies and would later distribute the spoils of war; the Reichs Kredit Gesellschaft managed credit for companies profiting from public funds, and Rowak, one of its subsidiaries, organized barter deals with foreign countries. The big general banks were also gradually coming under the Nazi thumb; first the Deutsche Bank with its 490 branches, then the Dresdner Bank with 368, then the Berliner Handels-Gesellschaft, Commerzbank and the Darmstädter Bank. As Jewish emigration went on, investment banks— among them Stein in Cologne and Delbrück, Schickler, which had become a subsidiary of Metall Gesellschaft—also fell into Nazi hands directly or were bought very cheaply by the big banks, which had themselves become Nazi, in exchange for payment in New York of an absurdly small fraction of their true value.

At this point a misunderstanding between Schacht and Hitler began: to the führer and Nazi theoreticians, such as Gottfried Feder, the war economy was supposed to last until it made war possible. They thought that lessons should be drawn from the First World War in order to build a country able to withstand a blockade and cut itself off from all external sources of supply in the event of a prolonged conflict. Schacht, on the contrary, thought that the state should withdraw from the economy as soon as full employment was reached.[44]

For another two years Schacht believed that his view would prevail and did not see that he was allowed to act only within the limits of what served the ambitions of the military and the führer. He had no idea that he would be dropped as soon as Hitler had finished using him.

During these two years, Schacht believed that he was at least tempering Hitlerian madness, even though riots, pogroms and the killing of Jews was continuing. Preparations for the Olympic Games in 1936 and the need to develop the war economy led the Nazis to disguise their true aims and allow Schacht the illusion of victory.

Gradually, however, the ambiguity of the situation was dispelled. The first incident took place on 16 August 1935 in Königsberg at a public meeting where Schacht fiercely criticized "those who break the shop windows of Jews and who accuse of treason those non-Jews who work with Jews." Persecution of the Jews, he added, was "illegal and should stop, otherwise I shall not be in a position to bring about economic recovery."[45] He added further, "I criticize those who are in charge of Jewish affairs when, by their actions, they make it impossible to implement a program of economic recovery." Anyone else but Schacht would have been immediately arrested after such a speech, as the Berlin press emphasized the next day. On top of that the radio censured him. Schacht, angry, then had several hundred thousand copies of this speech printed and distributed by the Reichsbank. Hitler was outraged but let him carry on, because he still needed him. Without worrying about what Schacht was thinking or saying, Hitler then launched a second wave of anti-Semitic laws. In September 1935 marriage between Jews and non-Jews was prohibited, and Jews were deprived of their civil rights and of the right to employ non-Jews. That was only the beginning.

Max Warburg then lost some of his optimism. Though he was quite determined to stay in Hamburg, he wanted to help the 300,000 or so Jews still living in Germany to leave. He did not know and could not guess or imagine what the risks were, but he understood enough of

Jewish history to expect the worst. He continued to run the Palestinian network but found it too slow and complicated, and in fact it did not help get many people out.

In order to move further and faster, he devised a mass evacuation plan, which would become the Warburg Plan. At the beginning of October he went to see Schacht and proposed that the Jewish emigrants who handed over their assets to the German Treasury should receive in exchange, when they settled abroad, foreign exchange paid by a "foreign syndicate," i.e., a group of European and American Jews. This "syndicate" would then have a claim on the Reich, which would be repaid in German industrial products that could be resold anywhere the syndicate wanted, up to a value of 1.5 billion marks. Schacht found the plan interesting and wanted to effect it. He submitted it to numerous committees, to the Ministries of Finance and of the Interior; and it is said the plan actually reached Hitler's desk.[46] All to no avail.

Max then tried other means of helping the exodus; in mid-autumn he once more crossed the Atlantic to ask for the family's help with his plan. However, as he knew that even in New York he was being watched by the Gestapo, he said little in public.[47] Felix and Eric agreed to help him again and gave him the consent of the American communities to constitute the foreign "syndicate."

On his return to Germany at the end of November 1935, Max discussed his plan with Schacht once again. Schacht, however, could do no more, for, within the space of three months his position had very much deteriorated. Since his Königsberg speech he was persona non grata with Hitler, and the economic levers were being progressively wrested from him by Goering, the man of the army and the party.

From then on the worsening of the Jews' position went unchecked. A new decree dated 14 November 1935 confirmed a previous one and required the dismissal of all Jewish employees in both the public and private sectors, apart from teachers in Jewish schools, before 31 December 1935, compensating only those who had served at the front during the war. Max was horrified by this decision and went to see Schacht. Did this apply to his own Jewish employees? To himself? Schacht swore to him that it did not, that it covered only the poorest Jews, wage-earners in trade or agriculture. In exchange for a promise that the other German Jews would be left alone, Schacht asked Max to arrange through Siegmund and the Jewish bankers in London an end to British press articles that were hostile to the German government.[48] This said something of the influence Schacht still ascribed to Max, who promised to intervene but did nothing. He fully realized that Schacht's promises were now worth nothing.

This time the anti-Semitic laws were implemented, and within a few days the public services dismissed all remaining Jews. In private companies, particularly banks and top companies, dismissal of Jews took longer and was more difficult. Not only did they have to be dismissed, which was sometimes a painful act for those who had to do it, but replacements had to be found for jobs requiring advanced technical qualifications. That year over fifty thousand Jews left Germany.

By the time his power began to decline, Schacht had succeeded in improving the economic position of the country markedly. International payments were back in balance and full employment had been reached. Within three years he had put nearly five million unemployed back to work. However, Schacht now wished to slow down growth, stop the Mefo bonds and redirect the economy toward the production of civilian goods. The man who had twice saved the mark did not now intend to see it ruined. But Goering wanted to continue the war economy and prepare the army for a long-lasting blockade and conflict. In his opinion industrialists and bankers should become officers in the new logistics, and the state should take control of the whole economy.

The disagreement was clear and Schacht would soon lose the battle. In March 1936 he pushed the mark rate up and proposed that Hitler should reduce spending by the party and the various police forces and put an end to the Mefo bonds. The führer refused. Goering openly denounced Schacht as an "economic traitor." The führer then removed Schacht from control over disbursements of currency for military purposes. In April he relieved him of control of foreign trade, at the request of employers angered by his upward management of the mark. At a cabinet meeting on 27 May 1936 Schacht again opposed the draft plan presented by Goering. "We can have export markets," he said. "Autarchy is not necessary. The policy of developing ersatz products is absurd."[49] He also declared himself against the reoccupation of the left bank of the Rhine that had just been decided on, and opposed German aid to the Spanish insurgents. In order to prove that he could foster trade, Schacht went to Paris in the summer of 1936 to see Léon Blum, the new Socialist prime minister, to request the right to buy raw materials in the former German colonies that the French now controlled. However, Blum hesitated because of German aid to the Republicans in Spain. Goering then took advantage of Schacht's failure to strengthen his policy of establishing an independent national economy. On 9 September 1936 at the Nazi party congress in Nuremberg, Hitler presented a new plan; with arming as the objective and self-sufficiency as the means, the whole economy was placed under the authority of this plan for four years. Goering, sure of the führer's support, then developed an industry to make ersatz products and refused to allow any exports of arms. Schacht refused to finance this plan by printing money; from then on he clearly opposed the regime and even tried to win the support of the army against Goering. He frequently met with Max during this time. In May 1937 Schacht again saw Blum, who did not, however, have the power to make a decision regarding trade.

That year Hans W. Petersen, an employee of the Jewish Oppenheim bank in Berlin and half Jewish himself, decided to take the risk of setting up a bank in his own name in the middle of Berlin, choosing thus to "hide in plain sight." A former German officer in the First World War, he had a mother who was an Oppenheim and a wife from the von Ganz family, one of whom founded I.G. Farben. More will be heard of him, later.

Meanwhile the activities of M.M. Warburg dwindled more and more. The firm was doing no more than organizing the emigration of Jewish clients, liquidating foreign banks and issuing a few loans abroad on behalf of the Reich. The number of its clients nevertheless increased somewhat. It was a strange bank, borrowing on behalf of a state it was helping its clients to flee.

Schacht continued on his downward path. On 22 January 1937, before the German Economic Chamber, which brought together the country's leading industrialists, he made a violent attack on Goering. At the same time in London Siegmund was resolving to send Max his resignation from M.M. Warburg because he disapproved too much of what was happening there. Meanwhile, Max decided to dissolve the joint subsidiary with Berliner Handels-Gesellschaft, which was in ruins since the people in charge of it had not the slightest desire to enter into a business relationship with such a conspicuous Jewish bank as that of Max Warburg.

In March 1937 Schacht, whose mandate was running out, wanted to suspend Mefo armaments bonds and threatened the führer that he would leave the Reichsbank if he were not allowed to do so. Hitler delayed, promising to put an end to them in one year's time. Schacht agreed to remain in his post until then but told the führer that he would resign if he were then forced to carry on inflationary financing of defense.[50]

Germany was becoming impossible to live in for Max and Fritz, the last two German sons of Moritz Warburg, as for all Jews under the Nazi yoke. Many of their Jewish and non-Jewish friends had emigrated, others were in prison or dead. Despite letters and telephone calls from Felix, Siegmund and Eric, Max still did not want to leave.[51] Neither did Anna and Fritz, who transformed their Kösterberg house into a shelter for families about to emigrate, and a reception center for orphans.

In New York a harassed and distressed Felix now devoted all his time to the Jews of Europe. In the spring of 1937, when he learned that the Peel Committee had recommended to the British government the partition of Palestine and the end of the mandate, he saw the prospect of the Jewish state to which he was still hostile. When the Jewish Agency met in a plenary conference in Basel in August 1937 to consider the Peel report, he went there with difficulty and, although very ill, opposed the conclusions of Peel and Weizmann. He accused Weizmann publicly of having lied to him and having always concealed his true aims. A few days later, despite the hesitations of Weizmann, who did not want a rump state, and the hostility of Felix, who did not want partition, the Peel report was approved, and the conference called for the beginning of negotiations for the creation of a Jewish state. Felix, very upset, made a vain attempt to force Weizmann's resignation;[52] he died three months after his return to New York, on 30 October 1937, leaving his wife and four children a quarter of a million dollars each, plus one-fifth of the "balance." Nobody knows how much this "balance" amounted to, except that it was quite substantial.

In Hamburg the activity of helping emigration was enough to maintain the illusion of business transactions; from a financial and accounting point of view the year saw some stabilization, even though M.M. Warburg lost eighty of the board seats it still held. The Hamburg-America Line went so far as to rename the *Max Warburg* and the *Carl Melchior*, two ships built in the 1920s. Despite the support of Werner von Blomberg, the German minister of war, and the industrialists, Schacht was unable to win the power to export or to stop the production of ersatz products. He did gradually manage to stop the issuing of Mefo bonds, then resigned on 27 November 1937 from the post of minister of the economy, but not from the Reichsbank. Hitler accepted this resignation, while permitting him the title of minister without portfolio. The Ministry of the Economy was then integrated into the plan organization.

Beginning of the New Trading Company

At the same time, in the democracies, the world economic crisis was beginning to come under control. Unemployment was down slightly. All currencies were fixed in relation to the dollar, though many were still floating. The governors of the leading central banks consulted each other regularly, and that very September the United States, Great Britain and France undertook in an agreement, later adhered to by Belgium, the Netherlands and Switzerland, to set common aims in economic and monetary policy and to consult each other on major decisions, particularly devaluations, giving twenty-four hours notice. This was the first unintentional result of the failed London conference of two years earlier.

On 7 June 1935 MacDonald, who was ill, left 10 Downing Street and Baldwin replaced him at the head of a coalition government that was actually Conservative. He immediately called an election and campaigned in favor of preparations for war. The ballot of 14 November 1935 confirmed the dominance of the Conservatives in the coalition government, which was extended.

As for the City, it had not yet recovered from the shock of the Great Depression. Siegmund, settled in his small offices, was seeking his future. In these years of humility and exile, a stranger to this highly codified world, Siegmund's mania for success drove him to attempt everything in order to survive. Nobody brought him business apart from Brandeis-Goldschmidt and occasionally N.M. Rothschild. It was up to him to find clients, and as a German he had to be considerably better than his English counterparts. In contrast to the people in the City, where the merchant banker was a man of fashionable, distant and superficial contact, Siegmund's instincts led him, the Hanseatic trader with a horror of speculation, to take risks that were seemingly enormous but in reality very calculated. He knew that he would prosper only by continually inventing new services and that his success would depend on his nonconformity and imagination. Did he want success? To do things with style, be the first, make money for one's clients—such were his ambitions. He also liked to quote what Fürstenberg had said of one of his clients, "Not only are these people crazy enough to invest, but they have the *chutzpa* to expect dividends." For him the role of any investment banker was like that of a business doctor who can spot the symptoms of a sickness before the first pain, invent a remedial strategy even before going into battle and make money for those he advises.

At the end of 1935 Siegmund had his first big client in Britain, the film producer Alexander Korda, who was unhappy with the British film laboratories, wanted to set up his own and asked Warburg to arrange financing. This was a major opportunity for Siegmund as it gave him his first chance to approach British capitalists with a serious proposition. The attempt was a failure, however, and he would long remember the obstacles he encountered in a matter that he had thought straightforward.

Siegmund continued to make a living by accepting commissions that other banks could not or would not undertake. Sometimes these were elementary matters, like financing the movement of goods; sometimes they were complex arrangements that the British banks did not dare to make, as they did not know the business. Thus one day the London branch of Chase of New York sent him a client who wanted to discount letters of credit on German ships. Chase did not know how to value that kind of risk, but somebody knew that Siegmund, from Hamburg, was well versed in the value of this kind of paper. The business was sent to him, he appraised it, found a banker to discount the paper and took a respectable commission. He also did some work with M.M. Warburg and with Kuhn Loeb, now run by John Schiff and twelve other partners. Like the rest of Wall Street, the old firm was beginning to find its feet again and to settle into a new area: it was concentrating on loans to American and European industry attracted to Wall Street by the favorable interest rates. The pace of business quickened in 1937 when Treasury Secretary Morgenthau, in order to increase the profitability of American banks, introduced a "Q" regulation, which prohibited interest payments on deposits of less than thirty days and limited the return on longer-term deposits to 6.5 percent. This ceiling encouraged borrowing in the United States and thus contributed to reabsorbing the American surplus. However, Kuhn Loeb was not in on all the successes of this immediate prewar period. Jimmy Warburg, Paul's son, had just made another fortune by helping to set up the capitalization of Polaroid, which Kuhn Loeb had refused to finance.

Overall, Siegmund attracted attention because of his lofty view of the role of the financier—a view he could hardly afford at that time. However, even at Brandeis-Goldschmidt, where he kept his offices, this austere but enterprising foreigner who talked all the time about *haute banque* was not very popular. People were surprised when this less than affluent young man looked down on important people and preached to them. "Either a firm is in *haute banque* or it does not exist, whatever its size," he would say. If an individual did not have *haute banque* style, he did not deserve to be noticed, associated with in the smallest transaction or recruited. Siegmund was furious when the standards he set were not observed by the two, three and then four people who worked with him. As in Hamburg and Berlin, he hated incompetence and vagueness. Unlike City people, he judged a client not by a balance sheet or an address book, but by traits of character and future prospects.

Siegmund knew where he was going and talked freely to his friends about it. He thought war inevitable, even desirable. He thought that the old firm in Germany would disappear in the turmoil and for the first time in two centuries the name of Warburg would disappear from world finance. He wanted to be ready to restore it, when the time came, and so to show himself worthy of family tradition.

Henry Grunfeld remembered Siegmund's perfectionism in these first years of work together, the power of his charm and his capacity to inspire his small team, huddled for more than ten hours a day in three small offices. Others who knew him at this time recall his work style as a "mixture of Jewish dynamism and German thoroughness."[53]

All this was far from the shallowness, or rather the hypocrisy, of some people in the City at that time. For example, one Saturday morning in 1936, Siegmund and Henry wanted to see a city banker who was a friend of Harry Lucas and boasted of never being at work on Saturday. They went to his office and found him there. City people did work hard, but they concealed it.

Siegmund intended to be accepted by his new homeland. Immediately he set about improving his English and insisted that his writing style should be corrected. Any letter leaving the bank had to be retyped if it contained the slightest spelling or grammatical error. He also set out to discover English literature and, as with everything he did, applied himself to it systematically, spending all his leisure time during those years reading Shakespeare, Dickens, Trollope and Butler, and noting in pencil on the flyleaf the numbers of the pages he wanted to re-read. His life was still austere, though a little easier than at the beginning. Year after year he moved to larger flats. He usually dined at home. With Baffy Dugdale (Arthur Balfour's niece) he continued to concern himself with the committee for refugees.

When Baldwin resigned for the third time on 28 May 1937 and Neville Chamberlain became prime minister following the abdication of

Edward VIII, Siegmund moved again—this time to a rented house in Sussex. Then, at the end of that year, business was good enough for him to buy a pretty house, with the Welsh name of Deerhaddnn at Missenden, in a part of Buckinghamshire where the British banking elite then lived. He traveled to the City each day by train. By then Siegmund felt at ease in the London world of finance. He had recognized its strength, but also its limits, and knew how to stay ahead of it.

He was the first in the City to make of his quasi-merchant bank a quasi-investment bank along German or French lines. In order to be able to deal in the securities of the companies he advised, free of tax and without going through the Stock Exchange's various intermediaries, he set up a subsidiary specializing in securities dealing. He named it Mercury Securities, from the name of a company he had bought, and in which he saw an ironic allusion—Mercury, at once a banker, merchant, communicator and messenger.

His business was growing. The following year eight people were working with him and he had to move next door, to 10 King William Street and some spacious offices, where he would stay for the duration of the war.

At that time a bogus Warburg came on the scene. In Amsterdam a pamphlet appeared on "The resources of National Socialism, three conversations with Hitler," signed by one Sydney Warburg, who claimed to be Felix's son, although no Warburg had ever borne that first name. The Warburgs would not discover until much later the origin of this forgery, which at the time called forth many denials from the family. It was the work of a Dutch journalist in the mood for a scandal.

"Herr Hitler is a Gentleman"

As Siegmund did nothing by halves he now decided to request British citizenship. He was not lacking in advantages. He had the support of the chairman of M. Samuel, Lord Bearsted, the grandson of the founder of Shell, whom he had known since his first trip to London. He was also able to count on other prestigious sponsors: Anthony Rothschild, Olaf Hambro and Andrew Carnwath of the Baring family.

He was resigned to being excluded from politics, the area that most interested him, for he knew that a German Jew, even if naturalized, had no chance of becoming a statesman in England. Still, this did not prevent his following the political news with great interest. On arriving at the office he read the full reports of debates in Parliament, took notes and carefully recorded some of the great phrases from these debates, along with some from his other reading.

Harry Lucas introduced him to Anthony Eden, Stafford Cripps and Margot Asquith. He shared their fierce hostility to Chamberlain's pacifism, then a minority position. Concerned that Britain was so unprepared for a war they knew to be inevitable, they were still more worried to see German industry increasing its production without any reaction from London, or even any objection that certain British businesses were profiting from this development. As all this was happening, Max informed Siegmund from Hamburg that Schacht had lost his economic power to Goering.

As 1938 began, Siegmund, like Stefan Zweig, was devastated by the passivity of the political, financial and journalistic elites in the European democracies:

> Ever and again {wrote Zweig} there was the cajoling intimation that Hitler wanted no more than to absorb the Germans of the the border states, after which he would be content and would in gratitude exterminate bolshevism; this bait worked excellently. Hitler merely had to utter the word "peace" in a speech to arouse the newspapers to enthusiasm, to make them forget all his past deeds and desist from asking why after all Germany was arming so madly . . . . Besides a negligible number of Englishmen, we [immigrants] were then the only ones in England who did not delude ourselves about the full extent of the danger . . . with the difference that I was a stranger, a tolerated guest in England and dared not utter a warning.[54]

The painter Fred Uhlman's contemporary description was identical to Zweig's:

> This was a surrealistic country where a Minister of Defense could announce with pride that 436 volunteers had signed up for the army, while Hitler had millions of men ready for war. This was a country where people suspected that my only motive in urging my friends to take arms, to introduce conscription, and to help the Spanish Republic, was the thirst for revenge of a refugee![55]

During these years Siegmund often had conversations with Stefan Zweig, for whom he had unbounded admiration. "Zweig's position in politics," he was to note privately on the death of the writer, "and his view of life in general were totally exempt from partiality and filled with tolerance, a tolerance which encompassed everything, except intolerance."[56]

After the *Anschluss* of 11 March 1938 Siegmund and Stefan were enraged. Here was Austria taken over and nobody really reacted, either in London or in Paris or Washington. Zweig wrote:

> ... there [were] none to grasp the fact that Austria was the stone whose removal from the wall would cause Europe's collapse. I, however, experienced the naïveté, the good faith in which the English and their leaders let themselves be bamboozled, with the smarting eyes of one who had seen the faces of the Storm Troopers at close range at home and who had heard them sing: "Today we conquer Germany, tomorrow the whole world."[57]

But to whom could Siegmund talk about the danger? Whom could he tell that these madmen who were now running his native country were not to be trusted? When the threat to Czechoslovakia began in April 1938 the cup ran over. He saw that war was coming, while France and Britain were clinging to the least hope of peace.

This crucial time marked Siegmund's first contact with British politics and the beginnings of his illusions of influence in such matters. That month the Congress of the German Sudeten party called for the province to be declared autonomous by the Czech government and brandished the threat of secession if the Czechs refused. Czech leader Eduard Beneš was confident his French, British and Soviet allies would support his government, and refused to give in. But in fact none of his allies really supported him. Chamberlain was quite willing to threaten the Germans with war in general, so long as he did not have to carry the threat out; Lord Halifax, the new foreign secretary, said as much to Joachim von Ribbentrop who had just replaced Neurath. On 10 April in Paris, Edouard Daladier, who had become prime minister, repeated that France would keep to its commitments if Czechoslovakia were invaded. However, his minister of foreign affairs, Georges Bonnet, was of another opinion; like Chamberlain and Halifax, he did not think that Czechoslovakia was worth a war. Joseph Stalin also did not want to intervene. As for America, Roosevelt did not care about these "Central States" of Europe—about which he knew little.

At the end of May, like British statesman Stafford Cripps and a few others, Siegmund thought that conflict was not only inevitable but necessary before Hitler, who was daily threatening to occupy Prague, became too powerful and allowed his ambitions to expand beyond the

Sudetenland. The summer passed in an intensifying war of communiqués, with everyone still unwilling to precipitate events. At the end of August Chamberlain had the idea of meeting Hitler. On 12 September, in a blustering speech at Nuremberg, the führer called for the Sudetenland to be annexed to Germany. The next day he sent an ultimatum to the Czech government, which called up its reservists. On 14 September Chamberlain announced that he was leaving the next day for Berchtesgaden to meet Hitler. The interview lasted only a few hours and ended inconclusively. Chamberlain came away convinced that only the attachment of the Sudetenland to Germany would prevent war and that it was better to do this by self-determination than to run the risk of a military annexation. He met Daladier on 18 September in London and then decided to obtain Czechoslovakia's consent to this surrender. Chamberlain was insistent that Beneš's agreement should be obtained before 26 September, the date of the Nazi party congress, at which Hitler might announce that he had decided on annexation. On 22 September Chamberlain met Hitler again at Bad Godesberg. This time the führer demanded complete evacuation of the Sudetenland by the Czechs within eight days. Chamberlain proposed that the fate of the province be decided through a self-determination ballot—everyone knew in advance what the result would be. On leaving he thought he had won the the führer over, but on 26 September in Berlin, Hitler announced the immediate annexation, pure and simple, of the Sudetenland from 1 October. The next day Beneš fell in with the British self-determination plan, but it was too late. The Germans were preparing to invade and Prague was forced to decree general mobilization. On this same day, in an attempt to halt the war, Mussolini, prompted by Chamberlain, proposed a meeting in Munich of Chamberlain, Daladier, Hitler and himself. All accepted and met two days later in an extremely tense atmosphere. Hitler did not modify his intentions but agreed that the occupation of the Sudetenland should be postponed for ten days, that native Czechs would be allowed to sell their assets before being expelled and that a joint commission would be formed to draw a new border between Czechoslovakia and the Sudetenland. In exchange for these absurdly small concessions Chamberlain signed a nonagression pact that spoke of a common desire never again to make war. On arrival back in London Chamberlain waved the text of this agreement, watched by Halifax and a delirious crowd, shouting, "I've got it, I've got it!" In the car, amid the cheers, he confided to his minister, "This won't last three months."[58] But was he talking about the peace or the enthusiasm of the crowd?

Like Stefan Zweig and a few others, Siegmund Warburg observed this appeasement in desperation. Attached as he was to the forces of reason, he could see in this behavior nothing but cowardice, unawareness, shallowness, blindness—everything he deplored in certain Englishmen. "It looked like the triumph of the dogged will to peace of an otherwise unimportant and leathery statesman, and the immediate reaction was universal gratitude to him."[59]

Some Britons were as lucid as the émigrés. That night Lord Baldwin wrote to Chamberlain, "Make the best of this time, for it will not last," and Churchill would say, "You had to choose between war and dishonor; you chose dishonor and you will have war." From his university, Keynes, who had published his *General Theory*, also protested against Munich as he had once done against Versailles. "The honor of our foreign policy had undergone a dreadful defeat."[60]

The dismemberment of Czechoslovakia began at once. The very day after Munich, on 1 October, Poland annexed part of Czech territory in Silesia; on 2 October Hungary took another piece of the country without Allied resistance. In a three-day debate beginning on 3 October, Chamberlain reported to Parliament on this "peace in our time," with the Shakespearean quotation, "Out of this nettle, danger, we pluck this flower, safety."

Not everyone at Westminster shared in the euphoria. Anthony Eden and Churchill both spoke against the agreement, and Sir Alfred Duff Cooper made a personal statement after resigning in protest from the Foreign Office. Stafford Cripps, who had returned from Jamaica a few days earlier and had had a long conversation with Siegmund, spoke against Chamberlain and his policy of "talking with sweet reasonableness about each dangerous issue as it arises, but always providing yourself with the maximum use of force to support your argument." Cripps added that Britain could make the greatest and most lasting contribution to world peace, not by building massive armaments, but by working out a new and better system for the cooperative economic development of world resources: "We can give a lead in working out . . . that new system which will make available to the common people of all nations commodities which now, though so bounteously produced cannot be obtained by many starving millions." He ended with a plea to the people of Britain to put into power those people "who will be prepared to rely for peace not on the word or forebearance of a foreign dictator, but upon the justice and progressiveness of their own constructive economic policy."[61]

Like Cripps, Siegmund would dispense advice of this kind to Britain for the next thirty years. However, on that day Stafford Cripps was neither listened to nor understood. On 6 October, by 366 votes to 144, Parliament backed Chamberlain, as did the whole of the British press. The day after this debate the *Times* wrote, "If the Government had been in less resolute hands, war would have been inevitable, and would have gone against the wishes of all nations."

Siegmund was crushed. He saw that war was coming and was convinced that after this agreement Hitler would think he could get away with anything. He wanted to influence the top British politicians. After much persistence, he arranged through the Rothschilds a meeting with Lord Halifax at the Foreign Office. The minister, pressed for time, received him from behind his desk and then, having seated Siegmund on one of the settees beside the fireplace, almost without looking at his visitor, got up and turned toward the window: "Well, Mr. Warburg, what can I do for you?"

"Minister, I should like to speak to you about Czechoslovakia. The only guarantee she has left is Hitler's goodwill, which will last no more than two months, unless Great Britain steps in now with troops, to prevent him going beyond the Sudetenland. You cannot trust that man, he will betray the agreement he has signed with you as he has betrayed the Germans themselves. An immediate war would have been preferable to this backward move, which has given him time to prepare himself better for attack."

"Mr. Warburg, I cannot do as you suggest. Your experience as a German refugee is certainly tragic, but it has altered your objectivity. Hitler has so far conducted himself with us as a man of quality; as long as he does so, we shall have no complaint of him and we shall trust him. Good-bye, Mr. Warburg."

Siegmund would always remember this first personal contact with a leading British politician and would comment on it to close friends, from whom this story comes. Five years after being ejected from the Reich's Ministry of Foreign Affairs because he had come to demand Hitler's dismissal, here he was again treated as "politically suspect," this time by the British minister of foreign affairs, for warning him against the Nazi dictator. Such were the initial limits of his influence in politics.

Events soon proved Siegmund right. It took only a few days for the disagreeable details to be made known of the completeness of the capitulation to Hitler, [wrote Zweig] of the shameful betrayal of Czechoslovakia to which solemn assurance of help had been made, and by the next week it was already notorious that even that capitulation had satisfied Hitler so little that he had violated its provisions in all details before the signatures on the treaty had dried. Goebbels no longer restrained himself from shouting to heaven that England had been held up at Munich.[62]

On 10 October, as agreed, Hitler occupied the Sudetenland, but there was no longer any question of a joint commission to establish the border. On 2 November Hungary appropriated twelve thousand square kilometers and one million inhabitants from southern Slovakia. Three months afterward the führer, who had thus far annexed only German-speaking territory, embarked upon imperial ambitions. In January 1939 he supported the Slovak independence movement and on 14 March met the new Czech president, Emil Hácha, in Berlin to force him, under threat of bombing, to request the intervention of German troops in Prague. On 15 March their troops entered Bohemia. That day Hitler took over Hradčany Castle, the seat of the kings of Bohemia and the symbol of Czech nationalism. Slovakia became independent and Bohemia-Moravia a protectorate, which Hitler entrusted to an old acquaintance of Siegmund's, Baron von Neurath.

Siegmund was dumbfounded to learn that on that same day representatives of the British and German employers' associations were calmly meeting in Dusseldorf to discuss future cooperation between the industries and banks of both countries, and signing an agreement providing for the "abolition of all unhealthy competition between them,"[63] while making "every effort to obtain the help of their respective governments in order that they should co-operate with a view to compensation of the advantages granted to their companies by other governments, and especially that of the United States." And he was really outraged when the chairman of the British employers told the Times on his return to London, "The conversations were conducted in a friendly spirit with, on each side, a great wish for mutual understanding."

On 26 March 1939, the Reich claimed the "free city" of Danzig from Poland, as well as a railway and a motorway across the "Corridor," created in 1919. Britain jibbed at this and on 31 March Chamberlain announced that he would intervene in the case of a German attack on Poland. On 7 April Mussolini annexed Albania. Intense diplomatic activity during the summer brought no détente.

Despite all this, cooperation continued calmly among British, German, Swedish and American companies. I.G. Farben and Sterling Products Inc., Bendix and Zenith set up joint subsidiaries; the shares of the Bosch foreign subsidiaries were all fictitiously sold in New York to some Wallenbergs, so that until the United States came into the war the Bosch companies would be protected.

In contrast with the previous prewar period, this time the Warburgs, whether in Hamburg, New York or London, did, and could do, nothing to reconcil Germany and Britain. They were out of the game.

The End of M.M. Warburg

While war was being declared or breaking out everywhere from Poland to Abyssinia, from China to Spain, Max's position in Hamburg was now becoming completely untenable. A few days after the *Anschluss* the final blow came. He was called to Berlin by Schacht, still at the head of the Reichsbank:

> So far I have been able to keep your bank in the Reich Loan Consortium because I have been able to impress on Hitler the usefulness of the Warburg name in placing Reich loans abroad. You know you were the last Jewish bank to belong. But I have almost no power left and Goering has decided that your bank must leave the Consortium unless you sell it to non-Jews. I protested in vain. I can do nothing about it, and I myself am going to resign any day now. Good-bye Max, and good luck.[64]

Max understood it was all over. A bank without a state guarantee cannot survive; it is no longer in a position to lend to anyone. If his old associate from difficult times was saying this, then everything was truly finished. That evening, on leaving the Reichsbank, Max noted somberly in his diary, "We said good-bye, having worked together for thirty years, in every possible way."[65]

Back in Hamburg he felt rather alone with only himself and his brother Fritz to make decisions. No longer with him were Paul, Felix, Aby and Melchior, all dead, or Ernst Spiegelberg, Eric, Siegmund and Karl, all emigrated. His was a dreadful choice. Should he close the bank or sell it to non-Jews? He knew that Siegmund would prefer him to close down rather than take a chance that the name would fall into the hands of the Nazis. But he saw things differently. "M.M. Warburg" should continue, even without the Warburgs. Within a few days he assembled a financial group, with a mixture of non-Jewish executives and some of the bank's major clients, led by Charles Wirtz, a brilliant young Hamburg wholesaler. They agreed on a selling price for the bank, obviously very low. Everything was done within the rules. Papers were drawn up: the bank would keep the name "M.M. Warburg" but the family would lose legal title to it. Max accepted the arrangement on behalf of all the Warburg shareholders. Quite naturally, he asked the most senior non-Jewish executive in the firm's hierarchy, Rudolf Brinckmann, "a faithful and valued employee,"[66] to run the bank. The people at Kuhn Loeb were reassured to see that a man chosen by them, exactly ten years earlier, now was responsible for taking care of the interests of the house.

Other Jewish bankers were making similar arrangements. Salomon Oppenheim entrusted his Cologne bank to one of his signatories, Robert Pferdmenges; Jacob Goldschmidt gave up the Darmstädter Bank to one of his executives. Everything happened tacitly. Nobody knew how long Max would be away from the bank, and the sale, though legally formalized, remained fictitious in the eyes of some witnesses. On 3 June 1938 all the Warburg staff attended a private dinner in the best restaurant in Hamburg.[67] Max and Fritz made speeches that included a message of hope for the future, and Rudolf Brinckmann responded gracefully. Though the two brothers reaffirmed their decision to stay in Hamburg, there was no promise they would return to the bank at a later date. What date would that have been? The Reich was there for a thousand years.

Leaving Germany

That year Max's son, Eric, divided his time between Hamburg and New York, where he had established a small financial company, E.M. Warburg & Co. Since he was now an American citizen, he was able to return to Germany without risk and landed there in June the day after the Hamburg dinner, hoping to persuade his father to leave the country. Max was still reluctant to go into exile. He was willing to go to New York and settle his wife there, but he intended to return to Hamburg and only then prepare for his own possible departure. They decided to sail as soon as possible, but a visa was needed first. As there was a wait for United States visas, they opted for a Canadian one.

To be able to leave the country, an even higher ransom than before had to be paid to the Nazis. The levy on capital owned by Jews had just been raised by the imposition of a 20 percent tax on the value of the capital, payable in two installments in December 1938 and August

1939. Once this tax was paid a Jew could still not get his money out of the country. Each emigrant could take with him no more than 10 marks in foreign currencies, or the equivalent of $8, plus 300 marks in goods, and his own personal belongings; a list of these belongings had to be approved by the police, who prohibited the export of jewelry and works of art.

Max could have used several of the methods then current to get his money out: changing money on the black market, even though this meant losing at least half of it; selling at a loss the marks blocked in a German account to foreigners or to Germans wishing to return to Germany; smuggling marks out and trying to get rid of them elsewhere, which was then very difficult. Marks were valid only in Germany; they would have to be reimported illegally by the buyer. He could also have given his capital to some Germans and once out of Germany had it repaid to him by friends of those who stayed behind. But in fact since 1936 few prominent Jewish families had been able to get large amounts out of Germany, Austria, Czechoslovakia or elsewhere. Thus Jacob Goldschmidt succeeded in saving his fabulous collection of Impressionists only by entrusting it to the Italian ambassador in exchange for his magnificent Berlin mansion.

Max, however, even in June 1938 managed to get sizable amounts of money out of Germany. Nobody knew exactly how much or what methods he used. Schacht could well have helped his old friend by ensuring that blind eyes were turned. At the end of June, Max sailed for Canada with his wife and son while Fritz went with his wife and two children to Stockholm. Once in Canada, Max was able to enter the United States freely with his son, an American citizen.

On arrival in New York Max told Kuhn Loeb that he had only come to settle his wife there and that he was going to return to Hamburg as soon as possible. He did not want to desert other Jews remaining in Germany. At the beginning of October, on hearing the news of Munich, he began to have doubts. On 11 November he nonetheless was preparing to sail when the *Kristallnacht* massacres finally opened his eyes. About the same time, Siegmund also persuaded his mother to leave Germany. On Christmas Day 1938 she took the train to Paris, where he went to meet her. In the notes he made at her death, he said:

Given the situation at that time, the decision to emigrate in 1938 was imperative. It was of course very hard for her to take leave of Swabia, the beloved country of her birth, and of the many friends she had to leave there.[68]

During that autumn of 1938 the last departures quickened. In September Gisela, Max's youngest daughter, who had stayed in Berlin to distribute contributions from American Jews to the Jews there, and to help them get out, sailed to the United States seeking still more funds that she intended to take back to the German capital. She planned to return to Germany with her father, but after *Kristallnacht* she, too, remained in New York, where she would marry soon afterward. Max's daughter Lola, after helping Jewish orphans in Hamburg for four years, founded the Children's Aliyah there before emigrating to England at the end of the year with her husband, Rudolf Hahn, an industrialist. To obtain authorization to take out her money, she had to give up her Berlin house to Funk, Schacht's successor at the Ministry of Economics. Max's daughter Renate had left Germany shortly before, to get married in India.

Despite the risks, some Jewish émigrés still returned to Germany from time to time. Thus in October 1937 Henry Grunfeld went to Berlin to fetch his father, using an old pre-Nazi passport, without the "Jew" stamp. On the road to the airport he found himself in a traffic jam, side by side with Heinrich Himmler. They stared at each other. This was enough risk for Henry, who decided never again to set foot in the capital of the Reich.

Similarly, Fritz Warburg, once settled in Sweden, returned to Hamburg in December 1938 after *Kristallnacht*, also with an old passport, to attend a secret meeting of the Council of Jewish Hospitals. Denounced and arrested by the Gestapo, he had his old passport confiscated and spent several months in prison. One story has it that it took the intervention of a leading Christian banker in Hamburg for him to be freed and allowed to leave Germany. Another is that he escaped, which is the version current in the family.[69] Kösterberg was then requisitioned by the Wehrmacht, who moved generals into the houses and antiaircraft batteries into the gardens.

The only Warburg still in Nazi hands, along with 250,000 other German Jews, was Otto, an eccentric professor of physics who lived in Berlin. The great-great-great-grandson of Samuel, Otto had become a biochemist in 1906 and won the Nobel Prize for medicine in 1931 for the discovery of the catalytic role of iron phosphides in biological oxidation. He was the first to have been able to combine organic chemistry and the physics of radiation. An old bachelor, he divided his time between his work, his dogs and his horses.

Nothing remained in Germany of the family financial network that six years earlier had been at the height of its power. All its clients, partners and directors were scattered across Europe, Latin America, Palestine and the United States. Gradually they would come together again. These renewals of friendship would stand out as landmarks in the history of the forty years that followed.

None is too Many

In the first four years of Nazism, only 150,000 German Jews had left Germany, 50,000 of them, like Siegmund, between Hitler's coming to power and the end of 1933, and the other 100,000 by November 1938. Another 100,000 were to leave between November 1938 and September 1939. In all, nearly 250,000 emigrated before the war to four main destinations: the United States, Palestine, Great Britain and France. In September 1939, 185,000 were thought to be still in Germany, out of which only 50,000 were under forty. The rest had perished in the prewar massacres.

It was increasingly difficult for Jews to get out of Germany or the occupied countries, as they were no longer wanted anywhere. Professional organizations, newspapers and even the government in Britain asked that their entry to Britain and Palestine be limited. On 2 September 1939, moreover, the British opened fire on a ship docking at Tel Aviv with fourteen hundred Jews on board. Two passengers were killed.

It was at this point, five years after his arrival in London, that Siegmund obtained his citizenship: the sponsorship of the leading British merchant banks had opened for him doors that would remain closed to many others.

Siegmund concerned himself with more unfortunate German-Jewish refugees and, when he was in London, often saw Baffy Dugdale and Chaim Weizmann, who were similarly concerned. By now there were numerous members of his family also in England, such as his cousins Anita and Lola, who were organizing help for refugees and later would work in a missing persons bureau.

Spared by the Holocaust, the Warburgs were an exception to most German-Jewish families of that time. Perhaps this should be read as the fate of uncommon seers, escaping, thanks to their centuries-old prescience, from the general tragedy.

In these prewar years, the West had little reason to be proud of the help it contributed to those persecuted by the Nazis. Hundreds of thousands of them sought to leave hell and were unable to do so, for lack of British, Swiss, French, American or Canadian visas; and all this despite the efforts of James G. MacDonald, and later of a few others like Raoul Wallenberg, who manufactured false Swedish passports in Budapest during the war.

There was one particularly dreadful example of the West's callousness. Edith Stein, a Jewish philosopher who had become a Catholic nun, would die in Auschwitz because nobody had been willing to accept her. Chaim Weizmann wrote that at the time "the world seemed divided into places where the Jews could not live and places they could not enter."[70]

Some Canadian consulates required a certificate of non-Jewishness before allowing entry, and a senior Canadian official told a journalist asking about the number of Jews to be admitted, "None is too many."[71]

The End of Schacht

By autumn 1938 Hjalmar Schacht, still minister without portfolio and chairman of the Reichsbank, was increasingly hostile to the policies of Goering, who was then at the height of his power. He was simultaneously head of the SA, SS general, president of the Reichstag, minister of the interior and of the Prussian police, air minister, commander-in-chief of the Luftwaffe, a member of the secret cabinet and finally—perhaps especially—chairman of Goering Industries. Schacht still wanted to put a stop to the Mefo bonds and decided to take up active opposition. On 28 September 1938 he became associated in a plan for a coup d'état by the chief of the general staff Franz Halder, but this was postponed by the announcement that day of the Munich agreement. Kristallnacht prompted Schacht to go further. On 12 November 1938, the day after the massacres, Goering announced that Jews would not be compensated for the damage, and would actually be held responsible for the repairs themselves "to restore the appearance of the streets on pain of a fine of one billion marks".[72] The same day another decree called on companies to dismiss immediately all Jews still employed, prohibited Jews from practicing as lawyers and required the closure of all Jewish shops before 31 December. In a fierce reaction, Schacht then denounced Kristallnacht and the latest measures before the staff of the Reichsbank.[73]

He had not yet lost all power. Through the Reichsbank he controlled the financing of the economy and could oppose the Nazis' economic plan. Thus on 21 November he refused to issue more Mefo bonds and would only authorize discounting of promissory notes for public works. Hitler had had enough. Goering, who claimed to have received the führer's order to step up production of arms and put more people to work, threatened, "If private companies are not capable of this, and if the banks cannot finance it, they will be nationalized."[74] When the first Mefo bonds fell due on 30 November an unruffled Reichsbank, on Schacht's orders, asked the state for repayment. Goering refused. This spending was not in the budget. Schacht was therefore faced with a *fait accompli*. He was forced to break the promise he had given to the lenders. He was absolutely beside himself, but he still hesitated to resign.

Meanwhile the removal of the means of economic existence of the Jews was gathering force. Thus on 3 December 1938 the state ordered the immediate sale of all industrial companies, land, property and anything else owned by Jews. Schacht was still attempting to oppose this measure and sought to reactivate Max Warburg's plan of the previous year. On 6 December, still chairman of the central bank, he left for London. There he met Siegmund, and then, on 17 December, Montagu Norman, the governor of the Bank of England, as well as representatives of the intergovernmental committee for refugees. He explained to them the details of his plan, largely taken from that of Max Warburg:

> I do not want to give an opinion on what is happening at present in Germany. But the fact is that Jews have no future there. They are soon going to be very badly treated, and chased out with no recourse. So for humanitarian reasons I have designed a plan to help them emigrate. I propose that each year for three years, 50,000 Jews should leave, not necessarily the richest first, on the contrary in fact. The proceeds of the sale of their belongings in Germany will be paid to a special fund, which will serve as guarantee for a loan from the world Jewish community to Germany. Money from this loan will serve, among other things, to finance the payment of 10,000 marks in foreign exchange to each emigrant family. In addition the world Jewish community will undertake to encourage German exports so that this loan may be repaid. You must take this plan or leave it; you must know that the present German Government will not accept any other, and that even this one has not yet received the führer's consent.

The Schacht plan was quite well received in London, and the Jewish community in Britiain agreed without too much hesitation to participate in financing it. Schacht then went to the United States, to put the plan to leaders of the American Jewish community. Those in charge accepted at once and decided to send a mission to Germany immediately to implement it. While in America, Schacht saw Max for the last time. At the end of December he requested a meeting with Morgenthau, but the secretary of the treasury refused to meet the chairman of the Reichsbank: so as not to displease Hitler, said some; for hatred of Nazism, said others. On 2 January 1939 Schacht returned from New York and went to see Hitler at Berchtesgaden, to obtain his final agreement. However, Ribbentrop, excluded from the negotiations, had persuaded the führer to keep to the straight ransom payments exacted so far. Hitler then told Schacht that all discussion of the subject must cease. Moreover, because of the assassination of von Rath in Paris the previous November, a special tax was to be levied on Jews and all securities handed over by Jews on departure would be converted immediately into marks for the Reichsbank.

For Schacht that meeting with the führer marked the ruin of his plan and a sign of what was still to come: a monetary creation that would permit the pillaging of Jewish property. He refused to Hitler's face to subscribe to this and on 7 January confirmed this refusal in a memorandum cosigned by all the directors of the Reichsbank.[75]

Meanwhile, as planned, two American Jewish leaders had gone to Germany, arriving on 10 January 1939 in order to work out with Schacht the details of an evacuation plan. They left empty-handed after eight days of rambling and polite refusals.

On 20 January Hitler decided to dismiss Schacht from the Reichsbank where he had reigned practically without interruption for nearly fifteen years. It was a strange procedure: Walther Funk was already appointed in Schacht's place the day before he was dismissed.

Still a minister without portfolio, Schacht then went somewhat into oblivion. In April he went to a BIS meeting in Basel where he still represented Germany, before being replaced by Schröder. He again met the governor of the Bank of England, Montagu Norman whom he warned of Hitler's ambitions in the Ukraine. On returning to London, Norman passed on the message to Chamberlain, who replied that Schacht no longer had the slightest political influence and that one should neither believe him nor negotiate with him. Schacht tried to get himself invited to America. The State Department refused, for fear of upsetting Hitler. Schacht then became a declared opponent of the regime.

Under Funk the German banking system integrated itself fully into the Nazi machine; the Reichsbank even prepared to store the gold teeth and jewelry from Auschwitz and other death camps. The Dresdner Bank lent money to an organization that managed concentration camps. Even M.M. Warburg, which kept scrupulously away from the Nazi party, took part in the war economy.

Jewish, German and British

Czechoslovakia was dismembered, Poland was under threat, Franco was in Madrid and the German-Soviet Pact had been signed on 29 August 1939: war was coming. On 1 September German troops went into Poland, and through their alliances, France, Italy and Great Britain entered the conflict. That day, Siegmund told his daughter, "Today is a solemn day, you will remember it all your life."

In Britain the carrying of gas masks and national identity cards became compulsory. Income tax increased. There was a major effort to increase farm production. London took on the appearance of a city under siege. Children were evacuated as a safety measure.

A sad awakening from her generous credulity had broken over England [wrote Zweig]. Even the plain uninformed people, whose loathing of war was a mere instinct, began to express embittered ill-humor. . . . Again the light barrage balloons, looking innocent enough like grey toy elephants, began to float over London, again air-raid shelters were dug and gas masks were distributed and carefully examined. The suspense equalled that of a year ago and was perhaps even greater because now it was not a naïve and guileless population but an already determined and angered one that stood behind the Government.[76]

For Siegmund, now a British subject, nationality was not a problem, but his wife, who had regained her Swedish citizenship in 1933, came under government supervision. She did not want British citizenship, which she could have had, because she did not want once again to renounce her original nationality.

The humanitarian organizations—the Central Council for Jewish Refugees and the Central British Fund for Jewish Relief and Rehabilitation—in which Siegmund was very active, no longer had the necessary funds to help thirteen thousand penniless Jews and turned to the British government, now frankly hostile to the refugees. No more British visas were being given to German citizens, except for relatives of German Jews living in a neutral country, or those who were only in transit through Great Britain. Those who were already living in Britain were closely watched by the police even if they had been there for a long time. On 4 September the government ruled that the courts would examine the cases of all Jewish refugees, including those who had become British citizens, and would intern those suspected of spying. The courts divided the refugees into three categories: those subject to internment, those subject to restrictions and those exempt from internment or restrictions. In October 13,000 cases were examined in this way: 186 people were interned, 189 were placed in the second category, among them Henry Grunfeld, and 9,656 were freed. In January 1940, 528 Jews were interned, 8,356 subjected to restrictions and 60,000 exempted from any supervision. About 8,000 were forcibly sent to Canada—among them Eugen Spier, a German Jew who had been living in Great Britain since 1922—or to Australia.

Siegmund himself, immediately after war was declared, had volunteered to work with the secret service or with the ministry in charge of the war economy but was considered suspect and rebuffed. He was furious.

The British attitude to the immigration of Jews to Palestine became just as strict. Despite the opinion of Churchill, who had joined the government when hostilities broke out, Chamberlain limited the admission of Jews to seventy five thousand over five years. In January 1940 a Foreign and Commonwealth Office report depicted illegal immigration into Palestine as "an organized" invasion of Palestine, inspired by political motives." Numerous discussions, aimed at finding somewhere to "put the Jews," took place between the United States and Great Britain. By turns approaches were made to Western Australia, to Eritrea, Ethiopia, Angola, the Philippines, Alaska, Madagascar, the Dominican Republic: all in vain.

The day after the German invasion of the Netherlands—which put an end to the activities of the Dutch International Corporation—Churchill replaced Chamberlain and the Labour party agreed to resume office as part of the new government. One of its first acts was to restrict from residence on the south and east coasts of England all Germans and Austrians aged sixteen to sixty. On 15 May suspect refugees were interned in camps on the Isle of Man and in Manchester. Siegmund had been crossed off the list thanks to his friend Andrew MacFadyean, and

Henry, warned on the eve of his arrest, had left his home at dawn and lived underground in London for four weeks, until MacFadyean could pull strings and gain his freedom.

By the beginning of June the internments were affecting everybody: a member of the Dutch government, a Norwegian general, famous musicians, even German employees of the BBC.

On 22 June 1940 an armistice was signed between Germany and France. From 7 September to 2 November 1940 London was bombed almost every night. Although over 11,700 people were killed, the bombings revealed in the words of Stefan Zweig, "England's profound, repressed power which discloses itself only in the hour of extremest danger."[77]

The journey between Buckinghamshire and the City became less safe, and the train Siegmund took every morning was sometimes bombed.

> During these war years my mother lived through several German bombing raids on London, but nevertheless did not change her serene attitude. What counted for her in this context was her presentiment and her certainty that the war would lead to the end of Hitler.[78]

When the Blitz began there was a need for all-night firewatchers. Siegmund and Henry often volunteered for the task and spent the night in their offices, talking of the war and the future. Not for a moment, at that time, did Siegmund envisage anything other than an Allied victory; with the coming of peace, he thought that Britain should lead a united Europe and relinquish its costly empire. As for himself, he knew his ambition: to create in London what Max had done in Hamburg. Siegmund's children teased him. How could he be watching for fires properly when he talked so much? Years afterward Siegmund and Henry would be nostalgic about those long nights; when they sometimes lacked the time to get to the bottom of some problem, one of them would say, "We need another of those fire-watching nights."

In occupied Europe the descent into hell accelerated for the Jews. At the beginning of 1940 those in Germany were confined to their homes. Every morning they had to report to the local police station. Then after a time they were arrested, assembled together and sent to the death camps, into which the other Jews of Europe were beginning to flow. Who in Germany knew what was happening? By the end of 1940,

Siegmund's favorite author, Thomas Mann, who had emigrated at the same time as he had, declared:

> No one in the world believes that the German people feel proud of the history its despots are making—a miserable charlatanism made of blood and tears. The accursed adventurers who are pursuing the enslavement of the world feel deep within themselves that from today they have lost.[79]

On 15 May 1941 the emigration of German Jews was officially prohibited. On 22 June Operation Barbarossa, the code name for the invasion of the USSR, began. That summer Schacht, who was in contact with the opposition and without official duties, wrote a final letter to Hitler advising him to seek peace as soon as possible.

At the same time, with German atrocities against the Jews of Europe becoming known in Great Britain, public opinion altered and the position of the refugees improved. Most of the internees were freed. Some were even called in to work for the secret service. Siegmund finally managed to start a dialogue with the war economy department, run by Hugh Dalton, and continued to work for the Central Council of Refugees.

In October 1941 he learned that M.M. Warburg & Co. in Hamburg had become "Brinckmann, Wirtz & Co.," that Brinckmann was running it properly, not overzealously though without any particular tinge of opposition to Nazism. Max, when he heard this development in New York, was happy that his name was no longer linked, in any way, with the regime.

On 23 October, on orders from Himmler, the emigration of Jews was effectively forbidden and a trap closed on all the Jews of Europe. Thomas Mann was still exhorting the Germans to wake from this nightmare:

> I know that at the end of these eight years of brutalization, you can no longer imagine Germany without National Socialism. But is it easier for you to picture it perpetuated by the final victory in which he is trying to make you believe? Do you want to be smaller, more cowardly and have less character than other people?[80]

Siegmund helped to erect barriers against German loans in America: none knew better than he the German borrowing networks on Wall Street. Patiently he explained to senior British officials where Germany's friends in America were to be found, and with his connections among American bankers strove to break up the Nazi networks in neutral countries. He may well have remembered the time thirty years earlier, ironically, when his uncle Max had been doing his utmost to persuade America to lend to Germany rather than England.

On Yom Kippur that year, for the first time since his childhood, Siegmund spent part of the day at prayer in a London synagogue. His two children went with him. Both still remember it as a very solemn day.

The City at War: "Cash and Carry"

The City was asleep, emptied of staff called to the colors. The war economy concentrated financial power in the hands of the state. The position of the banks had not been sparkling before war broke out and matters were obviously made worse by the near disappearance of bills of exchange, the suspension of bond issues, the ban on foreign trade and the reduction in lending. Some of the companies completely oriented toward foreign trade, like Brandeis-Goldschmidt, had to cut back operations, and Paul Kohn-Speyer then entrusted the management of these funds to Siegmund.

In order to finance its purchases, Great Britain could no longer count on ample foreign exchange. Her exports to Europe were cut off and she therefore had either to borrow or sell assets. However, the US Neutrality Act prohibited the granting of loans or sale of arms to a belligerent nation, and the Johnson Act of 1934 prohibited lending to a country having defaulted on its First World War debts, as was the case since 1931 with all European countries, including Britain. There were not many other possible lenders: neither the Commonwealth nor neutral countries were candidates.

So Great Britain was able to finance its imports only by selling its gold reserves—still equal to those of the United States—or its foreign assets, valued at £3 billion. These transactions were carried out on the New York market, where all British securities had been physically sent in May 1939. At the beginning of the war the British Treasury had an estimate made of the value of the shares that could be sold, and found to its disappointment that on Wall Street they were worth only £1 billion. Britain had to move fast, as all the countries at war would be hawking their own securities, driving prices further down. In October 1939 a British Treasury office was set up on Wall Street, run at first by Walter Whigan of Fleming & Co., then by John Gifford, a friend of

Siegmund's. At once sales of securities belonging to public or private
entities began, at the rate of £2 million a week. In November Congress
modified the Neutrality Act to enable Great Britain to buy arms, but
without withdrawing the ban on borrowing. Britain had to pay for its
merchandise in cash and transport it on non-American ships. This was
"cash and carry," in which Siegmund would play a major part.

The sale of assets continued. Despite the reluctance of the US
secretary of the treasury, who was preoccupied with the fall of the
market, the Treasury allowed foreign sales to quicken. On 17 February
1940 a first massive, though discreet, sale of British assets produced
£30 million (in dollars). After the fall of France in June, Wall Street
believed that Europe was collapsing, and the stocks of English companies fell on the New York market. For a while, it was then possible only
to sell American stocks or shares in subsidiaries of British companies
operating outside the war zone. But Britain's need for foreign exchange
remained desperate, and the British Treasury sought to convert assets in
every way possible. With everyone expecting a major German attack by
the end of the year, three thousand planes a month had to be ordered for
Britain's defense. It soon became obvious that the reserves were going to
be exhausted by December at the latest. To buy the necessary arms
Churchill then decided to go for broke; he ordered the immediate sale of
all securities and all reserves, including the deposits of the central banks
of Europe, and French, Belgian and Dutch gold, except for the minimum needed to finance the sterling area.[81]

Siegmund quickly understood the advantage of the new "Cash and
Carry" ruling. In May 1940, before anyone else, the New Trading
Company organized a "syndicate" to finance the imports of British
companies. New Trading Company was not a member of the syndicate
but was in charge of administration. Companies (especially those of
medium size) came to Siegmund to put together buying operations in
America, and the syndicate's three associated banks—Hambros, Rothschild and William Brandt—opened the necessary credit lines for them
to pay cash.

With his New York friends—and he had more than any other
financier in the City—Siegmund also undertook to sell to American
industrialists some of the American subsidiaries in London, and British
companies in New York. He even succeeded in selling to some Americans a few office buildings in London—an extraordinary achievement
during this time of the Blitz.

However, the foreign exchange was running out, and in November 1940 London asked the White House to authorize it to borrow dollars in exchange for pounds to be deposited with the Federal Reserve Board. The secretary of state, Cordell Hull, refused. This would be tantamount to America considering the pound a reserve asset; also, it would violate the Neutrality Act. Remembering the aftermath of the previous war, the British were not very keen to incur debt and did not persist.

On 2 December British reserves were exhausted, and Winston Churchill, in "one of the most important letters he ever wrote," sent Roosevelt an appeal for help. "We need ships, planes and arms," he wrote, "and the time is coming when we shall no longer be able pay." On 10 December Jimmy Warburg wrote in the *New York Tribune* that if the law forbade America to lend to Britain, she should give her the amounts she needed, and he campaigned for a positive answer to be given to the British requests. On 1 December Roosevelt replied to Churchill that one "cannot refuse to lend a firehose to a neighbor whose house is on fire," and prepared to authorize loans to Britain. He only insisted that before borrowing anew Great Britain should repay its previous loans and mobilize all her financial resources. Morgenthau, who feared Britain was hiding some of her reserves, insisted that the British assemble all their gold and send it to America. The British agreed. On 10 January 1941, in the greatest secrecy, the USS *Louisville* took on board £42 million in gold that arrived in the United States sixteen days later. However, this concession had a reverse effect. It convinced Morgenthau that Great Britain did not really need the additional help after all.

At the beginning of 1941, still waiting for a concrete reply to Churchill's letter, the desperate British sold in New York the Viscose Corporation of America. According to Siegmund, who was associated with others in this sale, this transaction was worth $120 million. According to the American bankers, it was worth only $75 million. The British Treasury in fact received only $40 million, with a promise to pay a further $14 million later.

As there was a delay in securing American loans, Great Britain also had to hawk around New York, from the beginning of March 1941, British-owned shares in Latin American companies and in Malayan rubber. All these brought the British Teasury around £70 million. Now, apart from the subsidiaries of British industrial companies and the insurance companies, Britain was at the end of her war fund. If something were not done, she would be on her knees.

Meanwhile, what Siegmund was doing was well known in Berlin. On the German radio Lord Haw Haw denounced him as the Jew who was financing the war.

Lend-Lease

On 11 March 1941, to keep the war away from America, Roosevelt decided to make a substantial increase in aid to Britain and pushed Congress to pass the Lend-Lease Act. The idea had first come from Jean Monnet, who with Siegmund Warburg was undoubtedly one of the greatest men of influence of this century. The innovation was this: since America could not lend, she should lease. Britain had only survived the last eighteen months by selling her securities; now she would receive semi-loans and even gifts to buy arms and equipment in America. However, before Lend-Lease was put into operation, a series of negotiations took place between London and Washington. Lord Keynes represented Britain. Congress effectively required that all British assets in the United States should be considered as collateral for the new loans and that all previous loans—i.e. $700 million—should be repaid before the new plan was implemented. In May Morgenthau even suggested to Keynes that he should ask the American government for a loan of $400 million to pay off the earlier British loans. With a presentiment of probable refusal by Congress, Keynes suggested instead that this loan should be granted not by the American government but by the Reconstruction Finance Corporation (RFC) created before the New Deal, which would be more discreet. On 10 June, in order to make this transaction possible, a bill increased the resources of the RFC and authorized it to lend to foreign governments. Thus it was able quietly to lend $425 million for fifteen years to the British Treasury, on the security of British assets in the United States.

The United States intended to prevent the British from profiting from the goods obtained and to prevent them from competing with American products, particularly in Latin America if reexported. They wished to distinguish between supplies destined for the war effort and other supplies for which the Americans expected something in return. Roosevelt asked the State Department to prepare with Lord Keynes a report precisely defining these two categories and proposing certain forms of compensation for the second. He did not really expect money —the Americans did not want to create war debts—but the renunciation by the British of their privileged trade agreements with the Dominions, and their help after the war in establishing a dollar standard.

All these negotiations were very difficult. Communications between London and Washington were slow. In winter it sometimes took six weeks to get a reply to a letter. Keynes noted felicitously, "Friendship and exasperation advanced hand in hand."[82]

The American Warburgs in the War

On 7 December 1941 the attack on Pearl Harbor was not a surprise to everyone. In London the United States' entry into the war was welcomed with both relief and irony. The British had been waiting for this for too long. In New York the investment bankers—Morgan, Kuhn Loeb, Dillon Read—swept aside from public business by the New Deal, came back in force to finance the war economy. The American government awarded $175 billion worth of military contracts and the military-industrial complex developed around the banks. The RFC financed Lend-Lease for the whole of the American economy and spent up to $5 billion. Some people in America, rather sketchily no doubt, identified six financial groupings then in control of the major part of the American industrial economy engaged in the war: the Du Pont group (General Motors, Du Pont, US Rubber), the Mellon group (Gulf Oil, Westinghouse), the Morgan group (United States Steel, General Electric, Kennecott Copper, AT&T), the Rockefeller group (Standard Oil, Chase National Bank), the Kuhn Loeb group (all public utilities) and the Boston group (United Fruit, First National Bank of Boston). Even if this is a simplified list, it does not misrepresent the situation.

At that time the attitude of American capital was not without ambivalence, and its links with Germany remained important. Thus even in 1942 some Americans, acting with French and German nationals, set up a syndicate of banks in Vichy to operate in occupied Europe under the name Société de Crédit Intercontinental. Among these were the Banque d'Indochine, the Banque Schneider, the Syndicat des Assureurs, the Deutsche-Kredit Bank and the French subsidiaries of Ford and IBM. The American government quickly applied pressure, however, and the association fell apart.

The American Warburgs, who now had far less power than their fathers formerly had, made their own contributions to the war effort. While Max was rewriting his diary in the form of memoirs (publication of which the family would prevent), Frederick enlisted in the marines. Eric became one of the few German-born American officers, a lieutenant-colonel in intelligence in the African campaign. Jimmy went to London and worked on propaganda directed at Germany for the Office of Information run by Elmer Davis. He often met Siegmund there and worked with the American ambassadors in London, first John G. Winant, then W. Averell Harriman, as well as with Sir William Wiseman.[83]

Paul, one of Felix's sons, a patron of and dealer in art, who had succeeded his father as president of the Joint Distribution Committee, also passed through London on his way to France. He was later to become assistant to Lewis Douglas, ambassador after Harriman.

Arms against the Empire

From October 1941 talk began about the management of the postwar world. Each American military concession was exchanged for a political concession from Britain.

The British and American establishments were then very much against a monetary agreement, i.e., the idea of organizing financial and monetary exchanges and coordinating economic policies in order to liberalize trade. British company chiefs in particular were very hostile to free trade, thinking that if it developed, America, which was going into a depression, would drag Great Britain down too. They also wanted to retain "empire preferences" and the role of the pound, thinking that two monetary zones should be maintained: one for the pound and one for the dollar.

The two leading monetary plans that were to clash over the next two and a half years were drawn up at the very beginning of 1942. The authors were, respectively, assistant secretary of the US Treasury Harry Dexter White and John Maynard Keynes.

White, in his "Program for inter-Allied monetary action," proposed the creation of two institutions, an inter-Allied fund intended to stabilize exchange rates, and an inter-Allied bank, aimed at assisting reconstruction and the development of international trade. The idea was to link this bank's granting of loans to the establishment of liberal trade and monetary policies. Nothing was said of the mechanism by which the exchange rates would be regulated, nor of the nature of the exchange standard, though it was implicitly admitted that this could only be the dollar, with or without theoretical reference to gold.

Keynes proposed a very different and extremely centralized system. In his "Proposals for an international monetary union," he wrote that the "ideal system would surely consist in the establishment of a suprana-

tional bank which would have with the national central banks a relationship similar to that which exists between each central bank and the
subordinate banks." As far as he was concerned:

> ... this world central bank with a supranational status, escaping the
> gold standard as well as the hegemony of one currency over the others,
> should have all the attributes of a central bank, with a supranational
> currency for settlements between central banks. This bank for central
> banks, known as "the Union" would manage accounts denominated
> in "Bancor," an international currency defined in relation to gold; the
> member countries would receive "Bancors" in exchange for their
> gold; balances would be repaid. In cases where authorized drawings
> were exceeded, the member country would be able to adjust its
> exchange rates in agreement with the Union and would have to take
> the measures of adjustment it recommended.

So began an extensive theoretical debate. But it was already certain that
the American plan, which ensured dollar control of the international
institutions, would be the winner.

On 23 February 1942, two months after the German rout before
Moscow, the British and the Americans undertook in a Mutual Aid Act
to encourage free trade, without explicitly mentioning "imperial prefer-
ence." In April 1942 White unveiled a more specific plan "in favor of a
United Nations Stabilization Fund and a Bank for Reconstruction and
Development (BRD) for the associated countries." For him the fundamental point lay in the limitation of America's obligations as a creditor,
and in its right, along with other creditors, to exercise a veto on any
important decision, particularly in the matter of loans. Constituted by
subscription, the Stabilization Fund would have the power to buy the
currency of any country. It would be in control of the exchange rates at
which transactions would be carried out, and would be able to impose
adjustment measures; an exchange rate should only be altered when this
proved necessary to correct imbalances; only countries with credit balances in gold would be able to benefit from Fund loans. According to
Keynes, this new version of the White plan, though better than the first,
still did not allow enough adaptation of international liquidity, and
again gave too much power to the Americans.[84]

In May 1942 Great Britain had to sell off its shares in the American
armaments industry in order to pay the latest installments on its earlier
loans.

Holocaust, Death of a Friend

At the beginning of 1942 Siegmund moved back to London, to a flat at 23 Fairacres, Roehampton Lane, which he would keep for more than ten years.

By then no one could be unaware that the Jews in Nazi Europe were being wiped out. In January 1942, at the time of the Wannsee conference, which was to decide explicitly on the Final Solution, Thomas Mann said on the radio, "Four hundred young Dutch Jews have been deported to Germany, so that poison gas can be tested on them . . . . But this story seems incredible and in the whole world, many will refuse to believe it."[85]

Siegmund, in the midst of this sea of troubles, was doing as much as he could for the German Jewish Refugees Aid Society; and among so many anonymous deaths, he suffered the death of friends: Harry Lucas died of tuberculosis, Paul Kohn-Speyer also died of an illness and finally Stefan Zweig, who had gone to Rio at the end of 1941, committed suicide in October 1942, shortly before the Allied landing in North Africa. That day, dumbfounded, Siegmund noted privately:

> His idealism did not indicate faith in earthly progress, but the firm belief in the eternal power of irrational forces and values which find expression independently of apparent success or failure in accomplishing good deeds, in artistic creation, and above all in the personality full of greatness and nobility of certain human beings. He was anything but a cynic and yet he had a coldly skeptical realism that is rarely found, even among the most cynical people . . . . This often went so far that, almost intentionally, he would pronounce prophecies in contradiction to his own wishes . . . . He had a dreadful presentiment that we should have to go through a dismal transition period, lasting several generations, before new concepts could be established. His hope was that after a long interregnum of turmoil and chaos, and in the midst of the planned management of new bureaucratic states which he saw dawning, a new cultural model of the individual would manage to emerge, and that this individualism would be at once more realistic and more unyielding than that of the end of the last century.[86]

On 22 January 1943, a week before the defeat at Stalingrad, Schacht was finally dismissed from his post as minister without portfolio and left Germany.

Dollar Peace

So it was that without any Warburg playing a part in it, a new phase in the world economic order was beginning. After the failure of the BIS, inspired by Max, and that of the IAB, inspired by Paul, came Bretton Woods. Siegmund would much later be able to foresee its faults and use them better than any of his contemporaries.

From now on America was unstintingly helpful, lending her allies nearly $13 billion a year. Between March 1941 and September 1945 Great Britain alone received the equivalent of $30 billion—in arms, munitions and foodstuff. Concurrently, the discussion on a future monetary order continued. White amended his plan, though very slightly. In May 1943 he sent a questionnaire to the Washington representatives of forty-six countries. In June 1943, shortly before the American landing in Sicily, unofficial monetary consultations took place in Washington among eighteen countries. In the autumn a meeting of British and American experts only resulted in a vague joint declaration.

In the spring of 1943 the Keynes plan was very badly received in the United States. The *Wall Street Journal* called it "a means of regimenting the world," while the *New York Times* called for "a return to the gold standard, the most satisfactory system ever devised."[87] Soon afterward the American Bankers' Association, also with great reservations about the White plan, said that the creation of "a system of quotas or shares in an international monetary pool which would give indebted countries the feeling that they have the right to credit is unhealthy in principle and raises unrealistic hopes."[88]

Meanwhile, thanks to American aid, the British were gradually rebuilding their gold and dollar reserves to meet growing external debt and to prepare for postwar reconstruction. Their reserves thus went from $40 million in July 1941, the depths of the war, to $1,200 million in winter 1943. They were even able to arrange dollar loans to some of the Commonwealth countries. The Americans then called for increased British participation in the war. On 23 February 1944, as the Russian advance was gathering pace and the Allies were marking time in Italy, Roosevelt wrote to Churchill asking him to reduce British reserves to $1 billion. Numerous discussions took place. British reserves continued to increase, however, reaching $1.6 billion by the time a decision was made for the Allied landing in Normandy.

In March 1944 further Anglo-American consultations took place on the monetary order to be instituted after the war. The idea emerged at a conference intended to set up an International Monetary Fund (IMF).

The British, who had not yet consulted the other Commonwealth countries, dragged their feet. But in April a joint declaration was worked out by British and American experts.

John Winant, the American ambassador in London, then cabled Washington that

> . . . a majority of the directors of the Bank of England are opposed to the agenda of the conference to be held at Bretton Woods. If adopted, it will remove from London its control of world finance and will dethrone sterling as a standard, in favor of the dollar.[89]

At the beginning of May a debate began in the Commons. Keynes's proposals were criticized by some of the Conservative members, who saw in them a return to the gold standard, which they did not want. On 10 May the Commons and House of Lords authorized the government to continue discussions on this basis.

Also on that day the American president of the BIS, who was imperturbably carrying on his supposedly neutral work, said, "We shall continue to keep the institution working so that when the armistice comes, the former enemies will find it an effective instrument."[90]

At the same time, Jimmy Warburg was called on by the assistant secretary of defense to study United States policy toward Germany in the postwar period.

In late May Morgenthau invited forty-four governments, and a representative of Denmark as an observer, to take part in a monetary conference starting on 1 July, with the aim of "formulating concrete proposals for an International Monetary Fund and possibly a Bank for Reconstruction and Development" (BRD). On 15 June, a week after the Normandy landings, a drafting committee including representatives of seventeen countries met in Atlantic City and worked out an agenda for the conference. The Americans, who feared that Keynes would make difficulties over the organizaion of the IMF, kept the offices of conference secretary and chairman of the Fund committee, appointing Keynes chairman of the committee on the Bank. On 26 June the British delegation (led by Keynes) and the American delegation (led by Morgenthau) met to discuss two of the major problems: control of parities and voting rights. The British wanted each country to be able to decide its exchange rate on its own, while the Americans wanted the Fund to control any significant change in parity. Nothing was decided. There was little talk of the exchange standard, which remained ambiguous, though war loans had established the hegemony of the dollar.

On 1 July 1944 the conference opened at Bretton Woods with seven hundred delegates. Morgenthau was elected chairman, assisted by three vice-chairmen—a Belgian, a Brazilian and a Soviet. The official language was English. As expected, three committees were set up: one chaired by White, devoted to the IMF; the second under Keynes, who supported the IBRD; the third chaired by Suárez, a Mexican, studied other means of international financial cooperation. The debates on quotas were heavily attended.

On 4 July public discussions were suspended. The statesman Pierre Mendès-France won a seat for France on the two bodies, but not the voting rights he asked for. In the Bank committee, Keynes rushed the proceedings at such a pace that nobody could really follow them. Then the fate of the standard came into play. The Fund committee decided that exchange rates should be expressed in gold or "in a currency convertible as of July 1st, 1944." However, the dollar was the only currency to be convertible at that date. This decision was pushed through, the American delegate having presented this draft as "insignificant," whereas in fact it was a recognition of the dollar standard. On 12 July at the request of a British delegate, but against the instructions of Keynes, the phrase "currency convertible into gold" was changed in the final text to "currency convertible into gold or into US dollars." This fundamental change was not repeated in the ninety-six page document signed by the delegates but reappeared in the text submitted for the approval of the various governments, which had been drawn up by the Americans alone.

So the dollar standard was born in ambiguity. As Michel Aglietta writes, ". . . political sovereignty took the place of religious transcendence. Convertibility came down from its pedestal. It became at the same time a commodity and a problem."[91] In sum, because the British and Americans rejected the idea of a balance of responsibility between countries in surplus and those in deficit, they ended up reducing almost to nil the control of the new bodies over the internal economic policies of each member nation.

On 14 July agreement was nevertheless reached on quotas. China, Egypt, France, India, New Zealand and Iran put into circulation their reserves. On 18 July it was decided that the headquarters of the IMF and the IBRD should be located in the United States. There was also a decision to liquidate the Bank for International Settlements because of the part it had played in receiving the gold plundered by the Nazis from Europe. This resolution would not be enforced.

On 22 July, at the final session of the conference, Henry Morgenthau declared that the agreements would allow "the money lenders to be chased out of the temple of international finance."[92]

Meanwhile, Schacht returned to Berlin to take part in organizing the plot against Hitler. On 23 July 1944 he was arrested. Miraculously spared, he was sent to Flossenberg concentration camp, and then on 8 April 1945 to Dachau.

These were insane times. Hermann Abs remembers being received on 2 February 1945 by Ribbentrop, increasingly in disgrace, who told him, "I saw Hitler yesterday evening and he told me that if we lose the war we shall place the working capacity of the German people at the service of the Soviets."

In March 1945, with the defeat of Germany imminent, the US Congress backed the Lend-Lease Act only for purely military purposes, and specified that the system should end with the war. On 12 April Roosevelt died. On 23 May, when Churchill asked the king for permission to dissolve Parliament, there was next to nothing left of the Warburg empire.

In Berlin a very few German Jews had actually hidden in plain sight. Hans Petersen had survived. He was still a banker, amid the ruins. Otto Warburg was still working in his Institute and would even have received a second Nobel Prize in 1944, had Hitler not forbidden any German to accept the award. When the Russians arrived in Berlin he was still there; he would later visit the United States, quarrel with his American colleagues and return to Berlin to die.[93]

The first Warburg to go back to Germany at this point was Max's son, Eric. In charge of captured German Luftwaffe officers, he was the first to interrogate Goering, the man who had got the better of Schacht, but whose turn it was now to be powerless.

4

Riches of Peace
(1945–1960)

Siegmund's Ambitions

When the war ended, Nazi terror had accomplished what no other financial crisis, pogrom or war had achieved in over two centuries: wiped the Warburg name from the doors of the world's banks and dispersed the family to the four corners of the globe. Max was living out his last days in New York; Eric, demobilized and back on the banks of the Hudson, was thinking of returning to Hamburg; Fritz was living in Stockholm and his children had joined a kibbutz in Palestine. Of the children of Paul and Felix, only Frederick was still working at Kuhn Loeb with John Schiff; Jimmy was on the university circuit; Gerald was a cellist; Edward was concerned with horses, and Paul with the Jewish Agency.

Siegmund, now forty-three years old, was living in London. Not for one instant did he consider moving back to Germany. Though he did not like everything British, he appreciated this land of affability, courage and rectitude.

His character was full of apparent contradictions: he was elegant but not sybaritic; ambitious but not pushy; a Jew but not a Zionist; an intellectual but not a writer; fascinated by politics but uncommitted himself; enthusiastic but pessimistic. Most of all, though the source of his ambition was not always clear to others, he possessed the "sacred flame."

In contrast with almost all other bankers of his time, it was not money that drove him. He said, with a force that recalled that of his father and his distant ancestors, that as far as he was concerned the love of money was a kind of sexual deviation in the same category as necrophilia:

> Often, when I go around this strange world, I come across people who have a sort of erotic relationship with money—a relationship as passionate as with a woman whom you adore blindly. I find this irrational relationship with money difficult to understand, but it amuses me: the proud feeling of some men that if they want to they can write out a check for a million dollars or two million dollars. In a way it is almost macabre. The older I am [he would say later], the more I feel possessions are a burden rather than an asset. To make one's life simple is for me a supreme urge.[1]

Even so, his tastes lead him toward fine furniture, and the old gold boxes that have always been liked by a certain elite in Germany, and especially, fine books. He held avaricious or selfish people in low esteem:

> I remember I once had to deal with a very important industrialist and a question came up about making a much-needed contribution to somebody in his own family. We had a long discussion and he wouldn't even part with half the sum I thought would be required. I reminded him he had been betting pretty large sums at the gambling casino, and he said, "You know Siegmund, I can do all sorts of things, but to part with money, except for gambling, is the hardest thing for me to do."[2]

Siegmund despised that man. Though he himself would earn large, even huge, amounts, the commissions his business brought in would never be an end in themselves, or a reason for doing business, but merely the by-product—to be mentioned as little as possible—of a successful deal. The money would stay in his firm to make it grow in power and influence and become an institution. Basically, money was for Siegmund what a paintbrush is to a painter: a tool. Neither was power the aim of his ambition. True, he would have liked power in Germany if the rise of Hitler had not blocked his political career, but he knew that a German Jew would never be a minister in Great Britain and, in his view, what was the good of being anything less?

If Siegmund had a declared ambition, it was to do his duty. He often quoted a maxim of his mother's, "Do not believe O child of man that your happiness is in wishes fulfilled; it lies in duty done." He certainly meant to remain faithful to the ancient ethics of his family while he moved in the world of business. He meant to be a man of Justice and Tradition. Much later he would be proud of what a friend said to him on the subject. "Your strength in business is that you don't change your coat when you leave home, you are always the same man." [3]

In these months when the world was adjusting to peace, he set himself three goals: to become the leading banker in London; to take back control of the family bank in Hamburg; and to regain influence in each of the countries where the Warburgs had been great.

To do this he knew that he would have to be ready to reopen the international connections he knew well, and whose postwar significance he would be the first to perceive. "There is no important business conducted for major clients that will not take on an international dimension." [4]

He saw the outlines of a new role for bankers: to help the defeated countries; to lend to medium-sized firms in Britain and, when the time came, to larger firms everywhere. He foresaw that credit and money management would become relatively secondary activities, and that mergers, acquisitions and "syndicated" loans would require the expertise of specialists whom he would gather around him even before such operations became possible.

Between the wars Siegmund had been the ablest of all at managing international state loans; now he saw the era of international company loans arriving. He was the first to predict that American capital would find its way to Europe by routes other than those of rearmament. Having been deeply involved in the Dawes and Young plans, as well as "Cash and Carry" and Lend-Lease, he saw that the postwar development of capitalism would imply a continued movement of capital from the "heart" to the "center," from New York to London; but this time it would go through multinational companies at least as often as through public treasuries. To speed up this movement he had the idea, which had come to him once before in Hamburg, of putting together the advisory, borrowing and placing capabilities of several banks, from New York to Hamburg, via London.

Finally, he set himself a more nebulous goal, the same ambition that all the great Warburgs before him had when politics tempted them: to advise the man in power, to exert over him the influence that Siegmund liked to say was "more important than power, as it emanates from nations as well as individuals"[5] and to attempt to succeed better than his ancestors in bringing about the triumph of reason.

However, a contradiction was woven into the very heart of this plan, one known by all men of influence: influence, even when exerted through finance alone, may mean appearing on center stage and showing oneself to others, which increases the risk of being treated as a scapegoat by those whom one serves. As the postwar period began, he tried to avoid this risk by staying in the background and cultivating secrecy. He refused to be photographed or to meet with the press. "Our clients come to us because they have heard about us from a third party. . . . What counts above all are personal relationships."[6]

"Siegmund" to Some, "Sigi" to Others

Because influence is exercised over men, not inanimate objects, he would work at developing his charm. Those who met him at that time mention his radiance, his affability, the friendly interest of his questions, the precision of his mind, his all-embracing curiosity, his steadfast spirit, his will, his easy manner. The charm of the man went hand in hand with infinite patience and a subtle use of flattery. People who liked to pretend that they knew him now called him Sigi, while to his real friends he was Siegmund.

If anxiety for his own fortune was hardly an incentive, he was already famous for the passion he showed when a client's business, even if small, had not been treated with the requisite attention. Careful to cultivate his relationships like a garden, he wrote a thousand and one letters, just to keep contact. He had a taste for apparently aimless travel and for casual friendships that would prove useful at the most unexpected moments.

Contemporary witnesses speak of Siegmund's charm, brusqueness, obstinacy and bluntness. "A mixture of humility and arrogance" emanated from him, said the French civil servant Paul Delouvrier. When Siegmund wanted something, nothing could distract him from his objective. In his eyes any method could be used to advance his goal, and his tactics did not exclude coaxing, firmness, indignation or anger. His thorough knowledge of men and affairs, and his deep attention to detail enriched his sometimes fierce interventions; he had an acute anticipation of the inner reactions of those with whom he was talking, and a sense of theater that made him a formidable negotiator.

When he got his hands on a deal he thought of nothing else, night and day. He was incomparable in getting around obstacles that blocked his firm's progress. "Failure, even if delivered by an apparently irrevocable event, stimulates his fighting spirit. This is how he has been able to restore a number of situations which would have been lost for other people,"[7] said Pierre Haas, one of those who knew him. This mixture of pugnacity and intransigence was often enough to turn around a wavering client or a dissenting associate.

Siegmund also had a few weaknesses that he knew well and allowed himself to enjoy. He adored above all kindness, and when he met someone "kind" he always overestimated what he could expect of that person.

> He could lose his temper easily, but he had a good heart and was never malicious. He never sacked anyone without finding them a job elsewhere. The best way to be well treated by him was to do two things: make a great mistake and then admit it profusely.[8]

This was said by Charles Sharp, one of his few associates to dare to contradict him in public.

He did have his dark side. He did not value those who did not stand up to him, and he could not bear those who did stand up to him, even showing a refined sadism toward some of them.

His intense curiosity about others, and his acute sense of psychology and the rational led him shortly after the war to an interest in graphology as a means, he said, of "gaining insight into the psychological structure of other people, to find out more about them than years of personal acquaintance or a spontaneous intuitive impression will tell us."[9] He read much of Jung, Freud and the great graphologists. "I learned that the handwriting of a person contains signs of tension that reveal more to the expert graphologist than that person's facial, muscular or verbal expressions tell the rest of us."[10] All his life he would remain faithful to this passion and no associate or friend would escape this sort of examination. For him graphology was a rational element in a wish to know reality better.

He led a very simple life: much business travel; a few friends; ten days' relaxation a year in an English hotel, where he played bridge with friends; and overseeing the education of his children. He also saw much of his mother:

> During the greater part of her stay in England she did not live with her children but stayed in almost daily contact with them. She often

told me one should never forget the different pace of life from one generation to another and that in consequence it was better that older people did not live with others who were appreciably younger.[11]

He did not like dinners or cocktail parties. Once, in New York, he even refused to go to a cocktail party given by his own subsidiary.[12] His life was not devoid of relaxation, and he knew how to exercise his charm elsewhere than in finance.

Although Siegmund admired the British middle class, which had been able to stand fast in the storm, while the German middle class gave way to Nazi delirium, he felt completely foreign to British high society, whose conformity he hated. "My experience of life has shown me that Establishment people are usually mistaken, because they only admire those who are like them," he would note later.[13] His portrait of them is exact, clinical and unappealing. "Most of the important people in the City," he wrote, "are so anxious to avoid any unpleasantness that they will knowingly make blunders, with the sole aim of sparing themselves any conflict."[14] He abhorred the atmosphere of the square mile, riddled with gossip and rumors, "a way of compensating for some sexual deficiency in those people."[15]

The City in turn kept him at a distance and was wary of this barely naturalized foreigner who still spoke English with an accent. His name was famous and the Rothschilds and others gave him some help, but for many people in the Establishment, he was no more than a strange man with haughty demands, odd relationships and strange concepts, whose capital and business were of uncertain origin.

Perhaps he was basically shy—an intellectual too conscious of the power of words to speak of himself or judge others? Reading remained his major passion; outside the bank he read books with a devouring and methodical passion. When he disappeared for a fortnight, refused dinner invitations, isolated himself, waited for a plane in some airport or crossed the Atlantic by boat, he forgot everything and read in English, French, German, Swedish, Latin or Greek, anything at hand—thousands of books, he would say one day with pride. He especially liked biographies and history; he knew most of Balzac, Dickens, Thomas Mann, Goethe and Dostoevsky; and while he strove to stay up to date, he preferred to reread his favorite books, noting in a copy book extracts that he learned by heart and would later use in his letters, notes or speeches.

He did not like to read newspapers and spent as little time as possible doing this. "Reading them leads to a progressive loss of memory inasmuch as people read them with the unconscious wish to forget what they have read as soon as possible," he noted.[16] Yet he did have one strange fixation: the reports of debates in the Commons, which he read every day with relish.

Awakening of the City

In Europe the victors were in almost the same situation as those who were defeated. Britain was bled white. Many of its young men had not returned from the front. Five million homes had been destroyed. Industry had grown old. The country had lost two-thirds of its markets, and its foreign trade earnings had dropped by half. The merchant fleet was down by one-third. The pound, which was worth no more than half its 1914 value, was scarcely used any longer for reserves or transactions. The sterling area had become a debtor to the rest of the world; the Empire had ceased to be a source of profit and had become a liability. London now had to find dollars, rather than create pounds, in order to pay for its imports.

Like the rest of the country, the merchant banks were greatly weakened and limited themselves to buying and placing Treasury bills.

Politics, too, was a *tabula rasa*. The dissolution of Parliament was declared by the king on 15 June while Winston Churchill, who had called for it, was leaving for the Potsdam Conference. The election campaign was bitter. The Labour party called for nationalization of coal, transport, steel and the Bank of England, though not banks in general, and won, to everyone's surprise. On 28 July Clement Attlee, who had accompanied Churchill to Potsdam, became prime minister. Siegmund had two friends in the government: the chancellor of the exchequer, Hugh Dalton, and the minister for economic affairs, Stafford Cripps.

The Bretton Woods agreements were then ratified by the US Congress. On behalf of the Republicans, Senator Robert Taft denounced them because they would oblige the United States to put "all its money in the International Monetary Fund like in a rat hole." The Association of American Bankers for their part were also critical. "[We] are abandoning to an international institution the power to determine the destination and duration of use of our money."[17]

On 11 August the British were informed that Lend-Lease would
come to an end on 20 August and that current deliveries would have to
be paid for:

> The President has ordered the appropriate services in the Administra-
> tion to take immediate measures to put an end to all lend-lease
> operations and notify all beneficiary foreign governments of this
> cessation. The President orders cancellation of all existing Lend-Lease
> contracts.[18]

At this time, Siegmund met with Lord Keynes, who said he was
convinced of a British decline unless Great Britain recovered its trade
balance and obtained massive aid from America. Siegmund was angry
that the great economist would not declare these sentiments publicly.
Britain no longer had the means to pay for its basic imports. At all costs,
she had to find dollars, the only exchange currency now recognized.

A British delegation, led for the last time by Lord Keynes, went to
Washington in October to negotiate further American aid in exchange
for new concessions in economic policy. Writing from Washington on
28 October, Keynes told Dalton what he had told Siegmund shortly
before:

> There is no way out compatible in the long term with the internal
> policy of the present government, other than American aid. The fact
> that some Americans are increasingly conscious of this is in reality one
> of the hidden obstacles we shall meet along our way.

In December 1945 an agreement was reached. America would pay
$650 million to Britain and in addition lend her $3.75 billion at a rate
of 2 percent. Canada on her part would lend $250 million. In exchange,
Great Britain undertook to ratify the Bretton Woods agreements, make
the pound convertible and not use the borrowed dollars to pay its debt
in the sterling area. Keynes had to accept in Washington what he had
worked unceasingly to avoid at Bretton Woods a few months earlier.

The rules of the International Monetary Fund (IMF) came into force
on 27 December 1945. Countries then freely chose their parities, denominated in dollars, almost always overambitiously. The inaugural
meeting of Fund governors took place on 8 March 1946 in Savannah,
Georgia. Lord Keynes was appointed as the British governor, but he
died on 21 April, before the first meeting of the council.

In the course of that year the merchant banks rediscovered part of their role: they again began financing commercial paper, medium-term loans and exports. However, they were still under close supervision. The state, the biggest borrower on the internal market, controlled the issue calendar for British industry just as tightly. Issues intended for the foreign market—the major part of their activity before 1914—were very thin and the management of reserves for Commonwealth countries was increasingly undertaken by banks in those countries. The exception that proved the rule was Hambros, which in 1946 arranged the first loan to a foreign borrower emanating from a British bank. This was for the purchase by a Czech company of raw materials from the sterling area. Britain, now a debtor, could no longer lend money to the rest of the world as before, except by relending the money she received on deposit. Because of the pound's lack of convertibility, government had to reserve these loans for the sterling area. As the dollar was stable and freely convertible, it was the New York banks that took charge of the first loans of capital abroad.

With the loans she received, Britain's economy slowly got going again. In 1946 her exports were 37 percent greater than their 1938 level. The year end was very difficult, however, and 1947 was, as Dalton said, "a dreadful year."[19] In spite of this, on 15 July 1947, in order to respect the agreement signed in Washington when the loan was granted, the pound became convertible. Capital had no confidence in the Labour party and there was an immediate payments crisis. Between June and July withdrawals of gold rose from $75 million to $237 million per week. A month later Cripps gave up, made the pound inconvertible again and strictly limited imports.

Meanwhile the Empire was breaking up. On 15 August 1947 India and Pakistan became independent and the king, who had reigned over 457 million subjects in 1945, now had no more than 70 million. Britain nevertheless continued to finance military bases in a number of its colonies and in Germany, which was very costly. As Dalton said, "the bill we had to pay in dollars to feed the Germans was steeper and steeper,"[20] and this weighed on the British economy.

At the end of the war [wrote Sir Stafford Cripps] we thought that the post war period would be easier than it turned out to be. Since then, we have been trying to get out of this through a series of temporary expedients which as soon as their effects are exhausted, lead to further crises.

In fact in September 1947, in order to hold up the pound, Cripps launched an austerity plan, the first in a long series. No one knows exactly what role Siegmund played in this, only that he saw a lot of the minister for economic affairs at that time and recommended a reduction of the British presence abroad. He also insisted that growth should not be slowed down, that there should be no clinging to an untenable parity, and that a European union should be created. None of this was done and when, in March 1948, the Canadian and American loans had run out, Keynes's prediction of disaster seemed close to realization.

New Trading Company Becomes S.G. Warburg & Co.

Siegmund did not yet have a real bank. The New Trading Company had good clients, and not only emigrants living in London. Siegmund did not have the capital to help either medium-sized British companies or large American companies. In this first postwar year he limited himself to advising his usual clients. His first big postwar deal was in behalf of the Kohn-Speyer family, selling their majority stake in Brandeis-Goldschmidt to Rio Tinto, which had owned a holding in it since the 1920s.

Siegmund himself now wanted to open a real bank and do business in his own name. His name? It had long been understood that there would only be one Warburg bank and that no one in the family would have the right to create another. But that bank was now called Brinckmann, Wirtz & Co.

On this subject there are two unverifiable stories. According to one, in June 1945 the first letter to reach Kuhn Loeb from Germany was a letter from Rudolf Brinckmann to Max Warburg. In essence it said, "Sir, you put your trust in me. I have maintained your bank as well as possible. Now that the devil is dead, the bank [it] is yours if you wish to return. I am holding it at your disposal." Max is supposed to have replied immediately, "How could you believe for a moment that a Warburg would ever set foot in Germany again. Do what you like with what is left of the bank. We will have nothing to do with it." Siegmund seems to have believed this version or at least gave some of the people he spoke to the impression that he took it to be the truth.

According to another more widely held version, there was no letter. Max did not go back to Germany, being fully occupied in trying to get his family's authorization to publish his memoirs—which he did not get—and he died at the beginning of 1946, without asking for or obtaining anything from Brinckmann.

With Max's death the main obstacle to the use of the family name by another banking institution disappeared. It is true that Eric, who was managing the family's interests from New York, wanted to keep the name for himself, but Siegmund did not have the same reverence toward him as toward his father. So he decided to transform the New Trading Company into a real bank and give it his own name, S.G. Warburg. Eric attempted to stop him, but Siegmund replied that there was no longer a Warburg bank in Hamburg, inasmuch as Eric and his father, Max, had let it become Brinckmann, Wirtz, & Co., "a scandal which should be ended as soon as possible." He pointed out that Eric had set precedence by giving his name to a financial establishment in New York before the war, and that nobody was more of a "Warburg" than himself, Siegmund. He was, moreover, ready, he said, to do everything necessary, with his cousin, to restore the name to the door of the Ferdinandstrasse building, and then to bring together the various Warburg banks in Hamburg, New York and now London into one firm, obviously to be named Warburg.

Eric did not reply, but was furious when in October 1946, the New Trading Company became S.G. Warburg & Co. of 82 King William Street.

Return to the United States

Now Siegmund meant to pick up the threads in the other Warburg countries. First in New York, which he had never fully left. Though the war had made communication by telephone and letter more difficult, he had not broken off all contact with Kuhn Loeb. With Sir William Wiseman he had worked to destroy the Nazi financial networks and with John Schiff he had financed prewar operations. At the very beginning of 1946, Siegmund had returned to America and had seen Max just before his death. He had also met with Eric, who was back at the head of his small, personal bank and was a director of about ten companies, but despite the advice of his father and his wife, was only waiting for the right moment to go back to settle in Hamburg.

Siegmund had also seen the other Warburgs again, the Americans who now had no banking influence, or almost none. Felix's house on Fifth Avenue had become the Jewish Museum of New York. Paul's son, Jimmy, with one foot in banking and the other in public life, was still writing books that were ahead of their time; he talked at length with Siegmund about such works as *Foreign Policy at Home*, on aid to the Third World, and *Germany, Bridge or Battleground*. Jimmy subsidized the publication of liberal periodicals. Very anti-Zionist and a Democrat, he would later support Adlai E. Stevenson in his campaigns against Dwight D. Eisenhower. Siegmund had also seen Frederick again, the only one of Felix's four sons working for Kuhn Loeb. Like his father, Frederick was more interested in the theater and the cinema than in the bank and lived in Virginia, where he had inherited his father's residence. To say the least, he would never be a banking colleague of Siegmund's. Frederick's three brothers were leading the lives of peripheral Warburgs: Gerald was a cellist and conductor; Edward, a patron of the arts and philanthropist, had taken over from his father at the head of various Jewish institutions. Paul, who had worked before the war at the International Acceptance Bank alongside his uncle, became a counsellor at the London Embassy and then launched the first humanitarian hospital ship of the postwar period, the *Project Hope*.[21] None of them, as the saying goes, possessed the "the sacred flame."

Siegmund had wanted to see what he could do with Kuhn Loeb, then a bank of enormous power. Most of its work lay in issuing stock for iron mines in Labrador, uranium mines in Utah and companies in television, electronics and photography. Kuhn Loeb did not care for buying and reselling shares and limited itself to arranging the placement of company securities, for which it received fees. It did not place these securities in the same way as before the war, with wealthy individuals, but increasingly with insurance companies and pension funds. Running the firm were some strong personalities. Admiral Lewis Strauss left to become a member and then president of the United States Atomic Energy Commission, but others became executives and then partners: J. Thors, R.E. Walker, and later J.R. Dilworth and J.C. Andersen. Sir William Wiseman, after working for MI5 during the war, was also there.

At the time the senior partner in Kuhn Loeb was still John Schiff, the son of Mortimer and grandson of Jacob. A polo player and sailor, one of the richest men in America, John was a man of widely varied acquaintance, with small interest in business, to which he devoted little time. His aunt said of him, "He grew up in the tradition of well brought up people from Long Island, which from time to time conflicts quite oddly with his German Jewish heritage."[22] His sister Dorothy owned the *New York Post*.

In a New York exploding with gaiety and power in the immediate aftermath of war, Siegmund had also met Berliners like Ernst Spiegelberg, Max's former partner, and Jacob Goldschmidt, former chairman of the Darmstädter Bank.

His first businesss contacts in New York had been unpromising. He did not feel he could work out a relationship with the collection of millionaires at Kuhn Loeb, any more than with Eric.

Nevertheless, he still intended to have a Wall Street presence. On his second trip across the Atlantic, this time with Henry Grunfeld, just after the creation of S.G. Warburg & Co., he set up American European Associates, a small subsidiary of his bank, and took on Ernst Spiegelberg to run it. For years it would place for Siegmund the capital that his clients wanted to invest in America.

First Return to Germany

Germany came out of the war in ruins. In Hamburg, which had been heavily bombed between 24 July and 3 August 1943, and had been taken by the British on 4 May 1945, the Ferdinandstrasse building had remained miraculously intact. Arriving there in 1945 with the American army, Eric Warburg had been pleased to find Rudolf Brinckmann, one of the few heads of German establishments not to have compromised himself with the Nazis. He had kept his post after the arrival of the British. As for Wirtz, death had taken him at the age of thirty-eight. The firm was unable to restart its activities at once. Like the whole of the German economy, banks were then effectively in default. Those in the Russian Zone were liquidated, those in Berlin closed (like that of Petersen, who had survived the Nazi terror) and of those in Hamburg very few were still in a state to function. There was neither capital nor production.

Just as they had thirty years earlier, the ideas of reparations and debt reappeared with postwar occupation. Roosevelt and Morgenthau did not intend to pardon Germany for Nazism and wanted to prohibit her from recovering her influence. "Too many people here and in England," said Roosevelt, "hold to the view that the German people as a whole are not responsible for what has taken place, that only a few Nazi leaders are responsible. That, unfortunately, is not based on fact."[23]

Consequently he decided to reduce the economic power of Germany to a minimum. A secret meeting, held in his office on 8 August 1944, adopted a plan put forward by Morgenthau: to dismantle the Ruhr factories and rebuild them elsewhere, and make Germany a medium-sized power, basically agricultural. A protocol signed in London on 14

November 1944 stipulated that the "commanders-in-chief of the Allied armies will exercise supreme authority in Germany in behalf of their respective governments, each in his own zone and all three jointly in matters concerning Germany as a whole."[24] As the Allied advance went on, German industry was placed under supervision, though the Allies did not always trouble to change the men in charge. So, for example, in March 1945 the International Steel Cartel in Luxembourg was placed under the protection of an American military mission led by Colonel Frank E. Frazer, but Hans Meyer, boss of the Cartel since the beginning of Weimar, was left in his post. In April 1945, when the Ruhr finally was occupied, the American general Staff, in accordance with the Morgenthau Plan, decided to greatly limit reconstruction, favoring the building trades, mining and agricultural operations; destroying the cartels; and excluding Nazis from posts of responsibility.

On the death of Roosevelt, Morgenthau remained in his post and continued to implement his plan. James F. Byrnes, who replaced Edward R. Stettinius, who had himself replaced Cordell Hull, remained Truman's secretary of state. After the surrender, signed on 7 and 8 May in Rheims and Berlin, the Potsdam Conference met on 17 July to decide the future of Germany. By this time, Morgenthau, who understood that Truman was not sympathetic to his plan, had resigned.

The economic interests of the victors were then somewhat contradictory: the Russians and still—to a degree—the Americans wanted to demolish Germany's factories in order to prevent her from regaining a dominant position in Europe. But the British, who needed German steel for their recovery, urged renewal of prewar industrial relationships. The agreement reached at Potsdam provided for the political decentralization of Germany. "At the earliest practicable date, the German economy shall be centralized for the purpose of eliminating the present excessive concentration of economic power. . . . And primary emphasis shall be given to the development of agriculture and peaceful industries," i.e., mining and transport. There was to be centralized management of agriculture, prices and incomes policy, foreign trade, currency, public finance, reconstruction and communications. The manufacture of war materiel was prohibited and chemicals and metallurgy placed under supervision. A Control Commission was set up, comprising the four Allied commanders-in-chief, to make decisions concerning the country as a whole.

The Control Commission met for the first time on 30 August in Berlin. It was equipped with "directorates," each a kind of ministerial department administered by senior Allied officials. "As it was more convenient to govern alone than among four, the zones rapidly became something like independent countries with frontiers that were almost impassable for men as well as merchandise.'[25] The machinery of reconstruction was already working. The Western vice-governors, General Lucium Clay for the United States, Sir Brian Robertson for Britain and General Marie-Pierre Koenig for France, established themselves in Berlin with the official mission of destroying the excessive concentration of economic power. Clay created an economic division headed by General William H. Draper, a banker and former partner in Dillon Read. His first task was to uncover and combat a Nazi plan that was intended to permit, in case of defeat, the repurchase by figureheads of German subsidiaries confiscated in Britain, the United States and Latin America, and the departure abroad of Nazi engineers. In August 1945 General Clay proposed to the Control Commission the preparation of an antitrust law to apply to the whole of Germany. The French and the Soviets agreed at once, and a Russian text was the basis of the discussion. Only the British were against this measure: nothing must reduce the strength of their future suppliers. In spite of them, I.G. Farben, which was implicated in the monstrous economy of the concentration camps, was dismantled in November 1945 into several separate companies.

During the month of August 1945 most of the senior managers of the German economy were interned at Nienburg. Among them was Hermann J. Abs, who had spent the war first as a partner in Delbrück, Schickler, then as director of the Deutsche Bank and I.G. Farben. He stayed at Nienburg only three months, as the French and the British were fighting for his advisory services.

Meanwhile, quite possibly against his father's wishes, Eric returned to the Germany he had just left as a soldier and resumed possession of Kösterberg, which had not been destroyed. Faithful to one aspect of his father's decision—assuming he knew about it—he did not ask for the bank to be restored to him. Rudolf Brinckmann continued to run it amid the ruins of the city.

At the same time Hans Petersen, whose son had disappeared without trace on the Russian front, left Berlin and set up a bank in Frankfurt —at the time no authorization of any kind was required—along with his brother-in-law Richard Daus, a German officer wounded five times at the Russian front, and Hans von Gans, another brother-in-law and heir of one of the families that had founded I.G. Farben.

Reorganization went on; on 18 December 1945 the British military government seized the coal and steel industries in its zone. Two conferences on reparations took place in Paris and London in November and December 1945. As a result, in March 1946 the Control Commission drew up a list of industrial activities the Germans were prohibited from engaging in. It was stupefying: "war materiel, ball bearings, machine tools, tractors, shipbuilding, aeronautics, petrol, synthetic rubber, ammonia, aluminum, broadcasting equipment."[26] Production not exceeding 20 percent or 30 percent of that of 1939 was authorized for automobiles, steel, heavy machinery, basic chemicals, the electrical industry, mechanics and optics—all sectors that were sources of industrial exports. The Americans in their zone decided to encourage only the following industries: "coal, coke, electrical equipment, leather, wine, beer, spirits, toys, musical instruments and textiles."[27] They planned to control production by alloting coal supplies only to companies that followed their instructions.

Despite aid from America and Britain, the economic situation in Germany quickly became untenable and absurd. On the one hand consumption was being subsidized, on the other the growth of production was prohibited. Meanwhile, the four-power discussions on an antitrust law were continuing in the greatest confusion; as the British persisted in their objections, an exasperated General Clay decided in August 1946 to promulgate the law for the American zone alone. However, in Washington, where the Morgenthau plan was gradually being forgotten, it was said that denazification was costing the American taxpayer too much by slowing down German economic recovery, and that, in the somewhat extreme words of J.S. Martin, a senior official in the American occupied zone, "The men who had had undisputed control of the German economy even under the Weimar Republic and had run it so far off the road that only a war and an organized looting program could save it were indispensable."[28]

At the end of August some of the restrictions on travel within Germany were lifted; on 6 September in a speech at Stuttgart, Secretary of State Byrnes limited the mission of the occupying authorities solely to the destruction of Germany's military potential and the revival of its economy. Thus the Morgenthau plan was finally abandoned. The five thousand American zone administrators installed by Morgenthau—mostly senior officials, soldiers and academics—were progressively replaced by American industrialists and investment bankers, then increasingly by Germans. Among the latter were, according to J.S. Martin, who was bitter at being replaced, "many Nazis and Nazi sympathizers who came back into key positions in the economic and administrative life of Germany."[29]

Relieved to see America come around to her way of thinking, Britain rid herself of the German economic burden, signing an agreement in New York to merge her zone with the American zone. This created a dual zone (Bizonid). The draft antitrust law was then buried for good; a law was promulgated in the dual zone that prohibited only "excessive concentration of economic power."[30] It would never really be applied.

That same year Hjalmar Schacht, who had been acquitted at Nuremberg, reappeared in the public arena and put forward a plan for German recovery. He proposed that British and American money should be used to buy minority holdings in German companies and that a European economic union should be set up, with Germany as its center and the Ruhr as its heart. This was not too different from what the European Coal and Steel Community would be in some eyes.

Meanwhile, Germany became one of the main theaters of East-West confrontation. The USSR forced through an agrarian reform in its zone, and the failure of the fourth session of the council of ministers of the four powers on 24 April 1947 marked the real beginning of the freeze in relations between East and West.

Everything then accelerated. On 25 May 1947 an Economic Council was set up in the Western dual zone with fifty-four German members; this gradually reduced the restrictions imposed on the cartels and allowed some of the former executives to return; the subsidiaries of some American companies in Germany—such as General Motors, Singer and International Harvester—began operating again from July 1947. The shortage of coal and steel that was holding back economic recovery in Europe now drove the United States and Great Britain, despite French opposition, to authorize a doubling of German steel production in the Ruhr. Hermann Abs became financial adviser to the Economic Council in the dual zone, and Hugo Stinnes, the brother of Siegmund's friend Edmund, who was still living in Switzerland, came back to take charge of his coal mines. J.S. Martin wrote felicitously, "This was a time when reforms had to be delayed in the interest of recovery and a time when delayed recovery was blamed on reforms. Looking back, it is hard to fix the particular moment at which the transformation took place."[31]

From then on Truman's intention was clear: to reduce subsidies to Germany and strengthen it into a bulwark against the threat of a Soviet expansion in Europe. To do that it was advisable to return the country to independence and put a brake on controls.

Siegmund from London had strongly opposed the initial American attitude. As he saw it, a line should be drawn through the past and Germany should be anchored to Europe to keep it away from Soviet influence. He thought that Germany must become strong again for "without a great Germany there will never be stability in Europe," as he later told the British essayist George Steiner, a confidant at the end of his life. He saw the key to the future of Europe in Anglo-German relations. If Britain and Germany quickly helped each other and built a united Europe, it could catch up to the United States economically.

Siegmund did not confuse the Germany of Thomas Mann, whom he met in Zurich at that time, with that of Himmler and Goering, now dead, or Flick and von Neurath, in prison; and though he persistently decried the nationalism of the German elite that had pushed the working class into dictatorship, he recognized that the country had had only fifteen years' experience as a democracy. As for himself, he felt both German and foreign, a citizen of nowhere, too universal to take sides.

Still, he would never lose the memory of the Holocaust, and shortly afterward he would say to a friend, looking at the crowds in the lobby of a big Frankfurt hotel, "I would rather not know what all these people were doing in Hitler's time."

In February 1948, with the Banque Nationale pour le Commerce et l'Industrie (BNCI), he set up the British and French Bank, the first postwar joint venture between two European banks. At the time he had no connections with France but saw this as a first link with the Continent, a move toward Germany.

The following month he returned to Hamburg for the first time in fifteen years but found very little of "his" country. Berlin and Hamburg were still in ruins. Uhenfels, which had been sold, was deserted. He saw his cousin Gerda, who had returned to join her husband Reinhart Mayer, then prime minister of Baden-Württemberg province. He saw Brinckmann, who was gradually reviving the former Warburg bank, with issues of securities and clever deals financing international trade with the Joint Export Import Agency (JEIA). He also met Eric, increasingly well-established, and asked his German cousin to join him in taking action to have the bank restored to the Warburgs. The plan was in vain. Eric had made his choice: not to alter the course of destiny.

Siegmund, who would spend nearly thirty years of his life trying to regain control of the old firm, was not dissuaded. As soon as he returned to London he made a plea to the British occupying authorities for the bank's return:

> In February 1948, Robert Pferdmenges returned the Oppenheim family's bank to them without hesitation. It was the same for Stein in Cologne, Trinkhaus in Düsseldorf and others in the American zone. Why should Brinckmann in the British zone not do the same for the Warburgs?

Germany was being reborn. In March 1948 the Allied Control Commission was dissolved following Soviet dissent; France then withdrew opposition to unification of the three Western zones; in June a Western conference in London laid the foundations for a Constituent Assembly in West Germany. On 20 June, to counter a flood of forged notes from the East, the Western powers decreed a banking and monetary reform. This was the end of the black market. Dr. Ludwig Erhard became administrator of the Western zone. First the Americans, then the British and the French, put into operation eleven regional central banks, one for each Lander. The deutsche mark was created, along with a federal issuing bank in Frankfurt, the Bank der Deutscher Länder (BDL) to control the issue of notes, fix the discount rates and the reserve requirements of the eleven central banks. The big three German banks, the Deutsche Bank, Dresdner Bank and Commerzbank, were split into approximately thirty lesser establishments, with a chairman appointed by the elected authority in each of the eleven Länder. They were given local names: the Hessische Bank, for example; but in fact each remained under the tutelage of its former center. The Americans offered Hermann Abs the post of director-general of the Bank der Deutscher Länder, with one of Schacht's former assistants as chairman. Because he would not have full control, Abs declined the offer. The Marshall Plan authorities then asked him to reorganize the Kreditanstalt fur Wiederaufbau, which he agreed to do. Shortly afterward, thanks to the support of the future director-general of Midland Bank, Tony Helmuth, then a colonel with the British occupying troops, Abs returned to the management of a reconstituted Deutsche Bank.

The Soviets replied to the banking reform with a monetary reform in their own zone on 23 June, and with a blockade of the Western sectors of Berlin. On 28 June General Clay responded by setting up an air lift that would allow the former capital of the Reich to hold out for the ten months the Berlin blockade was to last.

Abs then went to England to propose to the British that a single central bank for the whole of Germany should be set up in Hamburg. In London he might have been thrown back into prison, except for the intervention of Tony Helmuth and Siegmund Warburg, whom he was meeting after fifteen years' separation. Siegmund spoke to him then of his wish to see the Hamburg firm restored to the Warburgs: a law of restitution now made this recovery possible.

Subsequently Siegmund once again urged Eric to speak to Brinckmann about returning the name and the capital. Brinckmann supposedly replied to the effect that he had once suggested this but Max had rebuffed him. Now that he had revived the bank, he was saying no. Eric refused to exert any pressure on Brinckmann himself. He began to use his Kösterberg house for several months a year with his wife, Dorothy, who was still against permanent return to Germany, and he converted the other houses into rest homes intended for social work.[32]

All the same, the law of restitution did made Brinckmann give some ground, and he returned 25 percent of the bank's capital to Eric as representative of the family. The law obliged him to do no more. Brinckmann kept 20 percent and the Industriekreditbank took the same. Siegmund, who received a few shares and a seat on the bank's board, was not satisfied with this arrangement, which validated the 1938 sale and ratified the loss of the name in exchange for a few shares. Accordingly, he decided that the work he was doing in Germany at that time, for big companies like Daimler Benz, Gutehoffnungshütte (GHH) and Siemens would be done without the services of Brinckmann, Wirtz & Co. Although he went to Hamburg three times a year to attend board meetings at the bank, he realized his few shares could hardly enable him to influence the firm's direction.

Why did the Warburg name not return at that crucial period to the façade of the Ferdinandstrasse bank? The closest and most reliable sources say that this was probably because Eric did not want to do as Siegmund, other family members and many German friends suggested —threaten Brinckmann with an appeal to the occupying authorities or with the creation of a competitive bank under the Warburg name. Many people report hearing him say at this time, "My father would turn in his grave if my family left this building." On 18 May 1949 the assistant secretary of defense John McCloy replaced General Clay as American high commissioner. On 23 May the Federal Republic of Germany came into being. In the East, the German Democratic Republic saw the light of day on 30 May.

John McCloy had worked for Kuhn Loeb's law firm, Cravath, Henderson & Gersdorff, and had come to know Thomas E. Dewey there, as well as Benjamin Buttenwieser, a Kuhn Loeb partner whom he took as an assistant to Berlin. (In turn, Buttenwieser would encourage Eric to return to Hamburg as often as possible in order to help rebuild the city.) McCloy also asked Gert Weismann—who now had changed his name to Whitman—to come and work with him. Whitman, a cousin of Schacht's former private secretary, had known McCloy in the United States during the war. On his return to Germany Whitman signed a State Department document forbidding him ever again to make contact with Schacht.

On 14 August 1949 the first general elections took place in the Federal Republic, and on 15 September Konrad Adenauer was elected chancellor. McCloy then allowed the cartels to re-constitute. On 21 September the Allied military government ceased to act and was replaced by a tripartite commission. The "high commissioners" no longer held sway over the German government and occupation status ceased to apply.

On 1 April 1950 Germany resumed its two-seat membership on the board of the BIS, which had not closed down despite the resolution passed at Bretton Woods. Quite naturally one appointee here was Wilhelm Vocke, chairman of the Bank der Deutscher Länder and future president of the Bundesbank. Someone from the private sector was also needed. Siegmund, asked for his opinion, suggested three names in vain, among them Hermann Abs. He then suggested Rudolf Brinckmann, not because he held him in high esteem, but because he wished in this way to renew the prewar tradition that had given the BIS a close connection with the family bank. Brinckmann was accepted by the Allies. As Siegmund saw it, he was simply taking the seat left vacant by Carl Melchior, nothing more. Nevertheless, by acting in this way Siegmund strengthened Brinckmann's position and would regret it.

The First Dollars for Europe

This time the postwar period began with an abundance of dollars. Though debts were canceled, American currency continued to rain down on Europe, no longer to finance war but to build up the economy. Siegmund remembered his youth. He did not want to see again any reparations, bankruptcies, debts; he dreamed of seeing Britain hold out her hand to Germany, work together with France, help create a unified

Europe of which London would become the hub. He talked of this to everyone he knew in British politics. "In those first five years after the war, he would have crawled on his knees for Britain to agree to lead a united Europe with London as its capital."[33]

His efforts were in vain. Both Conservatives like Anthony Eden and Labourites like Ernest Bevin rejected the plans for economic union put forward by Jean Monnet, who after having organized Lend-Lease was now launching into the reconstruction of Europe. Siegmund saw in this a sign of the inexorable decline of Britain and would later say that "the British budget deficit with the Common Market is the price paid for not having undertaken the creation of the United States of Europe in the first five years after the war."[34]

In 1947 he met George Ball, then still a lawyer, one of the Americans most interested in European affairs, who would become a close friend and one of his main channels of influence in Washington at the time of the Kennedys. Siegmund did his utmost to convince all sides to use American aid to build a united Europe. Then came the Marshall Plan, named after George C. Marshall, who in January 1947 had become Truman's secretary of state in place of Byrnes. On 5 June in a speech at Harvard, Marshall put forward a plan for European reconstruction, which a year later would replace bilateral aid.

On 28 June 1948 President Truman signed the bill authorizing under the Marshall Plan $4 billion in loans annually, and $2 billion in different forms of aid to sixteen countries. The Organization For European Economic Co-operation (OECD), set up six months previously, was to be in charge of managing the distribution.

At the same time, the Bank for International Settlements began to resume its function as an agent for the distribution of American loans in Europe.

"A Religious Agnostic"

Though Siegmund shared with Felix and the other Warburgs a great distrust of Zionism, to the point of sometimes claiming to be anti-Zionist, he nonetheless followed with intense interest the affairs of the refugees he had helped settle in Palestine during the 1930s. The tragedy of the camps had made him a resolute supporter of the creation of a state of Israel.

He conferred with both Chaim Weizmann and David Ben-Gurion in England and did his utmost to persuade those he knew among British leaders to allow the survivors of the Holocaust to enter Palestine. This was in vain, as Attlee and Bevin "saw in the Jews the followers of a great international religion, and not a race or a nation."[35]

In August 1945 when Truman, under pressure from the Jewish communities in America, asked Attlee to admit a further hundred thousand Jews to Palestine, the British leader, to gain time, suggested an Anglo-American commission to enquire into the whole problem of Jewish refugees from Axis countries. A year later, in April 1946, the commission recommended that a hundred thousand Jews be allowed into Palestine, and that a binational state be set up. Bevin then tried delaying tactics to keep Palestine under British mandate, postponing the creation of such a state. On 22 July 1946 more than one hundred people died when a terrorist bomb blew up the King David Hotel in Jerusalem. With feelings between the Zionists and the British government running high, Weizmann again went to London where he met with Siegmund and asked him once more to put pressure on the British government to support the creation of a Jewish state. Meanwhile, the British referred the problem to the United Nations.

In June 1947 Siegmund received a visit in London that touched him deeply. His two nephews, Fritz's children, had been living on the Netser Sereni kibbutz for a year and had come to talk to him of their hopes for a Jewish state. On 29 November 1947 the United Nations in New York voted 33 to 13 in favor of the partition of Palestine. There were ten abstentions, among them Great Britain. The Arab countries then unleashed a war that would end a few months later, in a precarious armistice. On 14 May of the following year, on the expiration of the British mandate, the State of Israel was proclaimed.

Siegmund followed these events with the intensity and reserve of an agnostic, deeply enthralled by Jewish history, and characterized by an abstract attitude to religion, which was the heritage of his German Judaism. During this period God was often mentioned in his personal notebooks. He noted, for example, a phrase that had struck him. "We must be full of gratitude toward God because he never ceases to encourage that continual adventure which is the freedom to lead our own lives," and, "What a distortion of the spirit it is not to see that the affirmation of life and that of God are one and the same."[36]

He often went to Quarr Abbey, near Ryde on the Isle of Wight, to see one of his friends, Paul Ziegler, a German who had become a Benedictine monk. One of Siegmund's friends wrote:

> We often talked about Ziegler and we used to show each other letters we received from him. Because of that, we implicitly discussed religion. I would say that Siegmund was an agnostic with a very religious spirit; by which I mean that he did not believe in an anthropomorphic God, but that he always listened to a higher and watchful consciousness. He always identified with the cause of Judaism as a moral force, but he never hesitated to oppose the government of Israel when he thought its policy too nationalistic.[37]

Siegmund continued to prove himself a citizen of the world. He was moved to tears of happiness when on 27 September 1951 Konrad Adenauer, in a statement to the Bundestag, recognized that the war crimes committed in the name of the German people deserved "material and moral reparation," and when soon afterward the German president, Theodor Heuss, recognized the existence of "collective shame." He followed intently the talks between the Germans and the Israelis that opened in The Hague on 21 March 1952 in a very tough atmosphere, between negotiators who on each side of the table spoke English with a Swabian accent. On 10 September an agreement was signed between Adenauer and Moshe Sharett, then Israeli minister of foreign affairs, for the payment over twelve years of $800 million to the State of Israel and of lifetime pensions to the victims of Nazism. As for the German Democratic Republic, it refused any recognition of Israel or payment of the $500 million she claimed. David Ben-Gurion, who at the time thought that the West Germans would not pay these reparations, asked for a $500 million loan as well.

Siegmund was amused when Hermann Abs told him that, when consulted by Chancellor Adenauer about this loan, he had shown some reservations, but that the chancellor had then said with a wicked smile, "Well, my friend, let me have your opinion in black and white. But make it a positive letter. Then I can send a copy of it to David Ben-Gurion." The letter was of course positive, and the loan was granted.

Nationalizations and Repatriations
During these years, S.G. Warburg & Co. was launching its first operations. First Siegmund gradually bought back the Brandeis family shares

in the mineral separation company. Rio Tinto, which had acquired a majority share the year before, had proven incapable of managing the company properly. Brandeis-Goldschmidt was already a good source of earnings for the bank, notably in the high fees charged for advice and credit transactions.

Starting at that time Siegmund was developing new and avant-garde methods in the unexpected sale of state enterprises to private individuals in Britain or abroad.

This happened primarily at the time of the nationalizations, for which the British Labour party was ill prepared. Emanuel Shinwell, a friend of Siegmund's who had become minister of fuel, wrote in his memoirs:

> I was optimistic enough to believe that after twenty-five years of talking about nationalization at least an outline of a plan would have been available at Labour party headquarters. Nothing existed beyond a few pamphlets for party workers and the public and copies of resolutions passed at party conferences.[38]

Nevertheless, the government decided to move quickly. The easiest nationalization, that of the Bank of England, was carried out in February 1946 without difficulty. Stafford Cripps told the House of Commons at the time that it was a question of putting the law in line with the facts. Other nationalizations were more troubled, because of very combative opposition from company executives, which complicated negotiations on the compensation of shareholders. This gave Siegmund his opportunity. When the shares of these companies were at their lowest, and when everyone was expecting that nationalization would amount to robbery, he guessed that the eventual compensation had to be higher than the current Stock Exchange prices. He formed these companies' shareholders into "syndicates;" the private owners were relieved to allow him to negotiate with the state. Siegmund's guess was correct. When nationalization of the 800 private companies in the coal industry took effect, for instance, compensation amounted to £164.6 million, calculated in 1947 by two High Court judges at a level far above that of the market value of the shares.[39] So Siegmund and his friends controlled a significant proportion of these shares. In the same way, immediately before the nationalization of electricity, he profited from his control of a large proportion of the 195 private companies and the 375 municipal enterprises to be compensated.[40] He acted in the same way in the nationalization of iron and steel, of transport and of the gas industry. He invested the money he earned in his firm, adding young staff members and taking risks in other deals.

This business, which took much of his time at the end of the 1940s, also brought him indirect benefits long afterward. He made contacts in the Bank of England, whom he then kept informed of how he saw the probable movement of the commodity and stock markets. In return he was chosen by the bank as one of the bankers to these new public bodies.

In addition he arranged loans for local authorities and medium-sized British industrial companies whose business the other banks were neglecting. These arrangements sometimes involved four-cornered loans, passing through Sydney and Tokyo.

Siegmund's third operating sector was one that he had made his specialty since the 1930s: the sale to foreigners of shares in companies held abroad by Britons. Convinced like Cripps that Britain should rid itself of its colonial burden at all costs and as quickly as possible, he had the idea in 1948 with Victor Bloch, an Austrian banker he had just hired, of selling to local capitalists some of the British-owned companies that had become too costly to manage from London—an idea combining *haute banque* with sound economics. Over the next two years Siegmund sent Eric Korner to locate capitalists abroad with holdings of sterling earned during the war from their trade with Britain. In this way he sold a plantation and a coffee distribution network, the Brazilian Warrant Company, to Brazilians; a tea company to Colombians; a street car company to Argentinians; chains of shops to Indians and a railway company to Mexicans.

A fourth activity in these early days was the reverse operation: buying back for the British the companies they had sold to foreigners before or during the war. He was the first to have the simple idea of bringing these British securities "home," of repatriating to Great Britain the capital given up to subsidize the war. In this way he brought back to Britain a quarter of the capital of Associated Electrical Industries, bought before the war by General Electric, and found British buyers for the British office buildings he had sold to Americans during the war—that is, for those left standing. Above all there was the huge deal he made in 1950: Jacob Wallenberg, one of the foremost Swedish bankers and head of the Enskilda Bank, who was also a friend of Siegmund's uncle Fritz and of his wife, Eva, asked him to find banks in Europe for a placing of the 20 percent stake in Ericsson that ITT had owned since the Kreuger scandal, but could no longer keep for reasons connected with American law. This was a huge transaction for Siegmund, his first real *haute banque* deal since leaving Berlin. Placing securities for a very large company, whose banker until then had been Kuhn Loeb, and distributing them in the leading European centers would open up for him the financial world of the old continent; this was his first good reason to make contact with the Banque de Paris et des Pays-Bas (Paribas) in Paris, with the Deutsche Bank in Frankfurt and Credit Suisse in Zurich. He was still an unknown; when Ronald Grierson, one of the staff he had just taken on, went to the rue d'Antin (Paribas's headquarters) with the business proposal, he was asked to spell the Warburg name, but the deal was then accepted and Paribas took one-fifth of the total.

Iron Fist

In these years of building and accumulating, Siegmund set up an organization and procedures that were unique for the time. They deserve detailed description, since they were at the root of Siegmund's unique success: he is the only financier to have made his bank an international institution during his own lifetime.

He organized his bank, which still employed no more than about thirty people, around a single obsession: knowing everything. No piece of information was to be wasted, even if apparently useless; no contact must be neglected, even if secondary, for in the long term it could be at the basis of an idea, another contact, a deal. No client was to be considered lost if a transaction could be thought up for him, or a weakness he had not perceived could be shown to him. With this in mind, he turned his firm into a cage, made of glass as he saw it—of iron where the others were concerned.

He and Henry Grunfeld each had an office. Everyone else was grouped in twos, threes or fours in offices according to specialty: money management, loans, financial counselling, mergers and acquisitions, foreign exchange, group administration. Siegmund's cold and restrained office, decorated with a few antiques, was open to all. A red light at the door gave warning if—as rarely happened—he was not available. His lunch and dinner appointments, sometimes even telephone calls, were planned three weeks ahead. He usually lunched, very briefly, at the bank, with a client, an industrialist, a minister, a top civil servant or a writer who was passing through. The other directors also invited contacts of all kinds to the bank's two dining rooms. Some, like Eric Korner, were reputed in the City to have two lunches per day, one at twelve-thirty and the other at one-thirty—it was more fashionable to be invited to the second.[41] The talk was not of cricket or holidays, as at other bankers' lunches, but of markets and products: a guest was always surprised by the host's exceptional knowledge of his company and his competitors.

So that each deal could be known to everyone, it had to be handled by two people, or by four if it was big, even when Siegmund himself was concerned. Every morning the mail was opened by one of the employees who summarized each letter in one or two lines, then combined the summaries in a memo that was distributed to the whole bank. All telephone calls were also logged the same day by those who made them, and all letters before going out had to be countersigned by a second executive and summarized for general use. "Style" was his pride, and the word "elegant" applied to everything done in his firm. Even the internal notes, which he called "yellow bills," had to be written with much more style than those of other leading merchant banks.

As before the war, and as in nineteenth-century Hamburg, every morning at 9:15, when the City in those days was still asleep, the whole staff met to steer the day's course. For thirty minutes, current business was discussed and new business assigned. Siegmund asked precise questions, which were often unexpected and sometimes ironic.

Foreign contacts were treated with the same rigor. Warburg's staff did a lot of traveling. Those who were abroad had to report to Siegmund each day by telephone or coded telegram. When he himself was traveling—his trips were arranged down to the minutest detail several weeks in advance—he had sent to him every day, wherever he might be, two big files in a yellow envelope: one contained the summaries of mail, telephone conversations and the morning meeting, a list of shares bought and sold, the schedules of the main directors of the bank in London or elsewhere, a list of lunch guests at the bank and a review of the British financial press; the other contained a statement of the main accounts and current proposals, thoughts on strategies being worked out and the movement of funds.

In this way the smallest piece of information received by someone in his firm, even if it was not directly connected with business, was passed on to Siegmund. He would know how to make use of it.

"Uncles" and "Adopted Sons"

All this apparently collectively information was in fact made to serve an extraordinarily centralized management style. Siegmund alone ran his firm, with an iron hand and with the assistance of an inner circle of faithfuls whom he brought into everything. They were Henry Grunfeld, Eric Korner and E.G. Thalmann, and who were known as "the uncles," according to Ronald Grierson's quip. Their ambition was to join his great adventure and create a great institution with him. They admired and respected him but expected nothing of him. With them he had a deep friendship, combined with great mutual respect. All were German or Austrian Jews, and naturalized British citizens. All behaved as foreigners in the City, feigning ingenuousness to be able to ask the most outrageous questions. They often spoke German among themselves, sometimes in front of people who did not understand it.

As foreigners they were happy to be admitted, without trying, to worlds from which they should by nature have been excluded. They would laugh among themselves about the British officer covered with medals whom they had to employ after the war to please an important client, but managed to get rid of gently after six months. On leaving, evidently confusing Jews with Nazis, he spoke the magnificent line, "I did not think it would be so pleasant to work with the people I have been fighting against for five years."

Other émigrés apart from the "uncles" surrounded Siegmund. One was Charles Sharp, an Austrian he had met at A.E. Wassermann in Berlin, who had volunteered for the British army and joined S.G. Warburg on its creation to take charge of foreign exchange loans and share issues. Every year Sharp amused the bank with a parody of its senior directors. Another Austrian, Victor Bloch, had as his only task thinking and discussing with Siegmund the opportunities there could be in the future for new services and experimental techniques. Then came a second circle, opened or closed at Siegmund's whim to the best of the postwar recruits, all potential successors, whom he would call his "adopted sons": first Ronald Grierson, then his real son, George Warburg, Ian Fraser, Peter Spira, Eric Roll and finally David Scholey.

Finding and training such people was one of his passions: for him an institution was a team of the best possible men, all working together. He chose them by methods then unknown in the City. This was the first time that the staff of an investment bank was selected not by birth, connections or even education, but because of their originality of mind, intelligence, courage, strength of character, culture, sense of detail and above all their "style" and feeling for the "sacred flame."[42] When a candidate was picked out by Siegmund's assistants—he sent scouts to British universities to interview the best people—he would get the man to talk about literature or politics, not at all about banking. Then he would fire some tough questions at him. "Would you dare to contradict your boss if you did not agree with him?" and "Would you like to be considered a nonconformist?"[43] Many gave the wrong answer. Anyone who gave the correct answers would take the final test, that of graphology.

In this way he assembled some superior people, not hell-bent on profit, but people of style and imagination, who had come from everywhere. At the end of his life, mentioning the changes in recruitment since he had left the bank, Siegmund said, "If I were . . . fifty years younger and went to apply for a position at Warburgs, I think . . . I would have very little chance to be hired. People would say, "This fellow is much too nonconformist, much too eccentric."[44]

An "RAF Mess"

At the end of the 1940s perhaps ten new people joined the fifteen who had been working at Siegmund's side for ten years. The atmosphere, said one witness, was that of an "RAF mess." Working there, said another, "was like being in a chamber music ensemble." Siegmund contributed great drive and superb communication, spending much time personally supervising his staff. "In order to build a good team," he said, "the leader must at the critical moment not only defend but also protect it."[45] So as to instill the "sacred flame" in everyone, and make them more conscious of the business, he applied what he called the "nursery principle." One of the "boys" would write a report, edited by Siegmund before being distributed, of each important meeting. This immense archive, still mostly unavailable, could one day supply the material for a fascinating history of the City.

All this welded his staff into a team with conditioned reflexes. Some who worked there but who did not stay long said it was rather like "unending military service."[46]

It was also like a court, however, with people always around him— in the corridors or in the elevator. Siegmund knew how to alternate demonstrations of affection and consideration, of firmness and gentleness, indifference and fierceness.

> He knew neither pity nor even compassion [said Pierre Haas]. One lapse and one immediately saw his face close. If the fault was judged serious, it closed forever. Average transgressions entailed a period of penitence lasting from three days to three months. For others, he was pitiless, an attitude of permanent suspicion on his part would drive the wrongdoer to resignation within a few weeks or a few months.[47]

When he no longer liked someone, he sent him to a remote office, where the miscreant would find himself with nothing to do; meanwhile, Siegmund would write predictable notes to Henry Grunfeld. "This man is useless, why are we keeping him?"

This trial by fire produced precise, hardworking people who were demanding themselves, with team spirit and yet with a great veneration for the boss.

At the time no other investment bank in the world worked like this. No one else had people fully employed thinking about the business to be done in two years' time and the methods to be used five years ahead. Neither did anyone else have a clear view of the long-term economic outlook. Nobody else traveled to the other side of the world for lunch, merely to establish contact with industrialists who would turn out to be clients only many years later.

The 1949 Devaluation and Afterward

At the beginning of 1949 the British economic situation seemed to be improving. Industrial production was up by one-third and exports by half of their prewar best. These were only appearances, however, as imports had increased by 85 percent in the same time, and the balance of payments had not come back into equilibrium. In the spring the country was once more on the edge of external bankruptcy, and Stafford Cripps was too ill to run its finances effectively.

Britain was not the only country in Europe where things were going badly. The Bretton Woods agreements were hardly in operation before all the countries in Europe were in the grip of the first great monetary upheaval. The parity chosen by each state on joining the IMF was then shown to be unrealistic. Sweden, Norway, Finland, France, Greece, New Zealand, Italy, Argentina, China and Japan all changed theirs. That year Europe had a $9 billion deficit toward the United States, and although the Marshall Plan brought Britain alone almost

$1.2 billion it was not enough to make up for foreign exchange losses. The British payments deficit increased and withdrawals of gold quickened. An Anglo-American meeting at the beginning of September, aimed at reducing the imbalance between the dollar zone and the sterling area, resolved nothing. Surrender was necessary, and Attlee resigned himself to devaluing, the second leader of a Labour government to do so, once again after the parity had been set too high previously by a Conservative government.

On 18 September 1949 the pound sterling was devalued by 30.5 percent and its value fell from $4.03, held since 1939, to $2.805. A number of other countries, whether or not they were European, devalued in turn: the Commonwealth, France, Germany, Belgium, Israel. In Europe only Switzerland did not devalue.

For Britain, this devaluation was a technical success. Stimulating exports and discouraging imports, it improved the balance of trade as well as the balance of payments.

In November Attlee nationalized iron and steel, and brought about an election. At the beginning of 1950 the election campaign was at its height. Labour, the favorite, attacked with imagined nationalizations: some called for the nationalization of merchant banks, brick works, flour mills and margarine factories. A pamphlet entitled "More Socialism or Less," published by the Fabian Society, called for the nationalization of food wholesaling, the automobile industry, life insurance, aircraft engine construction, shipbuilding, port installations, coal distribution, as well as ICI and Unilever.

The election did not produce a clear majority, and with a lead of eight seats, Labour continued to govern but relegated most of the promises in their manifesto to oblivion.

At the end of October 1950 Stafford Cripps, still ill, resigned and Hugh Gaitskell succeeded him as chancellor of the exchequer. Economic policy, to Siegmund's sorrow, remained extraordinarily conventional. Thus at the beginning of 1951 in order to reduce the demand for imports, the chancellor of the exchequer proposed massive savings in the health budget. On 29 April Aneurin Bevan and a young trade minister, Harold Wilson, resigned in protest of these cuts. Wilson then served as an adviser to Montagu Mayer, a wood importing company, and often met Siegmund Warburg, to whom he had been introduced by Stafford Cripps.

Labour had run out of steam, weakened on the right and the left, and a new election in June 1951 brought a large Conservative majority. Winston Churchill became prime minister again at the age of seventy-seven, with R.A. Butler as chancellor of the exchequer. "It does not matter for the moment that you are not an economist," Churchill told him. "Neither was I."[48] One might think that he certainly was not, having reestablished the pound at its 1913 parity in 1926.

A few weeks after the Conservatives' return to power came the first overseas crisis—one that Siegmund had been expecting since the end of the war. The Cairo government denounced the Anglo-Egyptian treaty of 1936 and the Sudanese condominium agreement of 1899 under which British troops were stationed in Egyptian territory. So began events that would end in the disappearance of the international role of the pound.

Meanwhile, Siegmund developed his business with British companies who were as nonconformist as he was.

In 1951 Cecil King, a nephew of Lord Northcliffe, one of the architects of the modern British press, took control of the *Daily Mirror*, where he had been working since the war, with only 4 percent of its capital. Without knowing Siegmund, he chose him as his banker because he had heard it said that Siegmund was outside the Establishment, as he was himself. That same year, Siegmund met Roy Thomson, a Canadian who had just acquired his first newspaper in Scotland. He, too, was to become a client.

At the end of 1951 Britain, like the rest of Europe, needed capital. Devaluation seemed to have succeeded. The trade balance was back in equilibrium; Butler and the governor of the Bank of England reconsidered returning the pound to convertibility after the failed attempt three years earlier. In January 1952 rumors circulating at the Commonwealth finance ministers' conference set off speculation against the pound, forcing Churchill to pull back.

In the long term, however, [wrote Butler] I believe that the decision not to free the pound was a fundamental mistake. The absence of a floating rate of exchange robbed successive Chancellors of an external regulator for the balance of payments corresponding to the internal regulator provided principally by Bank rate. If such a regulator had existed and a floating rate had been accepted, the Conservatives would have been saved some of the uncertainties and indignities of stop-go economics, and Socialists the traumatic experience of a second devaluation.[49]

With the pound nonconvertible, the merchant banks lost their role in the Commonwealth to the Canadian and Australian banks; while control over issues of foreign shares went to the New York banks, which were less expensive than London because of the dollar's convertibility.

In July 1952 General Mohammed Neguib took power in Cairo and called for the departure of the British troops. By the end of the year the British balance of payments was once more in deficit. In 1953, road transport, iron and steel were to be partly denationalized.

Eurobank

Though the Eastern Bloc countries had refused Marshall Plan aid, it was American dollars held in reserve, some in central banks in the East, that would be the first used among European banks. This was the first postwar "Euromoney," far from the carefully marked out paths of Bretton Woods. From this money, created from nothing in the days of the Cold War, would come the debts still hanging over us today. The Warburgs had nothing to do with that situation, but Siegmund was later to make of this currency a formidable means of financing multinational industry.

It was a strange bank that first "diverted" the dollar, the Banque Commerciale pour l'Europe du Nord. Its story is worth telling.

On 30 August 1921 some Russian emigrants who wanted to set up as bankers in Paris bought the Comptoir Parisien de Banque et de Change at 26 avenue de l'Opéra and renamed it "Banque Commerciale pour l'Europe du Nord" (BCEN)—with "Eurobank" as its telegraphic address. Their clients at that time were Russian émigrés who wanted to put their capital into a new place. In spring 1925, when the Herriot government established diplomatic relations between the USSR and France, the bank was in difficulties.

The Soviets wanted to buy a banking establishment in Paris to facilitate trade and financial transactions with France. The creation of a Soviet bank in France would have posed a number of problems, notably because of a still fierce dispute over Russian loans, made at the beginning of the century, that had never been paid back after the Revolution. Moscow therefore decided to buy an existing bank and became interested in the Banque Commerciale pour l'Europe du Nord, where Russian was spoken and people knew about the Soviet Union. The deal was quickly done, and the bank passed from the hands of the White Russians to those of the Soviets, who kept most of its staff. Until the war came the bank managed what small trade there was between the USSR and France.

After the invasion of Russia by the Germans in June 1941 the bank was closed by the occupying power and a sequestrator was appointed. Reopening in 1946 at new Paris headquarters, 21 rue de l'Arcade, it developed hardly any financial activity in France (and it remained impossible for a French bank to establish itself in the USSR). BCEN therefore concentrated on international trade on behalf of Eastern countries, selling Bulgarian or Rumanian gold to the Bank of France, the Union Bank of Switzerland, the Banque de l'Indochine and other banks.

For two years things worked smoothly. The development of barter in Europe and, from April 1950, the creation of a European Payments Union, a substitute for previous bilateral agreements, did nothing to change the nature of the bank's activities.

On 24 June 1950 the Korean War began. Mao Tse-tung's troops, siding with the North Koreans, entered the battle the following year against the Americans, South Koreans and UN forces. It was then that the Eurodollar appeared.

The Bank of China feared that its dollar reserves, which had been on deposit in Western banks since the beginning of the 1930s and had not been repatriated, would be seized. In order to protect these funds against American enquiry, they were deposited with the BCEN and registered in a special account under the name of the National Bank of Hungary. The Chinese began by placing $5 million there for six months. Then came a notable—though at first marginal—innovation. The bank, eager to get rid of these dollars to protect them better, redeposited them at low rates with the BNCI, Banque de l'Union Parisienne (BUP) and the Bank of America. This transaction was partly renewed for six months more, then extended. Good came of this for the Chinese. As soon as they entered the Korean War, their funds still in other banks, such as the Banque de l'Indochine, were seized at the request of the American authorities.

So for the first time a dollar transaction took place outside the United States without being subject either to American banking regulations or to American interest rates. Also, unless they were used by the borrower to withdraw gold or pay a debt in the United States, these were dollars created ex nihilo, without reducing the American money supply and without limit, since the banks that received the dollars were able to relend them without even keeping a minimum.

This first erasure in the text of the Bretton Woods agreement was a very ironic business. In the middle of the Cold War it was the state banks of the USSR and China that were making *short-term* loans of dollars to Western Europe to finance its reconstruction.

In a quite different context, another operation that year was considered by some to be the first medium-term loan in dollars, the first Euro-issue. Philips NV issued a medium-term loan of $25 million denominated in dollars on the Dutch market. In fact this loan was not really an issue, since it was reserved for a few shareholders who were identified in advance. The first real issue in dollars outside America—conceived by Siegmund Warburg in London—would not take place for another thirteen years.

During the following year, 1951, the use of short-term Eurodollars grew. Eastern dollars continued arriving at the BCEN. The BNCI, Société Générale and Crédit Lyonnais thus benefited from deposits of tens of millions of dollars; and the BCEN several times helped the Bank of France meet its payments to the European Payments Union. Italy, Belgium, Holland, West Germany and Britain also received hundreds of millions of dollars, marks and Swiss francs from the East through the same channels.

Later, when the Korean War ended on 27 July 1953, Eastern accounts in the United States were freed. Nonetheless, the Eurobank continued to receive most of the Western currency holdings owned by the State Bank of the USSR, took them on sight deposit and lent them again to American and European banks. However, it was no longer the only one to do this, and a number of private banks were circulating among themselves the dollars that resulted from sales carried out in America. The Eurodollar was becoming a currency in general use.

Takeover of Kuhn Loeb

Since the late 1940s Siegmund had gone regularly to the United States, in theory twice a year, on one of the magnificent Cunard liners. His investment subsidiary in New York brought him a few German and British clients whose money he invested in the United States. He felt that times were changing and industrial growth would slow down in the United States, and that it would be useful for American companies and financiers to find outlets in Europe.

He decided to seek out potential clients in New York, and in order to do that, to retake possession of Kuhn Loeb, one of the family banks, then at the pinnacle of its Wall Street success.

The greatest financiers of the time were then vying for the honor of joining the firm. J.R. Dilworth became a partner; and John Schiff was still running this partnership of billionaires who shared profits among themselves without reinvesting the money. It was one of the four biggest American investment banks, with Morgan Stanley, Dillon Read, and Lehman. It sold its financial advice for huge fees, arranged capital increases, mergers and takeovers for the most prestigious companies—from air transport to shipbuilding and railway companies.

At the beginning of 1952 Alvin E. Friedman, a young man who had just joined Kuhn Loeb, was to find himself by chance at the origin of the first business relationship between the American bank and S.G. Warburg. Instructed by the directors of the Hudson's Bay Company—an unusual British public company set up in the seventeenth century by fur trappers, and which by its articles of association had to remain in British hands—to find private shareholders, he proposed to go through N.M. Rothschild in London, whose New York correspondent Kuhn Loeb had always been. Sir William Wiseman, a wartime associate, suggested on the contrary the choice of S.G. Warburg, and his advice was taken. Siegmund then arranged the placing of these shares in the middle of 1952 but found buyers for only a fraction of them.

In that same year, Siegmund was associated in the launch by Kuhn Loeb of a loan on the Swiss market of 75 million Swiss francs for International Standard Electric Corporation. He also arranged, again with Kuhn Loeb, for the sale to a British company, Imperial Gas, of a subsidiary of the Canadian company Gatineau Power Co. And gradually he slipped into the councils and committees of the American firm.

At the end of that year, when General Eisenhower became president of the United States, when McCloy left Germany and when Gert Whitman left Germany to settle in Zurich, Siegmund's takeover in New York was astonishingly swift. By his charm and his exacting ways, he thrust himself upon Kuhn Loeb, and even somewhat neglected his own New York subsidiary.

At the beginning of 1953 John Schiff suggested that Siegmund should take an office within Kuhn Loeb and advise him on all business, American or otherwise. Siegmund agreed, but the regulations of the New York market prohibited him from being a partner in a New York Stock Exchange company, as he was already a partner in a bank. So in November 1953 an executive committee was set up to run Kuhn Loeb, consisting of two American partners and Siegmund—all of equal rank. From the beginning of 1954 he spent several months of the year at the

Drake Hotel in New York, and tried to impose his methods and concepts on the Kuhn Loeb group.

Eighteen months later, on 5 May 1955, an internal memorandum specified that Siegmund be treated as a partner, with the title of "executive director," and spend half the year in New York.

At the time there were in Kuhn Loeb's luxurious building on Wall Street eleven partners, of which the most important were John Schiff, Frederick Warburg, Sir William Wiseman, George Bovenizer and J.R. Dilworth. Siegmund's name appeared in the bank's literature after those of the partners and before those of the signatories, among them Henry Necarsulmer, who was to become a partner two years later and emerge as his worst enemy.

Siegmund was unable to prevent the firm's brochure from minimizing the links with his own firm:

> In Europe, we have recently established a close relationship with S.G. Warburg & Co., while maintaining our other traditional contacts with banks in London and on the Continent. These links have led to our being consulted in the sale of European companies, and in supplying our American clients with maximum aid when investing in Europe.

In spite of the reluctance of the other New York partners to admit it, at that date only the loans Siegmund had arranged could justify such pride.

Mercury Securities and Private Television

S.G. Warburg was from now an active and imaginative little bank, and amazingly mobile. Its profits rose from £40,000 in 1945 to £60,000 in 1948, then to £160,000 in 1951 and £200,000 in 1953. This was still small by City standards, but everything was reinvested in the bank. The directors—Siegmund and the "uncles"—took out only £38,000 a year in total, which was very little compared to the income of the lords of the City and Wall Street, or even to their own profits for the year.

In August 1953, when copper dealing resumed, Siegmund Warburg took an increasing interest in Brandeis-Goldschmidt, which he wanted to concentrate on the production of copper and its by-products. Another company fell into his hands by chance that year. Masius Ferguson, a then very dynamic advertising agency whose chairman was retiring, was up for sale. This purchase, which he hesitated to make, might have seemed absurd on the part of a banker. It would be decisive, however, since it would allow him to introduce himself to a market that would later become significant for him, the media.

For with the help of a few friends, newcomers like himself, such as Lionel Fraser and Cecil King, Siegmund would within a few years become the country's most dynamic banker to the British press and begin to open the way for private television in Europe.

Private television had already existed for some years in New York, Los Angeles and Chicago. The Federal Communications Commission (FCC) had in July 1946 granted twenty-four licenses to radio stations to set up television stations that were supported by advertising. The FCC had then blocked for five years the establishment of any new stations, before authorizing a few hundred additional ones in 1953. European broadcasting was then in the developmental stage. Public television was only just being established in France and Britain. The Conservatives and the British employers saw in private television a chance to oppose the BBC's monopoly. So in January 1953 they produced a White Paper asking for the free play of competition to be favored and for private networks to be set up alongside the BBC. Within the Labour opposition and some other ultraconservative or left-wing circles, there were fears that the privatization of television would strengthen American influence, and in June 1953 a heterogeneous group, from the unions to the lords, launched a campaign against this plan.

At the time the City had little belief in the profitability of this sort of project and was not at all interested. Only Siegmund, at the request of the few friends he had made in the press, took an interest; though he did not himself like watching television, he saw an opportunity to enter a sector of the future. Moreover, Sir Robert Renwick, the former chairman of a nationalized electricity company who had become a stockbroker, was also anticipating a future law and beginning to plan for a private network.

At the end of 1953 the government asked Parliament to authorize the creation of private television stations. In March 1954 the bill was narrowly passed; a public body, the ITA, was placed in charge of building the broadcasting stations and granting licenses. Programs would be financed through advertising and through an annual subsidy of £750,000. An official document would set out standards on the quality of programs.

Siegmund now undertook a reorganization of the bank to have access to the capital market and buy tax-free securities, such as those of Brandeis or Masius Ferguson. He also decided to set up a new holding company and attach to it both the bank and the companies he controlled.

The transaction was quite complex. Siegmund found a very old wagon-leasing company, the Central Wagon Company, set up in the nineteenth century at a time when the banks were refusing to finance the British railways. It had become a subsidiary of British Railways upon nationalization and its wagons were then sold, leaving nothing but cash on the books.

On 1 March 1954 the shareholders of S.G. Warburg bought the company from the state for cash by selling what Siegmund owned of Brandeis-Goldschmidt and Central Wagon. The company was then renamed after the subsidiary of the bank: Mercury Securities. A legal notice was issued at the time. "The directors of MSL believe that the SGW company has a satisfactory income and that taking account of the unforeseen circumstances expect to be in a position to recommend for the current year a dividend not below 8 percent." The board of Mercury was an exact copy of that of S.G. Warburg, with Siegmund Warburg, Gerald Coke and the "uncles," Grunfeld, Korner and Thalmann. The capital of Mercury Securities was then spread among several hands. The biggest shareholder was Rio Tinto, of which Henry Grunfeld became chairman, which sold to Mercury its remaining holding in Brandeis.

Mercury Securities Ltd., only just set up, bought the advertising agency Masius Ferguson, and Siegmund started work with it on a private television project. Two impresarios, Lew Grade and Val Parnell, and an advertising agent, Suzanne Warner, helped complete the arrangement. Siegmund arranged financing in the summer of 1954. The ITA found the plan too angled toward advertising and only granted it a license at the end of 1954, after grouping it with another plan prepared by the journalist Norman Collins with Renwick. Thus was born Associated Television. It was a failure at the start and Siegmund soon afterward arranged a partial buy-out by Cecil King's *Daily Mirror*.

That year the British economic situation deteriorated further. Expansion brought excess internal demand, inflation grew and the beneficial effect of devaluation was at an end. At the beginning of spring 1955 Churchill stepped down in favor of Anthony Eden, who dissolved Parliament on 15 April. In their campaign, Labour limited themselves to demanding the renationalization of steel and transport: it was in vain; power stayed with the Conservatives for almost ten more years.

Family Life—the Death of Siegmund's Mother

Siegmund's family life was running smoothly, and it was clear that he valued his wife's opinion in many matters. In 1954 he moved from the small flat at 23 Fairacres, Roehampton Lane, to much more luxurious accommodations in Eaton Square that he would keep for twenty years.

His son joined the bank as did Milo Cripps, the nephew of Sir Stafford; his daughter left home to study literature at Oxford. A number of Warburgs passed through London at that time: Fritz, who was still living in Stockholm; Frederick, who was living in New York; Eric, who divided his time between Hamburg and New York; and James, who was working to elect Adlai Stevenson to the presidency.

Siegmund's mother, to whom he was very close, was now feeling her age. In February 1954, because of her health, he delayed leaving for America for several weeks and made one of his first trips by plane:

> She would have been quite wounded if she had suspected that I had changed my appointment or travel plans because of her. Obviously the weaker she became . . . the more difficult our goodbyes became on one side and the other. This was why I said to her as a joke on one of my last trips to New York, "You should really take the plane for America with me." There was no delay in the reply, "I would like to, if I did not have so many social engagements keeping me here."

He left, and in April his mother had a serious fall in her room and suffered severe shock and several broken ribs. "She required of everyone who was then at her side a solemn promise that they should not inform me of her state of health."[50]

She did not recover from this accident and died on 25 October 1955. "A particular wish often expressed by my mother in my presence was that no funeral ceremony should be arranged for her . . . . This was the reflection of her eminently modest behavior and her rejection of any show or ceremony."[51] In accordance with her wishes, she was cremated.

A few days after her death, he wrote a long essay on his mother "for those who were close to her. I am writing this in German, since that was her true language, just as her view of the world was impregnated with the art of Beethoven and Goethe."[52] It was from this essay that the extracts above concerning her were drawn.

The IMF Goes into Politics

The year 1956 saw the beginning of the Suez crisis, which would mark the first overt political use of IMF resources. On 26 July, Gamal Abdel

Nasser announced the nationalization and seizure of the assets of the Suez Canal Company. In Britain and France feelings were very heated. The *Times* said, "If Nasser is allowed to enjoy his coup, all British and Western interests in the Middle East will collapse." Simultaneously the position of the pound deteriorated. The 1947 parity had become untenable. The balance of payments deficit was becoming huge and the likelihood of devaluation accelerated the flight of capital. In the month of July alone the gold and foreign exchange reserves diminished by £50 million. A stabilization plan was then decided on and as always it was a plan for recession. For the first time since its creation, the IMF was to be put to open political use by America, and the weakness of the pound would bar Britain from any independent foreign policy. The United States, where Eisenhower was running for reelection, did not want to hear a word about a conflict of any sort with anyone, and was ready to use every means, including a breach of the Bretton Woods agreements, to avoid going to war over Suez. "Great Britain," explained R.A. Butler, "had to show herself extremely sensitive to the American threat to act against the pound."[53]

Twenty-four countries then convened in London from 16 to 23 August to achieve international status for the canal. This was to fail, as Eden, obsessed with the memory of Munich, would not give way. On 29 October, with Guy Mollet and Ben-Gurion, he agreed to an armed incursion into Egypt. On 30 October the British government gave Egypt an ultimatum. On 31 October Franco-British troops landed at Port Said. Eden chose this moment to go to Jamaica for a rest, leaving the government temporarily in the hands of Butler. On 2 November the United Nations called for the withdrawal of Allied troops and the Russians brandished the threat of a third world war.

Since the crisis began, Britain had lost 15 percent of her gold and dollar reserves, and by the beginning of November was forced to ask for repayment of her IMF quota, or a loan, both of which the United States blocked. "I regarded this then, and still do," wrote Harold Macmillan later, "as a breach of the spirit, and even of the letter, of the system under which the Fund is supposed to operate."[54]

Never, in fact, had the European signatories of the Bretton Woods agreements imagined that America would use them as such a means of pressure, although it should have been clear from the way in which the negotiations had been conducted.

Britain and then France finally gave in on 7 November 1956, and on 22 November Butler announced the withdrawal of British forces and the beginning of gasoline rationing. Everything was settled: Europe's colonial ambitions had ended. The pound had had its day. The IMF had imposed the law of the strong.

Entry into the Holy of Holies

As for Siegmund, he continued developing his business in London and New York, not only through spectacular coups but also through some very prosaic business arrangements.

In 1956 the bank employed sixty people, more than half of them executives. It was beginning to have an intriguing reputation. "The firm was well known for playing the part of a sort of catalyst in the City, because of its new ideas, its minutely detailed organization favoring internal communication and its working hours," noted Sharp.[55]

The City still did not like Siegmund, which hurt him. In this closed club he was considered a foreigner, the émigrés' banker.

For his own part, he still did not like some of the behavior of the British elite and in December 1956 noted, "One of the dominant attitudes in the City is tolerance toward mediocrity and pleasure in criticizing the least weaknesses detected in strong personalities." He also loved to quote an anecdote that described that attitude very well. "An Englishman visiting Paris around 1805 glimpsed Napoleon from afar and said, 'You can see at a glance that this man has never set foot in Oxford.' "[56]

He still hated official dinners as much as ever, notably those at Mansion House, to which he was now invited. "You have to dress formally, which is very uncomfortable, and listen to a long speech which you could just as well read next day in the press."[57]

The financial establishment poked fun at his "useless" trips, and at the "unemployed" people gathered in the sort of "syndicate room" that had been seen in a prewar Germany, when no "syndicated" loan yet existed in London. However, they were astonished to see Mercury Securities bring together a whole group of service companies, bought almost haphazardly from bank clients who had died without heirs. The business's pretax profits now amounted to £1 million, or five times as much as in 1951. Siegmund himself continued to draw little money from the bank: some £10,000 a year, the same as the "uncles" and a little more than the executives one step down in the hierarchy.

Siegmund recruited Ian Fraser, a young Reuters correspondent in Bonn who wanted to become a banker. The way he took him on is indicative of the climate then prevailing at S.G. Warburg in 1956.

Nobody in the City wanted the youthful journalist. Sir William Keswick had sent him to Siegmund, who at that point was looking for people with a good knowledge of Europe to develop business in Germany. Siegmund spent a long time talking to Fraser, then introduced him the same day to Henry Grunfeld, E.G. Thalmann, his son, George, Robinow, Grierson, Sharp and Bloch. Fraser was asked all sorts of questions, and at the end of several days of interviews, he was employed at £800 a year.

On 8 January 1957 Anthony Eden resigned for health reasons. Harold Macmillan succeeded him the following day. On 13 May the government decided only to intervene in the Middle East at the request of the states concerned and subject to American support. It did not go so far as to disengage itself from overseas commitments, or to take part in the building of the European community, which became fact with the signature of the Treaty of Rome.

It was at this time that Siegmund was admitted to the "holy of holies." In September 1957 Richard Jessel, a stockbroker friend who with Siegmund had set up the New Trading Company and who was always on the lookout for what was happening in the City, told him that Seligman Brothers, a firm in businesss in London since 1869, and a member of the Accepting Houses Committee since in 1914, was seeking a merger with another bank. It is true that seventeen merchant banks on the Committee must have been used to accepting foreigners—in fact only two of them had not been founded by immigrants—but this was the first time since 1907 that a bank from the City's holy of holies had been on the market. At the time Siegmund learned of this no other buyers had yet declared themselves. The idea fired him with enthusiasm. He would be the first founder of a bank to take his firm onto this Committee during his lifetime. When he met with the Seligman partners, they hardly knew him. Seligman was not the firm S.G. Warburg & Co. usually went through with bills for the Bank of England. Nevertheless, a price was agreed upon, and the deal was settled within four weeks. Seligman agreed that the purchase should be reflected in the title: S.G. Warburg & Co. Ltd. (incorporating Seligman Brothers). Bank of England authorization was also needed, and as there was no other candidate, this assent was easily obtained. By the end of 1957, the firms were smoothly joined. Four Seligman partners stayed on with S.G. Warburg. Two of them, Geoffrey Seligman and his brother Spencer, would remain there until their retirement.

Other than in the City, this incorporation might have seemed unnecessary. In fact it was the key that opened numerous doors in world finance, and the day after the agreement was signed, Siegmund noted, "An opportunity never presents itself twice, and that settles everything."[58]

Dollars from America for Europe: the ECSC

The dollar now was unquestionably the leading currency, even though one-third of world trade was still denominated in pounds and British banks continued to dominate international finance. More than half of bank branches abroad were still British, nearly five times as many in number as those of American banks.

As Siegmund had foreseen, on one side European borrowers now were thinking of seeking dollars on Wall Street, attracted by the lower interest rates, while on the other some American industrialists were becoming interested in buying European companies.

Nevertheless, the great event of 1956 was the appearance on the New York market of the first postwar, long-term, European loans in dollars, a sign of the thaw for free capital.

The first of these was carried out by Siegmund Warburg,[59] in the name of Kuhn Loeb on behalf of the European Coal and Steel Community (ECSC). It was strange that the first big European loan on the New York market should have been organized by a British banker acting for an American bank and on behalf of a body Britain itself had refused to join. The background of this loan is important. It demonstrates the way Siegmund used his powers of persuasion to bring off a "first," which opened the way to a completely new era in finance.

Britain was then explicitly hostile to the faltering steps toward building a European community. In the Commons on 27 June 1950, Winston Churchill, then still in opposition, correctly summed up the almost unanimous state of mind of the country. "With our position as the center of the British Empire and Commonwealth and without fraternal association with the United States in the English-speaking world, we could not accept full membership of a federal system of Europe."[60] Bevin also considered it vital that "the efforts deployed for the organization of Western Europe should not be allowed to replace or hamper the greater concept of Atlantic unity."

So when in October 1950 the French minister of national defense, René Pleven, put forward the idea of a European Defense Community

(EDC), the British approved the principle for others, but not for themselves.

> We do not propose to merge in the European army, [Churchill—prime minister again—told the Commons on 6 December 1951] but we are already joined to it. Our troops are on the spot and we shall do our utmost to make a worthy and effective contribution to the deterrents against aggression and to the causes of freedom and democracy which we seek to serve.[61]

After the conclusion of the EDC treaty in May 1952, Great Britain made a mutual security agreement with this body. When the French Parliament refused to ratify this on 30 August 1954 Eden got Pierre Mendès-France to agree on 28 September that the Western European Union should take in West Germany and Italy and thus serve as a substitute body.

To the distress of Siegmund, who was convinced that the future of Britain lay in Europe, Churchill would keep the same distance from another European project, the ECSC. The treaty, which followed the outline of the prewar Steel Cartel, was signed in Paris on 18 April 1951. It was again Pferdmenges, among others, who negotiated in the name of Adenauer. "One thing is certain," said Harold Macmillan shortly afterward, "and should be faced: our people will never delegate to any supranational authority the right to close our mines or our steelworks."[62]

The ECSC was run by a High Authority, of which Jean Monnet, then commissioner for the French Economic Plan in Paris, was appointed president, as soon as it was set up on 10 August 1952. Siegmund immediately saw its potential and from time to time, without any special reason, visited the directors in Luxembourg.

In November 1954, with the help of the BIS, the ECSC borrowed $100 million from the United States, represented by the Export-Import Bank, in the form of loans to companies within the six countries. In order to negotiate these loans, Jean Monnet and Jean Guyot, his financial director, called on the help of the Lazard Bank in New York and its head, Monnet's old wartime friend André Meyer, as well as on Crédit Suisse.

When Jean Monnet decided to leave the High Authority at the end of June 1955, to be replaced by former French prime minister René Mayer, he left behind quite a different project: not a state loan this time, but $40 million to be raised on the New York market. The idea must have seemed mad. This would be the first big foreign loan since the war to be floated in America and it would be on behalf of a largely unknown quasi-governmental body, which was not a business and lacked a profit motive. Before his resignation Monnet himself had chosen the bankers who would take the lead. To keep to the law that required him to choose American banks, since the borrowing was to be on the New York market, he picked two Europeans well established in that country: André Meyer and Siegmund Warburg, whose family name Monnet still associated with the bank that had arranged most of the German loans in the United States for a century. Monnet did not know Siegmund but had heard of him from John McCloy, Hermann Abs, André Meyer and from all the Luxembourg directors, with whom Siegmund had kept in contact for two years, without immediate benefit.

At the beginning of June 1956, after six months of preparation, René Mayer brought the two bankers together in Luxembourg with two ECSC executives, two exceptional personalities who were to make this body one of the foremost borrowers in Europe. They were a Frenchman, Paul Delouvrier, who had become a financial director of the ECSC after the departure of Jean Guyot to Lazard's, and an exotic character, Ivan Scribanovitz, known as "Scriba," a genius of prewar German finance who in 1942 had become minister of finance in the Vlassov government in Nazi-occupied Ukraine, before resurfacing in Luxembourg in 1950, also as a financial director of the ECSC. Siegmund, like many others in New York and London, did not care for Scribanovitz, and met with him only in the presence of Paul Delouvrier. Agreement was reached on the conditions of the transaction, and André Meyer and Siegmund agreed to undertake the placing.[63]

The venture was most attractive to a proponent of European unity like Siegmund. In 1956 persuading the international financial community that Europe had a future and that the institutions it was setting up deserved to be lent money, was for him a task both of *haute banque* and politics. As this was a dollar loan, however, it could at the time only be placed through a Wall Street bank. When in July he went to unveil the plan to Kuhn Loeb, the partners balked; it was impossible, they said, to place such an enormous loan in behalf of such an untried borrower. Moreover, whoever the borrower or the guarantor, placing such a loan was difficult in itself, since there were no longer the great prewar fortunes capable of taking a significant share of the risk. Siegmund's partners refused to guarantee the placing. For lack of this guarantee, the transaction became even more problematical. By telephone Siegmund then did the rounds of the few holders of dollars in Europe. This was equally disappointing. Nobody wanted to lend dollars in the long term, unless they had prior assurance that someone on Wall Street would be taking a large part of the loan. Siegmund now realized he would be unable to guarantee the loan unless he placed at least 5 percent with a big New York investor. In August 1956 he approached one of the big American savings institutions, the Metropolitan Life Insurance Company, going to see its director-general, Hagerty:[64]

"I propose that you invest $2 million at a good rate of interest, by lending it to the best borrower in Europe, more secure than the British or German Governments since it is guaranteed by all the steel and coal in Europe, the ECSC."

"I don't understand. To my knowledge these ECSC people you talk about don't own any of the coal or steel themselves, do they? They are civil servants in offices. . . . So what are their assets?"

"They do not have any assets in the true sense, but the repayment of this loan will be guaranteed by the tax which the ECSC will levy on European coal and steel. This tax has been the subject of legislation. It is therefore a real asset."

"I am not convinced, Mr. Warburg. For the moment, your ECSC is no more than a piece of paper. I don't see what guarantee you are giving me."

"You will see, Mr. Hagerty. The High Authority of ECSC can be compared with the authority that runs the Port of New York. You know it—it also owns neither ships nor docks, but administers the port and levies a tax to do it. Neither you nor anyone else would hesitate to lend the Port Authority money . . ."

"Give me ten days, Mr. Warburg. I will call you back."

Ten days later Hagerty telephoned Siegmund: "We have thought about your loan here and decided to take $2 million worth of bonds in the . . . what did you say? Port Authority of the ECSC?"

The balance of the offering was placed within eight days.

The loan was signed for in Luxembourg by René Mayer and Paul Delouvrier in the presence of Siegmund on 16 September 1956. Thus was born a long relationship between the ECSC and Kuhn Loeb—ten years later the former would become the main non-American client of the latter. The credit, of course, goes to Siegmund—his formidable contacts and his convincing arguments.

Subsequently, Siegmund continued to meet frequently with the people in Luxembourg, who soon became some of the most sophisticated financial experts in the world.

Personal Unity

At the end of 1956 an amendment in American tax law allowed Siegmund to become a partner in Kuhn Loeb, without leaving his own bank. John Schiff asked him to settle permanently in New York and run Kuhn Loeb with him. Siegmund refused. He wanted to build up his own firm and not work to enhance the name of others. He was happy to run the two firms, but only to bring them gradually under his own control. Moreover, though he agreed to become a partner in Kuhn Loeb, he did so in the name of S.G. Warburg & Co., and not his own name. Ten percent of the shares of one firm were exchanged for the same number of shares in the other, an arrangement that tacitly revealed the weakness of Kuhn Loeb's capital in relation to the strength of its reputation.

At that time Siegmund was the only European banker to be a partner in a New York bank and spent nearly half the year on Wall Street where he was regarded both with curiosity and jealousy. Although that year he was still discreet, he was recruiting his own men for Kuhn Loeb, putting them in place and imposing his methods. He was aiming—through an intermediary, J.R. Dilworth—to control the firm. It would be much more difficult, he knew, to dominate the millionaire partners of Kuhn Loeb than to build up a firm in London with penniless émigrés. By backing Dilworth, he helped to impose his will indirectly.

Siegmund's life became exhausting. In New York he spent his days managing the American business and part of his nights following the London business, studying in his hotel room the daily files he would receive by telex, and to which he would reply the next day. In London his timetable was the reverse, but just as crowded. These arrangements soon proved to be of the greatest benefit, both in making contacts and gathering information. Belonging to the circle of John Schiff's partners opened all doors for him, not only on both sides of the Atlantic but also throughout the world, and his legendary address book became even thicker.

Kuhn Loeb, like the whole of Wall Street, was concerned above all with loans to the big American companies. This was the time when General Motors launched an increase in capital of $325 million, up to then the biggest in American history; a little later, Ford launched one twice that size.

That year, 1956, apart from the ECSC loan, S.G. Warburg carried out another big transaction from New York. With the help of Eric

Korner in London, it launched the first loan on behalf of Austria. The country was then going through a dreadful time. Russia, which had just invaded Hungary, was supposedly thinking of reinstating the zone of occupation its soldiers had evacuated only the previous year. Austria's young secretary of state for foreign affairs, Bruno Kreisky, came to the United States to negotiate loans for the new republic. Understandably, he had difficulty in placing them. Eventually, he contacted Siegmund, who was referred to him by Dr. Grimm, the new chairman of the Vienna Kreditanstalt. Grimm was a friend of Eric Korner from his youth and had encouraged Kreisky's political ambitions after the war. Warburg and Kreisky had breakfast together at Kuhn Loeb, and Siegmund agreed to place the difficult loan. He succeeded and thus gained for the next thirty years the respect, confidence and friendship of the Austrian authorities.

By now Siegmund was almost in real control of Kuhn Loeb, which with Dillon Read and Morgan Stanley, was one of three leading New York investment banks. He was concerned with all its operations, whether in the United States itself, in loans or mergers in electrical equipment, telecommunications, electronics, aluminum, optics, chemicals, transport, oil, capital goods, the nuclear industry, consumer goods, the food industry and textiles—or in loans to governments in Latin America and Asia.[65]

As in London, he took an intense interest in recruitment, devoting considerable time to seeking out the most brilliant young people on Wall Street. Thus he took on a Frenchman, Yves-André Istel, whom he would make a partner a year later. He lost J.R. Dilworth, whom he did not succeed in making managing partner of the firm, and who left in 1958 to manage the Rockefeller money.

In these two years Siegmund arranged, again from New York, other dollar loans in behalf of Jamaica, took part in the placing of issues for ITT, Reed Paper Group and British Aluminium, and set up dollar loans for Scandinavian countries such as Norway and for the cities of Oslo and Copenhagen.[66]

Siegmund, incidentally, noticed that these dollar loans, emanating from European companies or countries, were in fact subscribed for by European lenders, especially the Swiss. This reminded him of the prewar years when he himself had placed in the United States loans intended for Europe and had been able to scoop up dollars circulating on the Continent.

He talked at length about this development to one of his executives, whom he had just called to London: Gert Whitman. This conversation heralded the birth of Euro-issues.

Second Failure in Hamburg

Order progressively returned to West Germany. In 1952 the ten regional banks that had succeeded the Deutsche Bank were grouped into three bodies: one in Hamburg, another in Düsseldorf and the third in Frankfurt. Schacht set up his own bank in Munich again and in 1953 went to the Philippines, Chile and Argentina as an adviser. By the strange force of the law, on 9 January 1953 the BIS and the Federal Republic of Germany came to an agreement that legally testified to the Dawes and Young loans. No doubt the signatories were the last to remember that these amounts had not been paid. In November 1954 von Neurath was freed from jail for health reasons and died soon afterward.

In Hamburg the old firm was still called Brinckmann, Wirtz & Co. and was developing well, under intelligent management. Siegmund continued to try to persuade Eric to finish once and for all with the New York bank E.M. Warburg, which had become E.M. Warburg-Pincus, and join him in insisting that the Hamburg bank be given the family name again. Nothing happened until 1954 when, according to some witnesses, Brinckmann asked Eric and Siegmund to become partners at the same time as his own son, Christian. Though Eric was ready to agree, Siegmund was not. Not only could he not bear another dynasty taking hold in his bank, he could not become a partner if the bank did not carry his name. He countered with the proposal that in exchange for making Christian a partner, Brinckmann restore the Warburg name to the bank. The latter refused and the status quo persisted.

This failure had a deep effect on Siegmund, who spoke to his mother about it before her death:

> I shall never forget the tone of deep conviction in which she replied, "If one turns all one's strength to something, in the end everything comes out for the best." I told her that I often had great difficulty in keeping to such a principle without weakening. She replied with Goethe's maxim, "Hold fast in adversity, never give in and the gods will help you."[67]

Unlike Siegmund, Eric did not long withstand the temptation of returning to Hamburg as a partner. Despite the opposition of his wife and of

Siegmund, he eventually accepted Brinckmann's offer and became a
"general partner" in the Brinckmann, Wirtz & Co. bank, settling in
Hamburg to live, though keeping his bank in New York.[68]

The End of the Pound

On 22 December 1956, one month after the Suez retreat, the money
initially refused by the IMF was mysteriously granted. With Eisenhower
just reelected to the White House and the Hungarian uprising finally
crushed, the United Kingdom received $561 million from the IMF, in
addition to a $739 million loan.

But the pound was not to recover from the humiliation of Suez. At
the beginning of 1957, just as the first British H-bomb exploded and a
White Paper of defense called for a reduction in the armed forces to
reduce the military budget, the pound came under attack. In September
1957 Harold Macmillan obstinately refused to devalue, raised the
discount rate to 7 percent and put a further brake on internal demand.
Monetary stability and the equilibrium of the balance of payments were
thus once more re-established to the detriment of growth. Moreover, in
order to limit the use of its national currency in the sterling area and thus
recoup its debts, the Bank of England asked the banks to restrict the
granting of sterling loans to nonresidents. Although the currency became transferable again the following year, London would never succeed
in recreating a sterling-denominated market. The pound thus tended to
disapear from international trade, though for some time it still had a
presence in Zurich.

Therefore, to continue to play a part in financing international trade,
the banks in the City had to get hold of other strong currencies and
accept short-term deposits in dollars from nonresidents. This short-term
borrowing of dollars was much easier in London than in New York,
where it was possible to obtain only three-month loans, renewable once,
whereas in the British capital it was possible to get an immediate
twelve-month loan, with infinite renewal. The financial genius of the
City was such that it succeeded in keeping control of the world capital
market by agreeing to run it in a currency other than its own.

Other cities were able to contest this role. So in 1958 Paris was still
the center of the Eurodollar market, where transactions, essentially
between banks, did not exceed $500 million that year.

In addition, another factor would quicken the use of the dollar in
Europe. In 1958, the United States, which for five decades had lent to
the whole world without knowing a deficit, saw its balance of payments

slip out of equilibrium. Internal stability and competitiveness were stagnating. The US reacted badly, trying to reduce its lending abroad, instead of increasing its borrowing. Paradoxically, the result was that the dollars already abroad did not return to America but generated lending among multinational banks—that is, the Eurodollar market. Many a catastrophe would follow from this error.

At the same time, interest rates were rising in Europe, and it was advantageous for the dollar to be invested there. Therefore the medium-term loans issued on the American market by American banks were increasingly fictitious. European or multinational companies were only loaned dollars originating with non-American lenders. Wall Street received a 1 percent commission, while the European banks who did all the real work of lending and placing in Europe received only 0.5 percent.

Siegmund Warburg, living in New York as he was for nearly half the year, in constant contact with those who were passing through the city, assimilated the latest financial techniques. Consequently he was the first in London to be able to understand what the American industrialists were trying to do: buy Europe's industry with European dollars. The time of the multinationals had come.

The Aluminum War

The fifty-six-year-old émigré attempted and succeeded in bringing off a great "first" in the history of world capitalism: arranging for a company to be bought up on the Stock Exchange by foreign interests, against the will of its directors. Siegmund succeeded by putting on the table more money than in the whole of the City and by using a strategy that was revolutionary for the capitalism of that time—an appeal to shareholders against directors, to public opinion against institutions. Then began the era of "capital migration" and the emergence of a new generation of bankers that he had been predicting since the end of the war and for which he had prepared his own bank.

After the war, the increased demand for aluminum and the rise of manufacturers in the East meant that the big American firms had to produce for the whole world; to do so effectively, they had to buy companies around the globe. The American companies were Alcoa, established in 1888; Alcan, set up by Alcoa in Canada in 1901; Reynolds and Kaiser's, who depended on military supplies; and American Metal, the American subsidiary of Metallgesellschaft.

In Europe the aluminum companies were relatively small; only Pechiney and Alusuisse were on a world scale. British Aluminium, which scarcely met national needs, was not only small but outdated. Run by two prototypes of the British Establishment, Viscount Portal of Hungerford, former chief of staff of the RAF, a national hero and gentleman to his fingertips, and Geoffrey Cunliffe, son of a former governor of the Bank of England, the company was to become the stake in this great battle. British Aluminium's initial mistake was an investment in Quebec that turned out to be a financial abyss; the price of its shares, spread among a great number of holders, fell over two years from 80 to 37 shillings. It was then, as the Stock Exchange saying goes, ready "to be picked up."

The battle for control of the company began in February 1958. Three companies had their eyes on it. First, American Metal, whose president, Hans Vogelstein, was a friend of Siegmund's from early years in Germany, which he had left at the beginning of Nazism: Vogelstein asked Siegmund to arrange the purchase of British Aluminium through Kuhn Loeb. Even before negotiating, Siegmund snapped up 10 percent of the company's capital on the Stock Exchange for his client. The British board, contacted in April, refused to sell the company to foreigners, and Lazard, American Metal's other banker, advised Vogelstein to give up, which he did.

Siegmund, however, did not intend to drop the matter. In June he bought Vogelstein's 10 percent of British Aluminium—half through Kuhn Loeb and half through S.G. Warburg. About this time Alcoa in turn made contact with the board of British Aluminium, which gave them an equally negative reply. That summer the two Reynolds brothers, Richard and Louis, were also searching for an aluminum company to buy in Europe—if possible a lossmaker for tax reasons. It happened that Louis Reynolds owned a house in Jamaica adjoining that of Sir William Wiseman, who told him in August of American Metal's abortive attempt. Louis seized the opportunity and urged his older brother to buy British Aluminium. Richard Reynolds agreed to make the attempt and asked Wiseman to find him a banker in Britain. Naturally, the reply was, "Only one man is capable of bringing this off and he is Siegmund Warburg."

At the end of August Siegmund, then in New York, met the Reynolds brothers and explained the situation. "You can't bid on behalf of an American company; I tried that and it did not work. I am quite willing to start again, on condition that a British company is brought in as a majority partner." Richard was reluctant. As far as he was concerned, it was all or nothing. He finally gave in. Siegmund then proposed bringing in Tube Investments, a British steel company. He approached the chairman, Ivan Stedeford, who was interested and consulted his own bank, Helbert, Wagg, & Co., Ltd., run by Lionel Fraser, a friend of Siegmund's. Siegmund and Fraser reached agreement at the end of September on a bid of 78 shillings per share, 51 percent from Tube Investments and 49 percent from Reynolds. With Chase they built up the cash reserves—partly in Eurodollars— which would be needed in the case of a price war. And they arranged buying British Aluminium shares on the Stock Exchange with the help of two stockbrokers, John Gilmour and Anthony Lyttleton. The "players," as the press would later call them, were ready to meet the "gentlemen."[69]

Siegmund did not think it would be possible to achieve an amicable purchase. He knew that Lord Portal did not want to sell, especially not to him. He tried, nevertheless, and in September offered him 78 shillings per share for the securities controlled by the groups that supported the board. Portal refused. At the same time, as Stock Exchange rules then still allowed, Siegmund was buying shares anonymously. By 15 October he already had control of 15 percent without too much of an upward trend in the price. The directors of British Aluminium felt the threat coming and were worried. At the end of October, without informing their own board, they asked Olaf Hambro and Lord Kindersley, the chairman of Lazard and also chairman of Rolls-Royce and a Bank of England administrator, to organize a counterattack. This involved having British Aluminium shares bought by Alcoa. After a month of negotiation, in mid-November, Portal sold Alcoa one-third of the capital he controlled for 60 shillings per share, far less than he knew he could get from Siegmund. But in this way he kept his seat.

Then began between Alcoa and Reynolds what the *Financial Times* later called a "fight between two vast empires for a distant province, almost like Russia and Austria-Hungary fighting one another over the Balkans in the old days."[70] Siegmund, informed of the negotiations between Alcoa and Portal at the beginning of November, left for the United States to meet the directors of Reynolds. On Friday 18 November, when he was still there, Portal invited Ivan Stedeford, Joe MacConnel, the managing director of Reynolds, and Henry Grunfeld to St. James's Place, where he received them at four o'clock and offered to buy back what they owned. They refused and offered to buy his shares at 78 shillings apiece. Strangely Lord Portal seemed hurried, as though this proposal, which had already been made to him and he was declining for a second time, left him indifferent. He was in a hurry. He had a meeting at 5:00 with the press. He cut the meeting short and went to announce to journalists the sale to Alcoa of one-third of the capital, apparently without reporting the offer from Tube Investments. "In concluding this agreement with Alcoa," he said, "our company could never have made a better deal." Henry Grunfeld, who had been present secretly at this press conference, tried to telephone Siegmund in New York but could not immediately get through. Stunned and angry, Grunfeld decided to declare open war, putting into action a contingency plan he had previously worked out with Siegmund.

He called a press conference that same evening at the headquarters of Tube Investments, so that the next day's newspapers would cover the two bids simultaneously. He put everything on the table, explaining to the London financial press, which had never been so well treated, that British Aluminium was hiding from its own board a bid of 78 shillings.

> In the language of the City, when Alcoa wants to buy one-third of the capital, it is called "American co-operation" and when Reynolds wants to buy 49 percent it is called "an American wish to dominate." They are selling more cheaply, but keeping themselves to themselves. I therefore state that from now on we are making all shareholders of British Aluminium an offer to buy their shares at 78 shillings . . . . They have only to let their stockbrokers know their wishes.[71]

The next day, 19 November, the British press was full of the affair. Less traditionalist than the City, it immediately chose the side of the "new men" against that of the Establishment. This was a turning point for Siegmund: the press was with him. For years he had been meeting jounalists, simply to talk with them, give them information or listen to them; as a result he would usually be able to count on their support.

On that day the *Financial Times* described Portal as "the author of a putsch against shareholder democracy." He was assailed with questions. Why had he not told shareholders of the Tube Investments proposal? He replied, "Those familiar with negotiations between great companies will realize that such a course would have been impracticable."[72] At the end of ten days of legal proceedings, on Monday 1 December, the Stock Exchange battle began. It would be brief, as the British Aluminium shareholders would soon make up their minds. Alongside the several tens of thousands of small shareholders, a few big shareholders would also make a decision. Siegmund would remember hearing at that time many openly anti-Semitic remarks directed against him, the foreigner trying to sell one of the nation's jewels to foreigners.

On 14 December Siegmund again attacked. In newspaper advertisements he repeated the offer of 78 shillings for each British Aluminium share. On 19 December, to encourage shareholders "not to sell to these foreigners," Portal boosted the price by fixing the dividend for the year at 17 shillings, instead of the 12 decided a month before by his board. The battle hit the front pages anew. Siegmund snapped up all the shares coming onto the Market that he could. On the opposing side Portal tried to do the same. To find the money, his bankers Olaf Hambro and Lord Kindersley gathered around them the fourteen other "gentlemen" members of the Accepting Houses Committee, among them Morgan Grenfell, Samuel Montagu, Hill Samuel, Brown Shipley and Guinness Mahon, to form a buying consortium against the newcomer. On 29 December Portal wrote to all shareholders and appealed in newspaper advertisements for resistance to the Reynolds and Tube Investments offer, "in the national interest," offering sellers the same price of 78 shillings for their shares, and well above the price at which he himself had sold out to Alcoa a month earlier. "We must save British Aluminium for civilization," Portal was heard to say. On 31 December the consortium announced that it controlled 2 million shares, or a little more than one-third of the capital and would now offer 82 shillings for any additional shares.

Siegmund Warburg was annoyed. He intended to win the battle but did not want to break the still tenuous links he had been weaving for fifteen years in the City, and which he had just consolidated by joining the Accepting Houses Committee. On 1 January 1959 he asked for a meeting with Olaf Hambro to find a compromise. Hambros and Lazard took this request for a meeting as a sign of weakness and refused to see him. On the same day Lord Cromer, governor of the Bank of England and patriarch of the most ancient British banking dynasty, the Barings, and the chancellor of the exchequer called on Siegmund at his office to advise him to give up his offer; they informed him that this was also the opinion of the prime minister, Harold Macmillan. Siegmund was furious that his spirit of conciliation should have been taken for weakness. From then on he was absolutely determined to go the limit, feeling again that distaste for British banking he had harbored since 1931. The battle became total.

It was to be short. Siegmund took his bid price up to more than £4 per share. The following day the managers of private fortunes began to sell and chose to sell to Siegmund. On 2 and 3 January he bought 1.3 million shares. By 4 January he controlled nearly 40 percent of the shares. The pace quickened still further in the next few days, and on 9 January Tube Investments and Reynolds were able to announce that they owned more than 50 percent of the capital of British Aluminium. The consortium had lost. The following week Lord Portal and Geoffrey Cunliffe resigned. Shortly afterward the former became chairman of the British Match Corporation. Lord Plowden, chosen by Ivan Stedeford, replaced him.

Though it could be explained by all he had done since his beginnings as a banker, Siegmund's part in the aluminum war had the effect of a thunderclap in the City. So here was what this man could do. From then on it would no longer be shameful to get up early or work late. Finance would cease to be confidentially mentioned in clubs; no management or heir would be safe from a coup d'état. The plush legend of City quality was in pieces, for better or worse.

The war had ended but the wounds were deep. The attacks had been fierce. Anti-Semitism had never been so evident. Lord Cromer remained angry. Lord Kindersley told anyone who would listen, "I will never speak to that fellow again." Twenty years later Siegmund would still relate how jubilant he was that day in January 1959 when, coming out of his office, he saw Lord Kindersley in Threadneedle Street— having hesitated to greet him, he crossed the street to avoid doing so. On 11 January old Olaf Hambro, his former associate, wrote a bitter letter to the *Times* that was published the next day. "It is very unclear why the majority of editors of the press seemed to be against City opinion and openly wrote in favor of the takeover bid." In the same newspaper on the following day a Labour member of Parliament, Anthony Crosland, replied, attacking the consortium: "Their outlook appears to be about as contemporary as the style in which the City is now being rebuilt. Both make one shudder."[73]

Siegmund Warburg then liked to say that "people of quality pardon others more readily than themselves."[74] He probably felt that at that moment there were few people of quality around him. He also noted, "Most of the triumphs of a man in adverse circumstances are triumphs of character rather than intelligence."[75] No one would contest his character.

In a few days Siegmund had thrown down before the eyes of other bankers the winning cards he had been accumulating for years: his network of contacts, his team, his own capacity for work, his daring and especially his insistence on perfectly prepared and executed work. He was the first to have made use of the press against the institutions, to organize companies on a world scale, to jostle elites who were settled in their certainties, and with an ordinary telephone call, move private capital from one country to another and sweep away company chiefs. Suspected until then, as he said himself, "as the Jew, the newcomer, the fellow who had not been brought up in British schools and who spoke English with a foreign accent,"[76] he was henceforward famous and nobody could do anything other than take him seriously.

Deep down, Siegmund himself did not like this at all. From his beginnings he had practiced the virtue of discretion, and this time he had been forced to move to center stage. He who liked to keep his distance now found himself admitted into orthodox circles, which he thought was "the most dangerous thing that could happen to the bank, as it would lead to a propensity for laziness and complacency."

In an obituary printed on 20 October 1982, the *Financial Times* would write on this subject that Siegmund Warburg

> was [at the peak of his career] bitterly resented by his opponents as a gun-toting, parvenu financier. This extraordinary distortion of the truth reflects both the stuffiness of the City establishment in the late 1950s and its isolation from the central stream of international finance.

His associate in the venture, Lionel Fraser, wrote of him in his own autobiography, *All to the Good:*

> I admire Siegmund, not only because of the courage he showed in beginning a new life in this country and making an extraordinary success of it, but also for his almost monastic indifference to ephemeral pleasures, which derived from a highly acute perception of what was fundamental in life.

In the end the wounds were forgotten. Three months later, in March 1959, a friend they had in common suggested a meeting between the adversaries. Siegmund agreed. Olaf did too, on condition that this took place in his office. Siegmund crossed the big partners' room in silence; the giant Olaf met him in the middle. Each was watching for the other's reactions. Olaf moved toward him, put his arm around Siegmund's shoulders and said, "Siegmund, haven't we been awful fools?"[77] Eight months later Alcoa merged with ICI to become Imperial Aluminum. Shortly after that Alcan and Kaiser Aluminum in turn each bought British companies. Olaf Hambro asked Patrick Dolan, a public relations man, to restore his image, which had been much damaged by the defeat. At the time some people would note, not without irony, that Dolan was an American.

From then on Siegmund's role and actions were clearly recognized in the City. On 19 January 1959 the *Financial Times* drew up a balance sheet of the house of S.G. Warburg:

> Behind almost every big transaction in London, one finds the rather mysterious figure of Siegmund George Warburg . . . for him publicity is a kind of blasphemy. His photograph must not appear in the press and has never appeared. However, once the curtain is raised, one discovers a charming, cultivated man whose supreme pride is to have brought together a talented team in the field of banking, industry, accounting and finance. . . . Mr. Warburg also maintains close links with the Continent where his firm was established until he had to flee the Hitler terror.

Siegmund could not resist putting the journalist on a false trail. "At present he has only one ambition left: to retire and enjoy his passion for history and philosophy, perhaps write a book or two . . . ." Naturally he would not do any of this. For it was now that the career of the greatest postwar financier was beginning in earnest.

First Withdrawal

Siegmund was swamped with business that year. He advised Chrysler in its purchase of Rootes, recommended by Lazard; he introduced Ericsson to the British market, arranged loans for the National Coal Board and the purchase by Timken of its British subsidiary.

The *Financial Times* was then able to write of Siegmund that "he specializes in clients with a taste for international business; thus he advises British firms who wish to get a foothold on the New Continent, and also Americans wishing to establish themselves in European industry."

Above all, he arranged the purchase of the Kemsley group by Roy Thomson. In the manner of Cecil Harmsworth King, who had chosen him as a banker in 1955 because he was, like him, a stranger to the

City, Thomson was an outsider. The son of a Toronto barber, he had bought his first newspaper in Scotland six months before. He loved to shock ("My hobby? Balance sheets.") and claimed to be very right wing. He asked Siegmund to help him acquire Lord Kemsley's press empire, which included in particular the *Sunday Times* among twenty-three other properties. Kemsley, a former entrepreneur turned gentleman farmer, lived in the country; he had asked Lionel Fraser, his long-time banker, to find a buyer for 40 percent of his capital. Apart from the shares held by the Kemsley family, 1.5 million were held by the public. The shares were then quoted at £2.2. Kemsley wanted £6. Fraser told him he could not ask more than £4 or £5 and contacted Warburg's, which he knew Thomson had chosen as banker. Siegmund set the price at £4.10, according to the estimated value of the group's potential profits, offering the same price to Kemsley and to the public. Henry Grunfeld then had the idea of proposing to exchange the Kemsley newspapers for the Thomson private television station in Scotland. The transaction went through smoothly, to the advantage of both sides.

By the beginning of 1960 the economic fillip of 1959, which had allowed the Conservatives to win that year's elections by a wide margin, was forgotten. Unemployment reached 2.4 percent, and was as high as 4.7 percent in the north of England. Coal, shipbuilding and cotton were no longer enough to sustain growth. The British Treasury had to borrow another $892 million from the IMF, more than half the amount lent during the year by that body. In exchange, Per Jacobson, Swedish director-general of the Fund, obtained a considerable increase in interest rates from the Bank of England as well as severe cuts in state spending. In Vienna two months later he said:

> Britain has received aid not so as to continue as in the past, but to have time to put her house in order. A change of policy is essential for the future role that Great Britain intends to play in the world. What good would it be if people said, "the British are very nice, but they don't have any money."?[78]

The British government then introduced control of incomes and limitation of credit. Investment suffered at least as much as consumption from this.

Warburg made many other deals the same year. He bought out client companies left without successors: the British Gallup Poll and Heacht, Levis & Kahn, a rubber company. For accounting purposes he gathered them into a subsidiary of Mercury Securities, British Industrial Corporation, bought to take in everything that did not belong either to the bank or Brandeis. Its profits rose to £2.5 million, or forty times as much as in 1948. Siegmund then decided to move the bank's head office, with those of Mercury and Brandeis, into new offices in Gresham Street, just as austere as the others, and to house about one hundred employees there. He had become a master of finance with his company in London and his influence in New York and Hamburg.

It was precisely from New York and Hamburg that he now had to retreat. In New York his protégé Dick Dillworth left Kuhn Loeb after opposition from Henry Necarsulmer, who had himself become a partner. Siegmund saw the beginning of the end of his ambition to control the firm. In Hamburg he had to be satisfied with a compromise. In exchange for the acceptance of Christian Brinckmann as a partner, he managed to get one of his own men, Hans Wüttke, into the bank in a similar post. He had picked out Wüttke, a young director of Mercedes Benz, two years before on one of his visits to Germany.

His personal life also changed that year. His daughter, after teaching for two years in a London school, left to get married and live in Israel. Siegmund himself bought a house at Roccamare, near Grosseto, north of Rome, where he often went to work on his autobiography, though he was to abandon this project soon afterward.

In March 1960 he left the chairmanship of the bank and had the *Financial Times* write that "as a fervent supporter of the Atlantic Community he will be able to devote more time to strengthening the links between Great Britain and the United States on the one hand and the Continent on the other."

In another article on him in the *Times* at this point, he had them write:

Instead of throwing a network around the world like other bankers, he kept apart from Asia and Africa and concentrated on North America, Great Britain and continental Europe. He is the only London banker to be numbered among the partners of a great New York bank.

On 13 June 1960, with the oldest of the two "uncles," Eric Korner and E.G. Thalmann, he actually retired, at fifty-eight, from the executive committee of the bank, giving up the chairmanship to Henry Grunfeld.

The next day the *Financial Times* published a strange article, typical of the indirect confidences Siegmund took pleasure in imparting at the time:

> Although he has spent all his life in banking, he claims to be more interested in history and philosophy than in his own profession. He owns, moreover, a very fine and immense library. He is a modern banker who believes in the importance of proceeding along nontraditional lines. To this end, with his four assistants, he has built up a team of great quality. His conviction that it is necessary to give young people a chance is shown by the fact that along with the two elders of the firm he has retired from the executive committee to devote himself henceforward to the deveopment of links between the United States and Great Britain.

Siegmund wrote at the time in his notebook, "The real object of the vital impulse is to bring the diverse potentialities of the human being to their highest possible level."[79] This, in his view, he had not yet done.

5

Contraband Dollars
(1960-1973)

When the country that originated the currency standard refused the
responsibilities that sprang from it, the idea of a substitute currency
arose. When none was found, the idea of contraband currency germi-
nated and free port activity began. When companies reduced investment and allowed dollars to accumulate, it was the beginning, though as
yet unrecognized, of the crisis that has lasted to the present.

Long before others had thought of it, Siegmund succeeded in
bringing to London the borrowers and lenders of the "Warburg" countries, turning the British capital into a sort of copy of New York, using
all the currencies of the world first as semi-contraband and then quite
openly, in an unfixed place, a market for world money and for dollars
without a home.

The Gold Pool
By the beginning of the 1960s the Bretton Woods system was holding
together only in appearance, its elaborate machinery too fragile ever to
be set in motion. The system had never really been put to the test. The
value of the dollar had not changed since 1934, and that of other
currencies had moved little since 1949. None of what White had
foreseen had happened. Most currencies had remained nonconvertible
or had been timorously freed, dollars in circulation outside the banks

had become more plentiful than the gold that was supposed to guarantee them and the alteration of parities took on such a solemn aspect that its achievement became almost impossible. The American payments deficit no longer served to rebuild Europe's reserves but to feed loans among private banks.

The balance established after the war thus disintegrated without it being possible for new parities to be reached within the Bretton Woods framework. Everyone thought that if one of the leading currencies— primarily the pound—gave in, the others would follow, causing a chain reaction of catastrophe. So nobody moved.

The decade began in Great Britain and elsewhere with euphoria. Harold Macmillan requested the opening of negotiations with a view to joining the EEC, and the pound at last became convertible. But in fact, the pound remained extremely fragile, since the United Kingdom's short-term debts already amounted to several times the value of its reserves, and its balance of payments deficits led to a continual hemorrhaging of foreign exchange. The new chancellor of the exchequer, Selwyn Lloyd, did not imagine, any more than his predecessors had, there to be any other solution than a rigorous monetary policy, a strict budget and an increase in the discount rate and income tax. On 6 February 1961 he told Parliament, "We have to choose between the Charybdis of ease and the Scylla of discouragement."[1] Siegmund would often quote this phrase.

At that time the United States was still benefiting from a big trade surplus, but her payments were in deficit because of the growth of military spending abroad. She allowed foreigners to hold dollars so that they would not demand gold. During those years the US managed not to pay three-quarters of its deficit in gold.

This deficit began to tarnish the reputation of the dollar, and at the end of Eisenhower's term the gold price surfaced again, even becoming a political issue. In October 1960 the gold price rose to $40 per ounce on the London market, and the rise was only stopped by sales of gold from eight central banks. On 31 October 1960 John F. Kennedy had to make a solemn statement that he would not touch the price of gold if he was elected. From that time a fateful course was set in motion. It would not be possible to make use of the mechanism set up at Bretton Woods, for fear of a political tragedy, but things were slowly falling into place so that this would indeed happen.

The dollars that were circulating and multiplying among banks outside America were developing the Euromarket. It had now reached several billion dollars and served all purposes. In 1961 Japan borrowed $1 billion; Italy made use of it to develop its exports and even its internal activities; Singapore and Germany drew on it in turn.

Gradually the idea spread that the dollar would not hold its parity and thus inversely that the gold price expressed in dollars would increase. The first pressures then appeared on the free gold market in London and Zurich. In December 1961, in order to steady the price, the central banks of West Germany, Belgium, the United States, France, Italy, the Netherlands, the United Kingdom and Switzerland decided to constitute a gold pool, managed by the BIS and the Bank of England, declaring themselves ready to sell part of their reserves to prevent the price from rising on the London market. In fact they were already doing this. Another line of defense was erected in the form of a network of mutual support facilities among central banks, intended to make reciprocal loans of gold or dollar reserves in cases of difficulty and withstand short-term capital movements. The IMF also gained the option of acting by borrowing foreign exchange from six central banks. The system immediately went into action to defend the pound, once more under attack.

In February 1962 the same central banks decided to coordinate not only their sales but also their purchases of gold on the London market, with a ceiling price of $35.08 per ounce. On 5 June general agreements on loans between central banks were at last worked out, with the aim of helping countries in crisis by giving them the respite needed to work out a recovery plan.

All this action would stave off the collapse of the system for another ten years, but already it was no longer allowing steady release of the capital the world needed.

S.G. Warburg between London and New York

At Easter 1961 the whole firm, by then consisting of more than one hundred people, moved into new premises at 30 Gresham Street, bought the previous year. Siegmund kept up his tradition of austerity there and as at King William Street refused to have a nameplate at the entrance to the building. This anonymity, he said, was necessary to avoid tempting fate. The bank's annual reports continued to be printed on ordinary paper and were unbound. "I don't believe for a minute that we will ever get one additional client through printing our reports in a more flamboyant way. . . . But I think if I die tomorrow they will start printing on elegant paper," he said later.[2]

He attended the morning meeting less often and contented himself with giving ideas from a distance. That year the New Statesman wrote of him, "It would be difficult to find in New York a success comparable to that of Warburg." The distance did not prevent him from supervising all decisions, involving himself in everything, taking a plane if necessary or telephoning if need be to a bank official or bank chairman to defend his interests.

British business during this time of illusory euphoria was above all a matter of mergers and acquisitions, financial concentration and capital increases. In six years the United States invested $2 billion in Britain. Sometimes two of his clients were on opposing sides and would then fight for his services. In January 1961, for instance, Odhams Press, one of the two biggest British newspaper groups of the time, with the *People* and the *Daily Herald,* was fearful of being bought by its then rival, the group led by Cecil Harmsworth King, owner of the *Daily Mirror.* This was indeed King's intention. To avoid this takeover, Odhams, on the advice of N.M. Rothschild, tried to merge with another smaller group, that of Roy Thomson, who, as well as the *Sunday Times,* owned fourteen dailies in Britain and eighty newspapers in the rest of the world. Thomson, interested, quite naturally asked Siegmund to help arrange the transaction. Cecil King, informed by some of the Odhams shareholders of what was happening, decided to rush the purchase of the group through, and also asked Warburg to help. Siegmund then had to choose between two old clients and gave preference to King, whom he had known two years longer than Thomson. Thomson took this very well and called on another great London banker of the time, Kenneth Keith, who was running Philip Hill Higginson.

The fight was rough. Once more Henry Grunfeld led the operation for S.G. Warburg. Lionel Fraser was to write in his memoirs that in this business, "Financial blood, newspaper blood, labor blood was spilled." In eight days the Odhams shares rose from 40 to 64 shillings. To the great astonishment of parliamentary circles, the prime minister and the directors of Odhams themselves, it was Cecil King who won, adding the biggest British press group to his own, thus securing control of 40 percent of the country's dailies and becoming the foremost newspaper proprietor in the world.

This success did not lose Siegmund the custom of Thomson, head of the second biggest British group. Within ten years he had become banker to the two biggest European press groups.

244   A Man of Influence

The day after this deal the *Sunday Times* wrote of him that he was "the marvel of postwar banking." He himself wrote that day in his notebook, "In finance one must be pitiless with oneself and generous with others."[3]

In fact, though, not everything was going well. In New York, as we have seen, he had failed to have one of his men appointed managing partner at Kuhn Loeb, and he could not rely on John Schiff or Frederick Warburg. In that muffled Kuhn Loeb world, neither man had the forcefulness needed to impose Siegmund's strategy, and there were increasing conflicts between Siegmund and his New York partners.

In London his bank was beginning to contend with Kuhn Loeb over some big clients, since it was becoming possible to do in London what had previously only been done in New York. It is true that when one of the two banks had transatlantic business, it was theoretically shared with the other. Yet it was difficult to decide who should take charge when Siegmund was the one who had founded the business—given his position in each bank. So, for example, when he broke Hambros's century-old monopoly on Scandinavian loans, he did it from London and did not bring in Kuhn Loeb. Also, without even mentioning it to Kuhn Loeb, he arranged City quotations for his contracts from Germany (Thyssen, Hoechst), Scandinavia (Ericsson), Israel (Bank Leumi) and Japan (Toray, among others).

He was not overworried by this turn of events, since he foresaw that the flow of capital from the United States would dwindle because of its struggle against the deficit, and that it would become difficult to float loans on Wall Street in behalf of European companies.

At the end of 1961 short-term foreign exchange deposits from small savers were authorized by the New York Stock Exchange in the form of certificates of deposit. This innovation encouraged the development of a speculative market. Faced with the growth of lending, Siegmund foresaw that companies would show huge requirements for long-term borrowing in order to improve their balance sheets, and that no currency but the dollar would be considered acceptable by the borrowers.

By traditional standards S.G. Warburg & Co. was still a small bank. Yet its influence was not measured in figures on a balance sheet. That year not one merger was uncontested, and Siegmund was in on many of them. But not on all: Courtaulds, with Barings' help, was buying almost one company a month; Imperial Tobacco, helped by Morgan Grenfell, was doing the same. With Siegmund's help, the *Daily Mirror* sold the Hazell Sun printing works to British Printing. Burmah Oil, aided by

Barings, repelled an attempted bid by Shell and BP. Company managements changed more and more quickly.

The following year, 1962, his team changed: E.G. Thalmann and
Gerald Coke retired. Younger men replaced them. George Warburg
and Ronald Grierson became board members at thirty-two and twenty-
seven respectively. Eventually, George left to set up his own firm of
financial consultants, first alone, then with Milo Cripps, another S.G.
Warburg director. This was a dreadful blow to his father, striking him
deeply, though he barely spoke of it. "Having the ambition of restoring
the dynasty, Siegmund had felt a disappointment. His only son has set
up his own firm and the two men are not very close," *Time* magazine
wrote shortly afterward. This was the only confidence he would ever
allow to filter out concerning this separation. That day he wrote in his
notebook, "In life one can change nothing other than oneself."[4]

On the surface he recovered quickly from this and chose an
"adopted son." Ronald Grierson was still the favorite, but someone else
had appeared on the horizon: Ian Fraser, appointed a board member in
place of George. Siegmund's intuition about Fraser's potential as a
banker was to be proved right, as some years later he was to become the
first director-general of the Takeover Panel, then chairman of the Lazard
Bank.

Italian Autostrade

In 1962 it became completely ridiculous to borrow long-term dollars in
New York for multinational companies, whether they were American or
not. On the one hand the American administration still required non-
American borrowers to give the appearance of proceeding through a
Wall Street bank; on the other it was making borrowing in New York
more and more costly as it saw this as the source of the American
balance of payments deficits.

Siegmund then made plans to arrange long-term dollar loans directly from London, with the help of Gert Whitman, Schacht's former
aide, and Ivan Scribanovitz, the ECSC financier. This would be nothing
new for them. They remembered Berlin and Hamburg at the tragic
beginnings of Weimar, when dollars were loaned directly from one
center to another in Europe, and not only for the short term. They also
remembered the loans of Lend-Lease dollars among Commonwealth
countries. Why not do it again? After all, there was no prohibition on
investing the dollars held by Europeans in Europe.

At the beginning of 1962, when nobody else had yet thought of it, Siegmund and his colleagues decided to make the legal and financial arrangements for a new ECSC loan, still in dollars, but to issue it this time directly in London, not New York, by approaching holders of Eurodollars. After two months' work, they gave up the plan as it would mean taking a client from Kuhn Loeb, banker to the organization since 1956, though it had become so through Siegmund. In *haute banque*, this was not done.

In the spring Siegmund and Gert Whitman, by then a partner in S.G. Warburg, were looking for another borrower who had had no previous relationship with Kuhn Loeb. They decided they needed a financially sound European company, with a need to invest for the long term. Time was pressing, for Douglas Dillon, the secretary of the treasury, was making an increasing number of statements encouraging the Europeans and the American companies in Europe to borrow in their own markets and not to take capital out of America.

At the end of the summer, Siegmund went to Washington to see his friend George Ball, who had become assistant secretary of state. Ball backed him in the idea of winning support from President Kennedy for European construction and encouraged him to create additional financial markets in dollars outside the United States. As far as Ball was concerned, the American economy was still in good shape. The interest rate was still only 3 percent. General Motors declared a huge profit that year—the biggest in the world—and Du Pont showed profitability of 18.5 percent; unemployment was only 3 percent. However, this zenith preceded the beginning of an American decline: the large deficit could not be run with impunity, when productivity was so low. From his friends at the World Bank, Siegmund learned that $3 billion were currently circulating outside the United States, of which $1 billion were outside official institutions, serving as bank-to-bank loans. These funds, he said to himself, could be used other than in the short term.

Then, on 22 October 1962, the Cuban Missile Crisis flared. Strangely, this saw the final reemergence in American political life of John McCloy, who had become a special adviser to President Kennedy and who would be a player in this dreadful game of strategic bluff.

By then Siegmund had his loan, and he knew to whom to take it: an Italian public body controlling state participation in industry, IRI, and especially one of its subsidiaries, Finsider, because this company needed investment money.

He sent Ronald Grierson to see the IRI chairman, Enzo Donatini, with a proposal for a $15 million loan over six years. Donatini hesitated. Finsider did not have a good balance sheet and was experiencing some difficulties. The money would of course be welcome, but the company had no means of guaranteeing it. Donatini regretfully refused the offer. That need not be an obstacle, was Siegmund's reply. We shall act as though the loan were intended for another IRI subsidiary; anyway it makes no difference since the real guarantor is IRI itself, endorsed by the Italian state.[5] All IRI needed to do was choose a more profitable subsidiary. Donatini agreed and suggested Autostrade Italiane, the prosperous manager of the motorway network. Agreement was reached for a $15 million loan for six years at 5.5 percent on 14 January 1963, the very day on which General de Gaulle broke off talks with Britain on joining the Common Market, which Eric Roll and Olivier Wormser had begun two years earlier.

Ian Fraser threw himself into the IRI paperwork and into obtaining the various legal and administrative authorizations. This took another six months. The final obstacle was the Bank of England, especially in the person of the governor. Reluctant and even hostile, the bank demanded exorbitant stamp duties that made the deal impossible. Sir George Bolton, a friend of Siegmund's and a member of the board of the central bank, managed to have the duties reduced. Despite this concession Siegmund decided to locate the issue legally in Luxembourg, where duties were almost nil. The law firm Allen & Overy pulled the whole operation together. Once the security was ready, two City stockbrokers were chosen to introduce it to the London Stock Exchange: L. Messel and Strauss, Turnbull & Co. It was, moreover, Julius Strauss who in the issue prospectus, describing at length and in depth the supposed advantages that the Italian motorway network would draw from the loan, replaced the expression "foreign loan in dollars," used until then for loans contacted in New York, by the word "Eurobond," which would pass into current speech.[6] S.G. Warburg's commission was set at 3.5 percent of the amount of the loan, or $520,000, to be shared with its associates in the placement: Banque Bruxelles, Deutsche Bank and Rotterdamsche Bank NV.

The contract was ready for signature on 1 July 1963: an exotic contract, drawn up according to British law, signed in The Hague, for a loan quoted in Luxembourg, issued in dollars in order to finance investment paid for in lire by an Italian company that was not the borrower!

The launch caused enormous surprise on the market, and the loan was difficult to place despite the efforts made in Switzerland by Eric Korner and Gert Whitman, and those of Robert Genillard, who placed much of it for White Weld. The loan eventually went to a five-point discount and for four months there were no further issues of this kind.

The time was ripe, however, and Siegmund had done no more than anticipate events. Eighteen days later on 18 July 1963, in the face of a worsening American payments deficit, John F. Kennedy announced to Congress the imposition of a tax on foreign loans contracted in America, which would amount to increasing their rates; the Interest Equalization Tax varied from 2.75 to 15 percent, according to the duration of the loan. The result would be the opposite of what had been expected. Instead of putting a brake on the outflow of dollars, it would put a brake on the return of those already abroad, thus worsening the American payments deficit. The center of gravity of the international capital market shifted away from the United States, though no other currency came to replace or complement the dollar, as had been the case fifty years earlier when the pound had been obliterated by the American currency.

This great divide was probably necessary and inevitable; if Siegmund had not been the first to foresee it someone else would have done so soon afterward. However, he was the first because of his long experience in Germany in the use of expatriate dollars.

Besides, in February 1963 the Morgan Bank had already issued an 80 million deutsche mark loan in Paris for Neckermann, a German company, topped with a 3 percent commission to be shared with fifty other banks. In June of the same year Morgan was actually on the point of arranging another loan from Paris, this time $15 million in dollars, for a Japanese chemical company, Takeda. Accounting problems and the innumerable obstacles raised by the Bank of France—which did not accept that in difficult times for foreign exchange, any currency other than the franc should be borrowed within the country—prevented Morgan from succeeding. The Takeda loan did not take place until 22 November 1963, the day of President Kennedy's assassination.

Paris thus lost precious, almost irrecoverable time in the reorganization of its financial market. Thanks to Siegmund, who had set the example, and despite the Bank of England, the City was to seize this opportunity and become the main free port for contraband dollars.

The bad start for his first such loan and the general scepticism of European central and private banks did not prevent Siegmund from being sure that this was a huge market. He knew that in Switzerland,

Japan, Italy, Israel and even Britain many people owned dollars and would like nothing better than to lend them long term outside America. As he saw it, without this market, industrial growth outside the United States would be paralyzed, or would have to be financed increasingly over the short term by the commercial banks, which would fuel inflation and weaken the financial position of companies.

In August he made a tour of the main European central banks. In London, Bonn, Rome and Paris, he told each governor:

> We can't let the whole international capital market die just because New York closes. Companies must be able to borrow without your having to create money. Anyway these dollars will arise anyhow, because only a reduction in the American payments deficit would make that source dry up. But that will not happen because instead of preventing the outflow of dollars from the United States, the tax will, on the contrary, worsen it. Therefore, the best thing is for you to allow the issue of long-term loans in dollars. Besides, I have just done it a month ago in London with the help of some of your banks. Let them join us in transactions of this kind.[7]

Everyone was hesitant to allow contraband dollars to be lent long term. But Siegmund was persuasive. If this were not done, he maintained, expansion would be blocked and the European and American multinationals would slow this growth. Gradually, he managed to get the central banks to remove the obstacles.

He noted that month privately, "From time to time obstructive measures are a challenge to find new ways."[8] The opening of "new ways" did not prevent him from using easy ways too. While the investment banks were still hesitating to go into Euro-issues, the Eurocurrency market was developing without controls or limits. Even the central banks began borrowing from it to rebuild their reserves and defend their parities. That year the Belgian Treasury borrowed $20 million in London.

Siegmund plunged deeply into his new plans. At the end of 1963 he arranged a second dollar loan from London for the city of Oslo, then carried out the Euro-issue he had not dared to continue the year before, for the European Coal and Steel Community (ECSC). In parallel, he set up his own network for placing such loans, choosing Banque de Paris et des Pays-Bas, still headed by Jean Reyre, the Union Bank of Switzerland headed by Hans Schaeffer, the Deutsche Bank with Hermann Abs at its head and Banca Commerciale Italiana still run by Carlo Bombieri. The five men saw each other regularly on visits by one or the other to

Frankfurt, Zurich, Milan, London or Paris. The emerging Eurodollar market supplied a structure for this network of friendships where each banker invited the other into issues that one or another was arranging.

It was still a very small market: a total of thirteen Euro-issues took place in 1963, for a total of $147.5 million, or three hundred times less than today.

Siegmund now knew that he could successfully make of the City what he had vainly attempted to make of Berlin before the advent of Hitler: a sort of extramural New York. After all, London had a long tradition of financing both international trade and governments; it had initially lent European savings to the United States; then between the two wars it had managed loans in the opposite direction. Moreover, when London became the free port for the dollar, prewar vocabulary was quite naturally taken up. A leader known as the "pen holder" took charge of a Euro-issue and undertook with other guarantors to place the loan either directly or through the intermediary of sellers. The banks' commissions were fixed by a scale of fees, according to the value of the loan. This income, in dollars, was the equivalent for Britain, the country of the bank's headquarters, of an export of services: the only profit for Britain from the City's operations.

Siegmund thus made his bank the foremost in the long-term Euro-market. He was to stay at the top. Without taking excessive risks he went out to find clients, approaching companies as soon as he thought that they were potential borrowers, often even before they really knew it themselves.

His methods were original, even shocking for the time. He worked from a single center, without offices abroad or subsidiaries around the world. "Offices are as useless as ambassadors," he said, like his uncle Max. His men lived in a constant state of alert; within a few hours of receiving information from a local source, a commando force of two or three would take off from London and begin to use the information to sign up a future client.[9] Siegmund also kept himself informed of what others were doing. In London he put together a small group under Sharp, responsible for following the top six hundred banks in the world and for knowing at all times who was issuing a loan, so that the bank could be associated with it. Or who had capital available, so that a loan could be placed with them.[10]

Another event made 1963 an important year: in Zurich Siegmund met a distant relative, Theodora Dreyfus-Schiff. An extraordinary character, she had been born in Vienna and had become a screenwriter; then after fighting heroicly during the war she had become, in Zurich at the beginning of the 1950s, one of the best graphologists of her time. Siegmund gave her, as a test, the handwriting of someone who was close to him. Her analysis astounded him, being much more precise than the one he had received in London. Theodora at once became the bank's adviser in this regard and was to remain so for thirty years. She had a great influence on Siegmund. A few years later, for instance Siegmund would approach Karl Kahane, the great Austrian industrialist and banker whom he hardly knew: "Theodora has seen your handwriting and she has told me you were a person of great quality and that we should do business together. I don't know what, but why not try since she said so?"

Siegmund often traveled to Zurich, where he helped to set up a European Foundation of Graphology at the University of Zurich.

The bank was now making more than £600,000 in profits after tax, or just one-quarter of the amount declared by the holding company. Its influence increased by the month, in London as elsewhere. Anthony Sampson wrote, "It was the most spectacular newcomer in the City." Everyone came to lunch at Gresham Street, from ministers—to whom Siegmund explained that Britain would one day pay for her postwar mistakes and her refusal to leave distant territories—to leaders of the opposition.

He was increasingly sure of having been correct in the definition of his profession: a banker, he thought, must be small if he wishes to be influential. "As for supplying money to industry, bankers have lost their importance; but in advising, what I call being 'financial engineers,' they have gained much."[11]

He viewed with an increasingly critical eye everything he saw happening around him. His demands on men became even more severe. In September 1963 he wrote:

> I still hope for a new aristocracy, a new élite, whose qualities will be a suspicion of luxury and the accumulation of goods, a respect for substance rather than appearances, for quality in preference to quantity, and finally nobility and independence of judgment.[12]

He felt himself increasingly remote from the money ethic and the prevailing norms of conformity. He confided to Anthony Sampson, "It is always said that the City is in mutation, but the revolutionaries of one generation become the conformists of the next."

Finishing with Kuhn Loeb

At the end of 1963 the first Euro-issues led to conflicts of interest with Kuhn Loeb. Incidents became commonplace, and each side accused the other of having made offers that were known to be unacceptable to common clients, to avoid bringing in the other partner. To try to reduce the conflicts, a coordinating committee was set up, comprising on one side Nat Samuels and Alvin Friedman and on the other Gert Whitman and Ronald Grierson. However, this did not ease the strain. John Schiff, increasingly remote, did not want to choose between Siegmund and his colleagues, now led by Henry Necarsulmer.

On 22 November 1963, Siegmund was in New York and saw in the tragedy of President Kennedy's assassination signs that a certain version of America was shaken, and the end of his own American dream.

In London the Euro-issue market was becoming organized. In 1964 forty-four loans totaling $680 million were issued; the major part was done by S.G. Warburg on behalf of the city of Turin, and again for IRI, this time explicitly for the Finsider subsidiary.[13]

But the market was still narrow. Each Euro-issue took several weeks of negotiation. The borrowers were well-known companies—German, Norwegian, Austrian, Italian and Japanese. The lenders were anonymous, which allowed for the investment of doubtful capital and for interest to be received without payment of tax—which was what made the market successful. Some said that former Nazis, the Mafia, deposed rulers or more simply tax evaders, aptly named "Belgian dentists," found in these issues an opportunity to launder their money.[14] The fact that Swiss banks placed most of these first Euroloans and that Luxembourg banks clipped the coupons, in other words paid the interest, lent some credence to this theory. But as far as is known the first buyers of these bonds were rich, honorable individuals, Greek or Scandinavian shipowners and the Central Bank of Israel, which was investing its export revenues. In the spring of 1964 they were joined by American lenders, such as the Fiduciary Trust Company, which bought securities in behalf of American company pension funds, and in behalf of the United Nations.

In addition the Moscow Narodny Bank and the Banque de l'Europe du Nord signed an agreement with the Commonwealth money managers to invest some of the Soviet-held dollars in these markets. Eurodollars were now buying Euro-issues.

Having a Name in Frankfurt

Simultaneously Siegmund pursued his other major objective: to revive his name in Germany. Since 1958, when Germany had become an exporter of capital for the first time since 1913, he had managed to introduce German companies to the London market and float Euro-issues with the cooperation of German banks. He had not succeeded in regaining an inch of territory in the old Hamburg firm, except that without justification some people now called the bank Brinckmann, Wirtz, Warburg & Co. Therefore he looked for an indirect way that might lead to the reconquest of Ferdinandstrasse, and decided to set up a bank in his name in Frankfurt, where most of German financial life now took place.

He chose to take control of a small bank already mentioned, that of Hans W. Petersen, the Jewish banker who had hidden in Berlin in the middle of the war. At the beginning of 1964, Gert Whitman, a cousin of Petersen's, told Richard Daus to sound Petersen out. H.W. Petersen would be given the name S.G. Warburg. Siegmund Warburg, he said, would call him the next day if he agreed in principle.

Subsequently, Siegmund met with Petersen at London's Savoy Hotel, where he candidly explained his intention to use Petersen to put his name back on a bank in Germany. "My family was stupidly too German to accept that Hitler would act as he did. Now I want to come back." The two men sealed the agreement and in April 1964 S.G. Warburg, Frankfurt, was created. Siegmund made Jean Reyre and George Bolton partners; Richard Daus became the resident partner. Siegmund was still a partner in Kuhn Loeb, and it was Gert Whitman who became a partner to represent the London house. It was decided that in the case of a disagreement between Frankfurt and London, Siegmund should be the one to leave, giving up the bank to Richard Daus.

In the following year, Siegmund also persuaded Brinckmann, Wirtz & Co. to become partners in Frankfurt. The bank developed. It made Euro-issues, loans to international trade and gave financial advice. Siegmund followed the details and visited occasionally. Other British bankers such as Hill Samuel did as Siegmund did, establishing themselves in Frankfurt.

In Hamburg neither Eric Warburg nor Rudolf Brinckmann were happy about this. "If the name returns to Hamburg," Siegmund told them, "I will give up the Frankfurt bank." But Brinckmann, who was also a partner in Hauck & Co., another small Frankfurt bank, did not give in.

Siegmund later brought Brinckmann, Wirtz & Co. into a number of deals, as, for instance, the first loan denominated in pounds and deutsche marks on behalf of New Zealand.

The Break with Kuhn Loeb

Siegmund wanted to avoid a complete rupture with New York. He saw that American companies would now want to finance their European subsidiaries through the City and to do so would use the subsidiaries of American banks. Therefore he wished to retain links with Kuhn Loeb and continue representing himself in London as the partner of a big New York bank. It was too late, however. Necarsulmer was doing his utmost to opposed him, and the American partners, primarily his cousin Frederick, no longer accepted Siegmund's methods.

He then attempted to join with another of the Wall Street greats, Lehman Brothers, and to set up with them, Paribas and various British insurance companies, a banking operation in London. This failed; Lehman barely took an interest.

In July 1964 conflict with Kuhn Loeb intensified over a new issue being launched by the city of Oslo. Nobody knew whether Siegmund had heard of this business in London or in New York, where he went less often. Each side thought itself the instigator. Each side went as far as suspecting that its partner might sabotage the business in order to preempt a profit for the other. This was indeed what happened: Morgan carried off the deal. Siegmund wanted to finish the problem one way or the other: bring Kuhn Loeb to London or break with it. He had few allies on the spot. Wiseman was no longer there; the New York Warburgs headed by Frederick were cool; Dillworth had gone to Rockefeller and John Schiff was less than supportive.

To give fate a hand Henry Grunfeld, without mentioning it to Siegmund, went one Sunday in August 1964 to visit John Schiff on his Oyster Bay estate. They talked until four in the morning. Toward dawn John Schiff summed up, "I would like you to stay and Siegmund to take power in the firm, but I cannot force my partners to accept your methods. It is up to you to choose. Either you stay and bow to the rules of Wall Street, or you go."

Henry reported this meeting to Siegmund and they immediately made a decision. They broke with Kuhn Loeb as of 31 December 1964 and sold American European Associates, which was still vegetating as an investment fund, and set up another bank, S.G. Warburg Inc., with a director from Chemical Bank, D. Mitchell.

Siegmund would bitterly resent this failure. Fifteen years later he would say:

> I was deeply attached to Kuhn Loeb and thought there was a great possibility of making Kuhn Loeb into an élite firm in New York. We were on the way, and I was terribly disappointed when it didn't work. . . . I was able to build up quite an important international business for them . . . . I was also involved in the policy of the firm as a whole. It engaged several of their leading people, such as Nat Samuels, Harvey Krueger and Yves Istel. . . . It was simply because of differences of opinion with other partners on policy matters that I finally resigned [on 31 December 1964]. But I still have many good friends there.[15]

The "Night Club"

London was once more showing itself a place of asylum. Everyone praised the capability of its bankers, its quality of life, the breadth of its cultural life and the certainty that no change of government or exchange control, whatever else might happen, would disturb the habits of the many players in the City. Yet the financial center increasingly came to resemble a stylized bouquet in a rambling English garden. All around it the economic and political situation of the country was deteriorating. The government plunged into austerity to avoid devaluation instead of cutting spending abroad. Selwyn Lloyd, unjustly made the scapegoat for this crisis, was sacked by Harold Macmillan.

Despite support given the previous year by the central banks of Europe, the pound had not stabilized and its parity no longer reflected its competitiveness. The structure of the budget, the state of industry and military spending abroad made even slight growth impossible without an external deficit. The reserves were being exhausted, debts were inflating and parity was no longer tenable.

In September 1963 Harold Macmillan, then on an official visit to Washington, told John F. Kennedy very clearly that if there were not an increase in the dollar price of gold or a devaluation of the dollar, the pound itself would have to devalue and the whole Bretton Woods system would be threatened. At the time it was sacrilege even to make such a suggestion. Kennedy had all trace of this conversation expunged, even down to the notes taken by his own assistants.[16]

On 19 September, eight weeks before the death of Kennedy, Harold Macmillan resigned after six years in government and was replaced on 29 October by Sir Alec Douglas-Home. Reginald Maudling, appointed chancellor of the exchequer in place of Selwyn Lloyd, also did not take the necessary measures. He did not reduce military expenditure abroad, as Siegmund and others recommended, and did not develop industrial investments. The situation deteriorated. In January 1964 the worst balance of payments deficit in British history was made public. Capital was increasingly flowing out of Britain and demanding gold or dollars in exchange for pounds. In February, to attract or retain fleeing capital, Sir Alec decided on an increase in the discount rate, but for the time this was such a big decision that he went himself to Washington to inform the new President, Lyndon Johnson. Johnson asked him to limit the increase to a half point in order to avoid a rates war. Sir Alec complied. The increase proved insufficient, and at the end of May a new outflow of capital had to be faced. The trade deficit for the month of July reached £60 million. On 8 October it was announced that the balance of payments deficit for the current year would be £650 million. Everything was going badly.

In Gresham Street the staff often worked until late in the evening. The wits in the City nicknamed the bank the "Night Club." S.G. Warburg bought several companies from clients and, apart from Brandeis-Goldschmidt, now included an advertising agency, Masius Ferguson, which had become Masius Wynn Williams; an insurance broker, Stewart Smith; and the British subsidiaries of an American opinion survey group, Gallup Poll. That year it also acquired the biggest British pension fund adviser: the Metropolitan Pension Fund Association. These companies paid fees to the bank for its financial advice and dividends to the holding company, Mercury Securities, their shareholder. The same year Siegmund arranged the first issue since the war of American bonds in Europe on behalf of Socony Mobil.[17]

He still feared that success might bring both complacency and over-rapid growth leading to bureaucracy and a deterioration in the quality of service. He encouraged everyone in the "Night Club" "to make a special effort to preserve the personal style and the character that we consider primordial in the activity of a merchant bank."[18]

Though the work was hard, it was better paid than anywhere else in London, and in addition it was prestigious to work for Siegmund Warburg. Lord Weinstock, for example, following the example of the elite in Britain or abroad, would later send his son to the firm as a trainee.

There was no longer any dynastic appearance to the exceptionally young staff: out of eighteen directors, seven were under forty-five and four under forty. Five were foreigners: two Dutch, one Irish, one American and one Canadian. There was a former journalist, Ronald Grierson; a former Ambassador to Paris, Lord Gladwyn; and two former senior civil servants, James Helmore and Andrew MacFadyean.

That year David Scholey joined S.G. Warburg at the age of twenty-eight. The career path of the present chairman of the bank is worth relating. Born on 28 June 1935 and educated at Wellington College, then Christ Church, Oxford, he served in the Lancers, then became an insurance broker, first in Toronto, then with Lloyd's in London. At the end of the 1950s he was still only a young broker, playing the guitar in the evenings at the Monrose Club. In 1959 he joined his father, Dudley Scholey, at Guinness Mahon and became a member of the board of the Orion Insurance Company. In 1960 he married the daughter of the Canadian ambassador to London. In 1963 his father became the chairman of Orion, which he sold in 1964 through S.G. Warburg to a Dutch company. Dudley then left Guinness Mahon to join S.G. Warburg and brought along his son, who became Siegmund's personal assistant. David was given the small office between Siegmund's and Henry's. He was witness to everything. Siegmund, charmed by his calmness and originality, gradually came to see him as a new "adopted son," alongside Ronald Grierson below him.

Second Departure

On 31 March 1964 (a day chosen out of superstition; he hated 1 April), Siegmund, four years after leaving the chairmanship of the bank, gave up that of Mercury Securities. That day he told his staff:

> It is essential constantly to modify the composition of a team in order to rejuvenate it . . . the old, who should be called in the Japanese way "the old sages" must make way for the others, well trained to succeed them. So I am convinced that my departure from the chairmanship will strengthen our group, not weaken it. With the years our team has developed into a body which now lives of itself and is stronger today than the sum of the individuals who comprise it.[19]

He was quite pleased with himself and noted privately, "A good fellow? Someone without whom things could or would have been worse." No doubt this was how he saw himself. He had brought off some good deals and had helped others to avoid the worst. He certainly did not see himself as someone who only had wanted to make money. "Money which should be the servant of those who possess it can become a tyrant if it is taken as an emblem of social status."[20]

The following year S.G. Warburg's profits made it the leading merchant bank, along with Morgan Grenfell. Under an avalanche of compliments, Siegmund above all asserted the originality of his method. "I don't want to do things like other people. I have no blueprint. I do things in my own way."[21] From then on he compared his profession with that of a lawyer in the United States. "We act like friends who help the client to formulate the instructions. We try to reconcile the differences between clients."[22] Yet he could be extremely savage toward those he did not like. In July 1964 he noted about someone, "With him, as often happens, verbal diarrhoea and triviality of speech are accompanied by a constipation in ideas and emotions."[23]

On 25 September 1964 Sir Alec Douglas-Home led the Conservatives into an election. Against him for Labour was Harold Wilson, his junior, a director of statistics during the war and a member of Parliament since 1945. Wilson won the election and on 16 October 1964 became prime minister.

Wall Street Comes to London

America entered an era of deficits. First because just as the economy was in full swing and as the "Great Society" was launched, return on capital was falling and no longer attracted investors. Next because escalation of the Vietnam War was beginning and would last more than ten years, leading to inflation and deterioration in external balances. Any American external deficit came back to create dollars for the world. They substituted for insufficient national saving without it being visible that these were American debts that one day, long afterward, would have to be settled. So the dollar remained king, but its preeminence rested on its contraband circulation and no longer in the guarantee of the ruling economy, which until then it had reflected.

True, the average trade surplus was still $2 billion a year, against $3.3 billion in the previous decade. Military spending abroad had increased by 70 percent, mainly for Vietnam, costing the balance of payments about $2 billion a year. And the payments deficits of 1965,

1966 and 1967 in total reached more than $6.5 billion, half of this still paid in gold. Europe and Japan, which were growing faster than America, also began to re-export dollars.

As Siegmund had foreseen, the Interest Equalization Tax did not reduce the balance of payments deficit, but on the contrary worsened it by slowing down the return of dollars to America's banks. Persisting in the belief that by reducing the outflow of capital, one would reduce the deficit, President Johnson decided additionally on 10 February 1965 to encourage voluntary limitation of investment and lending abroad. This measure—just as ineffective as its predecessors—in fact only encouraged American companies to borrow Eurodollars in Europe in order to invest them outside America.

This explosion in the movement of private capital, unknown in history, opened the golden age of S.G. Warburg & Co. As the first bank to have concerned itself with transatlantic industrial concentrations, and the first to have launched itself into Euro-issues, it now became the symbol of the new form of postwar totally delocalized world capitalism. London became the leading center for this. Although American banks were setting up subsidiaries in London, Paris, Frankfurt and Zurich, it was primarily in Great Britain that they took root, just as Harold Wilson was reaffirming Britain's wish to enter the European Community. In 1965, ninety-eight foreign banks established themselves in London, forty-eight in Paris and seventeen in Zurich. Their beginnings were hardly brilliant. Their relative youth and limited experience were at first handicaps, but soon also the source of new financial imagination that would make them masters of the offshore market in their own currency.

Siegmund was therefore no longer the only one in the market. He came up against others: Deutsche Bank, Kuhn Loeb and Morgan. To withstand this new competition, as in prewar years, he had to invent the needs of others before they were aware of them themselves.

For instance, on behalf on New Zealand, he arranged with Brinck-mann, Wirtz & Co. and Commerzbank, against Kidder Peabody, the traditional banker to that country, for a complex issue, of which he was very proud—£10 million over fifteen years, partly denominated in pounds, partly in deutsche marks, to spread the exchange risks. Borrowing was in one currency, repayment in the other. When he managed to place 10 percent of this with the American bank White Weld, in London, the initially risky transaction became an outright success.[24] He arranged another issue for Mobil Oil. In September 1965 the first dollar issue took place on behalf of an American company, American Cyanamid.

In relation to the previous year, the Euro-issue market increased somewhat in 1965. It reached $800 million for forty-five issues, of which half were for the subsidiaries of American companies; seven of the twelve main lead banks were American, three were British, headed by S.G. Warburg, still number one in the market for the number of issues, and second behind Deutsche Bank for the amounts.

Ridiculous rumors began to circulate about Siegmund's success. Sometimes openly anti-Semitic, they were fueled by the considerable amounts he undertook to place and by his purchase that year of a small Zurich bank, the Banque de Gestion Financiere. In fact there was nothing mysterious about his success. It had to do with the extraordinary network of contacts accumulated over two centuries by his family and carefully maintained and developed by him. "You have to become someone's friend to become his banker, and not the reverse,"[25] he said. There was not a single great banking or financial institution in the industrial world where he could not count on at least one friend at the top of the hierarchy. This was how he succeeded with issues of loans for the Austrian public sector. His issues in Italy resulted from his relationship with Guido Carli, an economist and banker. His part in the deutsche mark issues was connected to his friendship with Hermann Abs, chairman of the Deutsche Bank, and with the Commerzbank chairman Paul Lichtenberg. Carlo Bombieri at Banca Commerciale Italiana, Hans Schaeffer at the Union Bank of Switzerland, Jean Reyre at Paribas, Marcus Wallenburg at Enskilda, David Rockefeller at Chase, Robert Lehman at Lehman Brothers and Robert Baldwin at Morgan Stanley were all his very close friends. To enter the few circles still closed, he got his own bank in through other "door openers." None of this prevented him from having to be very competitive, for no friend, wherever he might be, of course ever rejected a more appealing offer.

This unique network made him one of the greatest seers of world capitalism of the time. He consistently foresaw opportunities better than anyone else who had money to invest or loans to arrange—whether they were states, banks or companies in Europe or Japan. He only concerned himself with big deals:

[If they are well organized,] the smaller wholesale houses are stronger than the big retail houses. If the Deutsche Bank puts away $2 million

in a big issue among ten clients, it's very nice. But if we can put two
clients in at $1 million each, that also has advantages.[26]

He would use any means, either applying pressure or charm, to secure
his share of a loan. He did not hesitate to make persuasive or threatening telephone calls to whomever his target might be: a minister, the
president of the European Commission or a low-level employee of
another bank. Moreover, speed and prudence went together. Since, like
an ordinary broker, he still never bought an issue until he had first sold
it, he had to be able to have rapid confirmation of the placing, to be able
to put forward an offer that would be secure for him and tempting for
the borrowers. This was the only way to beat the big banks who were
more easily able to run the risk of guaranteeing the placement of a loan
before knowing whether their network would in fact place it.

He also specialized in the more difficult transactions—competing
on the capacity to innovate rather than on interest rates, which was very
much to his taste. This was the only business to correspond with his
criterion of *haute banque*, and the only kind to arouse his imagination.

Sometimes his ideas were too far ahead of their time, and they were
not always successful. Thus in 1965 he attempted to place a loan on
behalf of Swedish borrowers, denominated in a basket of European
currencies that he named "Euromoneta," well before the ECU was
thought of. He did not manage to get the loan accepted.[27] Fifteen years
later the idea of mixed currencies would be almost commonplace.

The following year, 1966, short-term interest rates in London broke
through the ceiling imposed by American regulations on long-term
deposits in the United States. This drove investors from around the
world more than ever to deposit their foreign currency in London, and
the two European dollar markets were still developing: the short-term
market very quickly and the medium-term market more slowly.

That year the Euro-issue market amounted to $1.3 billion, or the
exact amount of the American balance of payments deficit. Despite its
growing fragility, the dollar remained the favorite currency by a wide
margin, though a quarter of the Euro-issues were by now denominated
in deutsche marks. The number of issues also increased, reaching sixty-
nine. They took less time to arrange. Each banker would add some
subtlety to the previous banker's method. So in May 1966 S.G. Warburg invented the first Eurobonds partly convertible into shares, which
reduced the cost for the borrower, Società Generale Immobiliare di
Lavori e di Utilità Pubblica.[28] In June N.M. Rothschild invented a

Euro-issue with a "zero coupon," in other words, a deferral of interest payments to the end of the loan, which fifteen years later would make a fortune for the insurers. The biggest American companies, such as Union Carbide, General Foods or Gillette, now began borrowing regularly on this market for their investments outside America.

The market was also becoming more democratic. On 23 June 1966 the sale in London of short- and medium-term Eurodollar securities was opened to small investors, as had been the case on Wall Street since 1961. The London banks were then able to issue dollar certificates of deposit and offer them to a wide public, as they were negotiable by the banks themselves without going through the traditional securities intermediaries. It was an enormous change. For the first time since Weimar Germany small European investors—no longer just the banks or big investors—would be able to invest their savings in dollars, and the banks would be able to remain attractive to depositors. The homogenization of capital markets crossed a threshold. The first bank to issue securities in London was the First National City Bank, and White Weld Ltd. set up a secondary market for them.

It certainly seems astonishing that the Bank of England should have given such an authorization in that year of difficulty for the pound—not the only mistake in those years.

The Death Struggle of the Pound

Having abdicated its leadership role in 1957 in order to hold onto its parity, the British currency was now at the end of its tether. With the collapse of the rate set sixteen years earlier came cracks in the whole Bretton Woods system. This death struggle would end after two years of futile obstinacy in a devaluation, the story of which is worth telling. Siegmund was closely linked with it, and the devaluation marks the real point of departure for the great monetary and economic crisis in which the West is still immersed today.

With great injustice, history has pointed the finger of blame at Harold Wilson and at him alone. In fact, long years of blundering and conservatism were to blame. No one participant could be held responsible. Siegmund was to play the almost absurd role of a man of influence swept away by the current. From the evening of his appointment, on 16 October 1964, Harold Wilson was confronted with the same speculation against the pound that all his predecessors in the previous ten years had known. Because he was a Labour man, discretion was no longer in style. The City, the financial press, the Bank of England and especially its governor, Lord Cromer, were openly hostile to the Labour government. The American banks started and spread alarmist rumors about the future of the British currency. There was talk of devaluation, floating, nationalization of merchant banks, a tax on capital, controls on capital, import quotas and the closure of the gold market. Several merchant banks seriously considered leaving Britain. Having refused either to devalue the pound, reduce military spending or withdraw from foreign bases, the Conservatives now preached a reduction in social spending and public investment that they had not had the courage to impose when in office. As for the Labour party, they had but one obsession, which would dictate the whole of their conduct during these dreadful years. Having been in power at the time of devaluation in 1949 and part of the coalition making a similar decision in 1931, they did not intend to become known as "the devaluation party," though the 1949 action had been the logical consequence of the parities chosen by Churchill at the end of the war, and the 1931 decision had been no more than the result of the same Churchill's absurd policy in 1926.

Wilson did not want to avoid reform by making the electorate pay for the accumulated blunders of previous governments, and he refused to cut social spending, which he thought was already insufficient. Sure of the help of Washington and Europe, he wanted, on the contrary, to stake everything on the success of a program of reconstruction for industry.

While waiting for this expansion to take effect, however, there was an exchange crisis to manage, which was growing more serious each day. The gold reserves were vanishing through the combination of deficits and speculation, all the more since everyone was expecting immediate devaluation.

In addition, from the day he arrived at 10 Downing Street, Harold Wilson had instituted an original system of controlling economic affairs. He split finance, by setting up a Ministry of Economic Affairs under George Brown and assigning the Treasury to James Callaghan Then, after consulting with his personal economic adviser Tomas Balogh, he had announced that there would be no devaluation of the pound. Instead of reassuring public opinion, this announcement merely revealed the existence of a financial crisis, until then carefully concealed by the Conservatives. It also gave an antagonistic press a chance to attack the Labour party.

The next day Wilson chose his Cabinet. Besides official advisers such as Sir William Armstrong, Sir Donald MacDougall and Robert

Neild, he would see Siegmund Warburg from time to time as an unofficial adviser. Thirty years after advising a right-wing minister of foreign affairs in Berlin, Siegmund was advising a Labour prime minister in London. He himself made no secret of this irony, through pride as well as the wish to provoke the City, which was shocked that a banker could work for the "reds" in this way. In the United States *Time* magazine limited itself to this version of the news. "Prime Minister Wilson, an admirer of Warburg's modernizing influence in British finance, has made him one of his close advisers."

Wilson then had to decide how to check the deficits and the flight of capital. Time was pressing: there was less than £1 billion left in the vaults of the Bank of England. The opinions he received were contradictory: the economic policy file left by the previous Conservative chancellor, Reginald Maudling, proposed a tax on imports. Professor Nicholas Kaldor, who had become Callaghan's adviser, thought that imports should be limited by quota and that the pound should be floated for several months until it found a stable parity. Eric Roll, appointed secretary general of the Ministry of Economic Affairs, thought that public spending abroad should not be reduced. Thomas Balogh, Lord Cromer, Sir Donald MacDougall, Robert Neild and Sir William Armstrong were all of the same opinion.

Siegmund then gave the Labour leaders his diagnosis. He thought that the Bretton Woods system had shown itself to be perverse, since it had removed the role of the gold standard without replacing it with any other regulatory mechanism. But since this situation had to be lived with, it was not appropriate to devalue since this would only worsen the country's position. The British deficit, he explained, was basically caused by public, especially military, spending abroad, which structurally exceeded the shrinking foreign trade surplus. The need was therefore to try to increase foreign exchange receipts and reduce spending abroad. Conservative governments, however, had only tried to increase these receipts, without doing anything to reduce expenditure. Macmillan had actually spent more on defense as a percentage of GNP than any of his Western counterparts, except the United States. This took no account of other expenses.

> If, for example, military spending in India and Egypt had been cut [explained Siegmund], Britain would have saved £2 billion. . . . I do not mean by that that we should cancel all our commitments abroad, or play only a passive role in world affairs; I think there is a mean

point to be found: such is the difficulty of the foreign policy decisions you are going to have to take. So far, however, no government, Conservative or Labour, has managed to adjust our foreign policy to our capacity to gather in foreign exchange.

Therefore reducing spending abroad would be enough to set everything in order, he told Wilson, for in fact

> British finances are in a good state and there is no reason to devalue. Our short-term reserves equal our short-term debts and our assets abroad are of the same order as our debts. Moreover, amounts due in sterling should not be counted as debts as these are not real claims against Britain. There are enough liquid assets to withstand an exchange crisis, even without committing all assets. The country must stop spending abroad more than it earned there, and stop saying that all our ills result from the weakness of our industry without doing anything to modernize it. Sacred cows must be slaughtered, ambitions we can no longer afford must be forgotten, and in order to encourage productivity and increase export receipts we must introduce VAT or a tax deduction on exports, as in France or Germany.

There was much sympathy for this very detailed plan, presented during the last days of October 1964. Wilson, though he did not want to devalue, did not feel he could touch the British military presence abroad, which was still the subject of a national consensus. On 26 October he confined himself to settling on a strict budget, without reducing spending abroad, and a 15 percent import surcharge, a semi-devaluation that unleashed protests from other European countries and worsened the flight from the pound. At the end of November 1964 the gold reserves were down to £876 million. Within the government talk began of reducing the British presence abroad but they lacked the courage to act, in the face of a right-wing opposition. In November, at one of those boring bankers' dinners held at Mansion House, Lord Cromer entered the fray firmly opposing such reductions, saying that overseas investments should not be considered as surplus or as the first target of economies in the case of blows from adversity. By 18 November Wilson was convinced of the need to increase the discount rate in order to defend the reserves. At one point he considered informing President Johnson of this but decided against it. Unlike his predecessor, he did not intend to ask the opinion of the American president on a question that rested, as he saw it, with national sovereignty alone.

On this subject, too, the government was divided. Callaghan was against the increase, which he thought would stifle growth, while Brown was in favor, thinking it would stifle speculation. In the end, after long discussions, Wilson decided to raise the rate by one percentage point. This was not enough to check the outflow of gold and foreign exchange. In the City, the center of rumor and speculation, antigovernment criticism grew. On 19 November Wilson attacked the City in a speech, saying, "If anyone here or abroad doubts our resolve and acts in consequence, may he be ready to pay the price for his lack of confidence in Great Britain."[29]

The same day, in a speech that became famous, George Brown denounced the "Gnomes of Zurich." The phrase struck home. It rekindled the argument over the responsibility of financiers in a crisis, as in New York in 1913, London in 1931 and Berlin in 1933. The Bank of England governor's response to Brown was that there were no gnomes, only people in the City and elsewhere who were defending their own interests by turning away from the pound because they had no confidence in the Labour party. That day the City saw devaluation as unavoidable; demand for gold increased on the free market, maintained with great difficulty and near exhaustion by the "gold pool."

Very late on the evening of 20 November with a perplexed Wilson examining his options, George Brown called Henry Grunfeld to Carlton Gardens. Grunfeld repeated his and Siegund's shared opposition to devaluation and suggested defending the pound by means of a big, international, long-term loan—the announcement of which alone would be enough to quiet the speculators. Meanwhile, the medium-term measures would be taking effect. The next day, therefore, the United Kingdom did borrow. It borrowed only $1 billion from the IMF under the general borrowing agreements never previously used. This was not what Grunfeld and Siegmund had recommended. For the next two days the reserves continued to drain away, and Cromer began to resign himself to devaluation, also thinking that it was necessary to act quickly in order not to default. There was no more than the equivalent of £500 million in gold left in the Bank of England.

Seeing speculation continue, Wilson raised the discount rate to 7 percent on 23 November. He did not understand why or how this was happening:

We are at war [he said], and we don't know who the enemy is. What more do they want? I have cut public spending and restrained monetary policy and the financial crisis is still going on. Devalue? Out of the question. Be harder on the working class? Also out of the question . . . . We shall hold on. Besides, the United States cannot allow a devaluation of the pound and will help us.[30]

The following day, Wilson finally accepted the solution Siegmund had suggested some days before: a long-term international loan. On the evening of 24 November he asked Cromer to set the amount that needed to be borrowed to ensure that speculation would be banished: $2.5 billion was the reply. In order to give the decision maximum impact, the money had to be found during the next day and the loan announced immediately. That evening telephones began ringing in all the central banks of the world. Alerted by Cromer, the chairman of the American Federal Reserve promised $750 million; the Export–Import Bank promised $250 million. That was $1 billion. Treasury Secretary Dillon and his deputy, Stuart A. Roosa, spent all night on the telephone to several American private banks, asking for their help. Their main argument was that if the pound collapsed the dollar would follow, dragging down the whole Bretton Woods agreement and the American banking system itself. From his side Siegmund first called Kuhn Loeb and Lehman, then the following morning, as soon as the European markets opened, Hermann Abs and Jean Reyre. The Bundesbank chairman, Karl Blessing, also called by Cromer, agreed to coordinate calls to the European central banks. General de Gaulle, irritated by the short time in which he had to decide, finally allowed the Bank of France to participate in the loan "for the last time."[31] By midday, Blessing had received the agreement of twelve central banks. By seven in the evening a total of $3 billion dollars had been assembled, but only for six months. The "Gnomes of Zurich" had helped the pound, but without excessive risk. There was a champagne celebration in Wilson's office. On this occasion at least, devaluation would not take place. Speculation died down.

The day after this partial success, Wilson was able to go to Washington with head held high. The loan was allowing him to hang on. It was no more than a reprieve: by the following January the balance of payments was still in deficit and foreign exchange was again draining away. On 1 February 1965 Lord Cromer began admitting publicly that to reduce the outflow of foreign exchange, further budget cuts would be needed, "including some in overspending by local authorities and abroad."[32]

Wilson and Callaghan then protested publicly at these statements. No, reducing public spending further was out of the question, as was a reduction of Britain's spending abroad, and Wilson wrote to the governor, "It would be politically irresponsible and economically useless to abandon our bases."[33] On 24 March 1965 the loan of 20 November 1964 was renewed by the central banks at a meeting of their governors within the framework of the BIS. Two days later, on 26 March, the pound came under attack. It only stabilized for a few weeks after the announcement on 6 April of a harsh budget for the coming year. On a trip to the United States at the end of April, Wilson gave a quite brilliant explanation to an audience of bankers in New York of the new economic program he had put together with Brown, Callaghan, Siegmund Warburg, Kaldor and Balogh: he confirmed the priority given to industrial modernization and to price and incomes controls. He renewed his "unalterable determination to maintain the value of the pound and the values that depend on it."[34]

There remained the problem of withdrawal from the foreign bases, and during this trip Wilson was hoping to get some idea of the United States' position on this subject. This was very difficult because the government was divided on this issue. Within the Administration there were some, like Robert S. McNamara and Dean Rusk, who wished Britain to continue to play her part as auxiliary policeman of the West, and thought that "Britain should stay East of Aden," though Rusk did add, "We alone can allow ourselves to be the engine of the world." Others, however, such as Dillon and Roosa, feared that this spending would inevitably lead to a devaluation of the pound, then to that of the dollar. They therefore thought that the pound must be defended, and that to do this, British military spending abroad must be reduced. Lyndon Johnson refrained from deciding between these two theories.

Wilson concluded from this that it was better to stay "East of Aden," for if Britain left her bases, she would cease to be considered a great power and the United States would lose interest in helping her. On 25 May, to repay the second November loan, Britain borrowed $1.4 billion from the IMF and the rest from private banks. Some slight confidence in the pound returned, and it was possible to lower the discount rate in London from 7 to 6 percent. However, the payments deficit was still not decreasing, and on 16 July 1965 the pound again came under attack.

Wilson no longer knew what to do. Advice came from every side. The French and German ministers of finance recommended a further reduction of spending. The United States advised freezing wages. Cromer suggested forming a coalition government. Wilson was furious at that: he would never cause the prewar betrayal of the Labour movement to be repeated.

The summer passed without a solution. At the beginning of September Britain had to borrow a further $2 billion from the central banks, to consolidate the IMF loans once more. It was the same scenario and involved the same calls, but this time France refused to take part. On 10 September Callaghan announced that he had obtained more international assistance, but without announcing how much: in fact it was only $1 billion. On 16 September he brought out a draft five-year plan and instituted a system of voluntary wage restraint. At the end of the month Lord Cromer's term of office expired and Wilson appointed his aide L.K. O'Brien in his place. Neither Wilson, Brown, nor Siegmund Warburg regretted Cromer's departure.

In October and November the attacks on the pound continued, and the borrowed reserves were gradually being exhausted. Nevertheless, Wilson's industrial policy began to have an effect, and by the end of the year the prime minister was able to show a creditable result: the balance of payments deficit was down to £278 million in 1965, against £757 million in 1964.

On 31 March 1966 Wilson called an early election and was re-elected for five years.

Calm had only come about through borrowing from the IMF and from banks. They would have to be repaid. The main amounts fell due in November 1967, and nobody yet knew how they would be honored.

Siegmund at that time was seeing the prime minister quite often and introducing him to all the world's great bankers when they passed through London. In May he was offered a knighthood. His initial reaction was to refuse. This had not been his ambition, and it was the sort of honor the family had been stubbornly refusing for two centuries. He noted that day:

> People are either hard on themselves or pleased with themselves. The former are those who make the world better. He who accepts higher challenges and who succumbs in the end in his effort to take up these challenges is the real victor in life.[35]

But finally he accepted. The *Financial Times* wrote, "Under his direction, his firm had experienced meteoric growth, but his appointment rather recognizes the value of his economic advice to the Government. He has in particular recommended a reduction in defense spending overseas."

In July the pound was again attacked and Brown began to consider devaluation inevitable. Wilson would not hear of it; he decided on budget cuts, control of profit margins and very strict control of wages, linking their growth for the first time to that of productivity. Brown's five-year plan, voided of substance by these new measures, was dropped hardly a year after being put forward. There were howls of betrayal from the Labour left, including Parliament member Ian Mikardo. Brown, embittered, resigned from the Ministry of Economic Affairs in August and became foreign secretary. The Ministry drifted. Eric Roll left. Austerity made the recession worse: there were six hundred thousand unemployed and the reserves, wholly borrowed, hardly covered the amount of short-term debts, i.e., $3 billion.

Siegmund then believed that the government was headed for the abyss unless it made a clear choice immediately between the pound and military presence abroad. He thought it must be helped to choose the pound, the key to British financial power, and in this way also save the Bretton Woods system and the finances of the West.

So for the first and last time in his life he intervened publicly in British political debate. On 2 October 1966, in the *Sunday Times*, he published a very long and considered article in which he made public the content of his advice to the prime minister during the previous two years. After setting out current severe criticisms of government policy, he explicitly declared himself in favor of it:

> I am not a socialist and I believe that private enterprise has just as important a role to play in our time—perhaps the age of the second Industrial Revolution—as during the first Industrial Revolution. However, I feel that those who are not socialists should as patriots have the duty not to assume and pronounce that everything which the Labour government does is wrong per se, and should specifically recognize that the courageous initiative of a policy to freeze incomes and prices pending an increase in productivity—which has now been started—is an act of great historical significance . . . . I would not want to advocate a coalition government nor the inhibition of free discussion in regard to any political subject where this concerns currency or anything else, but I wonder if there are not certain sections of governmental action such as some aspects of defence, currency, support of the United Nations and similar topics, whose removal

from the actual struggle or shadow boxing of the political parties is overdue . . . . I would like to quote Sir Roy Harrod in his letter to the *Times*: "It is not over dramatic to describe the present freeze policy as our last chance. It is a sort of economic Battle of Britain. This aspect of the government's policy should have all-party support . . . . We need at least a year in which all increases in productivity can go to making our prices more competitive."

Siegmund explained that the government's measures were designed in the short term to restore foreign confidence in sterling and in the medium term to produce on trading account a favorable balance of such dimensions that together with invisible net income from the private sector, a surplus would be arrived at; this surplus would initially cover the current foreign exchange outgoings in the government sector, but would also provide adequate sums

to enable us to begin the amortization of the foreign debt which we have incurred. If this new policy is properly carried out, it should be possible for us to achieve the intended result.

I do believe that those who are canvassing at present the devaluation of sterling have paid insufficient attention to the underlying realities of Britain's economic position in the 1960s and are prescribing a quite inappropriate cure for her current illness . . . . If sterling were devalued by 10–15 percent, it would not improve significantly our export or import position. We do not at present have the unemployed resources which are needed if devaluation is to lead to a marked increase in exports; nor would devaluation diminish the need for imports of an essential nature (e.g., food and raw materials) and our experience with the 15 percent import surcharge suggests that the volume of other, less essential commodities would not be significantly reduced either. Furthermore, there would remain the problem . . . of convincing the world of foreign exchange dealers that after a devaluation of this order the parity then established would be maintained and that further currency speculation was a loser's game.

. . . On the other hand any larger devaluation—and perhaps a lesser one—would cause a chain reaction, leading to other currency devaluations which would cancel out the temporary advantage gained, or should I rather say stolen by the UK.

Devaluation and equally the introduction of a floating exchange rate would demonstrate clearly that rather than having the courage to submit to unpopular but necessary decisions we prefer to rely on an economic device of doubtful efficacy. By doing this, we would be betraying the confidence of those who have heeded earlier reassurances on the maintenance of the parity of sterling; we would be giving an unwarranted reward to those who, whether governments or private individuals, have to an undue extent withdrawn gold from its proper function and have hoarded it to the detriment to the free world's economy.

Having ruled out devaluation as "at best a doubtful expedient," Siegmund restated his fundamental points: that the income and price freeze should be made to work; that the country should not continue to overspend its income; and that a value-added tax or export rebate should be introduced. He attributed the country's position partly to an accumulation of past errors, including recklessness with regard to the treatment of sterling balances after the war, or the repeated failure to reduce government spending, particularly overseas.

> This would have taxed any nation . . . if either the Germans or the Italians had been forced during the immediate post-war period to spend anything approximating to what the UK spent on defense programs at home and abroad, the German and Italian economic miracles might never have happened . . . .
> But our past errors can be forgotten as long as the lessons to be derived from them are remembered. I believe that our economic position is basically a strong one and that if we are prepared . . . to be resolute in making the required changes, we shall be able to catch up with and perhaps in some ways even surpass the other countries of the Western world, all of which have serious, though less publicized, difficulties of their own.

This article made an enormous impact in London. Wilson was very grateful for Siegmund's support. The City was angered by his lack of opposition to the "reds."

When he wrote the piece, Siegmund was at the zenith of his British influence: free of any conformism, without a set pattern or prejudices, expressing, he would afterward say "nonconformist left-wing views," and making "shocking, indeed provocative remarks." "Think of it," he said, mimicking his opponents, "the other day the fellow said he was a floating voter . . . !"[36]

Even so his article was to have no real effect, for it was too late to mold or divert the course of events, too late for Wilson to follow his advice. Siegmund would witness with fury the death struggle of the pound, then that of Bretton Woods. It was time for the debts to be paid and speculation would fuel the payments much faster than the structural improvements. But winter passed, and in March 1967 the United Kingdom managed to repay its debts to the central banks. Things were looking up; however, the closure of the Suez Canal and the Six Day War between Israel and its Arab neighbors in June, followed by a dockers' strike in September, caused British exports to fall while imports rose, so that more borrowing had to be done. This was the last straw. Wilson decided to renationalize iron and steel at a low price.

At the same time, still without knowing whether it was acting to "irrigate during a flood," as Jacques Rueff wrote, or to replace a shaky dollar, the IMF at its September annual meeting in Rio de Janeiro decided to create a new form of international liquidity, the SDRs (Special Drawing Rights). Bretton Woods was coming apart.

By October it was common knowledge that Britain would not have the means of paying her debt, and an imminent devaluation was expected. The outflow of capital accelerated. In November 1967 another payment date arrived, with no lifeline in sight. The choice was repayment or devaluation, in an attempt to reduce the deficit and staunch the capital hemorrhage. The decision was to devalue.

On 11 and 12 November the governors of the main central banks, meeting in Basel, discussed the extent of possible devaluation. On 14 November the British government published the figures for the October trade deficit, the biggest in British history, and two days later the cabinet discussed devaluation. On 17 November, in order to defend the pound, the Bank of England sold a further $1 billion, the equivalent of more than £300 million.

The next day, under pressure from the IMF, Wilson resigned himself after a three-year battle to a 14.3 percent devaluation. The pound fell from $2.80—its rate since 1949—to $2.40. The discount rate went to 8 percent, corporation tax was increased and public spending was once more cut, though without touching most of spending abroad.

What would have been no more than a technical readjustment six years earlier was now to unleash a financial disaster of global proportions.

The Dollar Adrift
The fall of the pound led to that of the Spanish, Danish and Israeli currencies, among others, and pushed the dollar into the front line. As

Siegmund had foreseen, the American currency immediately came under threat, as everyone expected a dollar revaluation of the gold price, following its pound revaluation. So for the first time in history, in order to defend the dollar, the central banks of Europe had to buy dollars and sell gold. Moreover, the Vietnam War was deepening the American deficit, which rose from $1.6 billion in 1966 to $3.2 billion in 1967.

The day after the British devaluation President Johnson published a restatement of his intent to maintain the price of gold at $35 per ounce. But no one any longer believed this: there were far too many dollars outside America. On 26 November in Frankfurt the governors of the "gold pool" central banks decided to continue sales of gold, to support existing exchange rates; on 30 November the IMF lent a further $1.4 billion to Britain, to help her stay on her new course, which at the start would inevitably worsen the deficit.

By the end of 1967, therefore, there was growing expectation of an increase in the gold price: a wave of gold sales brought the risk that the free market price and the official price would get out of line. The "pool" then sold gold bars worth a total of $2 billion. This situation could not last.

The argument over the gold price was now in the public arena. On 28 February 1968 Senator Jacob Javits openly called for dollar convertibility to be suspended and the gold pool to be abandoned. The effect was disastrous. As Siegmund had foreseen, the British deficits had been worsening. To reduce them, the budget presented in March 1968 by the chancellor of the exchequer, James Callaghan, tapped 2 percent from purchasing power and took up one of Nicholas Kaldor's old suggestions. To make imports more expensive without a further devaluation, importers would have to deposit foreign currency equal to 50 percent of the value of the goods imported as a guarantee for six months. The balance on services began to improve, but as Siegmund had also foreseen, exports had not picked up enough to compensate for the higher cost of imports caused by devaluation, so this led to inflation and wage demands.

In the United States, too, nothing could reduce the balance of payments deficit. There was still full employment, but the Vietnam War was increasing imports and inflation. The American trade surplus fell. Speculators attacked the dollar. Expecting a devaluation, everyone wanted to buy gold instead. There was therefore nothing to encourage industrialists to repatriate their capital to the United States, which also worsened the deficits. In January 1968 a strict legal limit was imposed on the previously optional foreign investment quotas, and to implement it the Treasury set up a Bureau of Direct Foreign Investment.

Siegmund by then thought that America, which no longer saved enough to invest in his country, was in danger; he thought that it would be lost because of the gigantism of its financial institutions and their desire for short-term profit. He wrote in his notebook that "An American only asks himself two questions, Where can I park my car? and How can I lose twenty-five pounds?"[37]

Gold was now being sold—a lot of it—to prevent the devaluation of the dollar. Between November 1967 and March 1968 the main central banks disposed of $3 billion worth of gold in an attempt to calm the market. It was in vain. In March, with the Tet Offensive a psychological setback for the Americans and General William Westmoreland asking for 200,000 more GIs, Johnson asked Congress to pass a tax surcharge to continue financing the war. Congress refused.

In London on 8 March the pool sold 100 tons of gold, on 13 March 175 tons; on 14 March at least 225 tons, and possibly as much as 1,000 tons in order to hold the rates. During the night of 14 March Johnson telephoned Wilson to ask him to close the London gold market, to avoid a hemorrhage of gold from Fort Knox; Wilson then called on Siegmund, who thought the measure unavoidable. On 15 March Wilson closed the market for a few days for the first time since it had been created. Confidence in the dollar then collapsed. On 16 and 17 March the leading finance ministers met urgently in Washington. It was expected that they would decide to raise the gold price, as provided for in the Bretton Woods agreement. In fact, caring more about political fiction than financial realities, they actually decided to allow gold to float, but without changing its official price, thus putting an end to the operations of their pool and instituting a dual market for gold. Honor was saved. The dollar was floating, but no one acknowledged this.

The fact was that conversion of dollars into gold was no longer possible; the monetary authorities allowed the price of commercial gold to come about, through the forces of supply and demand; the dollar became the real standard. Bretton Woods was dead without ever really having worked. America was now able to indebt itself without risk: there was nothing more to repay. The White plan arose intact from the ashes of Bretton Woods.

The pound was no more. Its share of international trade had fallen to 7 percent. "The legacy of the right," wrote Wilson, "weighed on almost all the Government's decisions for five years, for the five years and eight months we were in power."[38]

A month later, on 31 March 1968, Johnson announced his decision to seek peace in Vietnam and not to seek reelection in November.

Zenith in Britain

In these years when currencies were being torn apart, Siegmund earned money for his bank and brought it increasing influence. In March 1966 for the twentieth anniversary of the foundation of S.G. Warburg & Co., he allowed the *New Yorker* to publish a long article about him, later partly reprinted in a book:

> With the reputation of never having lost a single takeover battle, of spending more than half his time outside Britain, of being listened to just as much in Washington as in Downing Street, he is always surrounded by secretaries, dictating in his car, making telephone calls worth millions of dollars.[39]

Reading this flattering text, to which he had made no small contribution, one might have thought that Siegmund was taking himself seriously, that he had given up the modesty that had been his rule. However, he still also knew the truth of ambition and the absurdity of things, and noted privately, "The key to happiness lies in the illusion of seeing sense in nonsense."[40] And again, "Most things we do, happy or unhappy, slip between our fingers like sand. Some stay in our hands like pebbles, and these are the only ones that count."[41]

The following month, to mark the same event, *Time* devoted another article to him that summarized and completed the *New Yorker* profile; he was again presented as the "banker whose growth had been the fastest in the City" and who had "shaken the sloth of the City by introducing German organization and discipline."

He made many big deals that year, helping with a number of mergers and coups d'état against lazy managements. He was also at the zenith of his influence in British economic policy. Not only had he been at the center of the devaluation debate, but he was also much involved in industrial development.

At the beginning of 1966 George Brown wanted to facilitate company mergers, which he felt the merchant banks were neglecting, and had the notion of reviving the prewar Bankers' Industrial Development Company, run originally by Major Albert Pam of Schröder's. His plan was to create a kind of public investment bank to be called the Industrial Reorganization Corporation, to which he assigned the role of "industrial catalyst," when the necessary mergers did not take place naturally. Despite opposition from the entire City, which saw this as a threat of unfair competition from the public authorities, but thanks to the efforts of Eric Roll, the IRC was set up and given a budget of £150 million. Its services were free, and for detailed advice it directed people toward the merchant banks. Its first chairman was Sir Frank Kearton, also chairman of Courtauld, and George Brown asked Siegmund's protégé Ronald Grierson, whom he hardly knew, to become director-general. Siegmund allowed him leave from the bank, theoretically for two years. Several people asked before Grierson had refused, and it was probably a good thing, Siegmund thought, to have a man on the inside of the IRC. For in contrast to the City, Siegmund saw in the operations of the IRC the prospect of much new business for his house. He was right. Immediately he participated through this means in setting up ICL, the result of a merger of eight computer companies, also in Chrysler's purchase of a stake in Rootes Motors and in the merger of GEC and English Electric.

In the following year the IRC also brought him into the merger of British Motor Corporation and Leyland, which then formed one of the biggest automobile groups outside America. For months Siegmund was to negotiate subtly on the two major points crucial to the success of the talks: what was to be the relative weight of the two companies within the group, and which of the two chairmen, Sir George Harriman or Donald Stokes, would become chairman of the whole? It was he, after much discussion and after arbitration by Harold Wilson himself, who was to evaluate the weight of each firm within the whole; and it was he who was to dictate the choice of Harriman as chairman. Finally it was Siegmund who, following a plan he had made at the beginning, was to depose Harriman the very day he took office as chairman, in favor of John Black, the youngest Leyland director, after some merciless confrontations.

Ronald Grierson was against what he saw as this "shotgun wedding" and left the IRC to become vice-chairman of English Electric. This departure led Siegmund to choose another "adopted son," Peter Spira, who managed the international department. Again that year Mercury Securities helped Orion, where David Scholey's father worked, into the lap of Nationale Nederlanden, a big Dutch insurance company.

S.G. Warburg was still the leading seller of Euro-issues by number, and the third by amount.

The group's profits still made it the top bank in the City, along with Morgan Grenfell. Siegmund, less interested than ever in money, kept only a very small part of it for himself. In September he noted, "If money has any virtue in this world of perverse capitalism, it is only that of protecting our private lives in a society which suffers above all from excessive indiscretion."[42]

The following year he took on some prestigious executives: primarily Sir Eric Roll, who had left the administration when Brown resigned from the Ministry of Economic Affairs and joined Siegmund on 31 March 1967. Then there was Van der Beughel, a former Dutch minister of foreign affairs, and an Italian count. Nobody was safe from Siegmund's approaches. Thus he slipped word to Bruno Kreisky, then without a government post, "If you want to go into business now, do nothing without telling me first." Others, such as Sir Robert Armstrong, cabinet secretary, would later hear the same advances.

Eric Roll has recorded the charm of Siegmund at that time, and his ability to distance himself from events:

> He could be relaxed even in moments of great drama, appreciating the sporting aspect of any transaction, especially when the competition was rough. He often found this very amusing, exercising his sense of humor even in the tensest moments. When business required it, he spared himself no effort, including attendance at evening functions which he hated more than anything. One of the images which comes back to me is that of Siegmund at some important meeting or other (at Downing Street or Bilderberg, indeed even an annual conference for the Siemens bankers), I can see him standing still, apparently absorbed in his thoughts, in a corner, surrounded by the crowd. . . . In spite of that, people invariably came to him. One of those who knew him best said that he acted like a magnet, even in taxis, for example when he was leaving the opera on a rainy evening. He certainly exercised a kind of magnetic radiation, which attracted people, business and—although the media avoid saying so—news.[43]

His characteristics had become accentuated with age. His height, his head that was too big for his shoulders, his highly concentrated gaze at the person he was speaking to, as though nobody else existed, were all increasingly fascinating and impressive.

That same year David Scholey became director of the bank and made his appearance within the circle of "adopted sons." He urged Siegmund to take an interest in the insurance broker Matthews Wrightson, whose board he had joined the previous year. Siegmund was to buy it and merge it with Stewart Smith, the firm he had owned for some time. The transaction was to give him great placing power for his own loans. That year Morgan Grenfell took a similar step, buying 20 percent of the biggest Lloyd's broker, Willis Faber.

Mercury Securities then had more than 250 employees. The British elite still did not much like Siegmund, this ex-German who succeeded splendidly in any world business he touched, advising a Labour prime minister in London all the while. He hardly cared for the elite either. In August 1967 he noted, "Making an effort is considered bad taste by high society;" and again, "When dealing with people of no interest, one should concentrate on things of no importance."

This distance from his own environment no longer bothered him, since he was by now rich and powerful enough to do only what he enjoyed, and to choose his clients. The following year his firm, with the Plessey chairman John Clark, made a bid for English Electric, which was rejected and fought. Sensing that it was going to fail, Siegmund himself took over and suggested a merger instead. Clark refused, Warburg withdrew and the bid failed. Siegmund told the *Financial Times*, "We have only won all our battles because our clients have followed our advice. There are people we reject as clients. We ask of them only two things: to be honest and to be businessmen of quality."

The article presented him as "the banker who has turned the purchase of a firm into a work of art," and described him as "a man who speaks quietly, in a serious, almost somber manner, and whose slightly stooped appearance is more that of a professor than a money man."

At the time he himself valued his own fortune at £5 million, which he ostensibly left under the management of experts within his bank. He said, "I have no Rolls-Royce, no yacht, no racehorses and no property." Then aged sixty-six, he was the same age as Max had been when he, Siegmund, had left Hamburg. His son was no longer with the bank. He had left Great Britain to live in the United States.

The situation in Hamburg had not altered much. Eric's eighteen-year-old son Max left America, where he had been born, and joined Brinckmann, Wirtz & Co. as a trainee.

The clash between the two branches of the family was then at its height. In April 1966 *Time* magazine gave a shrewd picture of the difference between the two men: Eric was "athletic and uncomplicated," while Siegmund was a "rather mysterious intellectual." Both had the desire to "restore the family's glorious past." The Hamburg bank was prestigious. "Bankers from all over Europe send their most brilliant scions to train with Brinckmann," said Eric, but he had to "share power with the Brinckmanns and the other partners."

Siegmund, in London, shared his power with nobody. In sum, there were no longer any restraints on him. He himself described his team as his "family." "His legacy to his brilliant team is great," said the *Financial Times*, "but one may wonder whether several people will be able to maintain the success of one."

Israel Corporation

Siegmund did not know Israel well when he went there first at the beginning of 1960. Very affected by his visit to the Degania kibbutz, where his cousin Fritz had just joined his children, he began to follow the country's affairs with intense interest. He was neither a Zionist nor an anti-Zionist. He was interested in Israel and only helped organizations in which he believed. Not the United Jewish Appeal because "[it] has too many chauvinistic sides. I don't believe in German chauvinism . . . British chauvism . . . American chauvinism and I don't believe in Israeli chauvinism."[44]

He gave to the Weizmann Institute and in London to the *Jewish Observer* because it was liberal. He took a keen interest in relations between Israel and Germany, and when on 14 March 1960 David Ben-Gurion met Konrad Adenauer at the Waldorf Astoria Hotel in New York, Siegmund attached great importance to the event. He saw himself as a citizen of the world, attached to an ethic, not a nation. He scarcely mixed with the Jewish community in London, not caring for it. The feeling was certainly reciprocated. In 1961, he noted privately, "Half the Jewish élite in Anglo-Saxon countries is conservative, and the other half is reactionary."[45]

Religious devotion was an integral part of his life, though he was too universalist to attach himself to a single faith. In 1962 he wrote, "One must be able to fill the moral vacuum of our times with a religion based on aesthetic and ethical elements, but without the complex of sin."[46]

That year Fritz died at Degania, the last of Moritz's sons and the first Warburg in centuries—maybe a thousand years—to be buried in Israel.

Because of his close connection with Dr. Foerder, who had become chairman of Israel's Bank Leumi, it was only natural that Siegmund introduced the bank's shares to the London Stock Exchange. After diplomatic relations were established on 7 March 1965 between West Germany and Israel, Siegmund visited the country more and more. He saw Foerder and political leaders. In December 1966 Dr. Foerder said to him of a common enemy, "That man loses much on acquaintance."[47] He was taken with the phrase and noted it down. Then began the strangest financial transaction in which he was ever involved in Israel.

In the spring of 1967 Siegmund, André Meyer, John Schiff and other important bankers were invited by the Israeli governnment to sail from Gibraltar to Tel Aviv on board the *Queen Elizabeth*. The cruise took place after the Six Day War and everyone was then called upon to make a large donation to Israel. All agreed. Siegmund was very surprised to notice that the most handsome donations came from Mexico and Brazil, not from Europe or America. During this voyage, Pinchas Sapir, then the Israeli finance minister, spread the idea of setting up the Israel Corporation, a body designed to channel European capital toward Israel.

This was put into operation during the following winter. S.G. Warburg and Kuhn Loeb took charge. Siegmund became co-chairman with Astore Maier, an Italian banker, and Harvey M. Krueger from Kuhn Loeb became director alongside Jacob Tsur, an Israeli and former director-general of the Ministry of Commerce. The initial aim was to attract $100 million, but only $27 million were collected. The undertaking was difficult to manage, as anyone who contributed $1 million had the right to a post as administrator. Two big deals were arranged with this money: the purchase of ZIM, a shipping company, and of some oil refineries. Siegmund, who had involved himself heavily at the start, gradually began to distance himself from the undertaking, whose methods of operation he found inconsistent with his own. Jewish affairs continued to interest him nevertheless, though not from a financial angle. In 1970 he learned that Elie Wiesel, whose works had affected him deeply, was in London for the publication of one of his books. He called Wiesel's publisher, George Weidenfeld, and asked him to arrange a meeting. The conversation lasted two hours. They spoke about Israel, about Judaism. Elie Wiesel saw

> an extraordinary character, calm, curious, learned. There was in him a humanism of astonishing strength. This former refugee is a man of letters who has not written anything, a philosopher who has not constructed a system. . . . There is no small talk with him, no gossip. He speaks briefly, simply, intensely with authority, without ever a mention of himself or his family.

Siegmund offered Elie Wiesel his help in any project he wanted, for peace in the Middle East or the defense of human rights. Wiesel declined the offer, but his meeting marked the beginning of a long association between the great banker and the great writer, each one fascinated by the other.

That year, less money was coming into the Israel Corporation. Someone came up with the idea of attracting non-Jewish capital. Initially, this came from Germany, through Rosenbaum, a Geneva banker, because Germany was then allowing the same tax advantages for investing in Israel as in certain other areas. The money was to be collected by the German trade union bank. Siegmund no longer liked this at all. So when in April 1971 Edmond de Rothschild joined the board of the Israel Corporation, he suggested he should be replaced as chairman. Then he also left his board seat to one of his executives and tiptoed away. He sensed before other people that this whole affair would end badly.

Ahead on Japan

Isolated from American aid after the war, Japan in 1962 was still a Third World country in the eyes of European specialists. Siegmund went there for the first time with two other British bankers (Alexander Hood, one of the heads of Schröder, and Edmond de Rothschild). He met the heirs of the Mitsuis and Takahashis whom his uncle Max had advised at the beginning of the century.

> We were there for about three weeks [he said], and I must confess I was very impressed. I thought these people really put an enormous effort into what they are doing, much more than we Europeans. And they apply to their work a unique mixture of utter discipline and infinite self-criticism. At that time, it was very difficult to place a

single Japanese bond or Japanese share in Europe; people thought Japan was in a terrible state and it would take them another fifty years to recover.[48]

Siegmund saw from this first contact that Japan was a future great power, where he felt comfortable, because he found there the qualities he appreciated above all: seriousness, style, attention to detail, the long-term view, an interest in things beyond money. Like him, the Japanese knew how to combine ancient wisdom with great modernity.

There he met an extraordinary character, almost his Japanese double, Jiro Shirasu, the leading associate of Prime Minister Yoshida, and the wielder of extensive influence. A graduate of Cambridge and a former trainee in the City, he had founded MITI and had attended the San Francisco Peace Conference as adviser to the Japanese delegation, and had played an important role between General MacArthur and the Japanese authorities in the management of his country's financial affairs. The respect he had won during the negotiations and his absolute knowledge of people allowed him to exercise extensive power over the various postwar Japanese cabinets, outside of any ministerial or political office. Shirasu introduced Siegmund to Akamura, the chairman of Normura, the biggest financial conglomerate in the country, and also persuaded him to concern himself with the Japanese market.

On his return to Europe Siegmund alone of all Western bankers at that time made himself the advocate of Japan and persuaded several of his clients to put 10 percent of their money into that country. No one would regret this. His relationship with Shirasu became a friendship, and Shirasu's second son later came to Siegmund in London as a trainee.

As always Siegmund's interest in the country went beyond the ordinary realm of finance; he was deeply interested in Japanese culture and read everything he could find on the subject. In February 1963 he wrote down the Japanese proverb, "If the water is too pure, the fish won't swim in it."[49] He would have liked to have originated this phrase, which for him was an elegant way of expressing refusal of absolutes, hatred of totalitarianism and the strength of tolerance. He seemed to discover the similarities between two kinds of ancient wisdom, that of his people and that of the Orient.

Business was business, however, and he also decided to break into the Japanese market. At the beginning of 1963 he sent Peter Spira and Ian Fraser to Tokyo in search of clients and at the end of the year issued from New York a $22.5 million loan for the city of Tokyo, guaranteed by the Japanese government. This was the first postwar borrowing abroad by the city of Tokyo, and it was also the first Japanese loan guaranteed by the Japanese government. Then from London he made the first convertible Eurobond issue for Toray, a Japanese company.

From then on Japan became a regular client of the long- and short-term Euromarket and often went through S.G. Warburg for Euro-issues. In 1965 Siegmund launched a second Eurodollar loan for Toray, for a total of $15 million, then repeated the transaction for the biggest Japanese companies: Olympus, Mitsubishi, Fuji, the Bank of Tokyo, Tokyu and Tujo. Once again his passion for "gratuitous" contacts and his art of showing consideration to others were to repay him.

"Swindle" Issues

While the fiction of Bretton Woods was collapsing and Eurodollars were proliferating dangerously, the Euro-issue market experienced its first frauds and swindles.

In 1968 the American external deficit was down a little, at no more than $1.3 billion, but military spending abroad exploded as the country was bogged down in Vietnam. The Euro-issue market, which had stagnated around $1.5 billion in 1967, doubled the following year (130 issues totaling $3 billion). Among the borrowers were some who would soon default.

This was first the case with a $10 million loan arranged by S.G. Warburg for the Famous Schools Overseas Corporation, then with a $25 million convertible loan issued in June for a completely unknown company, ICC International. Nevertheless, its president, Robert Vesco, should have attracted attention—and we shall see why. Kuhn Loeb and other banks were victims of the same kind of trouble for which the lenders and the bankers picked up the bill. Such difficulties were fairly rare, in relation to the size of the market. This was a sign of the prudence of the investment banks, in contrast to the commercial banks who were lending as hard as they could in the short-term Euromarket at low rates, because no guarantee was needed there. The commercial banks were to lose much in bankruptcies and moratoria.

To satisfy the extensive demand for capital from multinationals in Europe and elsewhere, it was now necessary to arrange ever more enormous loans. It was at this point that Siegmund had the idea of a Eurofund, borrowing several million dollars in the form of convertible Eurobonds to further invest in the Euro-issues of companies not identified in advance.

At the end of 1968, faced with a continuing United States external deficit, Johnson, at the end of his term, again hardened America monetary policy. The administration even tried to restrict commercial lending abroad by the big banks, without, however, abolishing the limits set in 1937 on term deposits. These decisions caused a further rise in American interest rates, which was to worsen the financial crisis of the indebted cities and that of brokers such as Bache & Co.

Richard Nixon became president in January 1969 and continued the struggle against inflation, then considered top priority; but the Vietnam War was deepening the balance of payments deficit, which could be neglected insofar as there was no longer the need to take out gold to finance it.

The American economy had changed profoundly: that year 4,500 big mergers took place, and twenty-five of the five hundred biggest American companies were swallowed by conglomerates, with the investment banker playing a notable role. On Wall Street, too, the landscape was changing. New Deal legislation began to crack under the weight of competition and the profit requirement. Despite the Glass-Steagall Act the distinction between the two types of bank was becoming blurred. The big commercial banks saw a dangerous loss of profitability in their traditional markets and tried to outwit the old financial advice houses, which were themselves having trouble. At Lehman the founders' grandson, who was more interested in racehorses than banking, died in 1969, leaving a collection of paintings valued at $75 million. His death caused something like chaos and some departures from the firm. Kuhn Loeb, still run by John Schiff, suffered similar difficulties: its profits fell and its margins declined. First Boston, Morgan, Salomon and Kidder still held out against the giants. But there was the need to invest the enormous cash resources of American companies that were slowing down their investments for lack of profitability.

There began an era of speculation, a source of fantastic gains, maintained by the monetary vacillation of governments; Eurodollars were invested at this time, and their holders earned much more than in Euro-issues.

Ever since the gold price had been freed, an increase in its free market price had been expected. But to general surprise, the gold price stayed at around $40. Since impatient speculators had been wrong on the dollar, they turned their attention to Europe. On 29 April 1969 the German finance minister, F.J. Strauss, publicly suggested that his country would be able to revalue its currency within the framework of a multilateral realignment. Accordingly, there was immediate speculation on the mark and between 30 April and 9 May the Bundesbank had to take in 4 billion to hold its parity. On 9 May the German cabinet postponed revaluation indefinitely, and on 12 May instituted new controls on capital inflows. On 28 July just as the SDRs came into force, the franc in turn came under attack—its position had been deteriorating for several months. On 8 August France finally agreed to the devaluation rejected six months earlier. Speculation then moved back to the mark and on 29 September the Federal Republic of Germany, able to hold out no longer, decided to float its currency. On 24 October, once the position had stabilized, a new rate was fixed, revaluing by 9.3 percent. At the end of October the speculators left the mark, went back to the dollar and German reserves fell by $5 billion, including a $500 million sale of gold to the United States.

On the international capital market, Euro-issues, unlike Euro-dollars, scarcely increased at all, and the 1968 level would not be reached again until 1971. London remained the heart of the short- and medium-term offshore dollar market. Even Italian dollars lent to Italian companies were handled by the City. Meanwhile, American banks offered American multinationals all-round banking services: buying companies, picking investments, borrowing, asset management, short-term loans, investing money on the Eurodollar market. . . . they could do everything except place Euro-issues in the United States or with American citizens.

The all-round banks of Germany and Switzerland in turn began to compete on their home ground with these American banks, as well as with the British banks, whose placing capacity proved too weak. S.G. Warburg, unquestionably the leading bank in the market until then, had to give up its place to the Deutsche Bank in 1969, while still continuing to grow with the market.

Swindles proliferated. Thus Paribas-New York Securities placed $25 million worth of convertible bonds in the name of one Equity Funding Corporation, which was later shown to have padded its profits by declaring fictional sales of insurance policies. Along with most of the big American and British banks, S.G. Warburg was caught in this business and dropped part of its profit for the year.

This was the year of the failure that had the greatest repercussions in this market. It was the work of Bernie Cornfeld, who had set up Investors Overseas Services (IOS) in 1956 to sell investment fund shares to American soldiers overseas; by 1968 he was managing $2 billion worth of savings invested in issues of all kinds, with sizable earnings. Already, a little earlier, Bruno Kreisky had had a visit from a strange messenger who asked him to take over the running of IOS Austria at an enormous salary. Kreisky of course refused but telephoned Siegmund in London to tell him the story. "You were right, and not only as far as you are concerned: nobody should touch it. Within a few years it will be the bankruptcy of the century." Cornfeld had in fact begun a very dangerous cumulative process. Whatever the Euro-issue, even the least secure, he would buy 10 percent each time. Several bankers, some of the most honorable, helped him with placing, or included him in the syndicates they led. Trouble began for IOS in the spring of 1969 when rates went up and it had to bear the cost of the loans it had guaranteed until it found clients to place them with. In order to protect its cash, IOS itself then issued loans through the intermediary of complex structures, among them a ghost bank, the Investors Bank of Luxemburg. By July it was not even honoring these loans. In September the snowball continued to grow. In order to pay up at the beginning of 1970, it issued eleven million shares at a nominal value of $10. Six lead banks and 116 others agreed to take part in placing these shares. This seemed to be the validation of IOS. But first S.G. Warburg, then a little later Kuhn Loeb, Hambros and N.M. Rothschild refused to join in. Although the shares rose to $25 immediately after the issue, the credibility of IOS began to erode in April 1970 and the price fell back to $4. N.M. Rothschild offered to buy the lot for $1 apiece, which Cornfeld haughtily refused. Shortly afterward IOS was sold in the name of the company ICC to Robert Vesco, who appropriated $224 million from the assets of IOS and absconded. In 1972, IOS was declared bankrupt. Today Vesco lives in Cuba and Cornfeld in Los Angeles.

In 1970, while the interbank creation of Eurodollars was exploding, forming new and doubtful alliances, the Euro-issue market was still stagnating: only $2.7 billion were invested, while more than $100 billion Eurodollars were in circulation. More than 120 offers were made during the year. By now an offer could be arranged within a few days. The City was now attracting the biggest banks. Walter Wriston, president of the City Bank of New York, summed up well for Anthony Sampson the reasons why the American banks chose London. "The Eurodollar market exists in London because people believe the British Government is not about to close it down. That is the basic reason and that took you a thousand years of history."[50]

Paris was still in second place, far behind London. Other markets appeared in Frankfurt, Amsterdam, Zurich, Basel, Geneva, Milan, Vienna, and even Nassau, Beirut, Tel Aviv, Hong Kong and Singapore. In order to place securities there, several British banks—Schröder, Hambros, Rothschild—organized joint subsidiaries with local banks but gradually dismantled them to set up their own offices.

The United States' balance of payments deficit continued to deepen. The trade balance again showed a surplus of $5 billion. The capital revenue balance was also positive, thanks to the foreign income of American companies, but because of the Vietnam War the balance of services went deeper into deficit, in 1970 equaling the trade surplus. In the United States nobody was worried about the problem. The fashionable theory on Wall Street was that of benign neglect: in other words it was not the dollar that was overvalued but the other currencies that were undervalued. Walter Wriston even said, speaking of Germany, "Nobody has a balance of payments surplus that doesn't want one."[51]

The American labor movement, seeing unemployment grow with the external deficit, called for a return to protectionism in order to reduce imports. With a view to reducing the deficit, President Nixon finally decided not to oppose the outflow of capital, as his predecessors had done, but to attract it, and to this end raise rates and abandon the regulations set by Roosevelt.

There were those who thought that these measures would ruin London and send the Eurodollar market back to New York. Nothing came of it; the return on capital remained lower in the United States than elsewhere, and even though military spending began to subside a little, the damage was done. Inflation and a balance of payments deficit had brought about a trade deficit and compromised the last chances for Bretton Woods.

Forgetting London

Weariness comes from the lack of a reason for living. In November 1968 Siegmund noted, "One of the great weaknesses of our time is the anxiety to create an image for oneself."[52] He no longer wanted to give himself an image or anything else. Why go on? For whom? His daughter was living in Israel. His son had put an end to Cripps-Warburg & Co. to settle in the United States. Already Siegmund too was thinking of going away.

Without mentioning it to anyone in his firm, he entertained merger proposals from other banks—Hill Samuel and Jim Slater. He was not the only one at the time to envisage changes. Most families had lost their influence among the merchant banks they had founded in London. Guinness Mahon was no longer run by the family. Only Baring was still managed by the three Baring brothers, John, Nicholas and Peter. Everywhere the family system of management by a body of partners was giving way to specialized departments with hierarchies and salaried managers—responsible for investment, fund management or share issues. Moreover, the commercial banks, with their anonymity, bureaucracy and technology, were encroaching more and more on the preserve of the merchant banks. Their interests intermingled: National & Grindlay's bought Brandt, Midland Bank bought Samuel Montagu and Hambros itself sold 10 percent of its capital to the Prudential Insurance Company of America.

Siegmund made his choice; he attempted to merge with Hill Samuel; in the summer of 1969 there were discussions: would the company be called "Warburg-Hill Samuel & Co." or "Hill-Warburg-Samuel & Co.," and who would run it? An agreement was reached, then abrogated when the two general staffs proved incapable of reconciling their strategy. Siegmund wanted his firm to retain its specialization in financial advice and therefore to refrain from stockbroking; the latter was not *haute banque* as he saw it. Hill Samuel would say after the event, "We thought it was necessary to offer a wider spectrum of financial services than he did."[53]

Once the plan was buried Siegmund gave up further development in London. After all, one could continue to grow elsewhere. This was also the period when Britain was again beginning to concern itself with the Continent. After General de Gaulle's departure from the Élysée Palace in April 1969, the Common Market membership talks, interrupted two years earlier, could be resumed. On 14 January 1970, Wilson indicated the British desire to participate, but it was the next prime minister, Edward Heath, who actually took direct action in June, following the Conservative election victory. Nevertheless, when the British Parliament finally ratified membership of the EEC on 28 October 1971 Siegmund was pleased:

> I think I may say that I am a good European [he said later]. I thought it was in the interest of Great Britain to join the countries of the Continent well before the EEC existed, and I am sad that it should have taken so long. A pity: we should have been spared many of the protectionist elements of the Treaty of Rome.[54]

Hamburg by Halves

Despite thirty years of setbacks Siegmund had still not given up the idea of restoring the family name to the bank in Hamburg. Now that he was established in Frankfurt, he tried another stratagem: a merger between the two German operations.

He was having trouble with S.G. Warburg, Frankfurt, whose growth left something to be desired; he wanted to sell it and buy something bigger—Effecten-Bank, a provincial commercial bank in the Frankfurt area, founded by the Hahn family before the war and quite well established. Richard Daus was very much against this purchase. Siegmund decided to disregard the objection and made the acquisition without informing him. When Richard Daus learned of it he went to London to say that he wished to bring the aforementioned termination agreement into effect. Siegmund replied, "Can you afford to buy back your share?," knowing that Daus could not. Then with Paribas, the Vogt group and M.M. Warburg, S.G. Warburg set up a holding company, of which it owned 27.5 percent, but controlled 50 percent overall. Its name became "Effectenbank-Warburg." Richard Daus then became an independent, and Gert Whitman, who also was not in agreement with Siegmund's acquisition, went into partnership with him. Siegmund was furious.

To avoid fighting two battles at once, Siegmund reached an agreement with Brinckmann. Both names would appear on the Hamburg bank, though Siegmund did set certain subsidiary conditions that demonstrated once more his deep feeling for the name: the bank title was not to be "E.M. Warburg," but "M.M. Warburg," Warburg was to appear before Brinckmann and the name of Wirtz was to remain even though Wirtz had died long before. In addition, the link with S.G. Warburg in London was to be strengthened through an increase in the exchange of directors. At the end of six months of discussion, on 6 January 1970, the Hamburg bank became "M.M. Warburg-Brinckmann, Wirtz & Co." Eric Warburg also was delighted by this arrangement.

On the following day, under the heading "Name over the door again," the *Times* wrote:

> For the best part of 15 years since Sir Siegmund and his family again secured a stake in the Hamburg bank, he has been working to get the Warburg name included in the bank's title. The Brinckmann family,

headed by octogenarian Dr. Rudolph [sic] Brinckmann, we understand, did not welcome the change in the name of the Hamburg
bank.

That was putting it mildly.

Then came two coincidental deaths: on the way to register the
agreement at the city hall, Rudolf Brinckmann collapsed in the Hamburg Rathaus Platz from a heart attack. The same year saw the death of
Gert Whitman.

Even today a brochure from this opulent Hamburg bank summa-
rizes the episode in that inimitable style that allows bankers generally to
smooth over the rough edges, rendering the task of the historian nearly
impossible. "Eric came back to Hamburg in 1956. His name was later
incorporated into that of the bank, which had developed strongly after
the war under the title Brinckmann & Wirtz; the present name pre-
serves both traditions." One could hardly be more ecumenical.

On that same January day in 1970 Siegmund reached a new stage
in his retirement. Having finally dropped the idea of merging his group,
he left the effective chairmanship to become honorary chairman. Two
"uncles," Coke and Korner, left the boards of the bank and Mercury
Securities, where they still had seats; David Scholey, Peter Spira and Ira
Wender now were members with Eric Warburg and Hans Wüttke.

In November 1972 Siegmund was to note, "Human beings are
born and die like animals or plants—but friends never die."[55] Perhaps
he was thinking then of Gert Whitman, seeking to forget their final
quarrel.

Free Port, Floating Currencies

The foreign exchange markets had become very unsettled; the continuing Vietnam War had thrown open the way to inflation, deficits and
monetary insecurity. In June 1970 the Canadian dollar started floating.
All over the world the demand for capital from companies and states
was increasing faster than saving. Interest rates increased, worsening the
recession, and money was created on the Eurodollar market, worsening
inflation. Rates were expected to rise further. So the banks held back
from lending at a fixed rate for the long term, when there was so much
to be made from speculating in the short term; and Euro-issues were
difficult to place. Unprofitable companies were driven into short-term
borrowing, and the profitable companies considered speculating rather
than investing.

Siegmund did not care for this. He preferred real lending transactions and not to become involved in speculation.

Then came a notable innovation, which in the space of a few months and on a global scale would change the nature of all money markets, throwing them into complete uncertainty. For the first time in centuries there was to be long-term borrowing of money at a rate changing at short intervals. As always with an innovation, several financiers wrangled over the honor of having been the originator. What is certain is that all, at one time or another, acknowledged having submitted the concept to Siegmund Warburg, and all admitted that he had been the first to have understood it, refined it and made it work. The most probable of the initiators was a then-unknown financier, Evan Galbraith, a young director with Bankers Trust International Limited in London, and a future US ambassador to Paris. According to reliable sources it was he who in February 1970 conceived the idea of launching a Euro-issue with an interest rate that would vary every six months. His superiors were skeptical and did not see themselves proposing such a loan to one of their clients.

Galbraith then talked to other banks about the concept but received a similarly negative reaction. Only Peter Spira, then Siegmund's chief lieutenant and in fierce competition with David Scholey for control, took an interest in the idea. He showed Galbraith into Siegmund's office that spring, and a profitable conversation ensued; later Siegmund refined the idea with David Scholey, who had become an expert on the variable-rate concept. Within a few days he had settled on the client to whom the deal should be offered, the amount and the rate. He knew that the best possible borrower at that time for this type of security was ENEL (Italian Electricity) which, he thought, needed $150 million over ten years; he knew it could pay 7 percent, or 0.75 percent above the rate for six-month loans. As always, his wonderful market intuition proved accurate. Spira was dispatched to see the Italians, and the deal was made in May 1970. Similar transactions were repeated for Pepsico, then General Cable and the Argentinian government with Bankers Trust as joint lead bank.

This was the first floating rate issue, though some see the very small —$14.7 million—issue by Dreyfus Offshore Trust in July 1969 as something of a precursor. Since then the method has been greatly developed and more than half of today's Euro-issues are carried out in this manner.

Still there are those who maintain that someone else was first with the idea: a man named Minos Zombanakis, another of the strange adventurers in finance, who was also at Bankers Trust in London at the time. Others attribute paternity to Bob Genillard, who also worked in the City.

One observer, David Potter, was to write later:

> I remember that Siegmund, Bob Genillard of [of White Weld] and Evan Galbraith all claimed to have had the idea in their bath, to the point where a journalist had to wonder what sort of bathtub could have held these three maestri all together.[56]

End of Bretton Woods

This first issue turned out to be a mistake for the lenders, however, for in 1970, contrary to forecasts at the beginning of the year, interest rates fell in the United States for the first time in ten years—an American president had chosen to fight the recession rather than inflation. Capital then flowed massively toward Europe: in the first quarter $22 billion left the United States. There, under what now seemed to be double benign neglect—of the dollar and of inflation—the outflow of gold from Fort Knox continued, and American gold reserves were insufficient, against the Eurodollar mass, to make maintenance of convertibility credible. Despite American pressure too many people were demanding gold in exchange for their dollars.

At the beginning of 1971 Nixon set up an International Economic Policy Council, to try to draw up an overall diagnosis of the dollar situation. As its head he later appointed Peter G. Peterson, then the young president of Bell & Howell. Peterson wrote a report, without doubt the most influential document in postwar American economic policy, that put into words the ideas that were much in the air at the time. He put on record that America no longer dominated Japan and Europe and that there was a "risk of giving old answers to new questions."[57] He considered Bretton Woods a burden for the United States, where labor costs had become too high; but he did not mention the Vietnam War as one of the causes of America's difficulties. He criticized Europe's agricultural policy, among other systems of aiding trade, forgetting that it was the United States that excluded agriculture from GATT when it was drawn up. He recommended against protectionist measures that, he said, would amount to an admission of failure, but stressed that American productivity should be raised and international monetary institutions should be reformed so as to free the United States of the burden of Bretton Woods.

On 4 April 1971 John B. Connally, the American treasury secretary, told the press that the United States was not expecting an alteration in exchange rates. The markets did not believe this prognosis, and in that same month the Federal Republic of Germany took in $3 billion from speculators. On 26 April the German minister of the economy, Karl Schiller, proposed stemming the flood by organizing a concerted float by all the European currencies. The American treasury secretary repeated that "no change in the structure of exchange parities is necessary or envisaged."[58] The claim was disregarded. On 5 May the Bundesbank took in another billion dollars within an hour of the markets' opening, then suspended exchange transactions. On 8 and 9 May the EEC finance ministers, in emergency session, rejected the proposal for a concerted float presented by Karl Schiller. On 9 May Austria and Switzerland, unable to hold out, revalued their currencies by 5 and 7.1 percent, respectively. The next day the Federal Republic of Germany and the Netherlands each allowed their own currencies to float. On 28 May an unruffled Connally said again in Munich, "We shall not devalue. We shall not alter the price of gold."

He did have some reason for saying this, for in fact the position of the dollar was not catastrophic in itself, and American reserves covered a respectable percentage of public debt, as Michel Aglietta has pointed out:

> In 1913 at the zenith of the 'gold standard regime,' the ratio of British official reserves to cash commitments to foreign official institutions was 38 percent. For the United States that same liquidity ratio was 95 percent at the end of 1967, i.e., just before the first cracks appeared in the Bretton Woods system. By July 1971, on the eve of Nixon's shock tactics, it had fallen to 40 percent, perceptibly the same level as in 1913. The inevitable nature of abandoning dollar convertibility as a norm . . . is at least subject to guarantee, judging by this indicator.[59]

This analysis did not take in account the Eurodollars, which were to unbalance the economic boat, like so many badly stowed barrels.

On 20 July 1971, despite the ban on private gold trading that had existed since 1934, a forward market for gold coins opened in Los Angeles. This threw up a de facto devaluation of the dollar. The small market was closed the next day on orders from Washington, but the harm was done. Worse still, on 9 August a Senate committee publicly advocated devaluation of the dollar. France and Switzerland prepared to organize two-tier markets in order to withstand the speculation everyone now knew was inevitable. On Sunday 15 August Nixon called a working meeting at Camp David, with the ostensible aim of preparing the defense budget, with McNamara, Arthur Burns, John Connally, and Under-Secretary Paul Volcker. That same evening he went on television to announce measures for economic recovery, tax cuts and a wage and price freeze. In what he said could be found two of the arguments from the Peterson report. Five times he mentioned the "unfair" dealings of other countries and seven times the activities of "international speculators."[60] He announced the imposition of a 10 percent tax on all imports, until other countries adopted different exchange policies, altered their trade policies and increased their own military spending. He made no reference whatsoever to the Vietnam War. Lastly he said:

> I have ordered Secretary Connally to temporarily suspend the convertibility of the dollar into gold. . . . Now that other nations have vigorous economies, the time has come for them to carry a fair part of the burden of liberty in the world. . . . The United States need no longer meet competition with one hand tied behind its back.[61]

The next day every stock exchange, except Tokyo, was closed. Treasury Under-Secretary Volcker met the deputy governors of the central banks in London and told them, "The dollar is not devalued, it is floating." Connally, still just as unperturbed, said, "The official gold price of the dollar is unchanged." Dean Acheson wrote at the time, "You cannot import, pay interest and allow American capital to be available to all, without risking catastrophe." In effect, two simultaneous monetary systems were now extant: one for banks and another for trade.

There were still some believers: between 16 and 20 August the Bank of Japan, striving to maintain the exchange rate, soaked up $2 billion. On 19 August France once more rejected the German proposal for a concerted float by the European currencies and instituted a two-tier foreign exchange market. But on 22 August the director-general of the IMF, Pierre-Paul Schweitzer, suggested on American television that matters should be clarified, that the dollar should be devalued against gold and America should make its "contribution" to restoring monetary stability. By autumn, nothing had been stabilized.

For the first time in eighty-three years the United States experienced a $2 billion trade deficit, and the balance of payments deficit that year reached $9.2 billion. At the end of that year, 1971, there was even a bill in Congress aimed at reducing imports and American investment abroad by instituting what amounted to quotas.

On 13 December the American and French presidents, Richard Nixon and Georges Pompidou, met in the Azores and together announced their agreement on a devaluation of the dollar and a revaluation "of certain other currencies." On 17 December, at a meeting at the Smithsonian Institution in Washington, the Group of Ten agreed on a realignment of currencies and a 7.89 percent devaluation of the dollar. The Swiss franc and the mark rose; the dollar, the lire, the pound, the yen and the French franc fell.

On the Euromarket the role of the Swiss franc, the yen and the mark came out of this stronger. The creation of international liquidity was then completely left to the action of private banks. Euro-issues stagnated, since they were less profitable than short-term speculation. In 1971 they totaled $3.2 billion, or only as much as in 1968.

London, for the Last Time

In spring 1970, the Conservatives regained the government and set out to undo everything Labour had done in the City and elsewhere. The IRC and the limitations on credit were abolished, a system of compulsory reserves was set up and intervention in the government bond market was stopped. In January 1972 the fall of the dollar was the cause of another pound crisis, worsening inflation, which reached 8 percent. By then there were nearly one million unemployed. The 1972 budget, like that of the previous year, was a budget of recovery and tax cuts. In November, with inflation sliding up, the government imposed a wage and price freeze. The pound stabilized.

On 1 May 1972 the United Kingdom decided to join the European Community, and for a time it seemed there was a return to the spirit of Bretton Woods. On 12 May in a speech at Montreal, the governor of the American Federal Reserve, Arthur Burns, called for a "process of reconstruction" for a new monetary system. On 16 May George Shultz succeeded John Connally in the post of treasury secretary. In London once again the parity chosen was too high and nothing could stem the wave of speculation. In mid-June the United Kingdom lost $2.5 billion of reserves in six days. On 23 June the pound sterling left the EEC and began floating.

The City was then bubbling over. With the progressive lifting of controls and intensifying American competition, the British banks wanted the means of carrying on the war. Gradually there was a weakening in the century-old distinctions between merchant banks and commercial banks dictated by tradition and long-standing prudence, as protection for savers. All banks were now getting into leasing, factoring, insurance, and property. For example, a new law allowed bank profits to include those made in property, thus leading to an increase in authorized deposits. All the banks plunged in, either buying developers—like Hambros, which bought a property development company by selling them its own building—or like S.G. Warburg and N.M. Rothschild, which set up property investment funds. Also, in order to increase their capacity to place shares, the merchant banks sought institutional clients whose share portfolios they could manage. Here again S.G. Warburg was the first to think of this and do it successfully. From 1972, it managed the Post Office Pension Fund and bought for it the property group English and Continental Property for £95 million.

That year the Euro-issue market woke up: Siegmund issued a Euroloan for ICI. It was the first time the company had called on anyone other than Schröder Wagg. Siegmund was certainly one of the world masters of this market. The field was growing: 218 issues in total amounting to $5.5 billion in one year; only White Weld, Deutsche Bank and Morgan were ahead of S.G. Warburg. Since the transaction for Autostrade Italiane ten years earlier, Siegmund Warburg had directed 62 issues himself.[62] Borne by the wave, his firm grew at the rate of the market.

He was also foremost in London in financial advice, and top in takeover bids, and at the end of the year brought off one of his most notable exploits: Trust House Forte, the target of a bid, called him in to help. Siegmund managed to thwart the bid, despite opposition from half the firm's board. In November of the same year he also advised the Maxwell Joseph Group in its attempted bid for the brewers Watney Combe Reid, a well-managed company, supported by its staff, and without any connection whatsoever with the Maxwell Joseph Group beyond the wish of the latter to build up one of Europe's first conglomerates. In the middle of the battle in January 1973, Harold Wilson, back as opposition leader, publicly declared himself against Siegmund in a speech reported in the *Times*:

Many people are alarmed and frustrated by the extent to which they feel themselves to be pawns in other men's games. Their future and that of their families may be dependent not on their own endeavors, but on distant decisions over the allocation of financial resources, or on the subtle transactions of financiers.[63]

Here was Siegmund being called a "financier" by the man whose close adviser he had been against, the "gnomes"!

For the second time, after the Plessey business, public opinion and the press turned against him. He still won, nevertheless, having managed to secure assistance and capital from the Prudential Insurance Company.

Finishing with Hamburg

On the surface everything was going well for Siegmund in Germany. He had his name up in Hamburg and Frankfurt and he knew everyone of any account in banking and industry. When he went to Frankfurt all financial activities revolved around him. He stayed at the Schlosshotel in Kronberg, not far from the city, where bankers and industrialists called on him one after another.

Siegmund then once more proposed to Eric Warburg and Brinckmann that M.M. Warburg, Brinckmann, Wirtz & Co. should be merged with Effecten-Bank to create a large investment house reaching across Germany.

Their points of view were definitely too far apart and negotiations broke down in autumn 1973. The next day Siegmund telexed Hans Wüttke, who could no longer stand the situation, "Give up, leave Hamburg." At the same time he telexed Hugo Ponto, chairman of the Dresdner Bank, "Hans Wüttke is free, take him. Thank you." This was done, and Wüttke became a director-general of this bank. That day, Siegmund wrote down in French Metternich's magnificent phrase, "Cette affaire finira comme toutes les affaires, d'une manière quelconque."[64] (This will end as everything does—somehow or other.)

Passing through Paris

On the eve of the dramatic increase in oil prices, Siegmund now thought that London might lose its place as an offshore dollar center. Following the migration of dollars, he saw the money-free ports multiplying and New York reviving; he thought that international financial activity would return to America until Tokyo took over. After his break with Kuhn Loeb and the beginnings of the Euro-issue market in 1964 he had owned nothing more across the Atlantic than a small company, S.G. Warburg, Inc., which served as an operating base and where he received visitors when in America. He had to reestablish himself there and very strongly, in order to arrange the huge transactions needed by American and foreign companies. That year, for example, AT&T borrowed more than $1 billion. He resigned himself to returning to New York in strength. He did not want to do it alone or with a British bank. He had already tried shortly before to buy one of them and could see that his methods were too original for such a union to be possible.

Now that he had regained the taste for business, he looked for a European ally with whom to carry on business in *haute banque*. He looked first in Germany for a partner. This was the time when his final attempt at merging his bank with the Hamburg bank failed.

He then chose the Banque de Paris et des Pays-Bas. Almost nothing before had prepared him for this. He had taken small interest in France, apart from its literature, which he read in the original, and its history, which he knew well. He certainly had a close relationship with the Rue d'Antin, since the heroic times at the beginning of the 1950s, during the sale of the Ericsson shares, and his friendship with Jean Reyre. Several of the bank's executives, such as Pierre Haas, who had become a director of Paribas International, had been trainees with him and been initiated into the Eurodollar game from the beginnings of the market. And when in 1969 Jacques de Fouchier, the founder of Compagnie Bancaire, took Paribas by storm, Siegmund retained his links with the bank and found in de Fouchier another great financier who, like himself, had built up an institution from nothing.

Paribas was then a very large investment and deposit bank, ten times the size of Warburg, with forty offices in France, and more all over Europe, with powerful industrial subsidiaries and extensive power itself. Its Brussels subsidiary was the fourth largest Belgian bank and its Swiss and Dutch subsidiaries were also very powerful. It did not have a presence in Germany and had only a small investment bank, Paribas Corporation, set up in New York. Jacques de Fouchier also—for the same reasons as Siegmund—now wanted to establish himself in New York together with a British merchant bank. Given the links between the two houses, he thought of S.G. Warburg. So in March 1973 when de Fouchier and Siegmund lunched together at Paribas, it was natural for the question to come up. We shall never know which of the two was right in thinking that he first thought of proposing to the other that they should go into America jointly:

> Our two houses are complementary: one has a number of very mobile international professionals, the other has powerful subsidiaries and

large investment funds; one has very high-level clients everywhere in the world, the other has clients among the biggest industrial companies on the Continent.

They quickly reached agreement on the idea of looking for a business to buy jointly in the United States and on the immediate announcement of a prospective agreement between the two companies, which was made on 8 April 1973.

Siegmund, who was no longer on the boards of any of his companies, then agreed for the first time in his life to give a fairly brief interview to the London *Investors Chronicle*. He explained that as a European he had always been saddened by the absence of Britain from the Community, and now that she had entered, the banks of the ten countries should unite, without abolishing their independence of style, management or international network. Highly complementary with Paribas, he hoped in this way "to cover a much broader area [allowing] . . . slow, gradual growth of organic development. . . . All I feel is this is a case where one plus one should not be two, but should be considerably more than two."[65] Asked about a merger with Paribas, he said, "You can never forecast the future . . . but my first reaction would be no. I think it would be a pity if our two groups were to lose their individual character . . . in our kind of business, size can have great dangers." He also implied that they would be going to Wall Street together. "In this last chapter of my life, to be personally involved in putting life into such an Anglo–French organization in New York would be a task to which I would gladly contribute all I can."[66]

In fact, such was indeed the plan though no one on the outside yet knew of it. In the summer, discussions between Siegmund and de Fouchier continued, and they saw a lot of one another. At a dinner on 22 July 1973 Jacques de Fouchier had told Siegmund, "There are two kinds of imbeciles: optimists and pessimists."[67] It was the sort of biting aphorism he would have liked to deliver himself. They could definitely do business together!

At the end of August the technical agreement was worked out by Pierre Moussa, de Fouchier's assistant, and Sir Eric Roll. Shares would be exchanged in Europe, the subsidiaries each bank owned in New York would merge into a joint subsidiary and the subsidiary in turn would look for an American bank to buy. Then came a discussion about the name. Here Siegmund himself dealt with the matter. He insisted that his name should head the title of the New York bank; more familiar with Wall Street than the Parisians, he knew that common usage always reduced a multiple title to the first name on the list, and he wanted at all costs to avoid alphabetical order. De Fouchier agreed, against the advice of his executives. He said, "small before large."

By the end of the summer a compromise had been worked out and the deal was ready. It was announced in November. Two companies were set up: one in Europe: "Paribas-Warburg," with 25 percent of the Banque de Paris et des Pays-Bas, France, 20 percent of its Dutch and Swiss subsidiaries, and 25 percent of S.G. Warburg Inc.; the other in the United States: "Warburg- Paribas," which bought and merged Paribas Corporation and S.G. Warburg Inc. Lord Roll joined the boards of the bank and of Compagnie Financière de Paris et des Pays-Bas; Pierre Moussa became a director of S.G. Warburg & Co. and of Mercury Securities.

Excrement of the Devil

The dollar fared badly at the beginning of 1973. The worsening American trade deficit, which had reached $6 billion the previous year, led to the feeling that the Azores devaluation had not been enough. On 12 February the foreign exchange markets were again closed in Europe, and Japan and the United States announced a further 10 percent devaluation, which did not, however, calm the markets. Billions of short-term Eurodollars made up a huge mass. No one could see how to stop its growth, and it was linking all the banks in the world in a network of imprudence. On 1 March, faced with a dollar crisis, the European central banks bought $3.6 billion dollars and then immediately closed their markets. On 4 March the EEC finance ministers examined a concerted float in Brussels and on 11 March announced that six currencies would do this, the pound and the lire floating independently. The mark then revalued by 3 percent.

Siegmund had no illusions. He no longer believed that capitalist society was capable of extricating itself from this financial crisis without real control over its short-term debt, which would, he thought, be very difficult to achieve without tragedy. The proliferation of lending of all kinds on the Euromarket horrified him. He saw with misgivings the return to use of short-term credit to finance arms indirectly, as though Euroloans were now replacing the Mefo bonds of old.

As he saw it, all these evils arose from the meanness and shallowness that in Europe and America had replaced initiative and the spirit of enterprise, and from the fact that everything had become too big, too impersonal in the decision-making process of capitalism. In his view, as in that of all his ancestors, collectivity had always prohibited proper action.

He noted at the time, "The Second World War was supposed to be a battle between dictatorship and democracy. It has ended in a victory for bureaucracy."[68]

At this time he could well have become a Marxist, if Marxism in his eyes had not been so short on creativity. He dreamed of a social system where money did not exercise such domination of the world, where culture would allow another use of time. He was sure—and told anyone who would listen—that the present situation could not last. He already saw, beyond the disasters to come, the world reborn around the Pacific, where bureaucracy did not rule.

He then considered leaving Britain, which he loved and where he had built his career, but where he foresaw once again that matters were going to end badly. Not that he expected to see the rise of new dictatorships in Europe, but he felt everywhere the rebirth of an economy of violence after that of the debt economy. Not immediately a war economy, but already a demonic one.

In November 1973, just after the Yom Kippur War and the first increase in oil prices he noted, "Oil, that excrement of the devil. . . ."[69]

6

Last Refuge
(1973-1982)

Departures

In summer 1921, in the middle of the Weimar crisis, Max Warburg commissioned from Edward Rosenbaum, the Hamburg city archivist, a first version of the history of his bank. He defined precisely what he wished to find in it:

> It should be shown—and I attach great value to this—how much the development of such a firm is governed by chance and how the economic development is much more dependent on chance events and inherent tendencies than on the so-called consciously aimed activities of the individual. The description should be pervaded by a certain feeling of humility toward these forces. For most people suffer from exaggerated self-esteem, especially bank managers when they write their annual reports three or six months late are inclined to adorn their actions with a degree of foresight which in reality never existed.[1]

Rereading this document one day in 1973, Siegmund smiled: he and Max had much the same attitudes. His time, too, had not been devoid of "chance events" or "inherent tendencies." And like his elder relative, though more sincerely he thought, he took care to hide behind "events" and "tendencies," deny his influence over people and show himself as a

303

plaything of time, an unimportant observer of a history shaped by implacable forces.

He thought that the modesty displayed by Max on that day in 1921 did not correspond with what he had later done: stayed too long in business, ending by abandoning his bank.

He himself did not want to make the same mistake. He was to say, surely thinking of his second cousin:

> I did not want to repeat the mistake of others in similar positions who did not retire sufficiently early or who did not delegate responsibility. It's always been a nightmare fear for me, an obsession, that I might not have trained a sufficient number of successors who maintain originality and imagination. I have done my utmost to do that.[2]

This obsession was so near the surface that by then he had already taken three steps toward leaving the bank and was considering a final step. This time it would not be a withdrawal but, as forty years before, a sort of unconscious exile, a concealed rejection of the order to come, even perhaps a revolt against a world that had become in his eyes almost as unacceptable as the one he had once left behind in Berlin.

Siegmund's last step toward departure from the bank took place at the end of 1973. A thousand reasons have been given: his wife no longer much cared for city life, said some; he himself wanted to get away from a bank he saw, with some misgivings, growing bigger, at the risk of becoming petrified, said others; he wanted to escape the meetings that had taken on a formality he hated; he wanted to give himself time to make the choice of his successor. In fact he knew only too well how mistaken institutions could be in their choices.

> When the head of a big company resigns or dies, let's not kid ourselves, the shareholders have nothing to do with the choice of a new man. The new man is usually selected by the board a little bit like the way the Pope is elected by the Cardinals. He is co-opted by the system. Very often, I'm afraid, the board doesn't necessarily choose the man who is the strongest individualist, but rather the one who fits most easily within the bureaucratic machinery—a comfortable mediocrity.[3]

Some thought that he wanted to flee a crisis that would, in his opinion, cause such upheaval in his bank as to make it unrecognizable, and that he wished in repeating his exile from Germany exactly forty years

before, to become once more, without knowing it himself, an observer
—remembering past dangers, and watching for future threats.

After this departure he really did achieve the influence to which he
had always aspired: global and mysterious, invasive and undetectable.

Blonay

As in his first exile, once his decision was made, Siegmund proceeded at
a brisk pace. Scarcely settled in his new home, he was to note, "The
excessive analysis of a situation can easily lead to paralysis."[4]

The choice of his new property owed something to chance: Eric
Thalberg, an Austrian ambassador he had met through Bruno Kreisky,
invited him to spend a few days in Switzerland at his house in Blonay, a
small village near Vevey. He liked the location. Blonay was neither too
far from nor too close to the places nearest his heart; Germany, which
took up his time, and Zurich, which occupied his mind. He did not
particularly like Switzerland. He valued and respected its strictness and
hard work, however, and had several friends there, such as André Meyer,
the man he coyly said he recognized as the greatest banker in the world,
and who had long before settled not far away at Crans-sur-Sierre. In any
case, the attraction for Siegmund was not, as with some others, the low
Swiss tax rate.

Two years later, when Thalberg told him that some land adjoining
his was for sale, Siegmund bought it, sold his Italian property in
Grosseto, and unhurriedly had a house built to his design. He wanted a
real house, not a vacation home, gravitating around what counted most
for him, his books: simple architecture, a big reception room, guest
rooms, a huge terrace and especially in the center of the ground floor a
large library, finally assembling in one place and at ease all the books he
loved. In this library, permanently open to the dining room, he installed
a telex that rattled all day and part of the night, some fine furniture and
some fine pictures—nothing affected.

By the end of 1973 everything was ready. He sold his Eaton Square
flat and moved to Blonay. He found a Spanish couple to live in and keep
house. From then on he was often there, always with his wife. His
secretary came occasionally from London and stayed in Montreux. In a
corner suitcases were always ready for a sudden departure to London,
New York, Tokyo or Frankfurt.

His life in Blonay was one of semi-retirement. He read a lot, even
more than in London, and organized into book form the phrases—his
own and other people's—that he had long been collecting. But in fact he

also worked hard at supervising Gresham Street. He looked through numerous telexes, dictated others, telephoned around the world and saw many friends or clients of his bank. Almost all those mentioned in this book came to see him. It certainly was not the jollity or the cooking that attracted them to Blonay; the atmosphere was more than simple.

The rest of the time, that is for another six months of the year, he traveled at least as much as before, and when he came to London he stayed at the Savoy. In fact he felt less and less British, and more and more a citizen of the world.

He was not unhappy to leave London. Not that he did not retain immense gratitude and admiration for the country that had built up the City, beaten Hitler and saved freedom, and where he himself had built his own glory, but he remembered the irritations at the beginning, the rough jokes during the war, the irony in the 1950s and later the gossip about his methods. Often when he was depressed he inveighed against this to anyone who would listen, only to regret it later. With his inimitable gift for litotes, Sir Eric Roll reports that at this period he "hated cynicism and complacency, which he considered for many British weaknesses." Others heard him be even more severe, saying that Britain was condemned to decline "because there is nothing there but avarice and shallowness."

His criticism extended, moreover, to the whole of the Western elite, "arrogant, mediocre, full of uncertainty and shirking responsibilities."[5] He noted, "There are people there who are twisted enough to make it a point of honor not to be original."[6] He was worried to see the rise in Europe, in the banks and elsewhere, of gray and uncontrollable bureaucracies. "Promotion there is based, today more than yesterday, on the co-opting of mediocrity by mediocrity"[7]—everything that had always been rejected by the Warburgs.

When he left he wanted the break with his past to be complete. The great writer and thinker George Steiner, whom he had known at the beginning of the 1950s, when Steiner was a young professor of comparative literature at Cambridge, and who became a close friend at the beginning of the 1970s, was a witness to this. When he asked Siegmund if he should accept the post he was offered at the University of Geneva and leave Cambridge and Britain, Siegmund replied without hesitation, "Yes, of course; but if you leave you must leave everything: you don't play at exile, you must become a citizen of the country in which you live." This was what he had done on leaving Berlin and this was what he was doing again on leaving London; or almost, since he did not change nationality. Within a few months, thanks to his Swiss banker friends, he obtained the very privileged status that very few foreigners in Switzerland enjoy and that made him, as he felicitously said himself, "a distinguished foreigner."

Fleeing the War Economy

Siegmund's analysis of the world from which he had retreated was then very pessimistic. He had no taste for simple theories and said so in a phrase that suited him well: "I detest those who sum up the world in a single lie."[8] He did not like fashionable theories, especially not the idea that the "crisis" would be only temporary, just a difficult transition between two periods of stability. He noted with cruel humor in November 1973, amid a deluge of cheap comment on the oil price increase, "A period of transition is only a period situated between two other periods of transition."[9]

In fact his theoretical pessimism arose from practice. He had tried to move the world by means of money, which was, he thought, a tool of reason. In this way he had discovered the impotence of the rational. The archetype of a man of reason beaten by fanaticism and the laws of power, he did not like what he saw coming and analyzed it severely. He saw a further victory for the irrational, proof that the twentieth century was more a century of dictatorships and ideologies than one of finance. He was enraged to see world leaders incapable of avoiding the same mistakes, through carelessness and inertia, forgetting the lessons of history: those of New York in 1929, London in 1931, Berlin in 1933, Munich in 1938, London in 1967. "Some of the worst crimes," he noted, "are caused less by an action than by inaction or indifference."[10]

He remembered that when he had arrived, Britain was still lending money to the world and had been a great nation. He had seen her distanced from real power, rejecting new technologies, neglecting professional training. He had seen company bosses often become provincial officials or colonial administrators. After the war he had seen the whole of the Western World begin the same mistakes in different ways all over again—those his cousin Max had condemned forty years earlier. Europe had not been unified, gold had been forgotten, growth had been financed by debt. When, as before the war, the superpower in deficit finally decided to put the brakes on its lending, it could do nothing about the billions already circulating uncontrolled, outside the country, feeding the debt, which, in contrast with the situation in the 1930s, nobody knew how to repay, or even how not to repay.

He therefore saw capitalism caught in the toils of a gigantism that generated bureaucracy and blocked enterprises and freedom:

> . . . the amounts involved . . . are such . . . that it's no longer individ-
> uals but institutions that govern our world. . . . We still call this
> business system under which we work capitalism, but it's something
> quite different. It's something between the capitalism of the pre-
> 1914 era and the mercantilism of the eighteenth century. And the
> danger is that the bigger a company becomes, the more difficult it is
> to deal with it on a personal basis, and the more you become slaves of
> a big bureaucratic machinery.[11]

Siegmund expected that deprived of any resilience the rich countries would be obstructed in their growth by bureaucratization and waste. He already saw a great part of the world financial machine unable to function except through sales of arms, financed directly or indirectly by credit granted to the buyers of these same arms, opportunely rendered solvent, he thought, by the increased price of oil. As in the 1930s with the Mefo bonds, the debt economy was feeding on the war economy. He himself strove not to lend to such people and to warn the biggest American banks that were being lured into the trap of profit to cover their risks, and into risk in order to make profits. "If you go on like this, it will all blow up one day. And it will start in the shanty towns of São Paulo," he told his New York banker friends.

Few countries escaped his criticism: Germany? "Too dependent on exports." Britain? "Too shallow." America? "Too bureaucratic." Israel? "Too militaristic." He knew that the necessary action might prove difficult. "Sometimes you have to provoke one catastrophe to prevent another."[12] But in any case the reckoning could not be delayed beyond the end of the 1980s. There would either have to be a complete generalization of the dollar standard, or a war, or at best, cancellation of world debt and development of the Third World through the creation of a new currency that he wanted to see based on Special Drawing Rights and commodities. Beyond that, he thought that three countries would dominate world finance: Japan, the United States and Switzerland; and balanced growth would reestablish itself.

From the beginning of 1974 onward, he told this to everyone he met, including Bruno Kreisky, and announced that the crisis would be at hand for a long time. The Austrian chancellor, who wrote his thesis at the Univesity of Stockholm on the mistakes of the economists in 1929, was so impressed by this analysis that he reorganized his country's economy with a view to a prolonged crisis. It was as well that he did. For ten years Austria would have the lowest unemployment rate in the West.

Influence from Afar
Once settled in Blonay Siegmund did his utmost to have people believe that he no longer had any power. As he acknowledged in 1980:

> I have a certain influence but I'm not an executive. What do two—or ten—telephone conversations during the day mean? It's not much more than maintaining contacts with friends. . . . I have had nothing to do with [the big transactions done recently], except that they followed from relations which I built up years ago. . . . I've not been involved in one single external or internal discussion about those transactions. . . . [The directors] call me when old or new acquaintances of mine are in the picture. They are anxious to use my contacts. . . . But many very important promotions and appointments . . . are made without reference to me.[13]

The only thing he conceded was that he had had to fight to make some of his clients agree to work with his bank without working with him:

> One of the most difficult things was . . . when a big transaction was going on for one of our main industrial clients. And I had to tell him, "Henry Grunfeld and David Scholey will deal with you." He would say, "No, I want you," and I said, "Terribly sorry, you must be satisfied with my colleagues." He didn't want to accept it, but he soon reconciled himself to the situation.[14]

Matters were not really as simple as that; in fact he remained absolute master of his house. Every day he still received in the same yellow envelope the two files he had been given daily for more than thirty years. The telex clattered ceaselessly, bringing him notes, reports of meetings and current negotiations, market reports, commission levels. He was concerned with every last detail of business and made telephone calls ten times a day to Eric Roll, Henry Grunfeld, David Scholey, or even to junior executives or young people in the firm to ask questions or give instructions. Moreover, neither Scholey, Roll nor Grunfeld would take the risk of deciding anything important without telephoning him, or even, when it was critical, coming to see him. They would discover that he often knew more than they did themselves about the state of one deal or another. Sir Eric Roll remembered, "If I wanted to know from my office what was happening in New York, Frankfurt, Milan, especially in Gresham Street, the surest and quickest way was to telephone him in Blonay.''[15]

Petrodollars

The oil price increase diverted the flow of capital and worsened the disarray of currencies begun five years earlier. After the first increase in October 1973 the governors of central banks meeting in Basel on 12 November abolished the two-tier gold market, which had, in reality, already ceased to exist. On 23 December oil prices doubled again. Many other things changed in 1974. In February, the British miners' strike got the better of the Edward Heath government; in April Georges Pompidou, the French president, died; in May Willy Brandt had to resign in Bonn after the Guillaume scandal; on 9 August Richard Nixon left the White House after Watergate; Gerald Ford replaced him and denounced inflation as public enemy number one.

The oil-producing countries then truly became holders of capital and exported $55 billion the following year; as for the European countries, they ceased to be such holders. It was as if suddenly a considerable part of the savings of Europe and Japan had been given to the oil-producing countries.

There was uncertainty about the investments the oil producers wanted to make. Many thought that this money, since it was no longer European, would come to the United States. And America certainly enabled Wall Street to become once more a world storehouse for money. In February 1974 the last fragments of the 1963 interest equalization tax were scrapped and American banks were authorized to make loans abroad without restrictions. All controls limiting the exit of capital from the United States were abolished. The Employee Retirement Income Security Act actually authorized American pension funds to invest abroad.

Oil money was far from flooding into New York. In 1974 $14 billion petrodollars were invested there, against $7 billion in Europe, $11 billion in Third World countries and $23 billion converted into Eurodollars. The American banks did not want to take the risk of lending abroad in the medium term from New York and preferred to lend to Latin America in the shorter term. The volume of short-term Eurodollars exploded, reaching almost the equivalent of the total monetary volume of Germany and almost twice that of France.

The Euro-issue market shriveled for a time. Despite the turbulence, the City remained the prime free port for money. A first-rate observer of this period, Jean Baumier, noted:

There are more American banks in the City than in New York. At least a quarter of the Eurodollars circulating in the world are dealt in here, as well as half the transactions in gold, and the greater part of exchange dealings. The turnover of the Stock Exchange is higher than that of all the European stock markets put together.[16]

The appearance of the new lenders gave full meaning to the boycott from which such banks as S.G. Warburg, Lazard and Rothschild in London had suffered since the creation of the State of Israel. This "blacklist" was in theory a serious handicap, since it prohibited them from any participation in loans issued by member countries, or in the investment of their private wealth. Until then its effect had been almost unimportant, since these transactions were fairly rare. A lot of money was now involved, most of the market in fact; and no bank, even a very friendly one, could resist such a situation.

Overnight Siegmund's former colleagues—French, German, Japanese, Austrian and Swiss—ducked out of the numerous operations in which S.G. Warburg was the lead bank and refused to bring him into theirs. Everything was done with the purest hypocrisy. "Warburg" calls were not taken, they were avoided; any excuse was good enough. "I have nothing left for you in this loan, it has already been placed with other banks. . . . I cannot participate in your loans, I am overcommitted elsewhere." The Foreign Office, to which Siegmund turned, like the Bank of England, acted as though they saw nothing, and did nothing—anyway not enough for him.[17]

The results were soon felt. S.G. Warburg dropped to third place in the world in the Euro-issue Hit Parade in 1973, behind Deutsche Bank and Credit Suisse, and to tenth in 1974, even, in the first six months of 1975 to sixteenth place. This was a dreadful blow, as this market was the major source of profits, even when it fell back to $3.7 billion in 1973 and $1.9 billion in 1974.

Siegmund had already experienced something similar forty year earlier, and this time he was determined not to give in. From Blonay he made use of every possible means to force people previously indebted to him not to give in to blackmail, and did not hesitate to make use of threats:

> I hear you seem to be giving in to this blackmail of the Arabs. I think that is very unfair to us and it's wrong in itself. Shall I interpret that as meaning you sympathize with anti-Semitism? And don't kid yourself, we can—in the end—place just as well as those Arabs.[18]

He was as good as his word. For example, he immediately broke off all contact with a Viennese bank whose new chairman had given in to the boycott. He informed the chancellor:

> Not only has this gentleman allowed himself to be influenced by the boycott, but I would inform you in addition that he is criticizing you, a socialist government, while in control of a state bank. I do not find it acceptable that a manager should oppose his owner and I give you notice that I henceforward forbid anyone working with me to have the least connection with this bank as long as this gentleman is chairman.[19]

And thus it would continue, until the replacement of said gentleman.

London by Remote Control

When he left London he had left his house at a pinnacle of glory: A "service house," he said modestly—in fact the leading bank in Europe for mergers, ranked third in the world for Euro-issues. The position of his adopted country had grown worse. The oil price increase and slackness over wages exacerbated the old imbalances, inflation accelerated and in January 1974 the external balance, equal to twice that of the whole of 1973, was the highest in British history. Only a quarter of it was attributable to oil. Siegmund was dismayed. Wilson, immediately after the oil shock, had given the economy free rein and increased the purchasing power of wages by 6 percent in six months. Nobody was surprised that inflation first moved up to 16 then 24 percent. Wilson was to resign two years later, leaving Callaghan in charge of a crisis, shortly after Margaret Thatcher had become the new Conservative party leader.

Anthony Wedgewood Benn, secretary of state for industry, re-established the IRC that had been dissolved by Heath, under the title National Enterprise Board, a state holding company, this time with £1 billion to invest. In March 1975 Benn proposed the nationalization of Leyland, which, created by the IRC and very badly managed, was going through serious difficulties. Passed on 3 July 1975 with a £2.8 billion grant, this move did nothing to restore the firm's position.

Like all Western centers, the City was much affected by the oil price increase. All financial activity linked directly or indirectly with energy suffered. Hambros, for example, lost a great deal of money in shipping. Brandt, which had overinvested in property in the recent boom, was almost bankrupt and had to leave the Accepting Houses Committee. Siegmund, who remembered the near bankruptcy of M.M. Warburg in Hamburg forty years earlier as the result of similar errors, withdrew in time from the market almost unscathed.

The banks most under threat from the increased rates that had reduced their profitability had to sell out or merge with others: Montagu went to Midland Bank, Anthony Gibbs to Hong Kong and Shanghai Banking Corporation, Arbuthnot Latham to several foreign interests, Guinness Mahon to Lewis & Peat, a trading company. Several banking empires built up in the 1960s had become very shaky, such as those of Jim Slater or Pat Matthews. Slater Walker was saved by the Bank of England, but its founder had to resign. Luckily Siegmund's bank was not in danger—if it had been, few would have come to its aid.

In other centers investment banks were suffering as much from the rise in interest rates as from that of the oil price. On Wall Street, though Merrill Lynch, Salomon Brothers and Goldman Sachs held up, Kuhn Loeb and Lehman Brothers were in difficulty. W.E. Hutton, Loeb Rhoades, Hayden Stone, Hornblower and White Weld disappeared. In Germany on 26 June 1974 the Herstatt bank collapsed, and in September 1974 Credit Suisse announced that its Lugano subsidiary had lost £33 million in foreign exchange speculation. Only a few nationalized French banks came out of this relatively well, the reward of prudence.

During these difficult years all the changes, which had been germinating in the past, accelerated. There was a need for more specialization and large-scale organizations. The commercial banks overtook the investment banks and encroached increasingly on their territory. Organizational diagrams grew more complex, even in banks that stuck to investment or business. There were now forty directors at Warburg, thirty-seven at Kleinwort, twenty-seven at Lazard and thirty-one at Morgan Grenfell.

On leaving London Siegmund's firm wish was to establish a structure that would prevent his firm from increasing in size after he had left.

To do this, he first arranged his succession. Henry Grunfeld, who was seventy years old, decided to leave the chairmanships of the bank and of Mercury Securities to share with Siegmund the post of "president." Lord Roll succeeded Grunfeld at the head of both entities. Peter Spira left the bank to become the financial director of Sotheby Parke Bernet, and David Scholey, at forty-one, became the new successor designate. Two years later it would be Scholey who would hold the annual press conference presenting the firm's financial report.

Siegmund reformed the organization of his house by simplifying it. Masius Wynn Williams, his advertising agency, established in Europe, New York, Australia and South Africa, merged with an American agency, D'Arcy MacManus, which he owned only in part. He gathered all his insurance interests into just one of his companies, Stewart Wrightson, which he converted into a subsidiary of the bank rather than the holding company. Brandeis-Goldschmidt, which had made more than £1.5 million that year, was separated from the other interests.

Siegmund finally agreed that his group should take a part in advising the heavily indebted governments of the Third World, to which American banks persisted in lending unlimited short-term amounts; and he entered a group of three, with Lazard-Paris and Kuhn Loeb to help Indonesia, then Gabon, Nigeria and Costa Rica among others.

New York Once More

While other European firms, such as Hambros or Morgan Grenfell, were establishing themselves in New York, Jacques de Fouchier and Siegmund were constantly seeking an American partner for the same exercise. It was difficult. Kuhn Loeb, which was adrift after big losses on the mortgage market, could not be approached. Frederick Warburg died that year; and John Schiff, who was still more or less running the firm, tried in vain to merge it first with Shearson Hayden Stone, then Paine Webber, and Eastman Dillon.

Lehman Brothers also was out of the question. Paribas still invited the company routinely into the Euro-issue syndicate it ran, but Lehman was in a crisis. It was no more than a collection of elderly partners, each worth tens of millions and who would only be dictated to by someone richer. In October 1973 this galaxy of millionaires, whose one and only motive was profit, named as president a newcomer to the house, Peter G. Peterson, who after his report to President Nixon, just before the collapse of the dollar, had been appointed secretary of commerce. His assistant was Louis Gluksmann, a Hungarian employed as a trader in

1962 by Bobby Lehman, and who was now earning $2 million a year. When, in order to revive the firm, Peterson decided to go into partnership with the Banca Commerciale Italiana, neither Paribas nor S.G. Warburg had any more to do with Lehman Brothers.

As no other big New York investment bank was available, de Fouchier and Siegmund looked for a regional bank; this was how the idea for a relationship with A.G. Becker came up. Set up in 1893 in Chicago, it had later dealt in commercial paper and had then become one of the leading dealers on the American money market and stock exchange, and a leader, along with Goldman Sachs, in the national bond market. As a privileged intermediary for numerous European companies, acting as issuer or borrower on the short-term dollar market, it was also a not inconsiderable operator in the American Treasury Bill market. It handled 3 percent of the transactions of the New York Stock Exchange, a large amount.

At that point, the staff, who owned the whole of Becker's equity, was unable to meet the firm's need for additional capital. So at the end of 1973 their president, Paul Judy, came to London looking for the partners he could not find in America. He met Siegmund, who was interested. Simultaneously, Dan Good, one of the Becker managing directors, arranged a meeting with Paribas through one of his friends, a former financial director for Hammer and friend of Pierre Haas. Good informed them that Becker was looking for partners. In December 1973, a month after their own agreement, Paribas and Warburg jointly agreed to negotiate with Becker. Four months later in April 1974 agreement was reached: Warburg-Paribas was to put $25 million into A.G. Becker, receiving in exchange 40 percent of its capital, with an option to increase its holding beyond 50 percent at a later date. A joint holding company was set up between A.G. Becker and Warburg-Paribas, with three subsidiaries: A.G. Becker, for the money market, A.G Becker Securities for stockbroking and Warburg-Paribas-Becker for investment banking. Here again, Siegmund had supervised the naming of the firm.

It was high time for Becker to find capital. In the month that followed, the restriction of stock exchange commissions cut into the profitability of New York brokers, among which Becker was one of the biggest. The big American banks thought they had won. In fact they also suffered, since the increase in costs would lead to a rise in interest rates and thereby reduce the profits the banks thought would result from these reforms.

Siegmund was happy. He now had the ideal instrument with which to attempt what he had tried to do with Kuhn Loeb twenty years earlier: the equivalent of Morgan Stanley or Lazard today—a great and influential bank. He knew this would take a long time:

> I expect it to take at least ten or fifteen years. At least. After all it took André Meyer years to build Lazard of New York; it was a relatively small firm when Mr. Meyer came to New York in 1940, and Lazard only started to flourish in the beginning of the 1960s. I think he got their most important client, ITT, at the end of the 1960s.[20]

At the beginning, all went well between the two "divas" of finance. They did much business together. Contact between executives took place several times daily, and the directors met every three months. For three years the partnership was profitable on all sides: the Paribas securities brought in an increasing share of Warburg profits.

Success showed up ambiguities in the agreement: each side, though it might deny the ambition, secretly dreamed in fact of swallowing the other. Moreover, Paribas and Warburg did not put all their American business through Becker: they remained competitors in financing and guaranteeing loans. In addition, their management methods were radically different. While Paribas followed Becker only from a distance, like its other subsidiaries, Siegmund intended to control New York as he controlled London; he sent over a number of high-quality people and had detailed reports sent back to him. Siegmund himself often telephoned Paul Judy, the Becker president, from Blonay, and quickly got to know everything about the firm. Finally the parity of the two shareholders raised delicate operational problems, similar to those Siegmund had already experienced in 1930 with the Berliner Handels-Gesellschaft in Berlin and in 1963 with Kuhn Loeb in New York.

The Debt Economy Again

At the beginning of 1975 Gerald Ford made no fundamental change in Nixon's economic policy, and America went deeper into depression. The unemployment rate rose from 5.5 percent in January to 9 percent in May 1975. The drop in investment and the demand for housing was steep. The crisis brought about a shortage of capital and an increase in interest rates. So by the beginning of 1975 the city of New York, $7 billion in debt, was on the edge of bankruptcy. Securities were hard to place; the biggest American securities retailer, W.T. Grant, was on the edge of bankruptcy.

The dollar was unstable, and in order to support it, on 1 February 1975, the governors of the central banks of Germany, Switzerland and the United States decided on a policy of concerted intervention on the markets. That month the Federal Reserve sold $600 million in foreign currencies, held as a result of interbank agreements. Currencies were hesitant, all floating in relation to others. None of them had the means of forcing America back into balance. It was no longer possible to forecast anything.

The American banks, in search of profits on which to survive, launched into risky markets and competed against themselves through their foreign subsidiaries, which speculated more with the Eurodollar than they financed industry.

On 1 May 1975, in order to revive the economy, Ford reduced interest rates—they dropped from 13 percent in August 1974 to 6.5 percent in May 1975—and pushed through the biggest tax cuts in American history: $22.8 billion. As federal spending simultaneously increased by 19 percent, the budget deficit then rose to $71.2 billion, against $43 billion the year before. On the other hand the balance of payments improved. After the equilibrium of 1973 and 1974, it showed an $11 billion surplus in 1975.

Wall Street in this less oppressive atmosphere increasingly shed its restraint in order to attract money. Since banking and broking commissions were freely negotiable, investors began to haggle over rates, and banks and brokers saw a sudden drop in their profits. As in the previous year, short-term lending gathered pace, and the commercial banks, attracted by easier profits than they could find in developed countries, lent heavily to Latin America and Asia: more than $30 billion a year, i.e., more than was being granted to these countries by public development aid bodies. By 1975 they owed a total of $180 billion, nearly half of it to commercial banks.

Meanwhile everything was falling back into place with remarkable flexibility. The multinationals were increasingly abiding by American banking rules and cleaning up their balance sheets. Long-term lending recovered. In the black year of 1974 there had been only 81 issues raising $1.9 billion, but in 1975 there were 248 raising $8.3 billion, an absolute record, far above the $5 billion of 1972.

So after forty years the debt economy was back on top. And it was out of control: for example, the loan issued for the ECSC in October by Kidder, Peabody, Paribas, Credit Suisse and Nomura, first set at $50 million, was then increased to $100 million. There was three times as much business as in the previous year. By then it was taking less than two days from the first contact between a borrower and one or more possible lead banks to the point where—once the banks guaranteeing the loan had been found—the agreement was drawn up. The market was operating twenty-four hours a day, five, if not seven, days a week on a global scale. Thus Siegmund placed a $125 million ECSC loan on the telephone between Christmas 1975 and New Year's Day 1976, and as was his custom did not commit himself to take it until he was sure of placing most of it.

Nevertheless, in 1975, despite help from Becker, S.G. Warburg had climbed back only to twelfth place in the *Institutional Investor* ranking, though it remained the only investment bank to appear among the top ten borrowers of marks and the only British merchant bank among the top ten issuers in the European Community. Still, a year later it had regained its world ranking: fourth biggest lead bank in the Euromoney listing.

Thirty Years After

The year 1976 was a strange one. Three decades after the founding of S.G. Warburg the world was running into problems that could be thought akin to those of the immediate postwar period.

Just as thirty years before, there was talk of IMF rules. On 7 and 8 January in Kingston, Jamaica, the IMF's provisional committee organized increased quotas for the Fund. Just as thirty years before, the currencies were in difficulty. Just as thirty years before, America was worried by the threat of unemployment. Congress accused the president of not doing enough to stimulate the economy, even though the budget deficit was already at $66.4 billion and inflation was at 6 percent. Americans blamed their government for spending too much money in Europe.

Britain was in a monetary and economic crisis, with unemployment and inflation, and despite the oil beginning to flow from North Sea wells, the pound fell from $2 on 1 January to $1.56 by October. London requested a loan from the IMF, this time of $3.9 billion, in exchange for which, as it had thirty years before, the IMF insisted that the British government should in the future make strict budget cuts. A White Paper on industrial policy denounced the low level of investment, the weight of the state in the financial market, the scarcity of savings and the inadequate interest shown in this sector by the merchant banks. The paper recommended the development of a "dynamic, vigorous and profitable" private sector and a policy of recovery, "giving industrial development priority over consumption and even over our social objectives."[21]

Although Britain was floundering in the same difficulties and with a standard of living barely twice that of thirty years before, S.G. Warburg during that time had become a worldwide as well as British institution, a reflection of the gap between the position of the City and that of the rest of the country.

In April, S.G. Warburg's thirtieth anniversary was the occasion for a dinner with all the directors. Siegmund, who came from Blonay for the event, could be proud of himself. In terms of net profit, his was the leading merchant bank in London by far.

Organization of the groups was complete: Mercury Securities owned three-quarters of the S.G. Warburg bank, with the remaining 25 percent held by Paribas, the joint buyer in June 1976 of 20 percent of a small Canadian bank, Canadian Commercial and Industrial Bank of Edmonton. S.G. Warburg controlled Becker in the United States, a bank in Switzerland, another in Frankfurt and had interests in Tokyo, Hong Kong and Luxembourg. Mercury also controlled Brandeis (whose profits quintupled that year, and which bought International Minerals and Metals), insurance, shipping (three ships in Norway), 25 percent of Paribas, pension fund consultant MPA, with agents all over Europe and in Australia, Warburg Investment Management and finally two advertising agencies: Masius Wynn Williams and D'Arcy MacManus, which later merged.

That year the bank also arranged the purchase of Felixstowe Docks by European Ferries, defended Garton & Artagent against an attempted takeover and arranged the sixth biggest British increase in capital. Its list of British clients was impressive: British Petroleum, Imperial Chemical Industries, Reed International, Trust House Forte.

At the time the anniversary was celebrated, Siegmund could have been especially pleased to regain his ranking in a still exploding Eurodollar market—the interest rates were very attractive. In January 1976 alone there were as many Euro-issues as in all of 1974. Over 1976 as a whole 346 were launched, nearly one a day, totalling $15 billion, or double the amount for the previous year, itself already exceptional, though it represented only half the amount of short-term Eurolending. Huge issues were launched: S.G. Warburg shared the lead with Deutsche Bank on a $100 million loan for ICI; and on 14 March 1976 the EEC, with Deutsche Bank as lead bank, issued a $300 million loan, more than twice the previous record; another $500 million followed three weeks later for the same borrower: a long way from the ill-received $15 million loan for Autostrade in 1963.

That year S.G. Warburg & Co. had returned to first place in British banking, and to fourth in the world on the Eurodollar market; in 1976 it led fifty-two Euro-issues, or more than all the other British banks put together.

Salaries had remained reasonable: the chairman of the bank earned £39,000 a year, and the directors between £20,000 and £32,500, while their counterparts in the American subsidiaries of British banks earned three times as much before taxes. In his annual report that year the chairman, Sir Eric Roll, who had become Lord Roll, called on the British government to take action against excessive taxes that penalize bank executives.

Siegmund was worried that this success might lead to a paralysis in his bank. He was afraid that his executives would become like "these people who are more anxious to avoid failure than to achieve success," and he was worried about the size of the firm. "We are getting too big on both sides of the Atlantic. This is the punishment for success. . . . If you take on more and more clients, the moment comes when the quality of your service cannot fail to deteriorate. . . . You must be more choosy about what you do, and you must pass on certain things to other firms,"[22] he said for publication soon afterward. He noted a few days before the anniversary, "Our efforts are going in the wrong direction when we do not have the courage to say no."[23]

On the day of celebration the directors of Credit Suisse, which had just become his greatest competitor in Euro-issues by buying White Weld, sent him a silver cup. Engraved on it was the single word "Admiration."

The Gresham Street Elevator

The following year those who thought the crisis was transitory were disillusioned. America continued to plunge deeper into recession and the world financial situation did not improve. Jimmy Carter replaced Gerald Ford in the White House and began a more definite policy of economic expansion, hoping to reduce the unemployment that Ford had kept in check. Carter brought in a big increase in tax on oil products that cut the budget deficit to $45 billion. Profits increased, but the rate of inflation accelerated; growth and new jobs were less than had been hoped for. Above all, the balance of payments returned to a deficit of

$14 billion and the trade deficit reached $32 billion. The American risk began to deter some lenders. Europe, supporting the dollar by buying it, imported inflation. To use these dollars outside America, the banks vied with each other in inventiveness: certificates of deposit with floating exchange rates were created, guarantees of exchange rates and so forth.

Wall Street was not spared difficulties. The fallen Kuhn Loeb finally found in Lehman Brothers, with capital in the region of $60 million, a buyer at $18 million—a ridiculously small amount in relation to their business. It was the end of an era. Peterson, the president of Lehman, was appointed president and chief executive of the entity, which kept the Lehman Brothers name, and John Schiff was appointed honorary president. To preserve something of a name that evoked a whole vista of American financial history, an international subsidiary was created under the title "Kuhn Loeb-Lehman Brothers International."

Things went less and less well between Paribas and Warburg. Each side continued to use other American banks for its business, and S.G. Warburg reestablished its own offshoot in New York alongside Warburg-Paribas-Becker. In September Siegmund went to America. He did not like what he saw. Above all, Warburg- Paribas had not managed, as he had hoped, to break into the issue market in America, as European and Japanese borrowers preferred to use the services of American banks. He became angry with the directors and noted on his return that Mrs. Russ, a Becker secretary, had said to him, "You have to be hated a little to be respected."[24] He was respected.

In London, though weak, the dollar was still the currency in which two-thirds of Euro-issues were made, with the deutsche mark the only competitor. The European countries, driven into deficit by the oil price increases, borrowed more than half the total, with the remainder going to other consumer countries: Japan, Canada, Australia. The amounts of Euro-issues to be placed increased from one day to the next; it took backbone to stay in the market. To secure a deal, a lead bank even would commit itself within a few seconds to place a big issue without prior assurance of any partner. Union Bank of Switzerland, one day in 1977, took on alone the risk of placing a six-year $200 million loan for Mobil International. The most responsible governments also borrowed on these markets, avoiding short-term borrowing wherever possible. Thus in June the Swedish government issued a medium-term $200 million loan, and the Australian government issued a $250 million loan in September. That year 363 Euro-issues were launched, totaling $18 billion, even more than the 3,466 issues and $15 billion total of the previous year. S.G. Warburg arranged 66 of these, worth $3.7 billion, as lead bank; it became the second biggest placer in the world by number of issues, still behind Kredit Bank and Credit Suisse. Crédit Lyonnais, the top French bank, came ninth.

By now the City was a center with hardly any relationship with Britain or even British banks. S.G. Warburg was the only British bank to feature among the top twenty in the market. This was a token of the unusual capability of its men, the exceptional value of its analysis and the reliability of its placing.

In Great Britain the pound once more stabilized at the expense of investment. James Callaghan, who had replaced Harold Wilson, was unable to stem the increase in wages. In July 1977 Callaghan gave in to trade union pressure and brought the real increase in wages up to 14 percent.

That year *Business Week* drew a stark picture of the City, describing Siegmund as the "exceptional survivor," and his bank as the "leading power in the City, still run by telex and telephone from Switzerland by Siegmund, who has been able to specialize in the two most profitable areas—financial advice and international guarantees."

Despite success Siegmund kept the rules he had started with at Gresham Street. The annual report was still austere. Working hours were unlimited. In an electricity strike, it was said, work went on by candlelight. Commented one executive, "I was waiting for the lift when I was overtaken by a group of four people (Warburg, Grunfeld, Roll and Scholey), who were taking the stairs. After that I didn't take the lift for several months."

"Most City observers," wrote the *Times,* "attribute [Siegmund's] success to his fanatically demanding teamwork, with just enough innovation to stay always at the head of the pack." He was certainly as hard to please as ever. In February he noted privately, "One of the qualities of a good manager is to take as little account as possible of the mediocre,"[25] or again, "When mediocre people have influence, they exercise it in the wrong direction."[26]

David Scholey, more than ever the successor designate, then became vice-chairman of the bank. However, Siegmund did not give up control, and from where he was, attempted to reduce the size of the group.

Failure in Belgrade

In 1978 America plunged to the depths of the crisis that had begun more than ten years before. In spite of strong growth, American unemployment was still hovering around 6 percent, inflation was accelerating and the trade deficit had reached $39 billion, with the balance of payments deficit still at $14 billion. The fear of even worse inflation sent American interest rates into a dizzying upward spiral: they began the year at 7.5 percent and finished at 12 percent. Confidence in America was severely damaged, and it was the turn of the American state to be considered a risk borrower. In April, for the first time in the country's history, a company, Beatrice Foods, was able to borrow abroad at a better rate than the government itself. Washington had its back to the wall. Carter and his treasury secretary were at odds over the policy to be followed and were hardly speaking to one another.

It was at this point, on 1 June 1978, that Pierre Moussa replaced Jacques de Fouchier at the head of Paribas and Pierre Haas took over from Pierre Moussa as president of Paribas-Warburg, a post he shared with David Scholey. Also, Becker had by then become one of the leading American banks for commercial paper and financial consultancy, but it had remained somewhat regional and had not made a mark on the securities or loan markets and was suffering from the American recession.

Elsewhere, debt begot debt: Argentina, Venezuela, Mexico and the Philippines were borrowing hand over fist in the Eurodollar market and from commercial banks in New York. In London, as the dollar fell, the Euro-issue market slowed down; that year there were only 248 issues totaling $12 billion. The World Bank borrowed $500 million at a rate of 5 percent to consolidate its own debts.

By the beginning of October 1978 the American balance of payments crisis had become so glaring that nobody on the Euro-issue market wanted dollars and it was hardly possible to place anything but marks. Inflation was taking off again everywhere, fueled by the dollars the central banks were buying to support the American currency. In Great Britain, as in the previous July, Chancellor of the Exchequer Denis Healey again set a 5 percent target for wage increases, but this guideline was breached first by the Ford workers who won a 17 percent increase, then by truck drivers and railwaymen. The income policy started by the Labour party was annihilated.

In Washington confusion was at it height; at the end of October the situation on the foreign exchange markets actually became catastrophic. The dollar collapsed for lack of confidence in American policies. Jimmy Carter then, on 27 October, called treasury secretary Michael Blumenthal to the White House. This was the first face-to-face meeting between the two men in more than a year. Blumenthal gave a disastrous picture of the situation and threatened to resign unless something was done to reduce inflation and strengthen the dollar. President Carter, still obsessed with growth, continued to be much against these restrictive measures. However, he instructed Blumenthal to prepare a plan to support the dollar. Then there was a replay of what had happened in London thirteen years earlier.

The next day, Anthony Solomon, the assistant secretary of the treasury, contacted William Bale, one of the IMF directors, and requested a $5 billion loan in Special Drawing Rights for the United States. Solomon then left for Basel to set out the other measures envisaged by Blumenthal to support the dollar and build up reserves: issuance of $10 billion in foreign currency Treasury Bills, as well as loans of $6 billion in Germany, $5 billion in Japan and $4 billion in Switzerland. The total was $30 billion. The German, Japanese and Swiss governments agreed. The president of the central bank prepared for a one-point increase in the discount rate and an increase in the reserve requirements for banks in order to reduce the money supply. On Sunday 29 October the *Sunday Times* in London mentioned that very significant measures were imminent, which Solomon categorically denied. By Monday 30 October the plan was ready. On Wednesday 1 November, the opening day of the IMF general assembly in Belgrade, when European markets were closed for All Saints Day, President Carter, visibly upset, flanked by Blumenthal and G. William Miller, announced the creation of a $30 billion intervention fund to support the dollar. American Treasury gold sales were multiplied by five and the discount rate went up to 9.3 percent.

In the next few days the dollar rose. Europe continued to import American inflation by supporting the dollar and in December set up the European Monetary System. Great Britain remained apart from this. However, from the following month onward, events in Iran and the announcement that more oil price increases were to come turned the dollar downward again.

For Siegmund the highlight of the end of that year was a trip to Japan, during which on 6 November the emperor and then prime minister Takeo Fukuda presented him with one of the highest Japanese honors: the Order of the Sacred Treasure (2nd class). The citation was highly laudatory:

> ... the S.G. Warburg Bank has contributed very greatly to the economic development of Japan, thanks to the great lucidity and

immense capability of Mr. Warburg. There is every reason to continue to have confidence in Mr. Warburg and to expect much of one who knows Japan so well.

Return to Monetary Order

The failure of Belgrade should probably be seen as an important turning point in postwar financial history; by 1979 American inflation, into double figures for the first time, would exceed 11 percent, even though the growth of the money supply had dropped by half. And the fall of the dollar had not prevented the trade deficit from reaching close to $40 billion, even though the balance of payments was in equilibrium. At the beginning of the following year, the dollar continued falling even though the budget deficit had halved.

In October 1979 the new chairman of the Federal Reserve, Paul Volcker, adopted an even stricter policy. He decided on a further massive increase in interest rates from 12 to 16 percent and limited the growth in the money supply to 2 percent: by the time of the second oil shock in November, the external deficit had suddenly dropped to zero. Europe then stopped supporting the dollar and began the struggle against its own inflation.

On Wall Street that year uncertainty about the dollar made the markets feverish and aggravated risk. Competition became increasingly fierce and decisions had to be made in ever shorter periods of time. The banks regrouped to survive: for example, First Boston, which had already bought White Weld, merged its international activities with those of Credit Suisse, into Credit Suisse First Boston, a dramatic transformation.

At Becker, Paul Judy could no longer bear the dominance of Siegmund. In June 1979 he left the presidency, while remaining a consultant to the firm. Siegmund rejected the suggestion that a headhunter be used to find Judy's replacement. "Certainly not, that would be no use! We know all the good candidates . . . ." He consulted Ira Wender, his lawyer in New York, whom he had met in 1964. Wender had subsequently become one of his "adopted sons" and in 1970 the president of S.G. Warburg Inc., but had returned to law practice after the 1974 purchase of Becker. At his suggestion Siegmund formed a committee comprising the three top Becker executives and asked them to look for a president themselves. . . . None of the candidates they put forward sufficiently impressed Siegmund, and after six months the committee recommended Ira Wender himself. S.G. Warburg and Paribas agreed.

The greatest names in American, Japanese and European industry and finance, including the ECSC, which had left the defunct Kuhn Loeb, were now giving their business to S.G. Warburg. It was also doing good business where there was no competition, between Paris and London: in the realm of mergers and acquisitions of American companies by European companies attracted by the low value of the dollar, such as that of the American company Coplay Cement and Ciments Français, or the purchase of Illinois Prospectives Ltd. by UK National Coal.

In London the Euro-issue market had reached a very high level. Aside from the $200 billion worth of short-term loans arranged in the space of fifteen years to the Third World by the commercial banks, there had been in the same period 1,954 issues totaling $60 billion, of which Siegmund's firm had carried out 355 issues worth $12.5 billion. At this time it ranked fourth in the world for the amount of loans placed and seventh for the total amount.

In Britain the management of crisis by austerity took its toll. In 1979 the GNP excluding oil was 5 percent lower than that of 1975. On 3 May Labour lost the election, Margaret Thatcher became prime minister and soon abolished what remained of exchange control. The Banking Act brought British banking legislation into line with that of the European Community. A deposit protection fund was set up, managed by the Bank of England and by Treasury-designated bankers, among them David Scholey. In spite of these efforts, inflation accelerated and recession and unemployment spread.

The City reflected British reality less and less but influenced world events increasingly: among the 355 foreign banks established there, Japanese banks now supplanted the American banks, taking in more foreign exchange deposits; the French, German, Arab concerns (such as the Saudi International Bank or the Arab Banking Corporation of Bahrain) were also active.

That year, Effectenbank-Warburg set up with S.G. Warburg and Bank Leu of Zurich a joint subsidiary in Luxembourg, which had become a major center for Euro-issues, under the name Société des Banques S.G. Warburg et Leu. In the following year S.G Warburg again increased its British turnover by 30 percent. With Rothschild it arranged financing for the British National Oil Corporation, the purchase of Avery by General Electric and the issue of shares by British

Petroleum. Siegmund, however, claimed to have had no part in these deals.[27] Meanwhile, David Scholey then joined Eric Roll as joint chairman of the bank and vice-chairman of Mercury Securities.

In the United States in 1980, despite the austerity measures, the American engine had not restarted. Equilibrium returned to the balance of payments, but at a price: a budget deficit of $60 billion, inflation above 13 percent, lower growth and increasing unemployment. In addition, a sign of the depth of the recession, the creation of international money, in other words Eurodollars, slowed down noticeably. The oil-producing countries were lending less. The official dollar reserves of central banks, having grown at 20 percent a year throughout the 1970s, reached $300 billion at the end of 1980 and then stagnated. The dollar still represented 80 percent of foreign currency reserves. In all, the supply of Eurodollars in circulation probably reached $1,000 billion, though greater estimates were commonplace.

While the real economy marked time, the financial market was prospering: within one year 310 Euro-issues were launched totaling $18.8 billion, and S.G. Warburg still placed third in the world for these.

Anxious to establish himself better in Switzerland, in March 1981 Siegmund decided to buy one-third of the capital of a small but imaginative bank, SODITIC, run in Geneva by Maurice Dwek and already one-third owned by Paribas Suisse.

In mid-1981 oil and commodity prices fell and deflation began. Euro-issues for the year again increased above the 1977 record, reaching $26 billion, while short-term lending in Eurocurrencies reached $133 billion.

To withstand the consequences of removing exchange controls, which led to a mass flight of capital, the City decided to attract foreign banks: so the holy of holies, the Accepting Houses Committee, opened itself to foreign bankers.

In June, after two years of negotiation led by Henry Grunfeld and the Brandeis-Goldschmidt chairman A.O. Creutziger, Mercury Securities sold Brandeis-Goldschmidt to Pechiney.

Investment for Peace

Siegmund now felt that he was without ties; he finally accepted that he was without power in the affairs of the world. Basically, he thought, his influence had always been very small. Ever since he had been prevented from entering politics, first in his country of origin, then in his adopted

328   A Man of Influence

country, he had felt regret. The politicians in Wilhelmstrasse had not
supported him when he had been threatened by the Nazis; nor had the
Foreign Office when he had been boycotted by several oil-producing
countries.

His universalism then led him back to some extent to his Jewish
identity. He devoured the books of Elie Wiesel (such as *Night*, which he
read in German) for their "ethical value." But he was more emotionally
committed to ethics and the law than to the land. Israel, which he
privately called in German "our *Sorgenkind*"—our problem child—
greatly worried him: because it was Israel, because the Middle East
could spark a world war. His first years in England had left him with a
passion for helping refugees and uprooted people; as such, the Palestinians also interested him at the time.

He certainly did not wish to damage Israel and apparently stopped
financing the *Jewish Observer and Middle-East Review*, published in
London, when it became too hostile toward Jerusalem.[28]

During these years he went to Israel on a few occasions to see his
daughter. In 1974, when the Israel Corporation went into bankruptcy,
he was very happy to have no further connection with it.

At the time, however, most of his interest was in a rapprochement
between Israel and Egypt, in which he was to be an active witness and a
masked actor, as befits a man of influence: passing from one to the other
the important signals he received in London or Blonay, from Americans,
Israelis, Egyptians and Palestinians, he helped bring them together. This
essential page of postwar history is worth telling.

In November 1976 President Anwar el-Sadat told an American
congressman that he was ready to come to an understanding with Israel
and that it was up to President Carter to take the initiative. Reaction, as
much from the Arabs as the Israelis, was negative, with a few excep-
tions.

But the situation changed in April 1977, when the Israeli election
brought Shimon Peres up against Menachem Begin. Bruno Kreisky was
then on an official visit to Damascus, where President Sadat, whom he
knew well, telephoned him: "Come and see me in Cairo before going
back to Austria." Kreisky agreed. Sadat received him in Cairo with
great ceremony and said:

> I have thought about this. I am ready to meet the Israelis after their
> elections, in Salzburg or anywhere else. I want to talk to them without

preconditions. Meanwhile I would like to meet the important Jews in
Europe and America. Can you choose them for me?

Back home, Kreisky telephoned the Austrian industrialist Karl Kahane
and then Siegmund Warburg. He told them of his interview with
Anwar el-Sadat and asked them to assemble an appropriate Jewish
group. Enthusiastically the two men drew up an inital list: Edmond de
Rothschild in Paris, Marcus Sieff in London and several American Jews
who, when contacted, hesitated. The Americans then asked the opinion
of people in Jerusalem who were reluctant about the idea—a reaction
that made Siegmund bitter.

On 17 May Likud won the election. On 21 June Begin became
prime minister and his government won the confidence of the Knesset.
The situation seemed log-jammed, and Siegmund despaired of seeing
Israel react to Cairo's outstretched hand. By September and October,
despite intensive diplomatic activity, there was still no agreement on the
conditions in which an international conference might be held in Geneva. Siegmund was then in New York, concerning himself with A.G.
Becker, but he met emissaries from the two sides and began to envisage,
with others, an economic development plan for the Middle East.

On 9 November President Sadat, addressing the Egyptian Parliament, took a dramatic step. He said he was ready to go to Israel and talk
to the Knesset without any preconditions. Matters then moved very
quickly. On 11 November Begin replied that he favored the journey; on
14 November Sadat said he was waiting for an official invitation and
Begin extended an official invitation through American diplomats; on
17 November Sadat accepted and after meeting Hafez al-Assad in
Damascus two days later arrived in Jerusalem. On 20 November he
addressed the Knesset and after a joint press conference with Begin left
Israel on 21 November.

After this intense month the pace slowed. The supporters of peace
became impatient. Shortly afterward Siegmund, who was following
events with great interest, wrote to a very close friend about his impression of the attitude of the government in the country he still called "our
Sorgenkind."

> You and I were both plunged into joint despair when we sensed that
> the remarkable opportunity offered to Israel by the peace initiative
> was not seized by the Tel Aviv Government as a result of the strange
> mixture of narrow views, unreasonableness and self-intoxication.

He remained in close contact with Bruno Kreisky, who kept him fully informed, and several times met President Sadat's director of information, the Egyptian journalist Ali el-Samman, to whom he passed certain messages.

In this way a meeting at the Hotel Marigny in Paris was arranged for President Sadat and Jewish leaders. On 13 February 1978 alongside Siegmund were Edmond de Rothschild, Nahum Goldmann, Karl Kahane and Lord Goodman, but several other Jewish leaders had refused to attend. It was a long meeting. Sadat invited them to go to Egypt. Siegmund barely spoke; he considered that for the moment he had no part to play; the ball was in the court of the Israeli political leaders. The next day Sadat went to Rome to meet Pope Paul VI.

Siegmund tried to encourage Israel to accept Sadat's outstretched hand. He made numerous telephone calls to friends and decided to write an appeal for peace. He wrote it on the night of 17 February and sent it to some of his friends, but all refused to sign it. Very bitter, he resolved to publish it in his name alone, in the next day's *Times*. It was a true profession of faith, an expression of his relationship with Judaism and the Zionists. This is what it said in part:

> If President Sadat's initiative were to fail, no Arab leader would be in a position to renew a similar initiative for many years to come . . . .
>
> The two founders of Israel, Chaim Weizmann and David Ben-Gurion profoundly believed that the idealistic spirit and legacy of Judaism must direct the aims and the conduct of the State of Israel. I heard these two great men speak in such terms, both before and after 1948, but they often expressed their criticism of those strains of petty nationalism which seem today in dangerous ascendancy in the policies of the Israeli government.
>
> The creation of a secure existence for a community is not identical with nationalistic opportunism. . . . While every friend of Israel—and I have been such continuously—must be aware of the urgency of providing all possible means for Israel's protection, this is the opposite of striving for the kind of territorial gains which merely increase dangers and risks rather than improve safety. . . . the present government of Israel insists on the preservation and even extension of settlements outside the territories legally belonging to Israel . . . the maintenance and extension of such settlements are bound to expose Israel in general and the settlers concerned in particular to rules which are arbitrarily manufactured and senseless from the point of view of those who pray for a strong and forward-looking Israel . . . .

Many Jews inside as well as outside Israel who share the views put forward in this letter are reluctant to speak out publicly because they are afraid that this might be interpreted as lack of loyalty to the cause of Israel. However, loyalty to sound principles and moral precepts must override any other loyalties. . . . In the minds of all thinking men, there should be a vision of the immense possibilities open to the Middle East once it benefits from the joint endeavours of Arabs and Jews.

This statement caused an uproar in the City and in Britain's Jewish community. Siegmund was very proud of it: as a free man, certain of his ethics, he scorned those who kept quiet.

A few days after writing this letter, he wrote to President Sadat to explain his silence during their meeting. In his eyes, the importance and the scale of the visit had made words useless. He ended his letter by saying, "Be aware that whatever the future, no non-Jew has ever carried or will ever carry as much positive weight as yourself in the history of the Jewish people."

Some months passed before Begin agreed to begin talks, after lengthy mediation by Cyrus Vance. On 8 August 1978 the White House announced a meeting of Carter, Sadat and Begin on 5 September at Camp David. The agreement they reached was made public on 18 September. The Egyptian cabinet approved it, despite the resignation of the minister of foreign affairs. The Knesset ratified it on 28 September.

In February 1979, at the Pierre Hotel in New York, Siegmund met Dr. Ashraf Ghorbal, then Egypt's ambassador to Washington; he explained that he was considering an economic plan that he called "Investment for Peace," with a view to encouraging European and American investors to take an interest in the Middle East; the spirit of this was that people should be persuaded that peace would bring prosperity and that the economic stability of the region would be a guarantee of peace.

In September 1979 he sent a second letter to the Egyptian president. He stressed to Sadat how important it was that the negotiations with Israel should last. "Mr. President, the whole future of peace in this region of the world depends on your patience." Sadat replied to this letter with a message passed to Siegmund the following week by Ali el-Samman in Blonay. "I shall not spare my efforts," Sadat told him. "If one day you hear one of your friends in Israel say that I showed patience in the negotiations, be aware that this patience originated in the attitude of a man as noble as you toward me."

By January 1980 Siegmund's resentment against Begin was such that he even refused to receive the *honoris causa* doctorate from the University of Jerusalem founded by his uncle Felix, and refused to go to Israel for as long as Menachem Begin was in power. The following month, he confirmed his views in a letter to a friend:

> The only loyalty which is imperative is that which I owe to principles and not to nations or governments. I think that the policy of colonizing the West Bank [of the Jordan] is contrary to the interests of Israel, as not only does it expose her to great danger, but it also damages the great founding cause of Israel, that of an exemplary community built on Justice and Humanity. I believe that Israel must protect her security in every possible way, but I think that Begin's narrowly nationalist policy imperils the security of the country rather than strengthens it. I see no hope of improvement between now and the coming US presidential election. A new United States president, whoever he might be, will exert pressure from the spring of 1981.

At the same time, he wrote a third letter to President Sadat, which was delivered into his Sadat's hands at his country house in Mit Abu-Kum, his birthplace. This expanded Siegmund's proposals for an economic plan for the Middle East mentioned a year earlier in New York. One Saturday evening in March 1980, Sadat called him in Blonay to say, "Camp David represents not only an agreement between states, but a new era in relations between the people of Egypt and the Diaspora." Time would prevent them both from going further.

Siegmund continued to finance the Weizmann Institute and help all people of goodwill in the region. The time has not yet come to uncover the details of everything he did in this regard, or of what others were doing along with him, except to say that here as in other places, Sir Siegmund Warburg proved irreplaceable in the true meaning of the word.

Darkness over America

This is the story of the sudden destruction of a bank. At Becker the Anglo-French-American alliance had now turned completely sour. Since Wender's appointment at the end of 1979 the bank had been recruiting staff, but without earning enough commission to pay them. Like the heads of other New York investment houses, Wender tried to solve his problems by turning the bank toward a market that seemed promising, but in which it had no experience—the speculative issuing and selling of

American bonds. The situation did not improve. Moreover, joint management required the daily agreement of the two partners in Paris and London, and indeed Blonay, while many other Wall Street banks were making their decisions in minutes. At the end of 1980, informed by Ira Wender of the difficulties, the joint chairmen of the group, David Scholey and Pierre Haas, decided their two firms should commit more money to the Becker subsidiary; nonetheless, this strategy did not find unanimous support in London, where some doubted that either S.G. Warburg or Paribas had the financial capacity to deal with the matter.

A.G. Becker's position had become extremely difficult: for its last financial year, it announced a profit of $4 million on retail broking and international operations, which was very little in relation to a turnover of $251 million.

In the volatile banking business success can quickly evaporate. Several important Becker directors left, such as Paul Judy, John F. Donahue and Albert Kobin. Then in May 1981 the prospect of nationalization in France opened up for the parent company Paribas, and Ira Wender was not enthusiastic about this development. In October, while this decision was hanging in the balance, Siegmund Warburg, in agreement with Jacques de Fouchier, decided to retain his links with Paribas, but opposed Ira Wender and Pierre Moussa. On 26 October, in the middle of the crisis at rue d'Antin following Paribas's transfer of control of its Swiss banking and Belgian industrial subsidiaries to foreign interests, Jacques de Fouchier returned to Paribas to replace Moussa, his successor. Dr. de Fouchier saw his firm through nationalization, until the appointment to its head on 16 February 1982 of Jean-Yves Haberer, then director of the Treasury at the Ministry of Finance.

Siegmund at that time went to Paris and made known his acceptance of the new rules of French banking. He kept his stake in the nationalized Paribas, and Lord Roll was appointed to the board.

In New York A.G. Becker, continuing to lose money, dismissed 10 percent of its 2,500 employees between March and May 1982. Rumors began to circulate about its accounts. In June, trying to calm things down, Wender announced that the loss for the past six months was only $42 million, but this only heightened the general unease.

Siegmund, when informed of Wender's statements, was furious: he knew from experience that an investment bank is no more than a fragile network of individuals—bankers and clients—and that a few rumors, destroying confidence, could finally bring its downfall. Now more executives left, taking with them their skills and their contacts. Clients withdrew and accounts were closed. Siegmund, incensed at what he considered Wender's blundering, went several times to Paris to persuade his partner Paribas to call for Wender's resignation, which finally came on 1 July 1982. For his part, Ira Wender was convinced that he had been sacrificed for having tried to keep an equal balance between Paribas and S.G. Warburg.

At the same time, in order to dispose of the rumors that were harming the firm, and at the request of its shareholding executives, Warburg and Paribas increased their stake in Becker to 51 percent. A new chief executive had to be found. Paribas did not want a man from London to unbalance its joint rule with Warburg, but wanted the appointment of an experienced American. Siegmund did not favor an over strong personality, capable of escaping his control, and thus put forward the idea of a provisional solution from within the firm itself: John Heimann and Dan Good. On 9 July, at a Becker board meeting in Chicago, Pierre Haas announced the increase in capital and the appointment as co-presidents of these two executives and of a Paribas director-general, Hervé Pinet, alongside them. Daniel Good had been with Becker for eighteen years and it was he who had arranged the first contact with Paribas. Ironically, John Heimann had been a signing partner with E.M. Warburg-Pincus for eight years, before becoming superintendent of banks in New York, then Jimmy Carter's controller of the currency; he had joined Becker only the year before.

Jean-Yves Haberer asked Siegmund to go to New York with him to install the management team and demonstrate to the executives the commitment of their European shareholders. Siegmund equivocated: he considered that he had said good-bye to New York and suspected that his return would do Becker more harm than good. He suggested limiting his stay to a discreet meeting in a hotel near Kennedy airport, but Haberer objected that this semisecrecy would be the worst possible tactic. In the end a two-day seminar was openly arranged at the Pierre hotel. For two days Siegmund fought steadily to motivate the Becker executives, lend them his vision and answer their questions. Those present speak of his extraordinary vitality, his passion for persuasion, his wish to restore order.

Banks changed hands quickly on Wall Street at that time. On that same day, 17 July, Al-Saghan, an Arab fund, owned by Saudis, Kuwaitis and Bahreinis, paid $40 million for a quarter share in Smith, Barney, Harris, Upham & Co., parent company of the fifteenth largest American investment bank.

Last Acts

Most of 1981—Siegmund's last year—was devoted to his German interests. Blonay became a meeting place for leading Germans, and he himself often traveled by chauffeur-driven car to Frankfurt or Munich. But he no longer had many influential contacts in those places. Hans Wüttke, who had been a director of Dresdner Bank, had left in 1980 to become executive vice-president of the International Finance Corporation, a subsidiary of the World Bank in Washington. Predictably, he no longer wished to have any relationship with M.M. Warburg-Brinckmann, Wirtz & Co.

The old firm still shone at the time, ranked third among the eighty German private banks that had survived the two thousand existing in nineteenth-century Germany. Warburg-Brinckmann, Wirtz, said its literature, "works with sobriety and pragmatism, following the Hanseatic motto: substance rather than appearance, which could also be that of the bank." It owned one subsidiary in Frankfurt, another in Luxembourg and controlled a bank in Nuremberg. It had assets of $1.4 billion. Out of its four hundred employees, twelve had been working there since the 1950s. It was run by four equal and unlimited partners: Max Warburg, who had replaced his father when he retired to Kösterberg, Christian Brinckmann, H.D. Sandweg, also chairman of the city's Stock Exchange, and Hans Schecke.

The last months of Siegmund's life were also marked by his wish for a greater presence in Japan, whose growth he had watched for twenty years. He had the idea of getting a foothold there with Mercury Securities through a joint operation with Rio Tinto. Suddenly, he allowed Peter Stormonth Darling to negotiate in Hong Kong, the leading financial market in Asia, to set up a bank jointly with the Bank of East Asia, to be called East Asia Warburg Ltd: a name that he had some difficulty in accepting. In July 1982, in London, Scholey also set up a joint finance company with Dai Ichi Mutual Life Insurance Co., under the name Dai Ichi Warburg.

The last businesss Siegmund knew of was the breakup in September of an operation arranged one year earlier with the American insurance company Aetna Life. Aetna Warburg Investment Management had been set up to manage money for the Ford Foundation, Standard Oil of Indiana and IBM. Aetna was now keen to buy a British bank, but S.G. Warburg was not for sale. So they separated. Warburg resumed business under the name Warburg Investment Management International.

Siegmund's firm was stronger than ever. In July 1982 Lord Roll announced a net profit of £13 million for the 1981 financial year, 10 percent up on the previous year, and 30 percent up on 1979. The bank was now worth £140 million and had £5 billion under management. As usual, the dividend distribution was quite modest. It was still the most profitable merchant bank in the City, and the third largest in the world Euro-issue market which, doubled once more that year, reaching $47 billion.

S.G. Warburg had a presence in London, New York, Frankfurt, Geneva, Tokyo and Hong Kong. Siegmund was truly the only banker this century who personally made the bank he founded an international institution.

Considering His Life

On 20 July, returning from his New York trip, Siegmund showed some signs of tiredness. Did he know then that he was nearing the end? He had certainly entertained the idea for some time. "You will be glad when you are rid of me," he often told those around him. Like most people of his kind, he thought himself indestructible, and he remained forward-looking. Why should he do otherwise—he was not ill and there was no threat to his health.

Like any man of quality, he regularly reviewed his own actions and judged them severely in accordance with the demanding criteria inherited from his Hamburg Judaism. His conscience was clear. He thought that he had been both fair and efficient. "It is difficult to combine generosity with discernment, but it is worth trying," he said. He tried every day of his life.

He did not reproach himself for his actions. "In this terrible century, nobody could find anything reprehensible whatever in my behavior," he told a friend: nothing in his relationship with his wife, the education of his children or his attitude toward friends, even though with some his extremely demanding nature and pitiless judgment may have broken a few dreams.

In these last months of his life several people heard him say, quoting Thomas Mann, that fulfilled life was unthinkable without the highest degree of joy on one side and an equally high degree of suffering on the other. From this point of view he thought his life had been a success. The mental ruin of his father, then his own financial ruin had been followed by the spectacle of his mother's physical suffering during the last fifteen years of her life, of which he said, ". . . the suffering had to pay for all the joys I owed her."[29]

He knew he owed much to others, and primarily to Henry Grunfeld, his oldest friend still alive, who said to him one day in 1981, "We both believe in the same ethical standards," and to whom he replied, "You couldn't have done it without me and I couldn't have done it without you."[30] He knew that he had revived, perhaps for the last time, one of the greatest names in Western wealth, and that he had influenced the tide of history as much as a man could through reason. He also knew that, despite inventing the best of the century's finance, he had not been able to prevent others from pushing the new debt economy into a paroxysm, raising once more the specter of war.

He had "wished that the world with him might be less bad than it would have been without him." Perhaps that is the ultimate definition of his success, the most accurate identification of the influence for which he yearned.

He also knew, as Henry Grunfeld told him at that time, that his main contribution would have been "the example he gave in developing the bank." He had tried to make S.G. Warburg & Co. the "Morgan Stanley" of Europe and he succeeded. He accomplished what he always wanted: remaining as small in size as he was great in influence and carrying off magnificent deals without ever claiming the credit.

He did not see himself as the greatest contemporary banker: he put André Meyer, the richest, and Hermann Abs, the most powerful, before himself. However, he was happy to have remained the indomitable outsider, the victorious stranger, unpersuaded by any victory to enter the circles of conformity. A "puritan and romantic prince," George Steiner called him.

When he considered the state of his business, there was not a decision he regretted, except, he said two years before his death, "in a relatively small proportion of cases." In these cases he had sometimes taken losses, but "they didn't upset me deeply. . . . I have today more money than I ever expected to make. But money to me is completely secondary."[31]

As for money, he possessed several tens of millions of dollars, far less than most bankers or speculators in London, Tokyo, Hong Kong or New York. He had left the bulk of it in his company.

Neither had he collected much, apart from a few fine books, some valuable furniture and a few antique silver boxes. Charles Sharp said of him:

> What impressed me most was his lack of attention to his own personal or family financial interests. Having had to concern myself with his investments and with the transactions linked to his move to Switzerland, I always had the greatest difficulty in arousing in Sir Siegmund any interest whatever in his personal financial affairs, or in those of his family, even when large sums were at stake.[32]

He had known in advance his destiny: to make a fortune without loving money, and to think rationally in a world of madness, aspiring to wisdom in a century of savagery. He firmly believed that the reason why he, a man of high finance, had had so little influence in this century was that this was not a century of money but one of speculation and power. He liked to say that "life is no more than a fatal illness."[33]

He was conscious of his failures and knew that they lay in what he considered the essential point: his dynasty ended with him; he had not managed a true return to Germany; his passion for politics had remained a dead letter; and above all he had been disappointed by many people. He had, he knew, a tendency to overestimate the people he met, and to be too enthusiastic at the outset, always confusing the person with the image he created for him:

> If somebody is friendly and polite, I would often take the politeness as a reflection of kindness. But Grunfeld would wisely say the man in question might want something out of us . . . . What I have learned is not to take [disappointments] as much to heart as I used to. What bothers me is when I trust somebody and then he lets me down. That has happened several times. My wife says that in certain dealings I am a baby. That is one of my many weaknesses: I am too trusting. . . . [Bad businesss decisions] depressed me, concerned me . . . but the things that got under my skin were human disappointments. There . . . I take these too much to heart.[34]

As well as reflecting on his failures, he often thought of the books he had long in mind to write: first an autobiography, which he had abandoned ("someone else will do it," he told several friends), then a collection of aphorisms, almost finished and of which he was quite proud. He chose a title, *An Anthology for Searches*. He had written aphorisms or selected them from his reading and organized them into an amazing interplay of reflections, from Talleyrand to Butler and from Goethe to Dostoevsky, from Trollope to Balzac. He did not have time to publish the book, and after his death neither his wife nor his friends were willing to do so, actually concealing from everyone the manuscript.

He also had some thoughts for a book on education. Forty years of contact with young people and a passion for teaching had supplied him with the material. At the bank, up to the last day, he would meet new arrivals, for the pleasure of answering their questions and unfolding before them the wonderful picture of the interlaced networks of world finance. He planned to attack the mass training dispensed in many universities, with students in search of diplomas rather than knowledge. Instead, he would stress continuous self-education, generalizing the methods he had designed for his own executives.[35]

But these works would not be published. No doubt this was because he did not really wish them to be, working unceasingly to remove all trace of himself: no books, no foundation in Jerusalem ("that is for Felix"), Britain ("that is for Aby"), and no university chair in America either ("that is for Paul").

He was probably most pleased to have left behind the memory of having been able to charm others. "If I die tomorrow," he told a friend that final summer, "the thing I should be most grateful for in life would be my friendships." Often during long evenings on the terrace at Blonay, watching the day slip away, Siegmund thought of his family and its history. How much he had talked of this family since his childhood. How he had held forth on its decline, its history and its experiences. Deep down he had never really left it. He had never forgotten that youth, forever set in tenderness and nostalgia, like old forgotten toys.

That terrace. . . . Like the one where twenty years earlier, a hundred yards below, his aunt Olga had written her memoirs, while a Russian writer, also uprooted from a lost paradise, used to pass by, exchange a few words with her and, wearing his unfashionable straw hat, take the funicular to hunt butterflies: Vladimir Nabokov. Or the terrace at Aby S.'s house on the Baltic, another forty years earlier, where the children listened to family stories and quietly vowed among themselves not to become bankers, so as not to be sad.

The Death of Siegmund

In July 1982 he took another trip to the United States, to Germany in August and then the same month to Britain, where he met Japhet, the new chairman of Bank Leumi, with whom he talked at length about their youth—both had spent their early years in Germany. Soon afterward Siegmund sent him the notes he had written about his mother. In this reminiscence, Japhet recognized his own mother.

In mid-August, tired, Siegmund returned to Blonay, where a few friends came to see him. From there he witnessed the foreign exchange crisis that he had expected to break out in Brazil, but instead struck Mexico, which was unable to meet the interest payments on its $80 billion debt. To save its own banks America had to grant Mexico two loans of $1 billion each, and on 20 August the American banks, additionally, had to accept a three-month moratorium; discussions with the IMF then resulted in a rescheduling of Mexican debt, and the granting of loans from the BIS, the IMF and the commercial banks. The first cracks in the system—an event Siegmund had been expecting.

On 3 September he dined with Bruno Kreisky, Karl Kahane and Hans Thalberg at the Victoria Hotel in Glion. They discussed the Middle East and the tragedy of Beirut, where a battle was raging, and talked of the big party at Claridge's in London that Lady Warburg was arranging, for bank executives only, on the occasion of Siegmund's eightieth birthday on 30 September 1982. This date obsessed him as an insuperable barrier. The invitations had gone out two *months* before and many replies had already arrived, with good wishes, to which Eva Warburg responded, as Siegmund was too tired to do it himself.

For the rest of the month he did not move far; he read a lot and once again went through the Joseph tetralogy by Thomas Mann, which he had discovered nearly fifty years before. Illness had hold of him. Doctors bored him, apart from his own, an old friend who came from London. He hated to be an invalid. He noted in his diary a recommendation to doctors, "If you are not in a position to perpetuate health, you should shorten life rather than prolong it."[36]

On 22 September Siegmund went to Munich again to attend a meeting where he saw Henry Grunfeld, who had come from London; this was the last time they saw each other. Henry Grunfeld related soon afterward, "I referred to a remark which he had made at that meeting about his being worried and I asked him what worried him in particular. He was frail and tired and he answered, 'What worries me most regarding the firm is complacency and that some recent successes may make some of our friends in London too complacent.'" It was like listening to the things he had said half a century before.

On Tuesday 28 September Siegmund had the serious stroke that was to end his life. The London reception was cancelled. On Thursday, his birthday, he was able to read a last article about him by the Daily Mail writer Patrick Sergeant, who wished a happy birthday to

> ... the greatest banker in the City of London since the war. He remains an enigma. A placid, almost shy man, when you look at his high forehead and his magnificent head, you think you are in the presence of an intellectual or a philosopher rather than a hard and tenacious banker, a master of markets. Wherever he is, we wish him happiness. He deserves it, since he left this world in a better state than that in which he found it.

In these last weeks he spoke only German and some people recall that he still knew by heart the speech he had made on the day of his bar mitzvah, seventy years earlier in Urach. A few days after his eightieth birthday, on his doctor's orders, he was taken by air ambulance to London, where he died on 18 October. His body was cremated. Only his wife, two children, doctor and secretary were present. He had wanted it that way; he was in the habit of saying, "I never go to funerals, I would rather concern myself with people while they are alive."

He entrusted to his wife the task of arranging the bequest of his library to St. Paul's School, the private day school in London that Anna had attended, as well as some money to set up a fund for the education of the children of bank staff. Upon his death it was claimed throughout London that the best of his 1,180 employees would immediately leave. None did.

In the next few days the British press published just a few articles about him, highly laudatory.

It was as though Britain was still having difficulty in agreeing to honor one of the greatest financiers in its history. The *Times* wrote:

> He was a principal author of the rebirth of the City's effectiveness. Banking for Siegmund Warburg was not a business, it was a profession and indeed a vocation, an art rather than merely a craft, the skills of which could be learnt. Siegmund Warburg's strength of character, his ability to apply sustained, systematic thought to a problem, his unique combination of boldness in conception, inventiveness and imagination in execution, together with an innate prudence and meticulous attention to detail soon became legendary in London and the world's other financial centers.

The *Financial Times* wrote almost the same thing:

> Sir Siegmund Warburg was perhaps the most influential financier in
> the City of London in the post-war period. . . . He brought about
> radical changes in the practice of corporate finance and was instru-
> mental in reshaping the role played by merchant bankers . . . . War-
> burg's lack of concern about the size of his balance sheet reflected his
> preference for influencing clients by acting in the role of consultant
> and guide rather than that of large-scale lender.

The Last of Siegmund

Within three years the last traces of Siegmund's presence were gone. His
wife died eight months after him. His daughter was living in Tel Aviv
with his granddaughter. His son was a banker in Connecticut. None of
his grandchildren was called Siegmund. His bank was transformed from
top to bottom. It left Frankfurt, became small once more in New York
and operated on the world market on a very large scale from London,
Geneva, Zurich and Tokyo.

Here ended, in effect, a history, a world and a culture. Upon his
death his bank was reorganized around an honorary chairman, Henry
Grunfeld, two chairmen, Lord Roll and David Scholey, and four managing directors. Five directors were now earning more than £150,000
each annually; the average pay for group employees was £16,000. Sixty-
five executives had a share of profits: austerity was no longer in style.
The bank left the Gresham Street building and moved back to King
William Street, this time to No. 33, a big new functional building
overlooking the Thames. The name still did not appear on the door.

The power of the group in Britain was extensive. Its profits went
from £13 million in 1982 to £17 million in 1983 and £23 million in
1984, i.e., a 15 percent return for shareholders. With reserves, profits
reached £35 million, or 25 percent on capital. It was then the leading
merchant bank in the City in terms of profitability, the third in terms of
profits and the seventh in terms of assets. With Morgan Grenfell it was
the leading British industrial adviser and dominated the share issue
market: GEC, Granada, Grand Metropolitan, Hawker Siddeley, ICI,
Reuter and Tate were its most constant clients. It was the banker to
British Telecom and would remain so after privatization, even though
the government was represented by Kleinwort, Benson in the share
issue. S.G. Warburg carried out twenty mergers a year, worth more

than £1 billion, and managed £6 million for its clients, among them the biggest pension funds, such as the Post Office, the National Coal Board and British Rail.

It remained the leader in the sterling Eurobond market and third in the world in the Euro-issue market, after Deutsche Bank and Credit Suisse-First Boston. In September 1983 it issued the first floating rate Euro-issue denominated in sterling on behalf of SNCF (French Railways), then another for the Irish government. On this market, which accounted for $47 billion in 1982 as in 1983, with 608 and 526 issues respectively, S.G. Warburg could be proud of its record. In all, within twenty years, out of 3,730 Euro-issues floated totaling $186 billion, S.G. Warburg as lead bank had placed nearly one-third, that is 906 totaling $60 billion. Overall, it was the fourth largest bank by number of issues and the fifth in amount placed, behind the Swiss and German giants, while the top French bank BNP came only sixth.

Finishing with New York

In New York lower inflation, the end of regulation and the increase in interest rates made loans to America more profitable. There was a need for increasing bank size to allow collection of maximum savings at the least cost, and speculation without too many risks. So one after the other the barriers erected after the 1929 crisis were lifted as the banks grew and financial supermarkets opened.

The first was created by Bank of America. On 25 November 1981 it paid $53 million for Charles Schwab, the biggest wholesale broker in America, which managed the servicing of securities and pension funds. The next day the Los Angeles Security Pacific National Bank set up a subsidiary of the same kind. In May 1982 the Federal Home Loan Bank Board authorized savings institutions to sell securities. In September the administration lightened the constraints set by the Glass-Steagall Act, excusing certain banks from them altogether, with the exception of the six thousand members of the Federal Reserve System. The American banks were then borrowing in the short term without restraint. With their communication technology, the centralization of information and market management, they became truly worldwide and were now able to offer American investors securities from every country. To be sold, albeit in part, to American residents, a foreign security had always to pass through an American bank; therefore a section of the securities market returned to New York, even though American savings continued to flow abroad at the same speed. So one-third of the capital of

British Aluminium and ICI and half that of Glaxo switched to New York.

On the other hand, and this became fundamental, the Wall Street banks were able to offer public or private American securities to foreign money. Wall Street, which still represented two-thirds of the world securities market (against 17 percent in Tokyo and 7 percent in London) again became a magnet for money of all kinds.

To attract and manage such enormous amounts, it was now necesary to arrange the issue and placing of securities in an increasingly standardized way. So there was less need for the specialized expertise of the small investment banks and an increasing need for large networks capable simultaneously of drawing off mass savings and managing a large portfolio of securities. So American Express offered eighteen different services, Prudential and Sears fourteen, Merrill Lynch, whose balance sheet had risen to over $1 billion, offered twelve and the big commercial banks, five. Merrill Lynch, which in the 1960s had only placed mutual funds, now had four thousand salesmen across the country selling insurance policies, Treasury bills, state bonds and property. Stockbrokers, investment banks and commercial banks saw their activities come into competition. The commercial banks indeed hoped to regain the right, which they had lost in 1933, to guarantee the issue of bonds and to establish themselves all over the American continent. Only Morgan Stanley and Goldman Sachs, controlled by a small number of private shareholders and unquoted, remained apart from the general changes.

In this enormous New York explosion, as sudden as that of the Euro-issues in London in 1976, reputations were staked and lost within a few hours and it was necessary to attain global scale in order to withstand the shock. In 1982 Lehman, which was still making $15 million before tax each month with capital of $250 million, was in difficulties. That year Peterson finally clashed with Gluksmann, who demanded that his boss leave the firm. Ten months later Lehman was sold to Shearson, itself bought a few months later by American Express. In this turmoil nearly all the foreign investment banks were neatly expelled from Wall Street. A few months after Siegmund's death, S.G. Warburg, which then intended to concentrate on London, decided to leave Becker, which was to pay dearly for the decision.

By the end of 1982 it had seemed that Becker had returned to some small profit. Having become the fourteenth ranking American investment bank, it appeared able withstand the competition. At Warburg, however, David Scholey, Henry Grunfeld and Eric Roll had already decided on separation. It was no use being in New York without being dominant. In London one had to be very big to be able to do everything, so the dead or useless branches had to be cut off. In March 1983, almost twenty years to the day after the launch of the Euro-issue on behalf of the Italian highways and less than six months after the death of Siegmund, S.G. Warburg sold Paribas its stake in Becker and contented itself with reopening a small office in New York. Warburg's few executives in New York returned to London. The links between Paribas and Warburg were not immediately broken, as each still retained 25 percent of the other and maintained joint businesses in Australia and Canada. Two months later there was a decision to finish even this arrangement, though Paribas still kept 6.5 percent of Mercury and the two former partners still treated one another as the most favored house.

In New York the company renamed A.G. Becker-Paribas held up fairly well at the beginning, despite being deprived of business from London. In June Heimann, who was still vice-president, told the press, "The firm must develop towards international banking." That was the least that could be said. Hervé Pinet, who was president, added, "Things are going well. The firm is in good form and making money."[37] In fact, six months later in the face of competition from the big companies, themselves in crisis, Becker began losing money—a lot of it. A year later, on 5 August 1984, Paribas agreed to merge Becker with the Wall Street giant Merrill Lynch, half broker-half banker, and became a major shareholder with 3.3 percent of the capital.

Greatness from London

It is the nature of banks to adjust to the financial demands of the times. Before the war the American and British governments had to issue loans abroad to make good their deficits, and found the banks they needed, of which Kuhn Loeb was the outstanding example. At the time of Bretton Woods they had to borrow their own currencies from other central banks, and the commercial banks did this for them. Today they can borrow freely on the markets of New York, London or elsewhere, and for this they need the financial supermarkets.

Since no other nation was ready to take over from the dollar in lending its own currency to deficit countries, the world, gorged with Eurodollars and American dollars, saw its debt increase limitlessly. Added to the American trade deficit was a payments deficit due especially to the servicing of debt, which overturned the law of the twentieth century. Once more, as in the nineteenth century, America had to attract world capital through its interest rates, a giant vacuum pump. On the other hand, its investments and loans abroad collapsed almost to nil.

Unlike the situation in the nineteenth century, America was also able to borrow its own currency from the world. Its debt led to its deficit and its deficit worsened its debt; in 1983 America's trade deficit quadrupled; in 1984 it redoubled, reaching $160 billion in 1985; all in relation to a budget deficit of $200 billion, half financed by foreign capital.

Overall, America, eleven times less populated than the Third World, was now seven times more indebted. From January 1985 it also owed the rest of the world more than it was owed, and owned fewer assets abroad than foreigners owned in the United States.

Then, as in all financial crises from the nineteenth century onward, exchange rates went mad: the number of days on which exchange rates moved by more than 1 percent went from three in 1982 to six in 1984 and eleven in April 1985.

In this turmoil, to remain at least the leading financial center in Europe, even in a country that was no longer the leading industrial power, the City had to counter Wall Street's drain on capital. There had to be a complete change of scale. It was now a question of investing fortunes not of $100,000 but $5 million; takers had to be found for loans not of $15 million but $500 million. So every means of attracting money from treasurers and speculators had to be made available. There was, for example, the London International Financial Futures Exchange, set up along New York lines outside the London Stock Exchange to manage long-term foreign exchange contracts—a place of speculative profit and enormous ruin.

In addition, to allow the London banks to grow as the New York banks had, by integrating domestic and international markets and also becoming giant financial brokers, there had to be an end to the barriers erected centuries before to protect savers from conflicts between those who placed securities and those who managed money. In April 1983 the British government called on the City to put an end to the distinction between brokers and jobbers, authorized groupings of British and foreign insurance companies, reduced stamp duty, deregulated commissions on foreign securities and abolished the monopoly of a few bodies on the introduction of Treasury bills. It initially limited to 29.9 percent the stakes banks were allowed to take in these Stock Exchange intermediaries, and delayed such participation until March 1986.

S.G. Warburg & Co. then decided to become the biggest firm in London, to be able to confront the four huge American firms: Morgan Stanley, Goldman Sachs, First Boston and Salomon Brothers. It sold out of Effectenbank-Warburg in Frankfurt and strengthened itself in Asia, where like all American and British banks it was intent on becoming established, and succeeded in making profits from the second year of East Asia Warburg's existence.

In November 1983 it went on the offensive. Having sold Becker, David Scholey paid £41 million (8 percent of it in Mercury paper) for 29.5 percent of the jobber Akroyd & Smithers, owned by the family of one of its directors, Andrew Smithers. Simultaneously, Akroyd on its part had been negotiating with Rowe & Pitman, a stockbroker 29 percent owned by Charter—itself part of the South African Oppenheimer group. One of the biggest firms in the market, Rowe & Pitman, brokers to the Queen, handled 18 percent of the foreign securities in Great Britain but was greatly threatened by the deregulation of commission and the abolition of its part monopoly on placing state bonds on the Stock Exchange.

In January 1984 S.G. Warburg in turn bought Rowe & Pitman, and in February added to the group the Treasury bill specialist, Mullens & Co., whose chairman, Nigel Althaus, then left to join the Bank of England and thus compete with the new group.

There were fifty other alliances of this kind that year: Samuel Montagu bought the stockbroker W. Greenwell & Co.; Charterhouse Japhet joined with Kitcat, another broker; Rothschild with Smith, a jobber; Buckmaster & Moore with Credit Suisse; Quilter Goodison with Skandia; Hambros and Société Générale with Strauss, Turnbull. Only Lloyds Bank refrained from buying a broker.

On 14 August 1984, under pressure from the market, the 29.9 percent limit was removed and a full merger of the four firms was decided upon. Mercury Securities therefore bought the rest of the capital of the other three for a total of £126 million, partly paid in Mercury paper. Akroyd was valued at £75 million, Rowe and Pitman at £42.5 million, Mullens at £8.6. By spring 1986 a new holding company controlling the whole group would be 73 percent owned by Mercury (this stake was to decrease later), 20 percent by Akroyd, 2 percent by Rowe & Pitman and 0.5 percent by Mullens.

Warburg has more than 130 industrial clients; Rowe & Pitman is the leading broker in London and has £1.3 billion under management that, added to the funds managed by Mercury Securities, doubles its capital. S.G. Warburg will become the first British merchant bank to equal the scale of Wall Street's Morgan Stanley, with seventeen hundred employees. Barclays, with ten times the deposits, will remain its only British competitor.

Siegmund's last "adopted son" became chairman. "The boat will cross the line when the off signal is given," David Scholey said. This was in April 1986, forty years exactly after the founding of S.G. Warburg & Co.

The name given to the overall group long remained in question. At first Mercury International, Rowak (from Rowe, Warburg and Akroyd) were used alternately, like Swarm . . . or, as a journalist suggested, it could have been "Pegasus, the winged horse with four legs, replacing Mercury, the winged messenger with two legs." In the end Mercury International Group was chosen. Some people saw risks. Wasn't it too big? too complicated? too London-oriented? too anonymous? too subject to conflict?

"While the world is really becoming internationalized," said an American banker, "Warburg is in danger of imploding into Great Britain. It could be one of the great victims of the international capital markets in the eighties."

What would Siegmund have said today? In 1982 he said:

> . . . we are getting too big on both sides of the Atlantic. This is the punishment for success. . . . If you take on more and more clients, the moment comes when the quality of your service cannot fail to deteriorate. This is our problem, we are in a way too big. In London we are definitely too big.[38]

Perhaps Siegmund would not have acted any differently, seeing no other way of meeting the spread of the American giants. In any case, if he had not done the same, he would have been one of the very few in the City to stay "small," for today almost nothing is left of the 18 merchant banks, 17 jobbers and 205 brokers who held sway there only two years ago. There was no reason why these changes in the size of banks should help solve international financial problems. On the contrary, as in previous crises they probably did no more than precede and accelerate disasters.

On a world scale the greatest uncertainty is still to come. A return to equilibrium without a financial crisis would imply that bankers made a virtue of necessity and continued lending to indebted countries, that developing countries implemented more severe policies, that the industrial countries maintained equilibrium in their payments without damaging their growth, that budget deficits everywhere decreased and that there was a massive fall in interest rates: an unlikely scenario.

History teaches us that it is most probable that debt will one day get the better of the debtors—or of the creditors. If the Third World does not pay its debt, the American banks will bear most of the burden and will be put under federal protection or indeed be nationalized. If, on the other hand, America defaults on its debt, through a massive fall in the dollar, and through protectionism, it will be Europe and the Third World that will suffer.

The gigantic mechanisms of the financial industry will then painfully give birth to another world, and beyond further falls in the dollar and extensive social, financial and military disasters will appear a new universe of giant banks, holding sway over a unified, computerized, uninterrupted market, where a single currency might prevail. In this complex of great mechanisms, money would become a commodity like any other, mass produced and based on any security imaginable.

It should be understood that despite the apparent rationality of figures and the huge amounts at stake, the influence of the financier will be no greater than it is today. Gambling, speculaton, the irrational and politics will be the law of the world, and the law of wealth. No doubt in the intervals between the great banking and speculative organizations, new financiers, seers of their time, will manage to make a place for themselves. They will try once more, still in vain, to help reason prevail against madness, calculation against risk, but without being too much concerned either with the dignity of nations or the labor of men.

Years ago Siegmund was impressed by a line of Oscar Wilde's. "In this world there are only two tragedies. One is not getting what one wants and the other is getting it." He himself had probably experienced both situations, going to the peak of *haute banque*, attempting to influence from there the course of events, succeeding, perhaps for the last time, in reassembling the shattered family and giving value to a name and power to memories.

The catalyst of a revolution that overtook him, a sensor for the madness of this century, an austere adventurer, a bold man and an old sage, he had been at the heart of the insanities, one of the few men of influence in this century—in the end, a man of charm. It could be said that Siegmund Warburg was the best that Europe and the Jewish people have given our time.

Bibliography

Abella, I., and Tropper, H. *None Is Too Many: Canada and the Jews of Europe (1933–1948)*. New York: Random House, 1983.

Agar, H. *The Saving Remnant: An Account of Jewish Survival*. New York: Viking, 1960.

Allen, W.S. *Une petite ville nazie, 1930–1935*. Paris: Laffont, 1967.

Attlee, C.R. *The Labour Party in Perspective and Twelve Years Later*. London: Gollancz, 1949.

Balbach, A.B. *The Mechanics of Intervention in Exchange Markets*. St. Louis: Federal Reserve Bank, 1978.

Barnouw, E. *Tube of Plenty: The Evolution of American Television*. New York: Oxford, 1975.

Baron, S.W. *Histoire d'Israël: Vie sociale et religieuse*. 5 vols. Paris: PUF, 1957–64.

Barry, E.E. *Nationalization in British Policy: The Historical Backround*. London: Cape, 1965.

Baumier, J. *Ces banquiers qui nous gouvernent*. Paris: Plon, 1983.

Belin, J. *Problèmes monétaires*. Paris: IEP, Les cours de droit, Fascicule 3, 1954–55.

———. *Problèmes monétaires, 1929–1945*. Paris: IEP, Les cours de droit, Fascicules 5, 6 et 7, 1958–59.

Bentwich, N. *They Found Refuge: An Account of British Jewry's Work for Victims of Nazi Oppression*. London: Cresset Press, 1956.

Berstein, S., and Milza, P. *L'Allemagne 1870–1970*. Paris: Masson, 1971.

Bevan, A. *In Place of Fear*. rev. ed. London: Macgibbon & Kee, 1961.

Birmingham, S. *Our Crowd*. New York: Harper & Row, 1967.

Bloomfield, A.I. *Monetary Policy under the International Gold Standards*. New York: Federal Reserve Bank, 1959.

———. *Short-term Capital Movements under the pre-1914 Gold Standard*. Princeton: Princeton University Press, 1963.

———. *Patterns of Fluctuation in International Investment before 1914*. Princeton: Princeton University Press, 1968.

Blum, J.M. *Roosevelt and Morgenthau*. Boston: Houghton Mifflin, 1970.

Boyer, R., and Mistral, J. "Economie en liberté," *Accumulation, inflation, crises*. 2d ed. Paris: PUF, 1983.

Brandon, H., *In the Red: The Struggle for Sterling, 1964–1966*. London: Deutsch, 1966.

Braudel, F. *Civilisation matérielle, économie et capitalisme*. 3 vols. Paris: Colin, 1979.

Brittan, S. *Treasury under the Tories, 1951–1964.* Harmondsworth: Penguin, 1964.

Brown, M.S., and Butler, J. *The Production, Marketing and Consumption of Copper and Aluminium.* New York: Praeger, 1968.

Burns, J.M. *Roosevelt: The Lion and the Fox.* London: Secker & Warburg, 1951.

Butler, R.A. *The Art of the Possible: The Memoirs of Lord Butler.* London: Hamish Hamilton, 1971.

Cairncross, A.K. *Home and Foreign Investment.* Cambridge: Cambridge University Press, 1953.

Calder, A., *L'Angleterre en guerre, 1939–1945.* Paris: Gallimard, 1972.

Calleo, D.P. *The Imperious Economy.* Cambridge, Mass.: Harvard University Press, 1982.

Carosso, V.P. *Investment Banking in America: A History.* Cambridge, Mass.: Harvard University Press, 1970.

Castellan, G. *L'Allemagne de Weimar, 1918–1933.* Paris: 1969.

Caves, R., *American Industry: Structure, Conduct, Performance.* 4th ed. Englewood Cliffs: Prentice-Hall, 1970.

Cecil, L. *Albert Ballin.* Princeton: Princeton University Press, 1970.

Champion, P.F., and Trauman, J. *Mécanismes de change et marché des euro-dollars.* Paris: OEconomica, 1978.

Channon, D.F. *British Banking Strategy and the International Challenge.* London: Macmillan, 1977.

Charlot, M. *L'Angleterre, 1945–1980.* Paris: Imprimerie Nationale, 1981.

Chouraqui, J.-C. *Le marché monétaire de Londres depuis 1960.* Paris: PUF, 1969.

Clapp, E. *The Port of Hamburg.* New Haven: Yale University Press, 1911.

Clarke, W.M. *The City in the World Economy.* London: Institute of Economic Affairs, 1965.

Craig, Gordon A. *Germany, 1866–1945.* Oxford: Clarendon Press, 1978.

Cripps, R.S. *Democracy Alive.* London: Sidgwick & Jackson, 1946.

Dauphin-Meunier, A. *La Banque, 1919–1935.* Paris: Gallimard, 1936.

———. *La Cité de Londres.* Paris: Gallimard, 1954.

———. *L'économie allemande contemporaine, 1914–1942.* Paris: F. Sorlot, 1942.

Davis, S.I. *The Euro-Bank: Its Origins, Management and Outlook.* London: Macmillan, 1980.

Delmer, S. *Weimar Germany.* London: Macdonald, 1970.

Delvert, J. *Le Japan.* Paris: Centre de Documentation Universitaire, 1975.

Denizet, J. *Inflation, dollar, euro-dollar.* Paris: Gallimard, 1971.

Droz, J. *Histoire de l'Allemagne.* 4 vols. Paris: Hatier, 1970–76.

Duroselle, J.-B. *Histoire diplomatique de 1919 à nos jours.* Paris: Dalloz, 1978.

Einzig, P. *The Euro-bond Market.* London: Macmillan, 1969.

———. *Parallel Money Markets.* 2 vols. London: Macmillan, 1971–72.

Einzig, P., and Quinn, B.S. *The Euro-dollar System.* 6th ed. London: Macmillan, 1977.

Eisenberg J., and Gross, B. *Un Messie nommé Joseph.* Paris: Albin Michel, 1983.

Estorick, E. *Stafford Cripps.* London: Heinemann, 1949.

Farrer, D. *The Warburgs.* London: Michael Joseph, 1975.

Feingold, H.L. *The Politics of Rescue.* New Brunswick: Rutgers University Press, 1970.

Fistie, P. *La rentrée en scène du Japon.* Paris: Armand Colin et Fondation Nationale des Sciences Politiques, 1972.

Foot, P. *Harold Wilson: A Pictorial Biography.* London: Pergamon, 1968.

————. *The Politics of Harold Wilson.* Harmondsworth: Penguin, 1968.

Fraser, L. *All to the Good.* London. n.d.

Fritsch, T. *Mein Streit mit dem Hause Warburg.* n.d.

Gerbet, P. *La construction de l'Europe.* Paris: Imprimerie National, 1983.

Goddin, S.G., and Weiss, S.J. *U.S. Banks' Loss of Global Standing.* Richmond: Robert F. Damé, 1981.

Goetschin, P. *L'évolution du marché monétaire de Londres, 1931–1952.* Ambilly: Annemasse, 1958.

Goiten, S.G. *Letters of Medieval Jewish Traders.* Princeton: Princeton University Press, 1973.

Goldmann, N. *Memories: The Autobiography of Nahum Goldmann.* London: Weidenfeld, 1970.

Goldsmith, R.W. *Financial Intermediaries in the American Economy since 1900.* Ayer Co., 1975.

Gombrich, E.H. *Aby Warburg: An Intellectual Biography.* London: The Warburg Institute, University of London, 1970.

Gorce, P.M. de la. *La prise du pouvoir par Hitler, 1928–1933.* Paris: Plon, 1983.

Griffiths, B. *Competition in Banking.* London: Institute of Economic Affairs, 1970.

Gross, N., ed. *Economic History of the Jews.* Jerusalem: Keter, 1975.

Grosser, A. *Germany in Our Time.* Harmondsworth: Penguin, 1974.

Guillen, P. *L'Allemagne de 1848 à nos jours.* Paris: Nathan, 1970.

Haber, E.; Schiff, Z.; and Yarri, E. *L'année de la Colombe: Jérusalem, 1977; Camp David 1978.* Paris: Hachette, 1979.

Hackett, J. and A.-M. *The British Economy, 1945–1965.* London: Allen & Unwin, 1967.

Hart, P.E.; Vitton, M.A.; and Walshe, G. *Mergers and Concentration in British Industry.* Cambridge: Cambridge University Press, 1973.

Hermant, M. *Les paradoxes économiques de l'Allemagne moderne.* Paris: Armand Colin, 1931.

Hilberg, G.R. *The Destruction of European Jews.* New York: New Viewpoints, 1973.

Hobson, O.R. *How the City Works.* 8th ed. London: Dickens Press, 1966.

Hoffman, P. *The Dealmakers: Inside the World of Investment Banking.* New York: Doubleday, 1984.

Howson, S. *Sterling's Managed Float: The Operation of the Exchange Equalization Account, 1932–1939.* Princeton: International Finance Section, Department of Economics, Princeton University. Princeton Studies in International Finance, No. 46, November 1980.

Iacocca, L. *Iacocca.* New York: Bantam Books, 1984.

Israël, M. Ben. *Espérance d'Israël.* Paris: J. Urin, 1979.

Jeanneney, J.-M., and Barbier-Jeanneney, E. *Les Économies occidentales du XIX siècle à nos jours.* Paris: FNSP, 1985.

Kelf-Cohen, R. *British Nationalization, 1945–1973.* London: Macmillan, 1973.

Kedourie, E. *Le monde juif.* Paris: Flammarion, n.d.

Kellet, R. *The Merchant Banking Arena.* London: Macmillan, 1967.

Keynes, J.M. *The Economic Consequences of the Peace.* London: Macmillan, 1985.
———. "Carl Melchior" in *Collected Writings.* Nos. 10, 16, 17 and 18. London: Macmillan, n.d.
Klein, C. *Weimar.* Paris: Flammarion, 1968.
Laufenburger, H. *Crédit public et finances de guerre, 1914–1944.* Paris: Medicis, 1968.
Laverny, P. *L'Euro-dollar et ses problèmes.* Paris: PUF, 1975.
Lelart, M. *Les Opérations du Fonds Monétaire International.* Paris: OEconomica, 1981.
Lindert, P.H. *Key Currencies and Gold.* Princeton: Princeton University Press, 1969.
Macdougall, D. *Studies in Political Economy.* 2 vols. London: Macmillan, 1975.
Macrae, H., and Cairncross, F. *Capital City: London as a Financial Centre.* London: Methuen, 1985.
Macrae, N. *The London Capital Market: Its Structure, Strains and Management.* London: Staples Press, 1955.
Magnifico, G. *European Monetary Unification.* London: Macmillan, 1973.
Malan, F. *Les offres publiques d'achat: l'expérience anglaise.* Paris: LGDJ, 1969.
Mann, T. *A Sketch of My Life.* London: Simpkin Marshall, 1930.
———. *Appels aux Allemands.* Paris: 1968.
———. *Joseph and His Brothers: Joseph the Provider.* London: Secker & Warburg, 1945.
———. *Les exigences du jour.* Paris: Grasset, 1976.
———. *Reflections of a Non-Political Man.* New York: Ungar, 1985.
Martin, J.-P. *Les finances publiques britanniques, 1939–1945.* Paris: Editions M. Th. Génin, 1956.
Martin, J.S. *All Honorable Men.* Boston: Little Brown, 1950.
Mayer, M. *The Fate of the Dollar.* New York: Times Books, 1980.
Miquel, P. *La grande guerre.* Paris: Fayard, 1983.
Monnet, J. *Mémoires.* Paris: Fayard, 1976.
Morlot, H. *Banque de l'Empire d'Allemagne.* Dijon: Jacquot, 1911.
Morse, J. *How British Banking Has Changed.* London: University of London Press, 1982.
Morton, F. *The Rothschilds.* New York: Atheneum, 1962.
Mourre, Michel. *Dictionnaire Encyclopédique Historique.* Bordas, n.d.
Odell, J.S. *U.S. International Monetary Policy.* Princeton: Princeton University Press, 1982.
Olden, R. *Stresemann.* London: Methuen, 1930.
Ormesson, W. d'. *La Crise mondiale de 1857.* Paris.
Parkinson, R. *Peace for Our Time.* London: Hart Davis, 1971.
Pascallon, P. *Le système monétaire international.* Paris: Editions de l'Epargne, 1982.
Peterson, E.N. *Hjalmar Schacht: For and Against Hitler.* Boston: Christopher, 1954.
Piettre, A. *L'économie allemande contemporaine, 1945–1952.* Paris: 1952.
Plender, J. *That's the Way the Money Goes: The Financial Institutions and the Nation's Savings.* London: Deutsch, 1982.
Pollard, S. *The Development of the British Economy, 1914–1950.* London: Arnold, 1962.
———. *The Wasting of the British Economy.* London: Croom Helm, 1982.

Porter, M.E. *Competitive Strategy: Techniques for Analyzing Industries and Competition*. New York: Free Press, 1980.

Raphael, F. *Judaïsme et capitalisme*. Paris: PUF, 1982.

Redslob, A. *De l'hégémonie à l'intermédiation du centre financier de Londres*. Paris: Thèse Sciences Économiques, 1976.

———. *La Cité de Londres: structures, marchés, réglementations*. Paris: OEconomica, 1983.

Reich, C. *Financier: The Biography of André Meyer*. New York: Morrow, 1983.

Reid, M.I. *The Secondary Banking Crisis, 1973–1975*. London: Macmillan, 1982.

Revell, J. *Changes in British Banking*. London: Hill Samuel, 1968.

Rivaud, A. *Les crises allemandes, 1919–1931*. Paris: Colin, 1932.

Robbins, K. *Munich 1938*. London: Cassell, 1968.

Robson, W.A. *Nationalized Industry and Public Ownership*. London: Allen & Unwin, 1960.

Roll, E. *Crowded Hours: Memoirs*. London: Faber, 1985.

Rosenbaum, E. *M.M. Warburg and Co., Merchant Bankers of Hamburg*. London: Leo Baeck Institute Yearbook, No. 7. 1962

Rosenbaum, E., and Sherman, J. *M.M. Warburg and Co*. London: Hurst, 1979.

Rosier, B. *Croissance et crise capitaliste*. 2d ed. Paris: PUF, 1984.

Roth, C. *The Jewish Contribution to Civilization*. Cincinnati: Cincinnati Union of American Hebrew Congregations, 1940.

———. *Histoire du peuple juif*. 2 vols. Paris: Stock, 1980.

Rueff, J. *Oeuvres complètes*. Vol. 1: *De l'aube au crépuscule: autobiographie*. Paris: Plon, 1977.

———. *Oeuvres complètes*, Vol. 2: *Théorie monétaire*. Paris: Plon, 1979.

Salama, M. *Les marchés financiers dans le monde*. Paris: PUF, 1980.

Sampson, A. *Anatomy of Britain*. London: Hodder and Stoughton, 1956.

———. *The Changing Anatomy of Britain*. London: Hodder and Stoughton, 1981.

———. *The Moneylenders*. London: Hodder and Stoughton, 1981.

———. *The New Anatomy of Britain*. London: Hodder and Stoughton, 1971.

Sautter, C. *Japon: le prix de la puissance*. Paris: Seuil, 1973.

Sayers, R.S. *Financial Policy, 1939–1945*. London: Longmans, Green, 1956.

MacScammel, W. *The London Discount Market*. London: Elek, 1968.

Schacht, H. *My First 76 Years*. London: Allan Wingate, 1955.

Schlesinger, A. *The Age of Roosevelt*. 3 vols. Boston: Houghton Mifflin, 1957, 1959, 1960.

Sédillot, R. *Histoire de l'or*. Paris: Fayard, 1972.

Shaw, E.S. *Money and Finance*. New York: M. Dekker, 1976.

Shinwell, E. *I've Lived Through It All*. London: Gollancz, 1973.

Shirer, W.L. *The Rise and Fall of the Third Reich*. New York: Simon and Schuster, 1960.

Shonfield, A. *British Economic Policy since the War*. Harmondsworth: Penguin, 1958.

Simonnot, P. *L'avenir du système monétaire*. Paris: Robert Laffont, 1972.

Simpson, M.A. *Hjalmar Schacht in Perspective*. The Hague: Mouton, 1969.

Solomon, R. *Le système monétaire international*. Paris: OEconomica, 1979.

Spiegelberg, R. *The City: Power without Accountability*. London: Blond & Briggs, 1973.

Stevens, Q.W. *Vain Hopes, Grim Realities.* New York: New Viewpoints, 1976.
Thompson, R.W. *Generalissimo Churchill.* London: Hodder and Stoughton, 1973.
Triffin, R. *Gold and the Dollar Crisis.* New Haven: Yale University Press, 1960.
Tuchman, B.W. *The March of Folly.* New York: Knopf, 1984.
Turner, G. *The Leyland Papers.* London: Eyre & Spottiswood, 1971.
Turner, H.A. *Stresemann and the Politics of the Weimar Republic.* Princeton:
Princeton University Press, 1963.
Uhlman, F. *Reunion.* London: Adam Books, 1971.
Vagts, A., M.M. *Warburg & Co. Ein Bankhaus in der Deutschen Weltpolitik
1905–1933.* Wiesbaden: 1958.
Van Dormael, A. *Bretton Woods: Birth of a Monetary System.* London: Macmillan,
1978.
Wallich, H.C.; Morse, C.J.; and Patel, I.G. *The Monetary Crisis of 1971.*
Washington, D.C.: The Per Jacobson Foundation, 1972.
Warburg, J.P. *The Long Road Home.* New York: Doubleday, 1964.
Wasserstein, B. *Britain and the Jews of Europe, 1939–1945.* Oxford: Institute of
Jewish Affairs, 1979.
Wechsberg, J. *The Merchant Bankers.* London: Weidenfeld, 1966.
Weizman, E. *The Battle for Peace.* New York: Bantam, 1981.
Weizmann, C. *Trial and Error.* London: Hamish Hamilton, 1949.
Wiener, M.J. *English Culture and the Decline of Industrial Spirit, 1850–1950.*
Cambridge: Cambridge University Press, 1981.
Wiesel, E. *Night.* London: Robson Books, 1974.
Williams, L.J. *Britain and the World Economy, 1919–1970.* London: Collins, 1971.
Wilson, H. *The Relevance of British Socialism.* London: Weidenfeld, 1964.
Worswick, G.D.N., and Ady, P.H. *The British Economy, 1945–1950.* Oxford:
Oxford University Press, 1952.
————. *The British Economy, 1951–1959.* Oxford: Oxford University Press, 1962.
Yaffe, J. *The American Jews.* New York: Random House, 1968.
Young, G.K. *Merchant Banking: Practice and Prospects.* London: Weidenfeld, 1966.
————. *Finance and World Power: A Political Commentary.* London: Nelson, 1968.
Zweig, Stefan. *The World of Yesterday: An Autobiography.* London: Cassell, 1943.

Miscellaneous

Auboin, R. *25th Annual Report of the BIS,* 13 June 1955. BIS, 1930–55.
The Bank for International Settlements and the Basel Meetings, fiftieth anniversary
publication, 1930–1980. Basel: May 1980.
The Power of the Last: Essays for Eric Hobsbawm. Cambridge: Cambridge University
Press, 1984.
Les problèmes actuels du crédit: Lectures organized by the league of former students
of the École Libre des Sciences Politiques. Paris: Alcan, 1930.
Reynolds, C.W., and Tello, C., eds. *U.S.–Mexico Relations.* California.: Stanford
University Press, 1983.
Sobel, Lester, A. ed. *Peace-making in the Middle East.* New York: Checkmark
Books, 1980.
Sutton, Eric, ed. and tr. *Gustav Stresemann: His Diaries, Letters and Papers.*
London: Macmillan, 1935.

Periodicals

Abadie, J.-P. "Les règles monétaires imposées aux banques centrales à travers l'édification d'une zone monétaire." *Cahiers du Cernea* 7 (March 1985).

Aglietta, M. "L'endettement de l'émetteur de la devise-clé et la contrainte monétaire internationale." CEPII Document de travail 85-03 (June 1985).

———. "Le système monétaire international est-il possible?" *Critiques d'Economie Politique* 26–27 (January–June 1984).

Auletta, K. "Article on Lehman Bros." *Fortune* (1984).

Cooper, R.N. "The Gold Standard: Historical Facts and Future Prospects." Brookings Papers on Economic Activity 1 (1982).

Coussement, A.M., "When the Bonds Went round Luxemburg in a Van." *Euromoney* (February 1981).

Crane, D.B., and Hayes, S.L. "The Evolution of International Banking Competition and Its Implications for Regulation." *Journal of Bank Research* 14:1 (Spring 1983) 39.

Dudley, L., and Passel, P. "The War of Viet-Nam and the U.S. Balance of Payments." *Review of Economics and Statistics* (November 1968) 437–42.

Helmann, J. *New York Times*, 11 June 1955 "A History of Eurobond Market." *Euromoney*, special issue.

"Interview with Siegmund Warburg." *Investors Chronicle* (13 April 1973).

Reich, Cary, "The Confessions of Siegmund Warburg." *Institutional Investor* (March 1980).

———. "Warburg, S.G. Inc." *Institutional Investor* (1983).

"Warburg, S.G." *Time* (April 1976).

"Warburg, S.G.: The Exceptional Survivor." *Business Week* (14 March 1977) 62.

Unpublished Documents

Bank of France. Lecture at l'Insitut Supérieur de Banque by the governor of the Bank of France, 5 July 1985.

"A gathering of the members of S.G. Warburg and Co. Ltd. to commemorate Sir Siegmund George Warburg, 1902–1982. London, 12 January 1983, in the Guildhall."

Gardner, R.W. *Sterling Dollar Diplomacy*. Aspen Institute for Humanistic Studies, August 1985.

Kuhn Loeb & Co. *A Century of Investment Banking*. New York: 1967.

———. *Investment Banking through Four Generations*. New York: 1955.

Warburg (Melchior), Elsa. "Random Memories," a journal.

Warburg, Max. *Aus meinen Aufzeichnungen*. New York: privately printed, 1952.

Warburg, Sir Siegmund. Personal notes.

"An Anthology for Searchers."

On his mother, Lucie Kaulla.

On Carl Melchior.

On Stefan Zweig.

Personal note from P. Haas.

Personal note from C. Sharp.

Notes

Introduction

1. "A gathering of the members of S.G. Warburg and Co. Ltd. to commemorate Sir Siegmund George Warburg, 1902–1982, London, 12 January 1983, in the Guildhall" (unpublished).

1. Fortune in a Name (1559–1902)

1. E. Rosenbaum, *M.M. Warburg and Co., Merchant Bankers of Hamburg.*
2. N. Gross (ed.), *Economic History of the Jews.*
3. Ibid.
4. Ibid.
5. E. Kedourie, *Le monde juif.*
6. Gross, *op. cit.*
7. Kedourie, *op. cit.*
8. Gross, *op. cit.*
9. Ibid.
10. Kedourie, *op. cit.*
11. F. Braudel, *Civilisation matérielle, économie et capitalisme.*
12. Gross, *op. cit.*
13. C. Roth, *Histoire du peuple juif.*
14. Gross, *op. cit.*
15. Roth, *op. cit.*
16. Gross, *op. cit.*
17. Ibid.
18. S.G. Goiten, *Letters of Medieval Jewish Traders.*
19. Gross, *op. cit.*
20. Ibid.
21. Ibid.
22. Braudel, *op. cit.*
23. Gross, *op. cit.*
24. Ibid.
25. Braudel, *op. cit.*
26. Gross, *op. cit.*
27. Braudel, *op. cit.*
28. Roth, *op. cit.*
29. Gross, *op. cit.*
30. D. Farrer, *The Warburgs*
31. Ibid.
32. Rosenbaum, *op. cit.*
33. Farrer, *op. cit.*
34. Rosenbaum, *op. cit.*
35. Ibid.
36. Ibid.
37. E. Clapp, *The Port of Hamburg.*
38. Braudel, *op. cit.*
39. M. Ben Israel, *Espérance d'Israel.*
40. Braudel, *op. cit.*
41. Gross, *op. cit.*
42. Farrer, *op. cit.*
43. Rosenbaum, *op. cit.*
44. Gross, *op. cit.*
45. Rosenbaum, *op. cit.*
46. Braudel, *op. cit.*
47. Clapp, *op. cit.*
48. Ibid.
49. Ibid.
50. J. Baumier, *Ces banquiers qui nous governent.*
51. Ibid.
52. Gross, *op. cit.*
53. Clapp, *op. cit.*
54. Ibid.

55. Rosenbaum, *op. cit.*
56. *Ibid.*
57. *Ibid.*
58. Farrer, *op. cit.*
59. Braudel, *op. cit.*
60. Rosenbaum, *op. cit.*
61. Clapp, *op. cit.*
62. Gross, *op. cit.*
63. Rosenbaum, *op. cit.*
64. Farrer, *op. cit.*
65. Rosenbaum, *op. cit.*
66. *Ibid.*
67. J. Droz (ed.), *Histoire de l'Allemange.*
68. Clapp, *op. cit.*
69. Rosenbaum, *op. cit.*
70. *Ibid.*
71. *Ibid.*
72. R. Sédillot, *Histoire l'or.*
73. Elsa Warburg, "Random Memories" (unpublished journal).
74. Farrer, *op. cit.*
75. E. Rosenbaum and J. Sherman, *M.M. Warburg and Co.*
76. Droz, *op. cit.*
77. Rosenbaum and Sherman, *op. cit.*
78. Droz, *op. cit.*
79. P. Guillen, *L'Allemange de 1848 à nos jours.*
80. Droz, *op. cit.*
81. *Ibid.*
82. *Ibid.*
83. Baumier, *op. cit.*
84. *Ibid.*
85. P. Hoffman, *The Dealmakers: Inside the World of Investment Banking.*
86. *Investment Banking through Four Generations* (unpublished).
87. Rosenbaum, *op. cit.*
88. Warburg, *op. cit.*
89. Rosenbaum and Sherman, *op. cit.*
90. Farrer, *op. cit.*
91. W. d'Ormesson, *La crise mondiale de 1857.*

92. *Ibid.*
93. R. Olden, *Stresemann.*
94. Rosenbaum and Sherman, *op. cit.*
95. Rosenbaum, *op. cit.*
96. Max Warburg, *Aus meinen Aufzeichnungen* (privately printed, unpublished).
97. Elsa Warburg, *op. cit.*
98. *Ibid.*
99. *Ibid.*
100. Farrer, *op. cit.*
101. *Ibid.*
102. Droz, *op. cit.*
103. Farrer, *op. cit.*
104. Sédillot, *op. cit.*
105. Gross, *op. cit.*
106. *Investment Banking through Four Generations.*
107. S. Birmingham, *Our Crowd.*
108. J. Yaffe, *The American Jews.*
109. *Ibid.*
110. Farrer, *op. cit.*
111. J. Wechsberg, *The Merchant Bankers.*
112. Rosenbaum, *op. cit.*
113. Guillen, *op. cit.*
114. Droz, *op. cit.*
115. Elsa Warburg, *op. cit.*
116. *Investment Banking through Four Generations.*
117. Birmingham, *op. cit.*
118. *Investment Banking through Four Generations.*
119. M. Aglietta, "L'endettement de l'emetteur de la devise-clé et la contrainte monétaire internationale".
120. Baumier, *op. cit.*
121. *Ibid.*
122. Max Warburg, *op. cit.*
123. H. Morlot, *Banque de l'Empire d'Allemange.*
124. Max Warburg, *op. cit.*
125. E.H. Gombrich, *Aby Warburg: An Intellectual Biography.*
126. Rosenbaum and Sherman, *op. cit.*

127. Max Warburg, *op. cit.*
128. L. Cecil, *Albert Ballin.*
129. Rosenbaum and Sherman, *op. cit.*
130. Elsa Warburg, *op. cit.*
131. Farrer, *op. cit.*
132. *Ibid.*
133. Rosenbaum and Sherman, *op. cit.*
134. Farrer, *op. cit.*
135. *Investment Banking through Four Generations.*
136. Birmingham, *op. cit.*
137. *Ibid.*
138. *Ibid.*
139. *Ibid.*
140. Elsa Warburg, *op. cit.*
141. Rosenbaum, *op. cit.*
142. Farrer, *op. cit.*
143. Rosenbaum and Sherman, *op. cit.*
144. Farrer, *op. cit.*
145. Gross, *op. cit.*
146. Elsa Warburg, *op. cit.*
147. Rosenbaum and Sherman, *op. cit.*
148. *Ibid.*
149. Gombrich, *op. cit.*
150. Elsa Warburg, *op. cit.*
151. Farrer, *op. cit.*
152. Elsa Warburg, *op. cit.*
153. Sir Siegmund Warburg, personal notes on his mother, Lucie Kaulla (unpublished).

2. Power at Court (1902–1933)
1. F. Uhlman, *Reunion.*
2. Sir Siegmund Warburg, *"An Anthology for Searchers"* (unpublished).
3. Sir Siegmund Warburg, personal notes on his mother, Lucie Kaulla (unpublished).
4. *Ibid.*
5. *Ibid.*
6. C. Reich, "The Confessions of Siegmund Warburg," *Institutional Investor*, March 1980.
7. J. Wechsberg, *The Merchant Bankers.*
8. *Ibid.*
9. *Ibid.*
10. *Ibid.*
11. Personal note from C. Sharp.
12. C. Weizmann, *Trial and Error.*
13. D. Farrer, *The Warburgs.*
14. *Ibid.*
15. A. Vagts, M.M. *Warburg and Co. Ein Bankhaus in der Deutschen Weltpolitik 1905–1933.*
16. L. Cecil, *Albert Ballin.*
17. E. Rosenbaum, M.M. *Warburg and Co., Merchant Bankers of Hamburg.*
18. *Ibid.*
19. *Ibid.*
20. S. Birmingham, *Our Crowd.*
21. Farrer, *op. cit.*
22. *Investment Banking through Four Generations.*
23. Farrer, *op. cit.*
24. Hoffman, *op. cit.*
25. *Investment Banking through Four Generations.*
26. Max Warburg, *Aus meinen Aufzeichnungen* (unpublished).
27. Rosenbaum, *op. cit.*
28. J. Helmann, *New York Times*, 11 June 1953.
29. Rosenbaum, *op. cit.*
30. Max Warburg, *op. cit.*
31. Rosenbaum, *op. cit.*
32. *Ibid.*
33. *Ibid.*
34. E. Rosenbaum and J. Sherman, M.M. *Warburg and Co.*
35. Farrer, *op. cit.*
36. Rosenbaum, *op. cit.*
37. Hoffman, *op. cit.*
38. Rosenbaum, *op. cit.*
39. *Ibid.*
40. *Ibid.*
41. Max Warburg, *op. cit.*
42. B.W. Tuchman, *The March of Folly.*

43. Rosenbaum, *op. cit.*
44. Cecil, *op. cit.*
45. Rosenbaum, *op. cit.*
46. P. Miquel, *La grande querre.*
47. Rosenbaum, *op. cit.*
48. Miquel, *op. cit.*
49. *Ibid.*
50. *Ibid.*
51. Rosenbaum, *op. cit.*
52. Miquel, *op. cit.*
53. Rosenbaum, *op. cit.*
54. *Investment Banking through Four Generations.*
55. Birmingham, *op. cit.*
56. *Ibid.*
57. Max Warburg, *op. cit.*
58. Miquel, *op. cit.*
59. MaxWarburg, *op. cit.*
60. *Ibid.*
61. Tuchman, *op. cit.*
62. Farrer, *op. cit.*
63. Rosenbaum and Sherman, *op. cit.*
64. Tuchman, *op. cit.*
65. Max Warburg, *op. cit.*
66. Miquel, *op. cit.*
67. Uhlman, *op. cit.*
68. *Ibid.*
69. Siegmund Warburg, personal notes on his mother, Lucie Kaulla (unpublished).
70. *Ibid.*
71. *Investment Banking through Four Generations.*
72. Tuchman, *op. cit.*
73. *Ibid.*
74. *Ibid.*
75. *Ibid.*
76. *Ibid.*
77. *Ibid.*
78. Rosenbaum, *op. cit.*
79. Tuchman, *op. cit.*
80. Elsa Warburg, "Random Memories" (unpublished).
81. Birmingham, *op. cit.*
82. Hoffman, *op. cit.*
83. Max Warburg, *op. cit.*

84. Rosenbaum, *op. cit.*
85. Max Warburg, *op. cit.*
86. Wechsberg, *op. cit.*
87. Birmingham, *op. cit.*
88. Farrer, *op. cit.*
89. Max Warburg, *op. cit.*
90. Miquel, *op. cit.*
91. Farrer, *op. cit.*
92. Cecil, *op. cit.*
93. Birmingham, *op. cit.*
94. C. Klein, *Weimar.*
95. Max Warburg, *op. cit.*
96. Farrer, *op. cit.*
97. J.M. Keynes, "Carl Melchior," *Collected Writings.*
98. *Ibid.*
99. Sir Siegmund Warburg, personal notes on Carl Melchior (unpublished).
100. Max Warburg, *op. cit.*
101. Keynes, *op. cit.*
102. *Ibid.*
103. *Ibid.*
104. Max Warburg, *op. cit.*
105. Farrer, *op. cit.*
106. Keynes, *op. cit.*
107. Max Warburg, *op. cit.*
108. Elsa Warburg, *op. cit.*
109. Wechsberg, *op. cit.*
110. Reich, *op. cit.*
111. Sir Siegmund Warburg, personal notes on Carl Melchior.
112. *Ibid.*
113. Farrer, *op. cit.*
114. Keynes, *op. cit.*
115. *Ibid.*
116. Wechsberg, *op. cit.*
117. M.A. Simpson, *Hjalmar Schacht in Perspective.*
118. Max Warburg, *op. cit.*
119. Hoffman, *op. cit.*
120. Simpson, *op. cit.*
121. Rosenbaum and Sherman, *op. cit.*
122. Max Warburg, *op. cit.*
123. Rosenbaum and Sherman, *op. cit.*

124. Max Warburg, *op. cit.*
125. *Ibid.*
126. Wechsberg, *op. cit.*
127. Max Warburg, *op. cit.*
128. Rosenbaum and Sherman, *op. cit.*
129. A. Dauphin-Meunier, *L'économie allemande contemporaine, 1914–1942.*
130. Elsa Warburg, *op. cit.*
131. Sir Siegmund Warburg, personal notes on his mother, Lucie Kauller (unpublished).
132. Simpson, *op. cit.*
133. E.N. Peterson, *Hjalmar Schacht: For and Against Hitler.*
134. Simpson, *op. cit.*
135. Max Warburg, *op. cit.*
136. Wechsberg, *op. cit.*
137. Peterson, *op. cit.*
138. *The Bank for International Settlements and the Basel Meetings* (fiftieth anniversary publication, Basel, May 1980).
139. Rosenbaum, *op. cit.*
140. Rosenbaum and Sherman, *op. cit.*
141. J.-M. Jeanneney and E. Barbier-Jeanneney, *Les économies occidentales du XIX siècle à nos jours.*
142. Simpson, *op. cit.*
143. Hoffman, *op. cit.*
144. *Investment Banking through Four Generations.*
145. Rosenbaum, *op. cit.*
146. Rosenbaum, *op. cit.*
147. Farrer, *op. cit.*
148. *Investment Banking through Four Generations.*
149. *Ibid.*
150. Farrer, *op. cit.*
151. Helmann, *op. cit.*
152. Weizmann, *op. cit.*
153. *Ibid.*
154. *Ibid.*
155. *Ibid.*
156. Farrer, *op. cit.*
157. Wechsberg, *op. cit.*
158. Reich, *op. cit.*
159. *Investment Banking through Four Generations.*
160. Hoffman, *op. cit.*
161. Simpson, *op. cit.*
162. M. Aglietta, *"L'endettement de l'émetteur de la devise-clé et la contrainte monétaire internationale".*
163. Rosenbaum and Sherman, *op. cit.*
164. G. Castellan, *L'Allemagne de Weimar, 1918–1933.*
165. Weizmann, *op. cit.*
166. Max Warburg, *op. cit.*
167. Farrer, *op. cit.*
168. *Ibid.*
169. Aglietta, *op. cit.*
170. Simpson, *op. cit.*
171. *The Bank for International Settlements and the Basel Meetings.*
172. Max Warburg, *op. cit.*
173. *The Bank for International Settlements and the Basel Meetings.*
174. *Ibid.*
175. Jacques Rueff, *"Les problèmes actuels du crédit,"* 1930.
176. Max Warburg, *op. cit.*
177. Rosenbaum, *op. cit.*
178. Castellan, *op. cit.*
179. Max Warburg, *op. cit.*
180. *Ibid.*
181. Rosenbaum, *op. cit.*
182. Sir Siegmund Warburg, personal notes on his mother, Lucie Kaulla (unpublished).
183. Aglietta, *op. cit.*
184. *Ibid.*
185. Rosenbaum, *op. cit.*
186. Personal note from C. Sharp.
187. Wechsberg, *op. cit.*
188. Sharp, *op. cit.*
189. Rosenbaum, *op. cit.*
190. Simpson, *op. cit.*
191. Peterson, *op. cit.*
192. Simpson, *op. cit.*
193. Wechsberg, *op. cit.*

194. Farrer, *op. cit.*
195. Wechsberg, *op. cit.*
196. *Ibid.*
197. Aglietta, *op. cit.*
198. *Ibid.*
199. Farrer, *op. cit.*
200. *Ibid.*
201. *Ibid.*
202. Helmann, *op. cit.*
203. *Ibid.*
204. Farrer, *op. cit.*
205. Elsa Warburg, *op. cit.*
206. Max Warburg, *op. cit.*
207. Castellan, *op. cit.*
208. P.M. de la Gorce, *La prise du pouvoir par Hitler, 1928–1933.*
209. Aglietta, *op. cit.*
210. J.S. Martin, *All Honorable Men.*
211. Dauphin-Meunier, *op. cit.*
212. Sir Siegmund Warburg, personal notes on his mother, Lucie Kaulla (unpublished)
213. Simpson, *op. cit.*
214. *Ibid.*
215. Max Warburg, *op. cit.*
216. *Ibid.*

3. **War Money (1933–1945)**
1. P. Hoffman, *The Dealmakers: Inside the World of Investment Banking.*
2. *Ibid.*
3. J. Helmann, *New York Times,* 11 June 1955.
4. J.M. Blum, *Roosevelt and Morgenthau.*
5. D. Farrer, *The Warburgs.*
6. *Ibid.*
7. *Ibid.*
8. A. Schlesinger, *The Age of Roosevelt.*
9. E. Rosenbaum and J. Sherman, *M.M. Warburg and Co.*
10. *Ibid.*
11. Max Warburg, *Aus meinen Aufzeichnungen* (unpublished).
12. *Ibid.*

13. M.A. Simpson, *Hjalmar Schacht in Perspective.*
14. Max Warburg, *op. cit.*
15. Rosenbaum and Sherman, *op. cit.*
16. H.L. Feingold, *The Politics of Rescue.*
17. E.N. Peterson, *Hjalmar Schacht: For and Against Hitler.*
18. Max Warburg, *op. cit.*
19. Blum, *op. cit.*
20. Rosenbaum and Sherman, *op. cit.*
21. *Ibid.*
22. Max Warburg, *op. cit.*
23. R. Hilberg, *The Destruction of European Jews.*
24. J.S. Martin, *All Honorable Men.*
25. Farrer, *op. cit.*
26. *Ibid.*
27. *Ibid.*
28. Max Warburg, *op. cit.*
29. Rosenbaum and Sherman, *op. cit.*
30. E. Rosenbaum, *M.M. Warburg and Co., Merchant Bankers of Hamburg.*
31. Simpson, *op. cit.*
32. Peterson, *op. cit.*
33. Farrer, *op. cit.*
34. Max Warburg, *op. cit.*
35. Stefan Zweig, *The World of Yesterday: An Autobiography.*
36. F. Uhlman, *Reunion.*
37. Zweig, *op. cit.*
38. *Ibid.*
39. Rosenbaum and Sherman, *op. cit.*
40. Note from Henry Grunfeld.
41. C. Reich, "Warburg S.G. Inc.," *Institutional Investor,* 1983.
42. Simpson, *op. cit.*
43. Peterson, *op. cit.*
44. Simpson, *op. cit.*
45. *Ibid.*
46. Peterson, *op. cit.*
47. Max Warburg, *op. cit.*
48. *Ibid.*

49. Simpson, *op. cit.*
50. *Ibid.*
51. Farrer, *op. cit.*
52. *Ibid.*
53. J. Wechsberg, *The Merchant Bankers.*
54. Zweig, *op. cit.*
55. Uhlman, *op. cit.*
56. Sir Siegmund Warburg, personal notes on Stefan Zweig (unpublished).
57. Zweig, *op. cit.*
58. K. Robbins, *Munich 1938.*
59. Zweig, *op. cit.*
60. Robbins, *op. cit.*
61. *Hansard* (House of Commons), October 1938.
62. Zweig, *op. cit.*
63. Martin, *op. cit.*
64. Farrer, *op. cit.*
65. Max Warburg, *op. cit.*
66. Rosenbaum, *op. cit.*
67. *Ibid.*
68. Sir Siegmund Warburg, personal notes on his mother, Lucie Kaulla (unpublished).
69. Farrer, *op. cit.*
70. C. Weizmann, *Trial and Error.*
71. I. Abella and H. Tropper, *None Is Too Many: Canada and the Jews of Europe (1933–1948).*
72. Hilberg, *op. cit.*
73. Simpson, *op. cit.*
74. *Ibid.*
75. Peterson, *op. cit.*
76. *Ibid.*
77. *Ibid.*
78. Sir Siegmund Warburg, personal notes on his mother, Lucie Kaulla (unpublished)
79. T. Mann, *Appels aux Allemands.*
80. *Ibid.*
81. R.S. Sayers, *Financial Policy, 1939–1945.*
82. A. Van Dormael, *Bretton Woods: Birth of a Monetary System.*
83. Farrer, *op. cit.*
84. Van Dormael, *op. cit.*

85. Mann, *op. cit.*
86. Sir Siegmund Warburg, personal notes on Stefan Zweig.
87. R.W. Gardner, "Sterling Dollar Diplomacy," Aspen Institute for Humanistic Studies, August 1985.
88. *Ibid.*
89. *Ibid.*
90. Hoffman, *op. cit.*
91. M. Aglietta, *"Le système monétaire international est-il possible?"*, *Critiques d'Economie Politique*, No. 26–27, January–June 1984.
92. Gardner, *op. cit.*
93. Farrer, *op. cit.*

4. Riches of Peace (1945–1960)

1. C. Reich, "The Confessions of Siegmund Warburg," *Institutional Investor*, March 1980.
2. *Ibid.*
3. J. Wechsberg, *The Merchant Bankers.*
4. *Ibid.*
5. *Ibid.*
6. *Ibid.*
7. Personal note from P. Haas.
8. Personal note from C. Sharp.
9. Wechsberg, *op. cit.*
10. *Ibid.*
11. Sir Siegmund Warburg, personal notes on his mother, Lucie Kaulla (unpublished).
12. Reich, *op. cit.*
13. Sir Siegmund Warburg, "An Anthology for Searchers" (unpublished).
14. *Ibid.*
15. Wechsberg, *op. cit.*
16. Warburg, "Anthology for Searchers."
17. R.W. Gardner, "Sterling Dollar Diplomacy," Aspen Institute for Humanistic Studies, August 1985.
18. A. Van Dormael, *Bretton Woods: Birth of a Monetary System.*

19. M. Charlot, *L'Angleterre, 1945–1980.*
20. *Ibid.*
21. D. Farrer, *The Warburgs.*
22. J. Helmann, *New York Times,* 11 June 1955.
23. J. S. Martin, *All Honorable Men.*
24. *Ibid.*
25. A. Grosser, *Germany in Our Time.*
26. Martin, *op. cit.*
27. *Ibid.*
28. *Ibid.*
29. *Ibid.*
30. Grosser, *op. cit.*
31. Martin, *op. cit.*
32. Farrer, *op. cit.*
33. C. Reich, "Warburg S.G. Inc.," *Institutional Investor,* 1983.
34. "Interview with Siegmund Warburg," *Investors Chronicle,* 13 April 1973.
35. Charlot, *op. cit.*
36. Warburg, "An Anthology for Searchers."
37. Personal note from C. Sharp.
38. E. Shinwell, *I've Lived Through It All.*
39. Charlot, *op. cit.*
40. E. E. Barry, *Nationalization in British Policy: The Historical Background.*
41. Reich, "The Confessions of Siegmund Warburg."
42. *Ibid.*
43. Wechsberg, *op. cit.*
44. Reich, "The Confessions of Siegmund Warburg."
45. Wechsberg, *op. cit.*
46. Reich, "Warburg S.G. Inc."
47. Personal note from P. Haas.
48. Charlot, *op. cit.*
49. R.A. Butler, *The Art of the Possible: The Memoirs of Lord Butler.*
50. Sir Siegmund Warburg, personal notes on his mother, Lucie Kaulla (unpublished).

51. *Ibid.*
52. *Ibid.*
53. Charlot, *op. cit.*
54. H. Macmillan, *Memoirs.*
55. Warburg, "An Anthology for Searchers."
56. Wechsberg, *op. cit.*
57. Personal note from C. Sharp.
58. Warburg, "An Anthology for Searchers."
59. Reich, "The Confessions of Siegmund Warburg."
60. *Hansard* (House of Commons), 27 June 1950.
61. *Ibid.*, 6 December 1951.
62. Charlot, *op. cit.*
63. Reich, "The Confessions of Siegmund Warburg."
64. *Ibid.*
65. *Investment Banking through Four Generations.*
66. *Ibid.*
67. Warburg, personal notes on his mother, Lucie Kaulla (unpublished).
68. Farrer, *op. cit.*
69. A. Sampson, *The New Anatomy of Britain.*
70. *Ibid.*
71. *Ibid.*
72. Wechsberg, *op. cit.*
73. *Ibid.*
74. Warburg, "An Anthology for Searchers."
75. *Ibid.*
76. Reich, "The Confessions of Siegmund Warburg."
77. *Ibid.*
78. A. Sampson, *The Changing Anatomy of Britain.*
79. Warburg, "An Anthology for Searchers."

5. Contraband Dollars (1960–1973)

1. Sir Siegmund Warburg, "An Anthology for Searchers" (unpublished).

2. C. Reich, "The Confessions of Siegmund Warburg," *Institutional Investor*, March 1980.
3. Warburg, *op. cit.*
4. *Ibid.*
5. "A History of the Eurobond Market," *Euromoney* (special issue).
6. *Ibid.*
7. Reich,, *op. cit.*
8. Warburg,, *op. cit.*
9. Personal note from P. Haas.
10. Personal note from C. Sharp.
11. A. Sampson, *The Changing Anatomy of Britain.*
12. Warburg, *op. cit.*
13. *Euromoney, op. cit.*
14. *Ibid.*
15. Reich, *op. cit.*
16. H. Brandon, *In The Red: The Struggle for Sterling, 1964–1966.*
17. *Euromoney, op. cit.*
18. J. Wechsberg, *The Merchant Bankers.*
19. Warburg, *op. cit.*
20. *Ibid.*
21. *Ibid.*
22. Wechsberg, *op. cit.*
23. Warburg, *op. cit.*
24. *Euromoney, op. cit.*
25. Wechsberg, *op. cit.*
26. Reich, *op. cit.*
27. *Euromoney, op. cit.*
28. *Ibid.*
29. Brandon, *op. cit.*
30. *Ibid.*
31. *Ibid.*
32. *Ibid.*
33. *Ibid.*
34. *Ibid.*
35. Warburg, *op. cit.*
36. Reich, *op. cit.*
37. Warburg, *op. cit.*
38. M. Charlot, *L'Angleterre, 1945–1980.*
39. Wechsberg, *op. cit.*
40. Warburg, *op. cit.*
41. *Ibid.*
42. *Ibid.*
43. E. Roll, *Crowded Hours: Memoirs.*
44. Reich, *op. cit.*
45. Warburg, *op. cit.*
46. *Ibid.*
47. *Ibid.*
48. Reich, *op. cit.*
49. A. Sampson, *The Moneylenders.*
51. *Ibid.*
52. Warburg, *op. cit.*
53. Sampson, *The Moneylenders.*
54. "Interview with Siegmund Warburg," *Investors Chronicle*, 13 April 1973.
55. Warburg, *op. cit.*
56. *Euromoney, op. cit.*
57. Q.W. Stevens, *Vain Hopes, Grim Realities.*
58. R. Solomon, *Le système monétaire international.*
59. M. Aglietta, *"Le système monétaire international est-il possible?"*, *Critiques d'Economie Politique*, No. 26–27, January–June 1984.
60. P. Simonnot, *L'avenir du système monétaire.*
61. Stevens, *op. cit.*
62. *Euromoney, op. cit.*
63. D. Farrer, *The Warburgs.*
64. Warburg, *op. cit.*
65. *Investors Chronicle, op. cit.*
66. *Ibid.*
67. Warburg, *op. cit.*
68. *Ibid.*
69. *Ibid.*

6. **Last Refuge (1973–1982)**

1. E. Rosenbaum, *M.M. Warburg and Co., Merchant Bankers of Hamburg.*
2. C. Reich, "The Confessions of Siegmund Warburg," *Institutional Investor*, March 1980.
3. *Ibid.*

4. Sir Siegmund Warburg, "An Anthology for Searchers" (unpublished).
5. *Ibid.*
6. *Ibid.*
7. *Ibid.*
8. *Ibid.*
9. *Ibid.*
10. *Ibid.*
11. Reich, *op. cit.*
12. Warburg, *op. cit.*
13. Reich, *op. cit.*
14. *Ibid.*
15. "A gathering of the members of S.G. Warburg and Co. Ltd. to commemorate Sir Siegmund George Warburg, 1902–1982. London, 12 January 1983, in the Guildhall" (unpublished).
16. J. Baumier, *Ces banquiers qui nous gouvernent.*
17. Reich, *op. cit.*
18. *Ibid.*
19. *Ibid.*
20. *Ibid.*
21. M. Charlot, *L'Angleterre, 1945–1980.*
22. Reich, *op. cit.*
23. Warburg, *op. cit.*
24. *Ibid.*
25. *Ibid.*
26. *Ibid.*
27. Reich, *op. cit.*
28. D. Farrer, *The Warburgs.*
29. Sir Siegmund Warburg, personal notes on his mother, Lucie Kaulla (unpublished).
30. Note from Henry Grunfeld.
31. Reich, *op. cit.*
32. Personal note from C. Sharp.
33. Warburg, "An Anthology for Searchers."
34. Reich, *op. cit.*
35. Wechsberg, *The Merchant Bankers.*
36. Warburg, "An Anthology for Searchers."
37. P. Hoffman, *The Dealmakers: Inside the World of Investment Banking.*
38. Reich, *op. cit.*

Index

changes in chairmanship, directors,
246, 280, 303, 348
proposed merger with Hill Samuel,
289-90
boycotted, 311-12
praised in Japan, 324-25
after Siegmund's death, 342-45,
347-48
mentioned, 277
Warburg (S.G.), Frankfurt, 254, 291
Warburg (S.G.), Inc., 256, 399, 302
Warburg, Samuel (cousin of Aby), 19
Warburg, Samuel (grandson of Elias),
27
Warburg, Samuel Elias (son of Elias
Samuel), 15
Warburg, Samuel Moses (son of Moses), 12, 14
Warburg, Samuel von (son of Simon),
9
Warburg, Sarah (1805-84, daughter
of Moses Marcus), 18, 19, 22,
24, 27
Warburg, Siegmund (1835-89, son of
Aby and Sarah), 22, 24, 25, 26,
27, 29, 32
Warburg, Sir Siegmund George
(1902-82), *v-ix*
birth, 41, 43
childhood, education, 43-44, 45
religion, Jewishness, 45, 189-91,
328
relations with his mother, 44,
45-46, 64, 155-56, 181-82,
217, 227, 340
fatalism, premonitions, supersti-
tions, 46, 117, 258
and Rathenau, 85
on Melchior, 78-79
and M.M. Warburg, 77-79, 89,
106
and politics, 77-78, 146-47, 151,
177-79, 271-73, 338
and the press, 78, 183, 301
and father's death, 87
in London and America, 96-97
marriage, 97
son, *see* Warburg, George
and money, 110-11
on Brüning, 105
daughter, *see* Warburg, Anna

personal relationships, 107, 135,
203-6, 205-6
and 1931 crisis, 110, 112
and rise of Nazism, 114
leaves Germany for America,
117-18
reading, 117, 145, 181, 182
settles in London, 121, 130-32
in Britain, the British, 131, 146,
157, 182, 209, 219, 233
and Jewish emigration from Germany, 126-28, 145, 157,
159, 161, 164, 172
first company in London, *see* New
Trading Company
as banker, 143-46, 180-82, 200,
203-6, 212-14, 221-24,
225-26, 234, 236-38, 251,
253, 262, 298
and Warburg name, 145, 186-87,
196, 203, 227, 254, 291-92,
301-2, 315, 349
personality, 144-45, 177-79,
180-83, 207, 235, 257, 279,
280
buys house in Buckinghamshire,
146
and approach of war, 147-52, 161
in Second World War, 163,
164-65, 167, 168, 170, 172
moves to Roehampton Lane, 172
on Zweig, 172
postwar aims, 179-80
and postwar Germany, 194-96
and power, influence, 309, 322,
327, 337
and graphology, 181, 206, 252
and postwar economy, 186, 194
establishes S.G. Warburg, 186-87
and America, 189, 194, 212, 229
and France, 194
and European unity, 194, 197-198
and Israel, 198-200, 281-83
and television, 215
moves to Eaton Square, 217
aphorisms, philosophical ideas,
234, 242, 245, 246, 250,
251, 252, 258, 259, 261,
277, 281, 282, 284, 292,
299, 305, 307, 322, 336-39
autobiography, 238, 340

ABOUT THE MAKING OF THIS BOOK

The text of *A Man of Influence* was set in
Garamond by Unicorn Graphics of
Washington, D.C. The book was printed
and bound by R.R. Donnelley,
Harrisonburg, Virginia division. The
typography and binding were designed by
Tom Suzuki of Falls Church, Virginia.